How Birds Behave

DISCOVER the MYSTERIES of what BACKYARD BIRDS do 365 DAYS of the YEAR

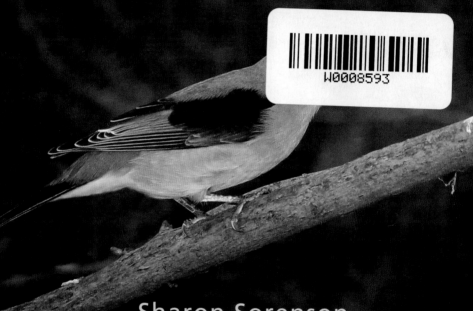

W0008593

Sharon Sorenson

STACKPOLE
BOOKS
Guilford, Connecticut

Published by Stackpole Books
An imprint of The Rowman & Littlefield Publishing Group, Inc.
4501 Forbes Blvd., Ste. 200
Lanham, MD 20706
www.rowman.com

Distributed by NATIONAL BOOK NETWORK
800-462-6420

Photos by Charles Sorenson and Sharon Sorenson

British Library Cataloguing in Publication Information available

Library of Congress Cataloging-in-Publication Data available

ISBN 978-0-8117-3863-7 (paperback)
ISBN 978-0-8117-6861-0 (e-book)

∞™ The paper used in this publication meets the minimum requirements of American National Standard for Information Sciences—Permanence of Paper for Printed Library Materials, ANSI/NISO Z39.48-1992.

CONTENTS

INTRODUCTION

Why do birds do what they do and go where they go? Why do some of them eat seeds while others sip nectar, gulp down berries, or catch bugs on the wing, and skip feeders altogether? Why do we see certain birds in January but never in July—or vice-versa? Why do we see several dozen of their kind nearly every day of the year but see others only in, say, April or October? Where do they spend the rest of their time? And why are they there? And here's a puzzler: Why do some birds change color from season to season, and how do they do that? Just out of curiosity, how do they choose a mate? Really, now, do they ever fight, then kiss and make up—or storm off and go their separate ways? Then to the practical: How do they know how to build a nest, where to find the materials and how to shape the nursery? So many mysteries! What if birds could explain why and how they behave as they do?

Well, in a way, they can explain. Biologists have done the studies. Sure, songbirds can't talk, but as the cliché goes: "Actions speak louder than words." A ton of research out there nibbles away at putting the actions into words. Now, after years of reading and listening to the pros, and after a lifetime of watching birds and asking questions, I've begun to understand some of the mysteries.

This book unravels and explains a year's worth of those mysteries about how birds behave. While I'm mostly a backyard bird watcher, anchored on a three-acre lot in eastern Posey County, Indiana, from time to time hubby and I venture out to bird elsewhere. Every day this year, for 365 days, wherever I found birds, I chronicled and photographed their behavior. You'll see how their actions change season by season, month by month, sometimes day by day—and definitely species by species. By following the saga, you, too, will begin to unravel the mysteries of birds' daily behavior. And there's this: Peeking into their secret lives enriches your bird-viewing appreciation, and thus your pleasure. You'll be thrilled!

As you join me in this romp through a year of watching bird behavior, may our kindred love for birds bring you joy. And above all, may understanding how and why birds behave as they do ever enrich your life as much as it has mine.

January

A male Northern Cardinal perches on a snow-covered hemlock bough, finding protection from the wind.

The sound of birds stops the noise in my mind.
—Carly Elisabeth Simon (1945–)

Welcoming the New Year

After last night's lovely full moon, the sun crawled up from behind the trees on a new year, clear, crisp, windy, a frigid 3 degrees. My eyes opened to see my first birds of the year: a Northern Cardinal foraging on the ground next to a White-throated Sparrow sipping at the heated bubble rock. What a perfect combination to represent the season. Our year-round bright cheer-me-upper and a regular winter visitor, bright yellow lores setting off its white-striped cap and white bib.

Around 7 a.m. each day, just at winter's dawn, the birds—especially Northern Cardinals, Tufted Titmice, and Blue Jays—expect their daily handout of a cup of split peanuts. So out the door I went in my PJs and hooded parka to add sunflower seed to partially emptied feeders and pour the peanuts into the ground-level platform feeder. As I cracked open the door, a half dozen Mourning Doves whirred to life, their flight a frantic reaction to my intrusion, costing them wasted energy on such a frigid morning. I hated that I disturbed them.

In the near distance, I caught the weak "Whee?" call of the Eastern Towhee. A ribbon of birds—likely a mix dominated by Red-winged Blackbirds but surely including among the hundreds at least a few European Starlings, Common Grackles, and Brown-headed Cowbirds—wove its way across the sky from south-southwest to north-northeast, scattered in a broad band that undulated overhead the entire 3 or 4 quick minutes I spent outside. Several families of American Crows angled west/southwest to east/northeast at an altitude below the ribbon of other black-colored birds. All had probably departed overnight roosts

A male Eastern Towhee, a typical ground feeder, forages for seed, both native and feeder-spilled.

near the Wabash River and were heading toward harvested agricultural grain fields, their feeding grounds for the day. Taking due note of their appearances, I finished the quick work of dispensing seed and darted back inside.

At 7:15 a.m., my morning vigil began at the kitchen window. Before tea was ready, a White-breasted Nuthatch picked its way across the midsection of our snag, the remainder of a fifty-year-old tulip tree that had to be cut to a skeleton a year ago last August to protect the house. The nuthatch darted from the snag toward the window feeder hanging near where I stood, snapped up a sunflower seed, and zipped away. At the hanging platform feeder a foot from the window, two American Goldfinches in drab olive plumage breakfasted on more sunflower seeds. Four male cardinals made it a feast. The little family of seven Blue Jays arrived to swallow and stuff their gullets with peanut splits, caching some against worse weather. Too many House Finches, probably over twenty, kept the scene active. A single Common Grackle wandered in. Really? When does anyone see only a single grackle? And the male Eastern Towhee that sang earlier now crept out, using his usual passage under the split-rail fence, to forage on spilled seed under the feeders.

The population of American Goldfinches increased, now eleven of them shoulder to shoulder. Camouflaged among them, a single Pine Siskin fed with the same enthusiasm, an avian combination enough to keep even the squirrels at bay.

Tufted Titmice finally arrived, four of them, slipping peanuts out when the jays were otherwise distracted.

A male Red-bellied Woodpecker permitted a female Northern Cardinal to join him at the hanging platform feeder but chased off a brazen jay that seemed to want everything to itself.

A minuscule Carolina Chickadee popped out from the backside of the bushes to take its turn at the bubble rock, drinking its fill.

With 15 minutes having ticked by, I moved, teacup in hand, from the north-facing kitchen window to a south-facing window and another set of feeders—seed cake, safflower seed, and sunflower seed. Three Dark-eyed Juncos foraged beneath the feeders and three Mourning Doves sat quietly, fluffed to almost double size, hunkered down amid leaves purposely left last fall. Feeding side by side were four more Pine Siskins, wing to wing with a single female or immature Purple Finch. At this season, it's usually impossible to separate Purple Finches, females from immatures, and we don't often see the raspberry-colored adult male Purple Finches. Come spring, the female/immature Purple Finches may sport a bit of pinkish red on their rumps, a telltale sign that they're molting soon into handsome males.

But I digress.

Above the ground-foraging birds, in another hanging platform feeder, five Pine Siskins joined six goldfinches, one much brighter than the others, already promising a new breeding season to come. They all fed facing into the wind. After all, wind whipping under feathers lets the cold inside all that insulation, but facing the wind pushes insulating feathers tightly in place! More House Finches, in various plumages, hung out, feeding, drinking, and chattering. Red splotches throughout the yard marked another half dozen male cardinals. Females blend in, so I waver, not quite able to get a handle on the count. They don't sit still when they're hungry!

A male Northern Flicker pounded the ground, an area heavily mulched with pine straw, likely hoping the mulch would offer a productive spot. I'm not sure what, if anything, he found there to eat, but he moved a short distance and resumed the search. Insects and his

A male Northern Flicker, preferring to dine on ants and beetles, digs deep in winter soil, his muddy beak showing effects of his work.

A Northern Mockingbird feeds on beautyberry berries, a fat-filled wintertime substitute for summer bugs.

version of filet mignon—ants—have to be deep now. Then he flew across the driveway to the flower garden, planted mostly in natives, now winter killed but still standing. I heard him call and wondered if he will get a response.

Four doves waddled along the garden path. Three White-throated Sparrows fed among frost-killed purple coneflower seed heads. Goldfinches gleaned among the late asters.

Back nearer the window, two Carolina Wrens foraged among the leaves, flipping their way through the buffet they found there. Last fall's leaves harbor eggs and larvae that sustain wrens and other foragers through the winter. Under the coralberry bushes, an array of White-throated Sparrows, House Finches, cardinals, and doves picked at spilled seed. Oddly enough, birds never eat these coral berries. While coral berries are native here, I think I must have inadvertently chosen some sort of hybrid. Big mistake. The fruits of hybrids are never viable, so they offer little or no nutrition to anything that eats them.

The Red-bellied Woodpecker landed on the suet pole.

Some European Starlings, white-speckled in their winter plumage and thus sometimes nicknamed "rice birds," joined a single House Sparrow, reminding me that no matter what I do, the big flocks of starlings will come later. Cold weather brings in flocks of everything, primarily for the only water in liquid form for miles around. Of course, they never pass up the opportunity to forage on some of the seeds as well.

I strolled back to the kitchen window just in time to see the Northern Mockingbird sail in to the native beautyberry bush. He'll no doubt finish off the last of the berries quickly, now that the weather dictates his need for the added nutrition these rich fruits offer. A single Red-winged Blackbird took his leisure at the sunflower seed. Three doves had settled in against the south side of the wooden fence, fluffed against the cold, taking advantage of the weak reflected heat. A few juncos arrived in the backyard, and five of the seven jays continued working on the peanut splits. A single crow flew in low, calling, then lifted to the tippy-top of the pine tree in which they built their last-summer's nest.

A second male Eastern Towhee arrived. Typically, of course, only one can stay. It's a territorial thing, even in winter. Probably the second male is an offspring of the other and thus tolerated, at least briefly. Finally I spotted the first Downy Woodpecker of the morning, picking along the bark of the bald cypress tree and then sailing to a quicker meal at the suet pole.

Now it's 7:45. For a half hour, I've caught up on who's who in the yard. This year of observing how birds behave is off to a bustling start. And breakfast is running late.

For the day, twenty-five species identified in the yard.

9 Canada Goose, flyovers
14 Mourning Dove
2 Red-bellied Woodpecker
2 Downy Woodpecker
1 Northern Flicker
7 Blue Jay
12 American Crow
4 Carolina Chickadee
6 Tufted Titmouse
2 White-breasted Nuthatch
2 Carolina Wren
1 Northern Mockingbird
45 European Starling
8 Dark-eyed Junco
5 White-throated Sparrow
2 Eastern Towhee
14 Northern Cardinal
2 Red-winged Blackbird
50 Brown-headed Cowbird
1 Common Grackle
30 House Finch
1 Purple Finch
11 Pine Siskin
13 American Goldfinch
4 House Sparrow
Species: 25 total in the yard to date for the year.

January 2

Interpreting the Inventory

Yesterday's inventory of birds in the yard represents this winter's constant population. In general, by January, birds have settled into their routine winter behavior in a habitat suitable for the long haul. Given sufficient food to maintain metabolism, and given adequate shelter against the elements, birds can survive the cold. Typically by now, they wander little, conserving energy, using every calorie to fight the cold.

While many of the species tallied yesterday were lured within my view by feeders, their presence is about far more than feeders and feed. Yes, feeders drew them to my windows, but something else enabled them to be in the larger yard. Winters here can be anything from mild to vicious, varying not just by the year but by the day. At the moment, the weather is trending toward vicious, so beyond food, birds must find adequate shelter. They need protection from wind, from precipitation—whether rain, snow, or sleet—and from predators. Without ready shelter, birds won't be in the area, much less visiting feeders.

So what kind of shelter do they find in this yard? Evergreens. Many of them of many kinds. Pines in two little groves, each harboring seven 80-foot trees, plus four more scattered about. Native eastern red cedars, a cluster to the south and a windbreak to the north, plus a half dozen individuals scattered along fencerows, their berry-cones also a favorite food for birds. More cedars, a group of five native gray owl cedars providing low and ground-level protection, not to mention more of those favored berry-cones. Native American hollies, two 70-foot trees and two shorter ones, all laden with berries that in another few weeks will soften after sufficient freeze-thaw cycles to offer a grand buffet. Hemlocks, three of them, also loaded with tiny cones, the seeds inside preferred by Pine Siskins.

Beyond the multiple evergreens, birds find other protective habitat: brambles, two patches, one to the south and another to the north of the house, offering thorny protection against predators. A loosely tended fencerow along our west and north property lines. A steep south-facing bank, unmowed and boasting dense grassy cover and the seeds the grasses provide. Three brush piles, all about chest high, offering cover in out-of-the-way corners of the property. And finally, a 100-foot by 40-foot native perennial, vine, and shrub garden, left standing, frost-killed, the stalks offering protection and the seed heads sporting another grand buffet from one end of the plot to the other. Across our little three-acre patch, then, birds find ample shelter, high and low, necessary to meet the unique demands of so many species.

The quirky thing about the sheltering vegetation centers on which birds use what. The birds that hang out in the high branches of evergreens are not the same birds that hunker in the brambles. The birds that seek shelter in the brush piles are not the same as those that scoot through the ground-cover cedars. And birds that forage in the tallest sycamores are not the same birds that shelter in the fencerow. They don't all like the same living arrangements or the same foods. They don't all forage the same ways. In short, their behavior sends a clear message: the more diverse the habitat, the more diverse the bird population. We'll see how the mantra plays out this year.

Finally, when bitter weather turns everything solid, however, birds also need water. Two bubbling rocks, each with a submerged, thermostatically controlled heater, provide ever-ready running water. Birds that would never come to feeders will flock to wintertime flowing water. Bird magnet!

January 3

Warring with Cold

With another bitter low of 3 degrees last night, the birds' behavior today showed their desperation. Flocks of European Starling that I estimated at 175 to 200 descended on the yard, not so much to visit feeders (although of course a few did) but really to shoulder their way into flowing water at the heated bubble rocks. Some birds clawed their way over the tops of others in a frantic and ill-mannered effort to get to water. We've not had above-freezing weather in well over a week, so there's little drinking water anywhere. Often when lakes and ponds turn solid, birds can manage to find necessary liquid by eating snow. While that's really hard on them, spending energy to warm snow to body temperature, the liquid helps them survive. Here, this year, we have an unusual condition. No snow. Just bitter, lingering, single-digit cold, a situation that dramatically affects birds' behavior.

Another sign of things to come today: a single American Robin. I rarely see robins in our wintertime yard, unless, of course, the native American holly trees have a ready-to-eat buffet. When the buffet is ready, robins come in droves; maybe this individual is scouting out the readiness. Holly berries must endure multiple freeze-thaw cycles before the rock-hard fruits become soft enough for birds to eat and digest. Now ice-coated, the berries hang useless but nevertheless attract the robin's attention. A few other birds have been checking the berries' readiness. Northern Cardinals flutter in, out, and about, so I suspect they're trying for a jump-start on the waiting robins. Since the trees are out of sight from any window in the house, though, I can only watch for evidence, like droppings on the sidewalk and scattered berries on the ground.

Although we're in the deep freeze now, it's possible that sunshine on the south side of the trees may have thawed the berries enough late this afternoon for the birds' consumption. If that's the case, this single male robin will be only the first of the parade. Some years I've counted over 300 robins floundering through the branches, finishing off berries on both 50-foot trees within a matter of days. On the final day, they forage shoulder to shoulder on the ground below, scavenging every last berry that they dropped or knocked to the ground in their feeding frenzy. Then, as a flock, they move on to someone else's berry production, maybe yours!

So add another species to the first day's total:
1 American Robin
Species: 26 total in the yard to date for the year.

A male American Robin flutters amid ice-covered holly, searching unsuccessfully for edible berries. After repeated freeze-thaw cycles, berries will become soft enough to swallow whole and digest.

January 4

Adding Two More

A family of Eastern Bluebirds has stayed with us since summer, the two adults and their offspring from summer's last brood. That's usual bluebird family behavior, for the offspring from the last brood to stay with their parents for the winter, and sometimes offspring from earlier broods join the extended family as well. Early springs affect bluebirds' nesting behavior, sometimes giving locals enough time to manage raising three broods for the season. Last summer seems to have been one of those years. At least three pairs moved among our eleven homemade Peterson-style nest boxes raising their multiple broods to fledging. Seeing bluebirds today, then, was no surprise. In fact, the surprise was that it took four days into the new year to spot them in the yard. Perhaps if I'd been outside listening, I might have heard them earlier.

The nicer surprise, however, came on the wings of the secretive Brown Thrasher. While thrashers nest here regularly, seeing them in the dead of winter makes for a real day-brightener. We're just on the northern edge of their winter range, so severe weather affects their behavior, often chasing them farther south for the duration. Too bad that today he's in no mood to sing his mockingbird-like song. In all honesty, though, research verifies that he has a larger repertoire than does the Northern Mockingbird—more songs, longer phrases, more variety, saying everything twice while the mockingbird says everything three times or more.

A Brown Thrasher hunkers against the cold, feathers fluffed to retain heat, very much the way a down-filled jacket retains heat.

Sadly, Brown-headed Cowbird and European Starling populations exploded today, probably at least 200 cowbirds and 100 starlings. These population explosions happen every time we have an extended freeze or snow cover. I'm hoping they'll follow their usual behavior and disappear—or at least dramatically diminish—as soon as temps climb above freezing.

3 Eastern Bluebird
1 Brown Thrasher
Species: 28 total in the yard to date for the year.

January 5

Gleaning Suet Crumbles

Desperate times cause birds to behave in desperate ways. Two male Eastern Bluebirds and a female worked for about a half hour to glean the last berries from the beautyberry bush. Not much remained, and what did was dried and surely of poor nutritional value. Earlier, the Northern Mockingbird had worked its way through the bush, day after day, feasting on what had been a luscious and abundant crop of berries. The high fat content of berries helps birds stay warm, so they're an important food source. Now, though, with almost no beautyberries remaining, the bluebirds likely found little sustenance. Little, however, is better than none. Winterberries and holly berries, however, hang ready—at least from my perspective. Maybe they're frozen too hard for the birds to swallow, especially since bluebirds swallow fruits whole. I hope, though, that the bluebirds find their way to those fruits soon. Their behavior and choice of sustenance, munching dried-up beautyberries, suggest their growing hunger as well as their growing desperation. They're bug and berry eaters. Seeds hold little interest for them. Given their bill structure, they can't crack open seeds. So it's berries they want now.

Meanwhile, I've put out another suet cake, a commercial one with seeds imbedded. The bluebirds don't eat the seeds, but the seeds help break up the suet, making the offering more manageable for them. And they do love the suet, a good substitute for bugs. But since bluebirds don't naturally cling to, say, a suet cage, they're not really comfortable—or adept at—eating there. Mostly, they forage below the suet feeders, on the ground, picking up crumbles that fall when other birds pick at the suet.

Of course, as soon as I put out the suet block, starlings found it. Rascals, all!

I caught sight of a stray cat prowling the backyard again this afternoon. This time I understood that the furry bird killer is hiding in the lariope, a dense 2-foot-high stand intended to serve as a photo background behind the bubble rock. While the semi-evergreen foliage indeed makes a pretty backdrop in photos and the purple berries never go begging among Northern Cardinals, Northern Mockingbirds, and other berry lovers, providing camouflage for a marauding cat will never do. So wielding a hefty hedge clippers and braving the cold, I whacked down the entire patch, making the bubble rock once again safe for birds to drink and bathe.

A pair of Eastern Bluebirds plucks berries from an American beautyberry bush in search of wintertime nutrition, native berries serving as the best substitute for bugs, bug eggs, and larvae.

After two more nights in the single digits, we're supposed to have a thaw. It will be fascinating to watch bird behavior the day the freeze finally breaks. What will they do differently? Dramatic weather changes always affect behavior.

Late tonight I heard the familiar calls of the Barred Owl, close enough to the house that it heard me flip down my recliner in order to pad to the door and listen. The stinker went quiet. But female owls control their territories and don't take kindly to intruders, even a male if it's the off-season. For several years already, this one has claimed an area here and to our immediate south for her own. I know she'll call again soon, perhaps dueting with a male, a pair's usual courtship behavior, staying in contact with one another. It's already pairing season for them.

1 Barred Owl
Species: 29 total in the yard to date for the year.

January 6

Relishing a Surprise

I had a nice surprise today, finding an unusual bird foraging among the whacked-down lariope, plucking the final purple berries! To wash down the few it found, it hopped up on the now-safe bubble rock for a quick drink, then dashed to cover in a vine-laden sapling. Typical Hermit Thrush behavior! But in early January? Photo files, however, showed that two years ago next week, the same unusual bird species paid a visit to our bubble rock. Gotta love that brave winter-resistant bird. In short, while an early January Hermit Thrush is unusual, it's not truly rare to find it here in winter; this is the northern edge of its winter range. Winter sightings simply verify the Hermit Thrush's normal behavior, staying as far north all season as possible so that come early spring, it can rush ahead to its breeding range in southern and central Canada. Right now, it's biding its time, saving energy to survive the cold, preferring not to fly any farther south than necessary. If the cold endures, though, it may have no choice but to move farther south to find the food it requires.

A Hermit Thrush sometimes spends the winter here, finding protection among vines and tangles.

1 Hermit Thrush
Species: 30 total in the yard to date for the year.

January 7

Staying the Course

The recent stretch of bitter cold raises the obvious question: How can birds weighing less than an ounce stay warm in subzero weather? In short, feathers and fat do the trick. When birds look fat, however, we're really looking at their fluffed-up feathers. The more they can fluff their feathers, the more warm air the feathers trap as it radiates from their skin. Birds also build up fat in winter, amounting sometimes up to 10 percent of their body weight. When they grow short of energy, however, their bodies can burn that fat in a matter of a day—or a night. Many birds also grow extra feathers in winter, adding the equivalent of a down vest, and you know how warm that is! Some even lower their body temperature at night by as much as 22 degrees, a process called regulated hypothermia. Both strategies save energy and lives.

Still, songbirds are so tiny that I have to wonder how they can maintain body temperature—normally about 106 degrees—during long winter nights. But they instinctively know the behavioral tricks: They eat high-fat seeds, building up reserves to get through the night (thus accounting for their heavy feeding just at dusk). Some birds snuggle against one another, a behavior that helps prevent loss of body heat. When they can, cavity nesters tuck into a cavity, either natural or man-made, often multiple birds together, even using nest boxes as winter roost boxes. Lacking boxes or other cavities, they scoot into dense foliage. Sometimes I'll note a bird with a bent tail, obviously one that tucked in a too-tight place overnight with a crowd. Note what all this behavior implies regarding the habitat we need to offer wintertime birds: rich seeds and berries, ample shelter, dense foliage, winter roost boxes—anything for protection against the elements.

During bitter-cold nights, multiple Carolina Chickadees sometimes huddle together in a crowded cavity to stay warm, emerging in the morning, like this one, with a bent tail.

Birds Do *That*?

Loggerhead Shrikes impale their victims. As brutal and medieval as it sounds, Northern and Loggerhead Shrikes skewer prey carcasses onto thorns or barbed wire and then tug them downward to keep them in place. Shrikes, about the same size as mockingbirds, take a wide variety of prey including large insects, rodents, lizards, snakes, even some small birds, almost anything up to their own size. While the mode of operation sounds a bit hawk-like, shrikes are actually songbirds—albeit ghoulish ones—that land on their feet and, using their hooked beak, grab prey at the base of the skull. According to a *Science News* magazine article, a rigorous shaking finishes off any prey not killed by the bite to the spine.

January 8

Feeling Relief

Temps yesterday soared to 40 degrees, the first above-freezing temps in over two weeks. This morning, awaking to this comparatively balmy day, I saw an immediate difference in the yard. The frantic flocks of 200 Brown-headed Cowbirds and 175 European Starlings have departed, returning to forage in more open fields where they find more abundant food. The usuals behave differently, too, feeding peacefully, alone among themselves. Faint songs wafted through the quiet when I put out the usual seeds. Songs in January, however, demonstrate behavior other than territorial claims or come-hither calls. Instead, songs are quiet acknowledgments of messages like, "I'm over here," and "Everything is okay," and "These are good berries." Singing behavior in January merely lets a mate know where the other is and signals to all that their world is safe.

A flock of more than 200 Brown-headed Cowbirds (about 50 shown here) swooped in yesterday, but they were gone today, off to more open fields and better foraging.

January 9

Repurposing a Christmas Tree

For several years, I've repurposed a live Christmas tree to serve as a colorful buffet in an otherwise drab winter yard. I've used everything from peanut-butter-filled pine cones; apple wedges; seed-head clusters from asters, goldenrod, sedges, and crape myrtle; and baby gourds filled with peanuts, chopped English walnuts, almonds, and sunflower and safflower seeds. Sometimes I tie on clusters of holly twigs or add a few rehydrated cranberries and raisins, strung and draped across the upper branches. Who comes to feed? As expected, Carolina Chickadees and Tufted Titmice behave in their usual foraging manner, going for the seeds in the baby gourds. Northern Cardinals pull down the switchgrass seed heads and run the stems through their beaks. Dark-eyed Juncos and American Goldfinches pluck the same seeds more delicately, one or two at a time. Mockingbirds love the holly berries and usually go for the cranberries and raisins.

The frustrating part, of course, comes when, in a single riotous night, raccoons rip into all the decorative pieces and spoil the whole appearance—and usefulness—for everyone.

A repurposed Christmas tree, designed to attract a variety of birds, is decorated with native "ornaments," including American holly, switchgrass, and other native grass seeds.

A Dark-eyed Junco dines on switchgrass seeds adorning a repurposed Christmas tree.

January 10

Venturing Outside

A high of 62 degrees today brought a perceived shift in bird populations, but the perception may have been the result of my venturing outside to watch and listen. Pine Siskin populations increased from one or two to a dozen or more. Some winters their numbers astound me, and some winters they never show their striped little faces. Their arrival or the absence thereof are behaviors determined by the seed crop in Canada's boreal forest. Only desperation drives them south. This has apparently been a desperate winter for them.

Early this morning, Snow Geese flying really, really high made me believe they're departing for their Arctic breeding grounds after spending much of the winter at Sauerheber Wildlife Management Area a few miles to our south. They have a long way to go, and the distance drives their behavior to start early. I guess it's nearing the time.

The biggest surprise for the day, though, was the appearance of two Red-headed Woodpeckers, the first we've seen in the yard in ages. And I do mean ages—probably fifteen years or so. Yes, they've been in the woods, but not in the yard. I'm guessing their hunger has driven them out to explore, and they've found our suet and sunflower seed. Here's also guessing they'll become regulars, at least during winter. Hunger drives birds to do the unusual.

A Red-headed Woodpecker sallies in for a surprise appearance after some fifteen years' absence from the yard.

Added to the list today:
50 or so Snow Geese, flying high, hidden by this morning's dense fog
1 Cooper's Hawk fly-by
1 Red-tailed Hawk
2 Red-headed Woodpecker
1 Hairy Woodpecker
1 Song Sparrow
Species: 36 total in the yard to date for the year.

January 11

Eating to Stay Warm

Last night, temps dropped to 20 degrees with freezing rain, then sleet, and then for most of the day today, snow, with flurries predicted to last throughout the night tonight. In spite of my best efforts, I simply couldn't keep the feeders open, so I swept snow off concrete areas—driveway, sidewalk, back stoop—and scattered sunflower seed, safflower seed, nyjer seed, and a few cups of whole corn in the open spots. Within a half hour, though, the snow covered the seed. Birds flocked in, trying to scratch open feeding spots. In late afternoon, I made a concerted effort to keep feed accessible. Birds must prepare for a cold night, eating enough to stay warm, gorging on enough calories to keep metabolisms going—indeed, eating enough to stay alive the night. Birds always live on the edge.

After an icy winter night, a female Northern Cardinal wears ice pellets frozen to her tail. The added weight and the iced-together feathers seriously hamper flight.

January 12

Counting Record Towhees

Snow piled up about 6 inches yesterday and last night, and now winds are whipping up sizable drifts across the yard and driveway. We're marooned unless a kind neighbor comes by with a tractor and plow. But the weather conditions make birds desperate to find food and liquid water. Today that desperation has brought an uncommon number of Eastern Towhees to the yard. Never in the yard have I seen more than a pair plus maybe an offspring or two, but today there were seven, five males and two females, maybe more, judging by the calls I hear a short distance from the yard's perimeter. Towhees are mostly ground birds,

A male Eastern Towhee, a ground feeder, faces life-threatening challenges in deep snow. Here he adapts by foraging on spilled feeder seeds scattered atop the snow cover.

rarely seen higher up, but foraging on the ground now means they must find protected areas, places where either the wind has whipped the ground clear or where minimal snow depths allow them to scratch for food. Scattered seed beneath feeders attracts them but probably rarely satisfies them. Friends reported seeing their towhees where they've never seen them before: picking at suet cakes. These are, indeed, desperate times.

January 13

Watching Birds' Resourcefulness

Eastern Bluebirds suffer perhaps as much or maybe more than other species during ice and snow. They're bug and berry eaters. Bugs, available now, of course, only as eggs and maybe larvae, are tucked underground, likely frozen, covered by multiple inches of snow. Any fruits remaining hang ice-coated. So bluebirds have two behavioral options: find another food source, or fly farther south, beyond the ice and snow, to seek sustenance. Of course, flying takes energy and puts them at risk for depleting their biological resources before they find an ice-free area in which they may—or may not—find bugs or berries.

So I'm watching their resourcefulness, which alternative behaviors they might choose. They've discovered crumbled bits under the suet feeder, leftovers from ravenous woodpeckers hammering at the frozen suet cakes, showering off flakes as they consume the larger chunks. While the woodpeckers do just fine pounding with their chisel beaks to break apart the suet, bluebirds can't hammer off even the slightest frozen-solid tidbits from

Five Eastern Bluebirds, facing dire times, feed on fat-rich chunky peanut butter smeared on tree bark and very finely chopped suet, apples, and rehydrated raisins scattered nearby. Because bluebirds swallow foods whole, suet and fruits must be offered in tiny pieces.

the cake. They lack the bill structure to do so. But ah, that suet is a great substitute for summertime bugs.

So in the late afternoons, they've been foraging on the ground under the suet feeders. Taking their cue, I've added a few tidbits of my own—some peanut butter and very finely chopped apples and equally finely chopped reconstituted raisins. They like the buffet. Perhaps they can survive because of it. I like to think so.

January 14

Adding to Birds' Misery

The severe weather continues, and we have another 3 inches of snow on top of the ice and snow from two days ago. As I suspected, the increasing severity worsens birds' misery and brings even more of them to the yard, behaving with more aggression than usual, whatever they find necessary to forage successfully. The Northern Flicker population zoomed today from one to five, all visiting suet cakes mounted at various locations. Flickers are highly migratory woodpeckers, so the added numbers in the yard right now are probably the result of wintering visitors from the north. Of course, they could also be offspring from the nesting pair we saw regularly early last summer. Whoever they are, they spent part of their foraging time staving off European Starlings at the suet feeders. At one point I watched a Downy Woodpecker, a Northern Flicker, and a starling vying for rights to the same feeder.

For a time I thought the starling was a sure-fire winner, but the flicker won. The poor Downy didn't stand a chance—although she hung around until all was clear.

A Brown Thrasher picked around seed scraps on the ground—probably the same bird that visited briefly ten days ago—but it didn't seem to find satisfaction. Thrashers are not seed eaters, but seeing it pick about in the debris suggested its desperation. It did, however, take a long drink at the bubble rock.

While nothing feeding in the yard paid much attention, a Red-shouldered Hawk circled the area twice, calling. She's not a serious yard threat unless she's starving, and she may be approaching that status. Mostly, though, she thinks of the little birds as too much trouble, too little food value for the effort. Still, I would have missed her entirely except for her persistent call, making me look to be sure it was the hawk and not a Blue Jay. Jays are notorious for their behavior of mimicking hawk calls, a habit that often scares everything from the feeders so the jays get full rein of whatever they want. Such stinkers, those jays, but so smart.

Behaving in his usual manner, the little Fox Sparrow showed cautious behavior, keeping to the underbrush, neatly concealed from any view from above, scratching about in the fallen cypress leaves, content to keep on keeping on, even amid the noisy jays and circling hawk. Wintering Fox Sparrows never like to be in the open.

New yard birds today amid the snow and ice:
1 Red-shouldered Hawk
1 Pileated Woodpecker
1 Ruby-crowned Kinglet
1 Fox Sparrow
Species: 40 total in the yard to date for the year.

A Fox Sparrow, a secretive ground-loving bird that tends to hide in evergreen foliage, forages on spilled feeder seed, camouflaged even in plain sight by its cryptic plumage.

Birds Do *That*?

Osprey align captured fish aerodynamically in their talons. In order to carry a heavy load more easily, Ospreys manipulate a captured fish to orient it straight ahead, head first, aligned with their own bodies, providing less drag as the birds fly. According to *Birds of North America Online*, the Osprey's reversible outer toe, which can move forward or backward, gives the birds the dexterity to rearrange the fish in midair.

January 15

Stripping the Hollies

The holly berries, having gone through sufficient freeze-thaw cycles, have now reached the perfect degree of softness for all those feathered berry lovers! At least the birds' behavior sent that message. Cedar Waxwings were the first to discover the perfect degree of readiness, and American Robins were quick to follow. The Northern Mockingbird tried in vain to defend the two 40-foot-tall trees, but it quickly reduced its efforts to one tree and finally to a single branch. The poor bird ultimately failed on all protectionist counts, and the robins stripped the trees. Three Eastern Bluebirds managed a few berries by feeding lower than the others. For whatever reason, robins start at the tops of the trees and work their way to the lowest branches—a behavior they follow every year.

19 Cedar Waxwing
Species: 41 total in the yard to date for the year.

A Cedar Waxwing snags a "ripe" holly berry that, after repeated freeze-thaw cycles, has softened sufficiently for birds to swallow whole and digest.

An American Robin gobbles down ripened holly berries. A flock can strip a huge tree of its berries in a matter of a day or two.

January 16

Sorting Sparrow IDs

This afternoon, out of the corner of my eye, I caught sight of an unusual sparrow in the platform feeder 2 feet from the kitchen window. Field Sparrow? No, its two-toned bill was distinctly different from the Field Sparrow's pink bill. Maybe a winter-plumaged Chipping Sparrow? No, that wasn't right either, especially given that most chippers have moved farther south to escape this winter's wrath. I managed a few photos before the stranger flew to the ground where it foraged through the scattered spilled seeds. Turns out that this bird is not a usual in my yard; its behavior more generally puts it in broad expanses of brush, feeding, as sparrows usually do, on the ground, foraging on tiny weed seeds. One wandered through our yard last year on January 24, under somewhat similar frigid conditions. It's a handsome bird, this American Tree Sparrow. Its behavior on both occasions, foraging at a feeder, sends a message: Finding food is tough out there.

After feeding for 5 or 6 minutes, it hopped onto the bubble rock, drank its fill, and zipped off toward the brushy hillside behind the barn. I caught up with it there, watching it forage in its preferred habitat, finding grass seeds to its liking.

An American Tree Sparrow munches on grass seed gleaned among the tangles on the unmowed hillside.

1 American Tree Sparrow
Species: 42 total in the yard to date for the year.

January 17

Hearing Nighttime Calls

The Barred Owl called three times tonight, at about 11 p.m. In the distance I heard his mate answer, her voice a bit higher pitched than his. She's likely getting her nest in perfect order, and he's letting her know he'll be around to bring her food from his stealthy nightly hunts. Their nighttime contact talk awakened me just enough in my snug bed to make me smile.

January 18

Catching the Melt Drops

With still winds and bright sun, we bundled up in as many layers as feasible and, in spite of the cold, spent several hours enjoying the sunshine, photographing birds, listening to song, and watching.

Desperate for liquid water, American Robins and Cedar Waxwings scattered along the snowmelt line on the south-facing roofs of the house and the garage, some eating snow, others catching the melt drops. The later in the morning and the warmer the sun on the roof, the greater the number of birds following the trickles. Nobody has to teach birds how to find water.

American Goldfinches and Pine Siskins were feeding on the sycamore tree seed balls. I can't imagine there's much nutrition there, but both species behaved similarly, flitting back and forth between the nyjer feeders and the tree, often dangling upside down from the seed balls as they fed. It was pure pleasure hearing the musical twittering songs of all the siskins, probably at least twenty-five or so, their song like tiny bells jingling from trees and bushes near and far.

American Robins, desperate for a drink of unfrozen water, find it at the drip line of sun-melted snow on the roof.

A Pine Siskin feeds on seed balls of a sycamore tree, perhaps preferring native seed to nonnative commercial varieties.

January 19

Checking Nooks and Crannies

With this the first day above freezing in several days, I had the incentive to wander the entire yard, checking nooks and crannies I can't see from any house window, watching for behavior and listening for clues about who's where. One good find for the day: Brown Creeper. Winter-only visitors here, they're hard to see as they spiral up the tree trunks, always up. Camouflage coloration lets them blend with the bark, and I'd never spot them if they didn't move. And I've never spotted them anywhere else other than foraging on tree bark, a uniquely creeper behavior. While there's nothing remarkable about their cryptic loveliness, they always make me study them for the plumage pattern. They're visiting my yard in winter, on vacation from their breeding territory along a relatively narrow band that more or less follows the US-Canada border. Watching them hold themselves against their little spiny tails as they hitch along the bark guarantees true respect for their athleticism! For them, it's a necessary behavior. How else could they poke into deep bark crevices to find spider eggs and other bugs, bug eggs, and larvae?

But I was also amazed today to discover how many White-throated Sparrows are hiding in the three little groves of red cedars, in the brambles, in the weedy patches, in the lightly tended fencerows, and in the woodland edge. I'm guessing there were at least thirty. Some were white-striped; some, tan-striped. Strange as it seems, the white versus tan does not depict sexual dimorphism. Rather, either color can be either sex. I have come to notice, however, that tan-striped birds seem also to have more streaky breasts. I saw lots of both today (see photos of both on March 4). They prefer dense cover and always forage on the ground, so they're spending little time in the open yard, uninterested in the feeders hanging there. Well, except for whatever spilled seed falls below.

Juncos surprised me, too, maybe twenty-five. Since only a few of each species show up at a time near feeders, it takes a walking count of the yard to figure out how many are really here as well as to gain insight into their behavior: how they react to the habitat, who's hanging out where in what kind of vegetation, and what provides shelter that they most prefer. Always a learning experience for me!

The one really great thing about the thaw: Starlings and cowbirds have gone on their way. Only five or six scavenged suet and seed feeders today. Yea!

> 1 Brown Creeper
> **Species:** 43 total in the yard to date for the year.

January 20

Ripping through the Yard

Yep, bound to happen sooner or later. With all the little songbirds enjoying the feast, a new predator arrived on the scene. My first clue came when I awakened this morning to an empty yard. I knew the trouble had to be a hawk, but which one? And where was it? By midday, after the songbirds made only guarded, off-and-on visits to the yard, I finally caught sight of a hawk ripping across the yard, landing in the maple tree. It was one of those mid-sized critters—either a small male Cooper's Hawk or a large female Sharp-shinned

A Sharp-shinned Hawk, here in my yard only in winter, tucks in among the branches, hiding, hunting lunch in our songbird-rich yard.

Hawk. They look so very much alike that I'm always hesitant to make the call, but by managing a few through-the-window photos and checking the field mark details, there was no question. A sharpie had moved in.

Sharpies love pine trees for shelter and camouflage. We have pines. Sharpies love feeding stations with an abundance of little birds. We have them, too. Sharpies love the jet-through situations that let them roar in and grab prey before the prey even know the hawk is around. We have that. Still, I wish it would take a few more starlings or House Sparrows rather than cardinals and bluebirds. At least sharpies hang out here in our immediate area only in winter. Range maps show their summer breeding territories begin in northern Michigan as well as to our east in the Appalachian range. For now, though, the rascal is a free-ranging terrorist here.

1 Sharp-shinned Hawk
Species: 44 total in the yard to date for the year.

January 21

Mimicking Bobwhites

While filling backyard feeders this morning, I heard the distinct call of a Northern Bobwhite. Really? I stopped my task and stood still, listening carefully. Could a European Starling be doing a close imitation? A second call, not the full ascending "bob white," but the contact call, the questioning that sounds to my ear as if it's saying "wha-at?" Several more times, clearly, the call came from the woods' edge to our east. So few Bobwhites remain in this part of the country that their call or song, either one, stops me in my tracks, grateful to know its presence. They've declined because of loss of habitat, the result of too-tidy farm practices that erase weedy fencerows, weedy roadsides, weedy creek banks, and generally shrubby patches within the grasslands.

So this morning's scenario seemed all wrong. The woods' edge along the one-lane road abuts the neighbor's yard. No grasslands here. No hedgerows, brushy ditch sides, and unmown or otherwise overgrown fields for wintertime hunkering down. In previous situations I've heard Northern Bobwhites across the hayfield or along the edges of the corn and soybean fields to our north. I've even had Bobwhites wander through our yard. In fact, once a covey of about a dozen fluttered into the maple tree to escape a perceived threat— me! But that was probably twenty years ago. Things have changed. Dramatically. Still, the Bobwhite's call could well be legit. I continued listening.

Given the starling population in our neighbor's yard, though, I'm reluctant to record the call as an additional yard bird. Starlings are just too blasted good at mimicking our precious Bobwhites. I couldn't convince myself.

A European Starling in winter plumage earns the nickname "rice bird," for the heavy white spots on its fresh plumage. The spots wear off by spring, leaving the bird in sleek iridescent breeding plumage. (See the starling in spring plumage on February 5.)

Birds Do *That*?

Chickadees shiver to keep warm. Their shivering, though, is not quite like our occasional shiver. Instead, it's an almost constant series of contractions of opposing muscles, minus the jiggling we humans exhibit. Such shaking helps the little guys produce heat up to five times their normal rate and then helps retain that heat, a process known as thermogenosis. According to the National Audubon Society website, to keep warm on cold winter nights, birds also fluff up their feathers to hold heat, put on fat for insulation, and even control blood supplies to vital organs, diverting warming blood away from extremities like feet and legs in order to keep their bodies toasty. In short, if they can find sufficient food to engage in their usual behavior, they can keep warm.

January 22

Foraging among Sycamore Balls
Finches, including American Goldfinches and Pine Siskins, were feeding like little piggies again today on the sycamore seed balls. It's hard to imagine that there's much nutrition there, given all the fuzzy parts, but every winter I find the birds munching away. Since birds love them, and since sycamores often have great nest cavities, they're good native trees for areas damp enough to support them. The one closest to the house, of course, brings me the most birds, but several more sycamores along the creek just inside our little patch of woods surely host other birds that wander into and through the yard that I don't see.

January 23

Washing Away Snowdrifts
Rain washed away the last of the snowdrifts; only a few piles remain where road graders left the heaps. Haven't seen anything new today, but with ongoing above-freezing temps, maybe the waterfowl will start moving. They've spent the winter with us, but now, by late January or early February, they're eager to return to their breeding range. Most will go to central Canada to breed, but the Snow Geese and White-fronted Geese will travel to the high Arctic.

The Northern Shoveler, one of our prettiest migratory ducks, arrives here in multitudes during winter.

January 24

Enjoying Flickers

Yellow-shafted Northern Flickers continue to visit the suet feeders now, even after the snow has melted. The odd thing about their ongoing visits is that most references claim that flickers never visit feeders, including suet feeders. Granted, they're not regulars at the bird buffet, but they certainly understand where to grab some nutrition during nasty winter weather. And they don't mind a treat during summer, either!

They're our most unusual woodpeckers in that they prefer to gather ants and beetles from the ground rather than hammer trees for bugs, although they do, of course, hammer on trees and carve out nest cavities in trees. Western flickers are called red-shafted, and that's because where our region's bird's feather shafts on wings and tail show bright yellow, in the West they're red. On both subspecies, males have a black moustache, but females lack the black facial pattern. Oddly enough, when nesting time comes this summer, they'll disappear, sneaking off quietly to breed somewhere private and secure. When the babies fledge and have their wings up to speed, the whole family will return. At least that's been their behavior in the past!

A Male Northern Flicker routinely visits to our suet feeder, even though authorities say the birds rarely do so.

January 25

Finding Emerging Daffodils

First glimpse today of emerging daffodils, one of the earliest plants to show green! I can't help wondering if birds see changes like that and let out a sigh of relief that winter must be close to ending. Okay, no, I'm being anthropomorphic. Sorry. But I certainly let out a sigh of relief!

January 26

Photographing a Hawk Overhead

Identifying hawks in flight can be a snap with a clear view of the under-wing pattern. Today a Red-tailed Hawk soared over the house, possibly checking out the territory. Since Red-shouldered and Red-tailed hawks don't like each other and compete for the same territories, I'm making an educated guess that the Red-tailed won't be around long. That's because a Red-shouldered lives here, and her territory includes our little corner of woods and its adjoining larger woodland, our yard, and the neighbor's hayfield. In previous years the Red-tailed has taken up residence farther to the north, including the neighbor's wood-lot, pasture, and surrounding agricultural lands. While the territories join, the two hawks seem to establish an uneasy truce about who stays where. Occasionally, however, the two hawks meet—no doubt unintentionally—at the unseen border of their territories. Inevitably, an aerial battle ensues until each sorts out the issues and returns to its proper place.

Today's photos of the Red-tailed's overhead flight make sense of the identifying under-wing pattern: the dark patagial stripe (the fold of skin between the body and wing) and the "comma" near wing's end. In addition, the Red-tailed's "necklace" serves as an excellent identifying field mark. While today's hawk is a mature bird with a namesake red tail, juveniles have brown tails, thus causing some confusion for folks. Amazing, isn't it, that birds can have such clearly defining plumages, all the result of a distinct color pattern on each individual feather.

A Red-tailed Hawk in flight, the sun shining through its tail feathers, shows off its signature red tail, a characteristic not evident on immature Red-taileds.

January 27

Scaring an Owl

Early this evening, just before 5 p.m., I startled a Barred Owl from what I assume was its day roost. I say I startled her, but in truth I expect I was the one more startled. She knew I was headed her way, her senses so keen that she had heard my every step from the time I stepped out of the house. The "Who cooks for you? Who cooks for you-all?" calls I've heard over the past few days have seemed to be coming from this general area, but I'd never been able to catch sight of her. She blended so perfectly amid the eastern red cedar foliage that even 20 feet away I didn't see her until she flew. If I hadn't been coincidentally looking her direction, I would never have known she was anywhere around. Her flight is absolutely silent. Most certainly that's why owls are called the "silent killers." Owl wing feathers boast an amazing construction that combines air passage and a structure akin to velvet that muffles all sound of movement. Prey never know what hits them.

This photo was taken in April 2016, but ironically it captures the exact spot she occupied this evening. Now I have to wonder if it's also the same bird.

A Barred Owl tucks into the dense branches of an eastern red cedar tree to afford itself safety during its day roost.

January 28

Wandering Afield

As we were out and about this afternoon, we made a foray to a wetlands to our south to check on waterfowl populations. The site is acclaimed for the tens of thousands of Snow Geese and White-fronted Geese that winter there. Smaller populations of dabbling ducks and a surprising several hundred Tundra Swans round out the general population. Of course, we usually manage to spot a few shorebirds like Killdeer and Wilson's Snipe, too. Typically watching over it all will be a dozen or more Bald Eagles, juveniles and adults. They dine on anything sick or injured or too slow to make an escape.

In short, we visit for the sheer numbers.

When I was a kid, we referred to Snow Geese and Blue Geese, rather mystical creatures that we only dreamed of seeing. Since then, things have changed. Now scientists have proven that Snows and Blues are merely different morphs of the same bird. But also when I was a kid, if you'd told anyone you saw Snow Geese here, you would have been considered a tad insane. Never did Snow Geese show either their white or blue selves here.

Migratory patterns, however, have changed. Now they're here in huge numbers. And huge numbers have caused the birds to become their own worst enemies, literally eating themselves away from the table. They nest in colonies north of the timberline in the Arctic tundra across Greenland, Canada, Alaska, and Siberia. Best estimates from the US Fish & Wildlife Service indicate there are about 5 million individuals, a population that exploded by 300 percent since the mid-1970s and continues to increase by about 5 percent per year. Best guesses suggest the population expansion may be the result of turning forest and prairie into agricultural lands, a change that attracts the geese. Because their vast numbers are destroying

Only part of the massive flock of tens of thousands of Snow Geese is shown here, lifting off from wetlands.

the arctic and subarctic tundra where they nest, and because that destruction is also affecting other wildlife that uses those lands, loosened hunting restrictions and the elimination of bag limits have been federally mandated in both the United States and Canada.

Still, seeing the birds lift off by the thousands, creating a vast blur of white, their black wing tips barely noticeable, makes me realize that at one time, before humans interfered, numerous species took off in equally blurred multitudes. The Passenger Pigeon makes the point: from tens of thousands to extinct over only two generations. My grandmother remembered Passenger Pigeons from her childhood when the skies would darken for days as the flocks flew over. The last individual, named Martha, died in captivity in 1914 at about age 29. We humans killed them all.

January 29

Visiting Lake Barkley

Surprisingly, Great Blue Herons hang out at Lake Barkley Dam in Kentucky year-round. Sure, sometimes the populations dwindle, but they're always there. Today was no exception.

There's something dramatic about Great Blues, something that causes most photographers to proclaim they can never get too many photos of the magnificent herons. Quite simply, the birds look prehistoric and awkward, gangly legged, dagger beaked, and long necked. But their behavior is anything but awkward. I'd call them stately. When fishing, they're marvelous stabbing machines, deadly accurate and wickedly fast. They can stand like statues for long minutes, stalking prey. They fly like graceful dancers, slow wing beats, neck bent into an S, and legs flowing straight behind. All those characteristics combine to make the big birds not only fascinating to watch but challenging to photograph, especially to capture them in flight with their catch in their beaks. We can readily spend hours at the challenge. And do. The images tell at least part of the story of the bird's behavior.

A Great Blue Heron flies with a sizable fish in its beak, heading to shore where it will manage to swallow the fish head first, whole.

Birds Do *That*?

Male Red-winged Blackbirds attract harems of up to fifteen females. According to the Cornell Lab of Ornithology website, in most populations, 90 percent of males have multiple females nesting in their respective territories. But here's the kicker: Even though the males are highly territorial and possessive about their respective harems, testing shows that up to half of the nestlings have been sired by some other male.

January 30

Peering at Pelicans

Continuing news from our Lake Barkley visit: Most folks would never dream they could see a pelican in the central Midwest, but they're here! These inland pelicans, however, only slightly resemble the grayish-brown ones seen along the coasts. In fact, American White Pelicans, all-white-bodied birds with contrasting black wing tips and edges, are among the largest birds in North America, weighing in at nearly 20 pounds with a wingspan of 9.5 feet. That wingspan is longer than our house ceilings are tall. One big bird!

The American White Pelican, a primarily freshwater bird, scoops its fish from the water rather than dive on it as do Brown Pelicans.

Why are they in the Midwest in January? They breed in central Canada and a few isolated colony areas in the US Northwest, but they love migrating through the central Midwest and hanging out during our generally now-milder winters. They've found man-made lakes like Kentucky's 134-mile-long Lake Barkley, restored wetlands like Indiana's Goose Pond Fish & Wildlife Area, and comfortable loafing spots along Ohio and Wabash River sandbars—all providing an abundance of fish the birds like to corral and swallow whole. Since the birds need about three years to reach breeding maturity, the sub-adults often hang out year-

Brown Pelicans, like this one preening, prefer saltwater habitats and are the birds most folks think of when they hear the term "pelican."

round, especially at Lake Barkley. After all, why would a bird be motivated to fly to breeding grounds in Canada if it's not of breeding age? An absence of hormonal drive lets the birds loaf here, much to our viewing pleasure!

January 31

Capturing the Unusual

Sometimes a photo reveals something too quick to see otherwise. Today, an image of a male Downy Woodpecker revealed something special—one of its eyelids. Birds have two sets of eyelids. One set moves up and down like ours. The other moves front to back and is translucent. Birds can see through the translucency. This secondary eyelid, called the nictitating membrane, protects their eyes in flight and against anything that might brush against their eyes while moving through their habitats. A blind bird, even a one-eyed bird, is a dead bird, so the extra eye protection is Mother Nature's way of keeping birds safe. Cool!

A male Downy Woodpecker appears to have its eye half closed but in reality is only blinking with its second eyelid, properly known as a nictitating membrane, that moves front to back instead of top to bottom.

February

A Short-eared Owl, adapted to high-Arctic summers and Midwest winters, hunts the reclaimed strip-mine lands that somewhat resemble its tundra home.

Look closely at nature. Every species is a masterpiece, exquisitely adapted to the particular environment in which it has survived.

—E. O. Wilson (1929–), American biologist

February 1

Relishing a Light Snow

Who would have guessed? More snow. Enough already, right? But this snow was lovely, not more than an inch, didn't stick to the roads, but clung to everything else and gave me one last (I hope) seasonal opportunity to photograph Northern Cardinals in the snow.

A female Northern Cardinal hunches, feathers fluffed against yet another winter snowfall.

Snow usually causes birds serious stress, burying their food. But they protect themselves by moving into a microhabitat, such as in evergreens or a dense hedge or on the lee side of anything. Closer to the ground is always warmer, so they also tend to stay low in snow. When they sense a change in air pressure, a condition that usually foretells bad weather, they go on a feeding frenzy, storing fat to keep warm. Of course, they've also evolved over thousands of years to survive the cold. Blood circulation to their feet, for instance, is diverted from circulation that warms internal organs, so their feet don't freeze, even perched on ice.

February 2

Counting American Goldfinches

While weather continues its roller-coaster ups and downs, backyard bird populations remain about the same. But there's one huge exception: American Goldfinches. This morning I counted seventy-two feeding in the yard, and I could hear more in the trees, nearby but out of sight. I'm not afraid to bet at least one hundred were foraging throughout the property.

So what's with the sudden uptick of goldfinches? Yes, of course, we have American Goldfinches year-round, but banding studies have shown they're not the same goldfinches year-round. While "ours" hang out almost full-time, breed here, raise their young in nests built of thistle fluff, and feed their babies regurgitated seeds, they're few in number—probably only a dozen or so. Goldfinches just north of us and way north of us, however, find their winters too harsh for survival. So, following their usual behavior, they meander south as far as necessary to find suitable cold-weather habitat. This winter they apparently overflew us, moving well to our south to avoid what has been—at least from the birds' perspective—a to-date nasty winter.

Now, however, the days are growing longer. Triggered by the sun's changing path, birds' hormones are beginning to pump them up, preparing them for breeding. Goldfinches that breed here are already here, among the one hundred. Goldfinches that breed to our north are on the move, some winging a few hundred miles, others many hundreds of miles, all heading toward ancestral breeding grounds. On the way, they've reached our southern

Forty-three American Goldfinches and three Pine Siskins feed at every available port on this snowy day, the weather driving them to quick sustenance.

Indiana yard only to discover that we're about as far north as they want to travel for now. Northerly conditions show no signs of welcome. So, as weather conditions determine their behavior, they've piled up. And they continue to pile up. Thus, the one hundred or so in the extended yard today.

February 3

Filling Nyjer Feeders

It's been an unusual winter for Pine Siskin behavior. Some winters I never see them; some winters they're here early and late. This winter, though, they've visited us almost every day. Sure, the populations varied, some days only a handful, some days a dozen or two, and some days forty or more. Now, among those one hundred goldfinches, I'd estimate at least forty siskins have piled up here—for the same reason the goldfinches are piled up. The longer days, but not necessarily warming temperatures, tell siskins it's time for them to return to their breeding grounds across Canada. The closest siskin breeding grounds lie 800 miles or more to our north, but few of these siskins will breed in the closest edge of their range. So some may fly in excess of 1,000 miles, and they're eager to be moving on, hardwired to reach breeding grounds early, to have first choice at the best territories and the strongest mates.

Between the goldfinches and siskins, then, the nyjer feeders drop about a gallon of seed per day. My yard is not unique in its abundance of finches, so area merchants' shelves are bare of nyjer seed this week. I probably bought the last 50-pound bag in the area this afternoon. Given the nyjer-seed price, I'm torn about how long I'd like the finches and siskins to stay!

February 4

Judging Juncos

Watching the multitudes of Dark-eyed Juncos today caused me to pause. Common birds, represented by nine subspecies, their numbers are estimated to range around 630 million across North America. Even locally, color variations—beyond the distinctive differences

A Dark-eyed Junco, showing more pink than usual along its sides, illustrates plumage variation among individuals and the difficulty of identifying subspecies.

between males and females—suggest not only possible local subspecies representations but maybe hybridizations as well. Subspecies typically are limited to specific geographic areas, but juncos migrate. When they arrive in our yard, they could have come from any number of locales. It's those sometimes pinkish sides on males, more pink than usual, that make me wonder who's who. Could it be an Oregon Junco? I know the Oregons are often misidentified, perhaps out of wishful thinking. Still, it's fun to sort them out, sometimes coming to recognize individuals that visit regularly. The little guy photographed today is certainly one of them! Wish I could somehow know where it's been, how far it's come, and whether it's going to stay until spring. Using geolocators, scientists have been able to tune in to a growing number of specific birds' migratory behaviors, and the results often boggle the mind.

February 5

Fighting for Food

In a battle this afternoon between a Hairy Woodpecker and a winter-plumaged European Starling, the winner takes all the suet! What determines who wins avian food fights? Mostly body size and beak size, but given this fairly even match today, pure feistiness did the trick. This suet feeder hangs near the center of the Hairy Woodpecker's year-round territory, so his natural behavior is to fight anything he deems intrusive—and this starling represented intrusiveness, big time.

By summer this speckled starling will lose its spots. In good light, its summer plumage of blues and greens will glisten with iridescence. Who thought I would ever admit to anything positive about nonnative invasive starlings, those birds that steal thousands of nest cavities from our native species, causing their populations to plummet. Starlings are to blame for the serious decline of Red-headed Woodpeckers and Eastern Bluebirds. Of course, ultimately humans are to blame for bringing the starlings from Europe. Yuck.

Oh. Who won the fight? You bet! The Hairy Woodpecker stood his ground, got in a few sharp pecks, and won the day—and saved his favorite suet feeder.

A Hairy Woodpecker engages in a face-off with a European Starling, each using its long bill to stab toward the other. Eventually, in this food fight, the home-territory Hairy Woodpecker won.

By summer, the European Starling's white spots have worn off, and the bird wears silky iridescent breeding plumage.

Birds Do *That*?

American White Pelicans herd fish. Close cousins of the oceanic Brown Pelicans, American White Pelicans live inland on freshwater lakes. Rather than dive for fish the way Brown Pelicans do, the white birds scoop fish from just below the surface. To make fishing easier, however, they cooperate in a team effort. Together, they chase schools of fish into shallow water, corralling them, and then scoop up dinner.

February 6

Coloring Spring

It's a sure sign that spring approaches: a European Starling with a yellow bill, spotted this afternoon at a suet feeder. After yesterday's tussle between the Hairy Woodpecker and the black-billed starling, it was a bit of a surprise to see the yellow-billed bird today. As winter wanes, starlings' bills turn whitish, then a dirty yellow, and by summer, in breeding plumage, bright yellow. Amazing, isn't it, that a bird can change the color of its bill!

February 7

Turning the Birds' World to Ice

No, it's not spring after all.

Only two-tenths of an inch of freezing rain fell last night; nevertheless, it turned the birds' world into a see-but-can't-eat state of crisis, their food encapsulated or frozen to the ground. Finches and sparrows can't manage to peck seeds loose. They fly to a perch only to slide along the stem until a bump, leaf, or twig halts their slide.

Even more disturbing to me, however, was seeing a group of Mourning Doves with iced tails. Because doves often roost in a protected spot on or near the ground, they risk the calamity of being frozen in place. One has lost about half of its tail feathers, but as unlikely as it seems, the feathers now yanked from its body are still iced by their tips to the tips of the still-viable feathers. The poor bird no doubt pulled out its feathers to escape its roost. Now, with a clump of feathers trailing behind, it can barely fly and crashed about awkwardly trying to land. As a result, it's highly vulnerable now to predation, especially by the Sharp-shinned Hawk that's been eating its daily kill in the yard. (Yesterday it took a Dark-eyed Junco right at the side door, scooting the door mat out of position in its furious floundering.)

In addition to the single dove with its severe handicap of lost but dangling tail feathers, a half dozen more doves sat, sunning, their backs to the weak warmth, their tails likewise ice covered. With their feathers stuck together, they can't fan their tails for navigational purposes, and added weight compounds the difficulty of flight. Some attempted to preen, but I fear they may cause more harm than good, perhaps breaking

A Mourning Dove, wearing an iced tail, exhibits serious aftereffects of overnight freezing rain. Ground roosters sometimes lose their tail feathers trying to free themselves from having been frozen to the surface.

the remaining feathers, rendering them useless. While temps remained below freezing, I hoped their sunning brought relief. As I watched out the window, considering their dire situation, I was saddened. With sunshine glistening on ice-covered trees, shrubs, garden remains, even every grass blade, we humans tend to thrill to what we perceive as a picturesque winter wonderland. Our comfortable lives let us slide over the harsh reality of the wonderland's effects.

February 8

Snagging a Buffet

Woodpeckers work daily on the snag in the backyard. We left the snag purposely when the old tulip tree had to be cut down to protect the house from falling limbs and the potential for uprooting. Tree service guys cut the tree to a snag that now pokes bare stubs to the sky, ready for woodpeckers to pound out the bugs and larvae. In fact, standing dead trees are essential for woodpeckers' survival, not only for food but, of course, for nesting and roosting. Today, a female Hairy Woodpecker and her mate, regulars at the site, checked for bugs among the bark's crevices. I'm betting they had a tasty buffet.

February 9

Helping Bluebirds

For the past two winters, I've worried about our Eastern Bluebirds finding enough to eat after the holly berries disappeared. Both last winter and this, I've smeared suet or a suet-peanut butter combo on tree bark near the ground, in a spot beneath a suet feeder. Since the bluebirds' customary behavior is to look for suet crumbs under feeders, they readily found my offering. And because they usually come to the yard in late afternoon, I wait until about 3 p.m. to put it out, hoping they get some before those rascal starlings scarf it all up. I'd love to feed mealworms, but again . . . those starlings.

February 10

Birding at a Distance

Getting out and about today to enjoy a break in the weather, we drove about an hour north to a reclaimed strip mine. Perhaps that doesn't sound very enticing, but every winter the Short-eared Owls come there for a several-months-long visit. They love the short-grass habitat throughout the thousands of acres of rolling land. More importantly, they love the moles and voles that thrive in the newly established grasslands. It's prime hunting, and the dozens of owls seem to stay healthy all winter dining on the little furry critters. Short-eared Owls engage in a low-light-specific behavior: They're late-in-the-day hunters, rising from ground-level perches a couple of hours before dark to sweep low in moth-like flight across the hunting grounds. What a joy to watch them doing what they do so well—all the while knowing that within less than a month, they'll be on their way back to the Arctic tundra to nest. Perhaps they overwinter here because the rolling grasslands remind them of their tundra home. Now it's become an annual ritual to visit them, hoping our satisfaction in seeing them matches their satisfaction in being here!

Among the Short-eared Owls hunting across the acres of reclaimed land, Northern Harriers exhibit a similar swoop-hunting behavior. But unlike Short-ears, harriers remain on task all day, not just at dusk and dawn. Voracious hunters, the sleek but muscular silver-plumaged males and the chunkier but equally agile rusty-colored females pursue little furry critters. Tonight we watched a handsome male take a not-so-little rabbit apart, bite by bite, swallowing hunks whole until the ground was bare. Because harriers and Short-eareds like the same foods, though, they often take offense at one another's presence. Aerial battles ensue. But Short-eared Owls don't like the presence—and, therefore, competition—of even another Short-eared, so foot-to-foot combat sometimes ultimately decides who hunts where. It's a behavior that sends owls on the run. Harriers outweigh owls; and although range maps show otherwise, since harriers live in the grasslands year-round, they're fighting on their home court. Who says those aren't great advantages!

All in all, we spent 3 hours watching the spectacle.

Short-eared Owls move south from their tundra breeding range to hunt in short-grass meadows, here across reclaimed strip mines.

A male Northern Harrier finishes a meal, having captured his prey in the short vegetation of a reclaimed strip mine.

Birds Do *That*?

The Ivory-billed Woodpecker was a finicky eater. According to bird columnist Jack Conner, the Ivory-billed Woodpecker went extinct because it was a finicky eater. It dined only on a certain beetle larvae. That larvae was found only in large, newly dead trees. Those trees existed only in virgin forests. And those preferred forests grew only in certain parts of the South. We humans, in our greed, cut those forests. The Ivory-billed Woodpecker, ecological specialist that it was, went extinct.

Now the Red-cockaded Woodpecker is considered our rarest woodpecker, and it, too, is an ecological specialist. It nests only in certain pines that have redheart disease. Similarly, Limpkins and Snail Kites feed only on apple snails. The decline of those snails will likely irrevocably mean the decline—or demise—of the ecological specialists that feed on them. Other birds exhibit equally limited ecological specialization. In short, because we humans make life difficult for many birds, only those that can adapt will likely survive. Ecological specialists may not.

February 11

Catching Kestrels

Capturing a digital image of an American Kestrel in flight makes for a memorable day and added to yesterday's pleasure in the field.

A male American Kestrel takes flight from its hunting perch, probably having caught sight of a rodent in the short grass.

Most often seen perching on utility wires, hunting short-grass habitat below, American Kestrels exhibit another unique behavior: They're one of the few birds that can hover during the hunt. When I was a kid, folks called them "sparrow hawks" because we thought they hunted sparrows. Actually, they prefer rodents and, in summer, dragonflies and grasshoppers. Our smallest falcon, the kestrel is a tad smaller than a Mourning Dove.

February 12

Accounting for Woodpeckers

A male Pileated Woodpecker made a somewhat rare visit to our suet feeder today, the one mounted on the old snag in the backyard. He roams the area and I hear him in our little woodlot, but bursting right out into the backyard—well, he surprised us. What a looker! The male Pileated is distinguished from his mate by his red moustache and fully red topknot, the red extending down to the beak. Their Woody Woodpecker size puts them in a class by themselves. Fortunately, over the past decades they seem to have adapted to their human cohabitants. When I was a kid, no one saw Pileateds; they stayed hidden, away from prying eyes. Now, with humans encroaching on their habitat, they've altered their behavior, becoming more tolerant of us—and now even come to our feeders.

Indeed, today was a deluxe woodpecker day. Simultaneously, at various suet feeders were Northern Flicker and Hairy, Downy, and Red-bellied Woodpeckers. How do I account for such behavior, five of our seven woodpecker species all showing up to feed at nearly the same time? Desperation. Their breeding season is just around the corner, and they need to eat. Their favorite foods, though—bugs and their eggs and larvae—are in short supply or frozen. Thawing temps predicted for later this week will be a lifesaver for woodpeckers that live where no suet feeders offer a ready substitute.

A male Pileated Woodpecker turns to a commercial suet cake to supplement a skimpy wintertime diet.

February 13

Feeling Balmy

This morning's above-freezing temperatures felt downright balmy, and birds were singing, I think, more loudly than since last summer. Of course, it's not about the warmer temps (although surely that weighs in on the action), but rather the lengthening days. Red-winged Blackbird behavior, the act of belting out their "konk-a-ree" song, always signifies spring to me, and the signal was the dominant song this morning. But Carolina Wrens, Northern Cardinals, Song Sparrows, and White-throated Sparrows added to the symphony. Perhaps more noticeable, however, was the rising twitter of Pine Siskins, dozens of them feeding in the hemlocks, picking at those tiny, thimble-size cones, my two long tube feeders inadequate to feed the flocks.

By late afternoon the Barred Owl was asking, "Who cooks for you? Who cooks for you-alllll?" perched in his regular spot in the eastern red cedar tree. The female may already be incubating or at least about to lay her eggs, so he's on watch. And he saw me watching, and lifted off to the south, away from my line of sight. Just then, however, I heard the Red-headed Woodpeckers start a ruckus, both of them chattering in unison. Assuming the owl had invaded their territory, I wandered that way. Sure enough, the owl set off again, continuing to the southwest. The instant he disappeared through the bare winter trees, the woodpeckers went quiet. I do hope they'll be able to raise their young on this new territory of theirs, one that apparently slightly overlaps that of the owls. Always the female owl calls from farther west, and that's what makes me believe the cedars mark the eastern boundary of their homestead. The woodpeckers are within 100 feet of those cedars, taking advantage of the old sycamore with its ready-made cavities. At least that's where I see them most often. Still, I've not seen them routinely duck into any particular cavity. Maybe they haven't decided yet.

February 14

Hearing the Bugles

Just before dark this evening, the bugles of Sandhill Cranes sent me scurrying across the yard for a view to the west. From the sound, I was almost sure they had landed in the neighbor's hayfield or in the adjoining corn stubble and were grazing there. Their calls, however, carry great distances, depending on wind direction. And indeed, the birds I heard were not in the adjoining field, nor were they in the field beyond that. In fact, they were in flight. High. Very high. So far away that I could barely make them out with my naked eye. A binocular view, however, showed about 175 to 200 birds, rowing in an imperfect V, no doubt returning to roost from wherever they spent the day grazing. "Roost" for Sandhill Cranes, however, is not the typical up-in-a-tree roost. Rather, they stand in shallow water for the night, safe from predators like foxes. Sleeping on their feet is an ingrained behavior!

175 Sandhill Crane
Species: 45 total in the yard to date for the year.

A flight of Sandhill Cranes cruises across the sky toward their overnight roost site in the marsh.

February 15

Checking Real Estate

Eastern Bluebirds spent much of the morning checking out the nest-box real estate. As part of their pair-bonding behavior, the two work together to choose the perfect nest site. One male seemed impressed by the Peterson-style box we have mounted on a post at the east end of the garden, the one somewhat sheltered by the eastern red cedar about 20 feet away. I never saw a female with him, but at least five bluebirds were in the area. Maybe she was one of the bashful ones. One pair seemed taken by a similar nest box at the west end of the garden, and I can't help wondering if they're the pair that made that box their home last spring. They raised two broods there and then moved somewhere else—perhaps to one of the boxes we have mounted in the neighbor's hayfield—to raise their last brood. I'm always amazed that our bluebirds typically manage three broods, although a few local folks claim they have pairs that produce a fourth brood. That would, indeed, exhibit amazing behavior. Without banding, however, I'm not sure how anyone could know that for sure.

While mid-February seems really early for the bluebirds to be actively ducking in and out of nest boxes, anticipating a nursery site, we usually have completed nests within four weeks from now. The lengthening days are driving the birds' hormones, giving us the start of a morning chorus, bluebirds among the choristers. Obviously, then, the lengthening day also triggers other behavior, including the home hunt.

In an effort to ensure the bluebirds' comfort, especially in terms of the nest box to the west, I took the liberty of whacking down the head-high now-dead stalks of prairie coneflower and fennel that obscure my view of the box. If my view is obscured, then their view is obscured, the stalks likely dampening the birds' satisfaction with the site. They like an open space, short vegetation in front and mostly around their nest site. As drop-catch hunters, they like to sit high, watch for insects, drop from their perch onto the bug or caterpillar, and return to the perch for dispatch. So even though the head-high stuff is perennial and in spring will re-grow from ground up, the stalks suggest to the bluebirds that they might be too enclosed once things green out. So whack, whack, whack.

A female Eastern Bluebird investigates a Peterson-style nest box as she considers possible nursery sites.

Watching these pretty birds that carry the sky on their backs always cheers me. Even though we've had a gloomy, rainy day, I found myself feeling sunny, not only because I see the birds enjoying the fruits of our labor in building the boxes but also because I know the activity represents something we're all quite ready to welcome: spring!

February 16

Sharing Care Instructions

When it comes to Eastern Bluebirds and serving as their hosts, there's no better resource than the North American Bluebird Society (www.nabluebirdsociety.org). Since bluebirds are checking out real estate now, it's time to review the "rules" for mounting boxes. According to NABS, never hang a bluebird nest box. Bluebirds don't like swinging nests. They evolved, after all, nesting in natural cavities, and natural cavities don't swing. Never mount a bluebird nest box on a tree, and never mount it on a fence post. Both locations give predators a "highway" directly to the box. And never mount one without a predator guard. All the details are explained and illustrated on the NABS's thorough and extraordinarily helpful website. It's my absolute favorite reference for all things bluebird.

February 17

Spying on the High Wires

Our usual route to town takes us along a straight, nearly featureless road paralleled by utility wires and railroad tracks, the road/track swath bounded on both sides by agricultural fields now in corn stubble, bean stubble, and greening winter wheat. Over the past couple of months, I've noticed two American Kestrels along the 3-mile stretch, perched on the utility wires, always facing the wind, usually about a mile from each other. Since they are of opposite sex, I like to think they're a pair, but of course I don't know that.

This stretch of road seems popular with these birds, our smallest falcons, and I'm always delighted to see them. Such pretty birds! Sadly, they're in decline. Their trouble comes from the fact that they nest in cavities. It's the way kestrels behave. No cavities, no nests. And given the chain-saw mentality of so many folks who whack down any tree that seems even remotely close to dying, cavities for all birds are in short supply. Since there are few trees along this vast, lonely, open stretch, I have to wonder where they nest. Perhaps they've found the perfect real estate in someone's barn or machinery shed, behind a beam or other coincidentally cavity-like structure.

Today, however, I did not see the pair. Instead, two Red-shouldered Hawks perched on the same wooden utility pole, one on top of the pole and the other, smaller hawk on the top cross-arm. Of course, it's the female's territory. She's in charge. Like most raptors, she's also bigger than the male. Puffed up against the cold, she looks to me as if she could strike fear in most anything, including the little kestrels, minuscule by comparison and just the right size for her lunch. Oh, my, I hope the little kestrels have gone somewhere safe. I know the Red-shouldered needs to eat, too, but I hope she chases rabbits or squirrels and leaves the pretty kestrels to breed again.

The blue-gray color on the wings distinguishes the male from the female American Kestrel, a small falcon seen most often perched on and hunting from utility wires.

February 18

Noting Trace Changes

Migration is just at the cusp.

A visit to the reclaimed mine area about an hour north this afternoon made clear that the Short-eared Owls have all but dispersed, winging their way back to their breeding grounds, mostly in Canada. Where they had been abundant, hunting the short grasslands a week ago, we saw none today. Rough-legged hawks were still hunting their respective territories, especially the light morph one that hangs out just east of the village. But they won't stay much longer, either. We're at the southern edge of their winter range—just about as far south as they ever go. Since they breed in the high Arctic, they have miles to go before they breed—many, many miles to go. That means they'll need to start the long flight north very soon in order to garner food-rich territories and set up housekeeping. I'm guessing today was my final date this winter season with these handsomely varied birds.

Spring peepers calling from isolated vernal puddles added a welcome orchestrated background, music that couldn't have better struck the mood for the afternoon as we issued more final good-byes to certain winter visitors and greeted others with a knowing nod toward their podiums. While not usually migratory here in southern Indiana, Eastern Meadowlarks have been tucked into sheltering vegetation much of the winter. Yesterday's sunny warmth in the mid-50s brought them out, front and center, singing on territory, seemingly one every 100 yards or so. What a joyous sound, those "Spring of the-a year" melodies. Likewise, Horned Larks hang out in area grasslands year-round and roam harvested corn fields in winter; this afternoon, in usual lark behavior, they picked their way

A grassland bird, the Horned Lark, its "horns" only feather tufts, often forages alongside unimproved roads, picking for grit.

along the rocky edges of the unimproved roads, darting into the grasses, disappearing instantly in their remarkable camouflage. In the reclaimed mine's random shallow ponds and streams, Mallards and Canada Geese paddled in pairs, exploring watery edges, most likely sizing up potential nest sites. Some do nest here.

Two pairs of Green-winged Teal angled among the Mallards, but they're not staying or competing in any way with the Mallards or Canada Geese for nesting rights. Again, we're at the northern edge of their winter range, and they'll head northward shortly, mostly into Canada or pothole country through the northern tier of states. In fact, these four birds probably are already on their way north, and the reclaimed-mine pools are merely a convenient resting and feeding stopover for them. It's almost certain that their usual migratory behavior takes them much farther to our south for the winter. Such handsome birds, those brightly colored males. I think they should be called green-headed teal, but nobody asked me.

Birds Do *That*?

Woodpeckers have Swiss army knives as beaks. So explains the Cornell Lab of Ornithology interactive exhibit called Beak Adaptations Exploration. Since woodpeckers hammer for their food, their bills are somewhat like wood chisels, chipping away at bark and inner layers to reach bugs, eggs, and larvae. As an added feature, the beaks are self-sharpening. When foraging in soft wood, however, they use their beaks more like picks, jabbing into the material to find tasty morsels. To snag those morsels, or to pluck tiny insects or eggs from leaves, the beak then functions like tweezers. It's the tool for all woodpecker trades!

February 19

Sighting Killdeer

Migration being at the cusp may best be headlined by this evening's sighting. I heard and then saw my first Killdeer of the season. While we live on the northern edge of Killdeer's winter range, and while I've seen them during some winters (including over one hundred in one stunning flock during a Christmas Bird Count), I really do believe that they would have had to move at least several hundred miles farther to our south to survive this year's nasty local winter weather. Too much ice and snow limited their ability to forage. Being the shorebirds that they are, they poke about in the ground, looking for bugs and worms. In fact, I've watched them tug at worms as much as 6 inches long, leaning backward to pull lunch free from the soil. With the heavy, soaking rain over the past two days, the soil was ready to yield morsels to meet their dietary needs. And so they're back! Without its namesake call, I doubt I would have recognized the Killdeer in flight against the setting sun. Silhouettes are hard. But call it did, repeatedly, as it sailed across the hayfield. I'm guessing it had spent some time in the adjoining harvested corn field, poking about amid the stubble as they are known to do.

A Killdeer forages among the remains of a harvested agricultural field, its camouflage plumage concealing it in plain sight.

Within the next two weeks, I expect to hear my first-of-the-season Eastern Phoebe. Some winters, when it's especially mild and they find a sheltered, secluded area that suits their fancy, they may not leave at all. But mostly they do leave. Their standard behavior, though, is to hang out close by, migrating no farther than necessary and certainly not venturing beyond the US southern border. The birds that don't go far obviously don't have far to return, so they're the first to arrive on their breeding grounds. And by the end of this week, I expect to see posted the first Ruby-throated Hummingbird sightings along the Gulf Coast, somewhere between the Florida Panhandle and the Texas coast. Spring! It's happening!

> 2 Killdeer
> **Species:** 46 total in the
> yard to date for the year.

February 20

Breathing a Breath of Spring

Record highs today in the mid-70s put another breath of spring in the air and motivated me to putter about in the garden, tidying up the west end where joe-pye weed, goldenrod, and fennel stalks stand head high but bare, offering strategic perches and tangled cover. Although I'd cut back the tallest a few weeks ago, I feared the remaining stalks still obstructed the bluebird box, situated only a few feet away, so I whacked down the remaining stalks, giving priority to the bluebirds. Ample tangles and strategic perches nevertheless remain for what is certain to be additional winter weather. Even though the maple trees are budding and the bald cypress trees have lengthy catkins dangling from every branch, I know winter is far from over.

An American Woodcock uses its long slender bill to poke into mud for tasty morsels, here, a hefty earthworm.

Still, a friend reported American Woodcocks winnowing and sounding off with their repeated buzzy, nasal insect-like "peent" in his yard this evening. We've never had woodcocks in our yard, but maybe someday . . .

To my mind, American Woodcocks are the magical messengers of spring. Their "peent" calls, made on the ground, precede the male's dizzying aerial displays as he spirals up, up, up in the sky, almost out of sight, and then zigzags down, his wings making a distinct twittering. He hopes, of course, to impress a female. Whether or not she's impressed, I am! It's a rite of spring!

February 21

Noting Pine Siskins' Lunch Choice

Pine Siskins were eating heavily today at the thimble-size hemlock cones. Yes, they're still visiting nyjer feeders, but apparently they'd rather eat their native foods. I'm just really glad I still have numerous big hemlocks. Unfortunately, with climate change, the hotter summers are stressing the trees. I fear they'll meet their demise in a few more years. Will the Pine Siskins visit us then?

A Pine Siskin forages among tiny hemlock cones.

February 22

Dismissing Harbingers of Spring

A little flock of ten American Robins foraged in the yard today, picking in the grass, calling "tut-tut" from the American holly trees—now completely devoid of berries. But the unseasonably warm days and the rain have apparently brought something to the ground's surface, and the robins relish the opportunity to feed.

Tradition has it that robins are the harbingers of spring. That's not quite true, depending on where you live. Here in southwestern Indiana, American Robins stay the winter—at least most of them do. Instead of hanging out in yards and parks, though, they form large flocks, often numbering several hundred, roaming together, foraging across open fields and meadows, more eyes finding more food for everyone. Mostly, they look for berries.

Now, however, with berries at the slim-to-none stage, robins hope for thawing temperatures that bring bugs (and worms), buried deeply in the soil for the winter, nearer to the surface. That little group of ten in the yard today is not "returning" from some distant migration, but they are "returning" to yards and parks, breaking off from the huge wintertime foraging flocks into small units, perhaps extended families, soon to form pairs and seek nest sites. Since robins are not colonial nesters, instead preferring their privacy and paired territories, they're looking to our yards and parks and other similar suitable neighborhoods for the perfect home to raise their brood. They're among the first birds each spring to mud together their signature nest.

February 23

Using Ultraviolet Vision

On the way to town today, I once again spotted both of the kestrels. I slowed the car to a crawl. I didn't stop; I would have frightened the birds. Moving cars are okay; stopped cars are a threat. So they would have flown if I had stopped, and I didn't want to interrupt their hunt. From their vantage point on the high utility wires, they can spot mice and voles scampering among the stubble. Mostly, though, because of their ultraviolet vision (most birds have that), they spot the little mammals by following their urine trails. As Mother Nature would plan it, the urine contains ultraviolet light. The trails must look like ribbons of code to the kestrels, pointing directly to lunch. But maybe that's too much information?

February 24

Watching Woodpeckers

Woodpeckers, the common five here—Downy, Hairy, Red-bellied, Pileated, and Flicker—have been gorging themselves recently at the pure-suet feeders. Given mostly above-freezing temperatures these days, I've traded in the seed-infused cakes for the pure stuff. I keep two cakes on 25-foot poles, the wire-cage feeders raised in place by pulleys. A third hangs against the trunk of the old snag in the backyard. At almost any time during daylight hours, one or more of the feeders will be hosting a customer, and once I witnessed a Downy and a Pileated

A male Downy Woodpecker (left) and female Pileated Woodpecker tolerate one another while feeding on opposite sides of a seed-infused suet-cake.

on either side of the same feeder, both eating in what appeared to be a peaceful agreement. Given the dramatic size difference, the juxtaposition seemed too unlikely to be true, but seeing is believing!

I expect the feeding-frenzy behavior may stem from the fact that woodpeckers are either preparing to nest or already nesting, and their food demands are high. Of course, they may also be suffering from a lack of natural food supplies. After all, they're bug eaters. Maybe they've searched and re-searched every likely place for bug eggs and larvae, and there's no denying they have competition for bark-hidden morsels. White-breasted Nuthatches, Brown Creepers, and all their fellow woodpeckers surely test every wrinkle of bark on every likely tree.

While they're now gobbling down at least one cake a week, come summer they'll largely ignore the offerings. Then, bingo, they'll bring their babies and teach them the advantages of fast-food meals.

February 25

Evaluating Suet Cakes

I should explain why I prefer the pure-suet cakes rather than the more common (and less expensive) seed-infused suet cakes. Woodpeckers aren't all that hungry for seed. They want the real stuff, the high-fat content to keep them energized and alive in the cold. On the other hand, not much else shows interest in the pure-suet cakes because they prefer seed. When starlings, for instance, peck apart seed-infused suet cakes to get at the cracked corn or other grains, the crumbles fall to the ground. In fact, seed-infused cakes crumble so easily that sometimes they break into pieces before I can place them in the wire-cage feeders. All those crumbles readily attract rodents. Who wants that?

While pure-suet cakes cost more than seed-infused ones, they better serve the intended birds—and at least to some degree repulse the nuisance birds. In the long run, in my opinion, the pure-suet cakes are actually more economical. In really severe cold, however, the

A female Downy Woodpecker feeding at a pure-suet cake shows tannin-stained plumage, the result of her frequently slipping in and out of her rain-soaked nest cavity opening.

seed-infused cakes may better serve birds other than woodpeckers, especially because they *do* crumble more easily and allow birds with non-chisel-like beaks—like bluebirds, for instance—to partake. It's a trade-off.

February 26

Noting the First Hummingbird

The first Ruby-throated Hummingbird of the 2018 season was reported along the Florida Panhandle Gulf Coast today. They're right on time! Typically, they reach our yard somewhere around April 10. Talk about predictable behavior!

They've spent the winter in Central America and launched themselves from the Yucatan Peninsula in an 18-hour, 700-mile flight across the Gulf of Mexico to the Florida Panhandle. Theirs is a protracted migration, however, each bird flying solo, each at its own timing, each with its own destination to its ancestral nesting site.

Male Ruby-throated Hummingbirds arrive several weeks before females, and this week brought the first reports of their return from Costa Rica, arriving along the Gulf Coast.

Birds Do *That*?

Male Northern Cardinals court females with food. He feeds her a seed, and if she accepts, they sing to each other. Charming, huh? According to Nature's Crusaders website, the courtship behavior of feeding his mate may continue all the way through the incubation period, a beak-to-beak show of attention, protection, and support.

February 27

Hearing the First Signs of Spring

Today along my drive into town, I heard an Eastern Meadowlark singing on territory. May I call it a sign of spring? Well, I may call it that, but really it's only a verification that the days are getting longer. Sure, it sounds better to say it's a "sign of spring," but for birds, seasons are marked only by length of day, not temperatures. Daylight hours determine behavior. An increase in daylight hours triggers hormones to react to the upcoming breeding season, while a decrease in daylight hours triggers fall migration. Still, gotta love that spring song!

An Eastern Meadowlark, shown here in flight, sings an announcement of "Spring of the-a year," a melody heard today for the first time this season.

February 28

Welcoming the Forecast

As House Finches hassled one another at a near-empty feeder, I saw a male lean down from his perch to feed a female on the perch below—courting behavior extraordinaire. Ah, love is in the air!

The weather forecast calls for sunshine tomorrow. After over a week of rain, flash floods, and a serious rise in area rivers, the forecast is welcome news.

March

A Red-headed Woodpecker assumes an aggressive stance, defending its territory.

There are no accidents in Nature. Every motion of the constantly shifting bodies in the world is timed to the occasion for some definite, fore-ordered end. The flowers blossom in obedience to the same law that marks the course of constellations, and the song of a bird is the echo of a universal symphony. Nature is one, and to me the greatest delight of observation and study is to discover new unities in this all-embracing and eternal harmony.

—John Muir (1838–1914), Father of the National Parks

March 1

Seeing Drifting Feathers

From the window I caught sight of more than the usual activity at the nearby seed-cake feeder. Seven male Northern Cardinals gathered there. Even though the commercial seed cake is designated for woodpeckers, almost everything likes to pick at its treasures. Among these early morning cardinals, two were on the feeder itself, one on top and one clinging to the side, and another sat atop the shepherd's hook from which the feeder hangs. Two foraged on fallen seeds beneath. Another perched, watching, on a winter-bare branch about 3 feet up, and the seventh waited his turn perched on the adjoining pergola. The seventh one, however, made me do a double-take. This cardinal lacked a black facial pattern. What strange plumage. He'll not do well in competition for the females since they will choose males with the brightest, most perfect plumage—a signal in their instinctive analysis of strong genes.

Nevertheless, what a bright picture they made, all seven red splashes decorating the mostly brown landscape. But they were serious about their feeding opportunities and certainly didn't see themselves as my yard decoration. Finding enough food in March, the meanest month of all for birds, is critical business. While I was attracted to their loveliness, they were attracted to a means of survival.

I kept an off-and-on vigil of the seed cake and the oddly plumaged seventh bird, watching over the next minutes, and shortly caught sight of a fluff of about ten feathers drift from the feeder to the ground. Oh, no! My stomach churned a bit because I was sure I knew the

This male Northern Cardinal, seed remnants on his beak, is missing his black facial pattern and will unlikely attain breeding success. Females instinctively choose mates based on bright, perfect plumage, an indication of strong genes.

cause and source of the drifting reddish feathers. The Sharp-shinned Hawk, here only in winter, must still be hanging around, and he's taken a cardinal. I just knew it.

Hoping I wasn't too late, I dashed to the door, ready to yank it open, looking for a cardinal, possibly wounded but maybe still alive. Before I could act, though, I saw that at least three cardinals still fed peacefully on and under the seed-cake feeder. Wait a minute. No sensible bird would be feeding if a sharpie had just killed one of their own—or even jetted through in an effort to kill.

So what had just happened here? Where did the feathers come from? What kind of behavior had I just witnessed? Finally I understood. Birds are beginning to pair up, choose territories, and defend their space. Seven males can't occupy the same territory during breeding season, and the first assault had just occurred, the first territorial behavior. Nobody died. Nobody was even injured, except perhaps his pride. They'll all work out the details soon enough, and I'll be unlikely to see seven startlingly red cardinals simultaneously at the feeder again. Well, maybe again next winter, when everybody's chummy once more.

March 2

Awakening to Song

A Carolina Wren woke me at 5:50 a.m. today, his song so vibrantly loud and robust that he sounded as if he were perched on the headboard of my bed. While it's easy to anthropomorphize and say he was happy, birds only sing about love and war. In reality, he was proclaiming his territory and renewing his pair bond with his mate. They've been a couple here for the winter. Actually, we've had a "couple" for years, but I know, of course, it's unlikely that it's been the same two birds for all this time. Still, they give me pleasure. Carolina Wrens are probably my favorite birds.

Within minutes of the wren's awakening me, a Northern Cardinal began his spring whistling. It's a different song from the few notes he sang in midwinter, more emphatic, enthusiastic, and far-reaching. He, too, is showing behavioral signs of commanding a territory. Soon, then, the dozen or so males hanging out here will scatter—at least some of them will, as each garners his own breeding territory. Cardinals don't stake out huge territories, and they will continue to feed together in the yard, a sort of public area where no bird has a breeding territory. But they'll be sorting out property rights, based mostly on "pecking order," dominant males defending first rights. Cautionary behavior from others will be in evidence.

At 5:55 a.m. the Eastern Towhee called his—or her?—"Where-are-you?" contact call, that rising "Wheeee?" that pairs use to keep track of one another. Unlike the cardinals, the towhees have apparently already staked out their territories, and the unusually high number of nine that fed in the yard during the worst of the winter is now back down to the customary single pair. That's all my little plot of land will support. Maybe it's the same pair that raised their brood in the tangles last summer. Of course, I can't be sure, but I'd like to think they're the same, that they've found good lodging here, like our native habitat, and call our place home.

With brightening skies, my eyes are drawn like magnets to the yellow splashes of budding daffodils, bright among their green spiky leaves, the only color in the frosty and otherwise brown garden. Temperatures were just below freezing last night, but warming temps and bright sunshine today have brought the blooming maple trees to my attention. I know full well that every bird has noted the buds as well. Buds serve up a fine, nutritious dinner for birds accustomed to munching wintertime seeds and berries.

March 3

Reflecting on Vultures

Friends reported seeing first-of-the-year Tree Swallows today! We rarely see them from the yard until well into spring when a pair often investigates the real estate for nest cavities. They get their name because historically they nest in tree cavities, but given the limited number of natural cavities available, they sometimes choose the bluebird box we mounted, with the neighbor's permission, out in his hayfield. It's near a pond, and water attracts bugs. Bugs attract Tree Swallows. The swallows are such acrobats, their feeding behavior almost entirely on the wing, that it's a joy to have them—even though they've commandeered a nest box intended for bluebirds. We hope they join us again this year, if for no other reason than for all the bugs they eat and feed their babies.

Maple trees have burst into full bloom; bald cypress trees sport masses of catkins; and many plants bear leaf buds showing a hint of green. While nighttime temps still drop below freezing most nights, the daytime highs in the 50s and 60s push us toward spring.

As I roamed the yard, pruning native buttonbush and cleaning a few tangled spots in the garden, a lone Turkey Vulture flew over so low I could hear the wind in its wings. When I was a kid, we never saw vultures here. Now we even occasionally see Black Vultures, a traditionally southern bird. Both sightings indicate the birds' expanding ranges. I'm reminded of the Blacks that cleaned up the dead skunk in the corn field last summer. Good to be rid of the smelly thing, but ewwww, eating a skunk?

1 Turkey Vulture
Species: 47 total in the yard to date for the year.

Last year, to raise their brood, a pair of Tree Swallows chose our bluebird nest box mounted across the hayfield.

Birds Do *That*?

Wild turkeys can run up to 25 mph. Turkeys have powerful legs that give them the strength to sprint. According to a summary of wild turkey trivia in *Smithsonian* magazine, the birds can also fly about 55 mph. Of course, domestic turkeys, bred to provide ample white meat for the Thanksgiving table, have less streamlined bodies and can neither run nor fly as fast as their wild counterparts.

March 4

Catching Imperfect Song

Many White-throated Sparrows look to be sporting new bright plumage these days. The streaky immatures are losing their streaks. The adults wear bright yellow lores. Their white throats and head stripes almost glisten with white, except, of course, for the tan-striped morphs. In either case, white or tan, their handsome transformations foretell their upcoming migration north to breeding grounds, primarily within Canada's boreal forest. Meanwhile, they're beginning to practice their "Oh, Sam Peabody, Peabody, Peabody" song. Now the notes waver weakly, not quite on key, but as hormone levels rise, the song will grow strong, sure, and vibrant.

The sex of White-throated Sparrows is not evident. Here, a tan-striped variety could be either a male or a female, and tan-striped individuals often mate with white-striped individuals.

Because white-striped White-throated Sparrows appear brighter than do tan-striped individuals, sometimes they are mistaken as males. Actually the white or tan stripes do not indicate sex.

March 5

Noticing Crows

From the kitchen window, I've been watching an American Crow for a few weeks now. Just one. It hangs out in the towering old native pecan trees along the north property line, and from time to time it flies to the cluster of pines to the west, always sailing low over or actually alighting in the tallest tree. Last summer a pair nested in one of the pines, but I could never see the nest. Standing directly under the trees, to any side of the trees, or at a distant vantage point from the trees, I could never spot the nest. Still, I saw them carry nesting material into the tree, saw them slip in from different directions during what I assumed was the incubation period, and then saw them making regular to-and-fro trips during what was assuredly the nestling period. Even so, the nursery itself remained an enigma. Now it seems the pair may be about to replay the mystery, carrying out once again their furtive behavior.

American Crows and their cousins—jays, ravens, and magpies—members of the Corvidae family, are recognized as the smartest members of the avian world.

Crows can live for a long time. The oldest known wild crow was just over sixteen years old when it was recaptured. Apparently no one knows how much longer the wild one lived, but another one in captivity survived fifty-nine years. There's certainly ample reason, then, to assume this crow I've been watching lately is not new to the neighborhood. It has likely made the pine trees and that part of the yard its personal family territory. The smartest of our birds, crows display strong family-tie behavior. The youngsters, for instance, hang out with their parents for a year or two, helping raise the new broods, serving as gofers until they learn the tricks of survival and are ready to breed themselves. Aunts and uncles also join the extended family, introducing cousins as they mature. The crow enjoys a cooperative community. So the one I'm watching from the kitchen window must be checking out details, maybe tidying up the real estate, before the family returns from winter roosting and feeding areas.

March 6

Naming a Hero

Last night I saw a male Northern Cardinal exhibit nearly unbelievable bravery. At least I interpreted his behavior as brave. For him, it was probably nothing more than survival instinct. Either way, here's what happened.

Sometime around 9 p.m., as I sat reading in my office, I heard a ruckus outside the front door. Something was rattling the aluminum awning, perhaps some critter climbing across, toenails screeching along the way. The winds, however, were fairly vicious, gusting to 35 mph, rattling the awnings, raking tree limbs across the roof's corner. Wind chimes clanged, a train whistle sounded from the south, the furnace blower kicked on, and voices murmured from the TV in the next room. So many noises blurred, a bit tricky to sort out. To check, though, I made my way to the door, flipped on the front porch light, saw nothing moving, and reached for the light switch to flip it off. Then I noticed the cardinal. He was perched under the awning, tight against a strut that extended from the edge of the door frame. His position looked unnatural, not a relaxed sleeping posture but an upright position, tilted, as if leaning against the support. In an effort to minimize my obvious disturbance, I flipped off the light, hoping I wouldn't cause him to fly, and returned to my reading.

Within a few minutes, however, the noise resumed, more distinctive and louder than before. My little female cat ran for cover under the bed. She's like a four-legged security system, always tuned into any unusual sound, and especially anything alarming. Off I dashed, returning to the front door, but before I could flip on the light or even glance out the door, movement at the adjoining window caught my attention. A raccoon hung by its hind legs along the window edge, inching its way downward. The feeder that had hung above was now missing, and the creature was well on its way to ripping apart the window screen. Surely it could see me, but it seemed unconcerned. I pounded flat-handed against the window frame, hoping to minimize damage and send the culprit on its way. And scamper off it did.

Flashlight in hand, I went outside through the garage door to make sure the raccoon was gone but especially to investigate the condition of my feeder, one of those expensive, adjustable ones, fearing it had broken to bits hitting the concrete walk or the stone edge of the planter box. Fortunately, it lay safely on the ground, unbroken. Sigh. Then, however, I remembered. What about the cardinal? The feeder had hung less than 10 feet from where the cardinal had been perched. Had he been startled from his perch, flown into the dark, unable to see, now on the ground and ripe for predation? Or had the raccoon snagged him before he could fly? Flicking my flashlight toward the spot where I had seen him perched, I was astonished to catch his brilliant red reflect in my light, still snug, still hugging the awning strut. Really? That bird stuck tight to his perch with a fat bully raccoon within feet of him? Instantly I dropped the flashlight beam to my feet and scurried away, wondering if the poor bird had simply succumbed to a heart attack but his clenched feet had kept him upright. Surely no bird alive would have remained in place under those death-threat circumstances. It was stunning behavior.

A male Northern Cardinal, perhaps the one that roosts under the awning each night, displays gray-tinged late-winter plumage. Within another month, he will be brilliant red, the gray tinge having worn away.

This morning at dawn, I heard him call. An answer from the other side of the yard inspired him to sing. My 5:30 a.m. cardinal-singing alarm clock, still alive. Perhaps the bird faced a death threat from the raccoon because, understanding that had he flown, he might well have faced death anyway. Since diurnal birds can't see in the dark, he would have been helplessly fluttering about, calling attention to himself, and likely facing his certain demise. Perhaps the risk of staying was the safer of the two alternatives, either almost certain death in the dark or possible survival on the perch. Can't imagine what his heart rate must have been.

March 7

Announcing a New Arrival

A friend 75 miles to our south reported his first Purple Martin today—surprisingly early! He hosts a big colony, usually approaching one hundred pairs, so he's keenly tuned in to the birds' comings and goings. Purple Martins have come to rely almost entirely on humans providing colony nest sites. Historically, of course, they relied on natural cavities, mostly in trees. As those cavities began disappearing, humans stepped up, mounting boxes and gourds for their use. Now, though, as human martin hosts grow fewer, the birds once again face a shortage of colonies. No colonies, no babies. Populations plummet. This spring, given the strange spring and lingering roller-coaster cold weather, I fear that

these birds will be living on the edge for yet another reason: Since they feed only on the wing, weather dramatically affects their food supplies. Wet bugs don't fly. Cold bugs don't fly. If bugs don't fly, Purple Martins don't eat.

These birds have been months on the wing, returning to their breeding grounds. Wintering in Brazil, they may come back by island-hopping across the Caribbean, traveling through Central America into Mexico and crossing the Gulf of Mexico, or following the eastern shore of Mexico all the way into the United States. Generally, they reach these parts in early to mid-March. They're early!

A Purple Martin pair lays claim to its chosen nest cavity.

March 8

Taking Note of Constancy

Yard populations have remained fairly constant for some weeks now, the same species with about the same number of individuals, but with one possible exception. Maybe, just maybe, the Sharp-shinned Hawk headed back north. Terror doesn't seem to empty the yard very often now, not like it did on an almost daily basis back when the sharpie habitually hung out in the pine trees. Now, of course, the Cooper's Hawk is taking up the slack and choosing a secret nest spot. I'm keeping my eye on a pine tree near the northeast corner of our place. There's a nest situated in an odd spot, well out on a branch, typical of a Cooper's preferred location. I'll know soon.

Odd thing about nests and nest sites: Each species has its preferred nesting location, from ground level to sky-high canopy, from inside a snug cavity to fully exposed on a cliff side. Each species also builds a unique kind of nest with reliably predictable materials, so specific, in fact, that field guides illustrate and describe nests by the species that build them. The remaining question: How do birds know how to build these species-specific nests? Ah, it's a behavior fully hardwired in their tiny brains. Still, practice makes perfect, and some pairs turn out a better product than others of their kind.

March 9

Missing the Turkeys

I'm thinking today about the eleven Wild Turkeys that roamed the neighborhood until last September. Suddenly we neither saw them nor heard them. One knowledgeable turkey hunter told me that if the flock is ambushed—perhaps by a coyote, fox, or dog—they'll never return to the site of the ambush. Granted a few neighbors have hunting dogs, but they never run loose. It's anybody's guess about what happened, but how odd that the entire flock would disappear simultaneously. Miss them.

March 10

Checking on Chickadees

While taking advantage of a warm, sunny afternoon, digging out some too-vigorous plants at the east end of the garden, I checked the bluebird box located there. Surprise! It holds an almost complete Carolina Chickadee nest, its mossy base the telltale identifying characteristic. It's the same box chickadees used last year, so it really shouldn't surprise me that they've chosen the same site. What is surprising is how early they've put all the pieces together. Above all, I'm surprised that they have a nearly completed nest, meaning they've made hundreds of trips in and out of the box and I haven't noticed the activity. Some bird watcher I am to have missed the behavior right in front of me. Birds keep nests secret.

When I recovered from my surprise, I whipped out my cell phone to get the picture and was immediately the target of scolding. Both members of the chickadee pair flitted from the cedar tree to the apple tree, fussing, coming from nowhere the instant the nest was

Carolina Chickadees build a foundation of moss before they construct the actual nest, a behavior that makes their nests readily identifiable.

A Carolina Chickadee peers from the opening of its chosen nest box.

"threatened." Up to that moment, I had neither seen nor heard chickadees during the hour or so I'd been working nearby. What clever behavior, keeping a low profile while a possible threat lingers, waiting until the threat is real, right at the nest, and then raising a big ruckus.

As soon as I closed the box and stepped away, the chickadees went quiet. After some minutes, one ducked inside the box, apparently making a security check, and then both birds left. I finished my gardening task nearby, again without seeing or hearing the chickadees. I'd bet anything, though, if I had returned to the box, they would again have appeared out of nowhere.

March 11

Preparing for Bad Weather

After reasonably warm weather this past week, with highs in the 40s, this afternoon's snow-fall gave us all a reality check—birds and people alike, I think. The snowflakes fell in what seemed like nearly fist-size blobs. Because temps hovered around 35 degrees, the snow piled up only on grass, branches, and other aboveground surfaces. So it was a lovely snow, and I think not too dangerous for commuters.

But all day, well before the snow began, birds fed heavily, and the populations at feeders were at abnormal highs. They knew. While scientists don't really understand how, they do know that birds perceive changes in the barometric pressure. As a result, they sense impending storms and behave accordingly, preparing for the threat. Today was proof of the claim. Around 1 p.m., I counted seventy American Goldfinches before I lost track of which birds flew and where. They were here in near-record numbers. Although I heard Pine Siskins calling from the high branches of the hemlocks while I was filling feeders this morning, I saw only a few picking at nyjer seed, even when the long tube feeder hung full to the brim. Later in the afternoon, as the snow began, strangely I saw no more siskins. Since I often see far more siskins in the mornings than in the evenings, however, tomorrow morning will bring the truth. Have the siskins gone? I rather doubt it. They wouldn't leave during the day (they migrate at night), and they wouldn't fly northward into a storm. So I'm betting tomorrow morning will show they're still here.

Other bird behavior also proved the birds' understanding of the upcoming bad weather. At least fourteen Dark-eyed Juncos and seventeen White-throated Sparrows fed much of the afternoon in and around feeders. They probably weren't always the same individuals, but their numbers clarified the intensity of their feeding. And about an hour before dark, I counted thirty-six Northern Cardinals, mostly in the backyard but some in front. I'm sure I missed a few because of the near-whiteout conditions, and the males were obviously easier to spot and count than the females. In spite of the high number, it's a far cry from my record count of fifty-two some years ago, a number I'll unlikely ever see again here. Still, the numbers reveal how much birds understand an upcoming change in the weather and how well they prepare for it.

March 12

Clearing Ice

Snow lingers on the ground tonight. After last night's low of 28 degrees, the 3 inches of wet snow turned crunchy. Today's high of 37 degrees melted anything dangerous on the roads but left enough white to remind us that winter remains. At dawn this morning, birds hung out nearby, hardly waiting while I filled feeders and bashed away ice covering feeder ports. Ice may be birds' worst natural enemy. Within minutes of my returning inside, birds lined the tube feeders, occupying every feeding slot. Of the eighteen birds on the feeder captured in one photo, half were Pine Siskins. For whatever reason, they're morning feeders! And they fulfilled yesterday's prediction.

Nine Pine Siskins and nine American Goldfinches feed together on a nyjer-seed-filled tube feeder.

March 13

Reporting Purple Martins

Neighbors reported that their first-of-the-season Purple Martins arrived today. In spite of the common misconception, there's no such thing as Purple Martin "scouts," birds that supposedly check out the nest sites and then go out and lead others to the colony. Instead, the first arrivals are just that: early birds, males or females. Most likely the early birds' behavior simply means they nested here previously, know the way, and reached their destination quickly. The early bird gets the best territory, or in this case, the best nest cavity. The neighbor's colony has been active for more years than I can remember, and the hosts regularly expand the number of nest cavities available. So who knows how many times some of these individuals have nested at the site. Perhaps some have nested here for more than ten years. After all, the oldest known Purple Martin was recaptured thirteen years and eight months after it was originally banded. That's also a lot of frequent-flier miles, from southwestern Indiana to Brazil and back—at least thirteen times.

Purple Martin colonies, especially those of manufactured gourds, are well received by these social nesters. Having the birds on one's property aids in the reduction of bugs—although not mosquitoes as commonly believed.

Every summer evening, as the martins crisscross the sky catching dragonflies, I hear their flight songs and I'm filled with nostalgia. The birds make me think of my dad. How he loved their musical calls! I've since wondered where the martins nested back in those days, in the early 1900s. Maybe farm folks mounted nest boxes for the birds even then. In fact, John James Audubon wrote in 1831 that he would select overnight lodging based on the beauty of the facility's Purple Martin box, usually tucked into the corner of its hanging sign. He felt that the nicer the martin box, the nicer the inn's rooms would be.

March 14

Understanding the Starling Impact

I caught a pair of European Starlings poking around, entering and exiting one of the gourd nest cavities hanging under the awning just outside my office window. They hadn't been nosing around for more than a minute when I heard the Carolina Wrens start up a fuss. I'm guessing the wrens already have dibs on that little piece of real estate and were having none of this starling intrusion. But a wren against a starling? Short of a David-and-Goliath miracle, the wren stands no chance.

And that's the problem with starlings. They don't belong here, and they're vicious thieves, robbing our native birds of nest sites. Think not only wrens but our owls, woodpeckers, titmice, chickadees, and bluebirds. In fact, the primary reason for the dramatic decline in Red-headed Woodpeckers is starlings robbing them of nest cavities. Ditto with Eastern Bluebirds that were extirpated in several states because of nest site competition with starlings. Given the starlings' beak size, there's rarely a question about who wins a battle with them.

So if they don't belong here, why are they here? In 1890, Eugene Schieffelin released sixty European Starlings and a year later released another forty in New York City's Central Park. Schieffelin wanted all the birds mentioned in Shakespeare's plays to be a part of his life in his new country. Little did he understand what havoc his releases would cause. A century later, starlings had become so prolific that they reached all the way across the continent to Anchorage, Alaska. With a population now estimated at well over 50 million in the United States alone, starlings displace an equal number of our native birds during breeding season. In addition, they destroy crops and, by shear multitudes, spread disease.

I chased them away this morning—for what little good that will do.

While it is illegal to do harm to any bird (outside of licensed waterfowl hunting), it is legal to eliminate three nonnative species: European Starling, Rock Pigeon, and House Sparrow. In fact, the National Audubon Society encourages homeowners to monitor nest cavities in their own yards, routinely ousting nonnative birds from them. I find it difficult to intentionally eliminate birds, but I have no hesitation whatsoever throwing them out of nest cavities in our yard, especially the nest boxes we've carefully built, mounted, and continue to monitor for our native species. I'm compelled to protect our handsome but vulnerable Eastern Bluebirds.

March 15

Sizing Up the Battle

Beware the Ides of March, Julius Caesar was warned. Turns out that the birds also heeded that warning this morning.

I watched a pair of Eastern Bluebirds investigating their usual preferred nest box at the west end of the garden. The male perched on a 6-foot garden stake while the female fluttered around the box, clinging briefly at the opening and then returning to the nest-box roof. Her behavior was somewhat unusual because she never ducked inside, and that's what they do when a pair is investigating a possible nest site. Her trips to and from the male on his perch seemed odd, too, I thought. After all, there were several other stakes she could have chosen on which to perch.

Then a pair of Carolina Chickadees arrived on the scene, and one of them went to the box opening, stuck its head in, pulled back, scolded, and flew to the nest-box roof. Really? Why is it behaving that way? The chickadees already have a nearly completed nest at the other end of the garden. That left me wondering: Did something happen to their nest and now they're trying to commandeer this box from the bluebirds? Or was something amiss in this box that somehow concerned the chickadees—as well as the bluebirds? The swooping, checking, and scolding continued from all four birds. Why would two different species scold about the same nest box, especially when one of the species already has an established nest?

Then a pair of Carolina Wrens arrived on the scene, hanging from the sides of the garden stakes, aligned with the nest-box opening. Okay, the European Starlings had threatened their nesting gourd yesterday, but generally the wrens don't nest in the bluebird boxes.

Instead, they prefer something smaller, like maybe the wren-specific boxes mounted under the eaves of the tool shed or—as usual—the gourds hanging under the house awnings. So why were the wrens joining the fray over this box? Something was surely amiss.

Mostly the wrens just scolded, but the bluebirds and chickadees made active dives toward the opening or hovered nearby. Neither species is adept at hovering, so that behavior was out of character and seemed odd to me. It also seemed odd that all the aggressive behavior, either physical or vocal, was aimed at the nest box, not at each other. But if birds are battling over a nest box, the battle is, ultimately, with each other. Strange.

The moment of clarity came after what seemed like a half hour but was probably closer to 10 minutes, when a European Starling's face showed at the entrance and the bird emerged from the box, alighting on the roof. Both bluebirds swooped over the starling, pecking it as they dove. One chickadee followed suit. Another starling appeared in the nearby cypress tree. Maybe it was there all along and, distracted by the ongoing battle, I missed it. But I really think it arrived only when what I took to be its mate emerged from the box and the aerial attacks began. It made no effort to intervene, however, only sat there in the cypress tree, watching.

In under 2 minutes, the pair of starlings left.

The wrens left; the chickadees wandered off; and the bluebirds made one last check of the box, both of the pair poking their heads in, then departing.

Unfortunately, the starlings didn't go far. They flew only to the other end of the garden where one landed on the box containing the nearly completed chickadee nest. Holding my breath, I hoped it would not trespass, invading the precious nearly completed weeks-long work of the chickadees. Then, zip, inside it went. Even from my recliner in the living room, I yelled, "Get out of there," having to then apologize to my husband, reading in the other room, for my outburst.

But I was enraged. So were the chickadees. Again out of nowhere, they appeared. They fluttered helplessly around, above, and in front of the box, scolding. In my mind, I could hear the starling inside laughing at the little chickadees. What brazen behavior for such a tiny bird to "attack" a starling. A starling outweighs a chickadee by more than seven times, has a wingspan and body length more than twice as long—and that's ignoring the starling's vicious beak compared to the chickadee's relatively minuscule bill. But many birds will risk their very lives to defend a nest, especially one with eggs or young.

Birds Do *That*?

Soaring birds fly in circles. When sunshine warms the earth's surface, the warming air rises in a columnar fashion called thermals. Because that rising air produces lift, soaring solitary birds like hawks, falcons, and eagles get an extra boost by riding the thermal air currents, taking them upward with little effort and extending their flight time as they eye the ground below for prey. Since the thermals form as columns, staying within the thermal means soaring within the column's circle. In addition, Aerospaceweb.org notes that flocks of birds also take advantage of thermals to gain altitude and expand their hunting range, most notably during migration.

For whatever reason, however, the starling emerged from the box and the pair left. Shortly, the chickadees alighted on the box, each ducking in, making another security check, and then departing. It's been 3 hours now, and I haven't seen them since, neither the starlings nor the chickadees. Again, though, I bet if I approached the box or peeked in to take a photo, the chickadees would be back in a flash, arriving out of nowhere, scolding. How do they do that?

Now that all had seemingly returned to normal, a female Eastern Towhee was left scratching among the leaves in the garden, uncovering (I hope) insect eggs or larvae for lunch. The bluebirds were back watching the suet feeder, garnering crumbles fallen from the various woodpeckers' poor table manners. A squirrel had taken over the platform feeder, but every perch on the nyjer-filled tube feeder was occupied by American Goldfinches. Dark-eyed Juncos scooted about below the nyjer feeder, foraging on spilled seed.

All was peaceful—until a Cooper's Hawk swooped past the window, grabbing my attention as it lifted up, swerving sharply right, ripping across the garden, then alighting in the pin oak. He was empty-clawed, having missed his luncheon goal. He rested a couple of minutes and flew on, through the woods, probably on to another feeding station somewhere else in the neighborhood. Slowly, the birds returned to their routine, ever alert, always on the edge between life and death, between eating and being eaten.

Ah, the Ides of March.

March 16

Delighting to Woodpeckers

Once again, hats off to the joys of the old tulip-tree snag in the backyard!

This morning, as I first padded into the kitchen for my morning cup of tea, I scanned the backyard. On the trunk of the old snag, a Hairy Woodpecker called "pic, pic." As he hitched across the bark, his mate flew in. Then—surprise!—a female Pileated Woodpecker arrived, parachuted her 27-inch wings for a landing, and made a beeline for the suet feeder. The feeder is a typical wire-cage affair attached about 5 feet above the ground and offers pure suet, not the seed- and cracked-corn-infused cake that makes such a mess. And now, three woodpeckers at once! But the Hairy pair, outsized by the Pileated by double digits, scooted around to the backside of the trunk and departed posthaste.

As the Pileated hammered at the suet, movement caught my eye. A bird I first took to be her mate had flown in to the back side of the trunk and hitched his way around toward the feeder. The two met, did a short bobbing "dance," and he zipped off. For an amazing minute, the two behaved in a thrilling way that's still plastered in my brain. What a delightful dance!

But after I uploaded the photos to my desktop, I realized that I'd been deceived by my quick look. The second arrival was not a male at all, but another, possibly more mature female. Photos showed that the first bird had bronze-colored primaries, an indication of fresh plumage. But the second bird, although it was also a female, lacked these bronze highlights, maybe a clue that the first bird had molted more recently or maybe that it was a first-spring bird. Identifying them both as females, however, changed the meaning of the bobbing dance. That was aggressive behavior! One female defending dibs on the suet

Two female Pileated Woodpeckers, perhaps an adult and a first-spring bird, dance around, darting and dodging, showing a form of woodpecker aggression, likely in a dispute over who gets this territory.

feeder caused the other to defer and depart. Anything to avoid a fight over one source of food when another was readily available nearby!

But back to the events of the Woodpecker Special: As the Pileated left the suet and continued exploring and shredding the snag's loosening bark, a pair of Downy Woodpeckers landed, edging their way toward the suet feeder. Since the female Pileated was preoccupied with her successful foraging higher up, no doubt gleaning insect eggs and perhaps larvae from the bark crevices, she ignored the Downys—and likewise they ignored her. But their behavior clarified their caution as they frequently cocked their heads her direction, no doubt making sure of their safety.

But then a female Red-bellied Woodpecker flew directly to the suet feeder, and the Downys gave way, inching upward, showing deference to the larger bird. Or maybe it wasn't just deference but a behavior more akin to a survival tactic. I wonder: Do little birds fear for their lives in the presence of larger competitors, or do they just want to avoid confrontation? I suspect it's really the latter, but it's hard to get inside those little birds' minds. We can only watch and guess, trying to interpret.

A female Red-bellied Woodpecker is distinguished from males by the patch of gray near the top of her head, whereas males are solid red (see photo on October 27). Both sexes have a wash of red on their bellies, but because the birds mostly cling against tree trunks, the red belly is usually hidden. By contrast, a Red-headed Woodpecker wears a red hood over its entire head, face, and neck (see photo on January 10).

What a morning, even before tea! Within less than 10 minutes, seven woodpeckers of four species feasted at the old snag. Granted, they apparently came initially for the suet feeder, but all except the Red-bellied stayed to forage across the trunk and limbs, picking in bark crevices, surely finding extra morsels along the way. What a shame it would have been, when the bulk of the tulip tree had to be removed to protect our house, if we had cut the tree to the ground. Instead, by leaving the main trunk standing about 25 feet tall and keeping at least the skeletal limbs to that height as well, we created a woodpeckers' paradise. It's Mother Nature's grocery store and nursery. Maybe one day a woodpecker will hammer out a nursery that I can watch right out the kitchen window! Even if that doesn't happen, it's hard to beat seeing seven woodpeckers in 10 minutes, enjoying the interaction among them, and knowing at the same time they're finding life-supporting vittles.

After all seven woodpeckers went on their way, a male Eastern Bluebird arrived on the scene. I watched his behavior as he scoured the ground under the suet feeder, plucking up tiny suet morsels and swallowing them whole. He's an amazing piece of work: Obviously he was watching the movements of the woodpeckers and knew they'd be dropping crumbles. Within minutes, he was there to gobble up the scraps. What an opportunist!

March 17

Looking for Phoebes

This afternoon, although temperatures reached the high 50s, uncomfortable 15 mph winds chilled me and kept me well under wraps as I explored the yard, listening, watching, wondering if anything was new. Sparrows were clustered by the dozens in the brambles, vines, and winter-crushed goldenrod. While the area is shaded, it was out of the wind, and the sparrows behaved in typical sparrow fashion: They fed on the buds of Japanese honeysuckle and hunkered down, tucked in out of the wind. I tried to sort them out. White-throated Sparrows were among the most numerous, probably around thirty or so. They'll be leaving soon, migrating north to their breeding grounds, so they're feeding heavily to support their molt and prepare for the journey. A Song Sparrow chased a second one from the bald cypress tree from which he guarded a newly chosen territory. They live here year-round, so they're sorting out who gets which territories for feeding and breeding.

The unusual song that I first attributed to a couple of the two dozen or so Dark-eyed Juncos turned out instead to be that of a pair of Field Sparrows, the first I've seen on the property since last year sometime. They live here year-round, too, but tend not to hang out in the yard during breeding season. They need broader grasslands than they find on my little patch of land. In addition to the two I saw, I could hear two others, one to the east and

The Field Sparrow likes to hang out amid grass stalks, brambles, and tangles.

another to the northwest. While I stood trying to sort out who was who, a Ruby-crowned Kinglet scampered through the poplar tree at the edge of the brambles. He'll be leaving soon, too. In fact, he may be here from farther south, only on a migratory stopover, perhaps for a day or two, to fuel up for the next leg of his journey.

2 Field Sparrow
(heard 2 more)
Species: 48 total in the
yard to date for the year.

What I was hoping to see or hear, however, was an Eastern Phoebe, usually our first migrant to arrive each spring. Other folks have reported seeing them, but I struck out on that goal today.

March 18

Fearing an Empty Yard

I counted eighteen Dark-eyed Juncos in the yard today and about an equal number of White-throated Sparrows along with nine Pine Siskins. When they all leave for parts north, the yard will look empty! Well, not entirely, of course, but the numbers will certainly drop, even with the addition of those lovelies that come here to nest.

Although I didn't know the secretive little Carolina Wrens had already built a complete nest in a section of horizontal PVC pipe, this morning I saw the nest's remnants hanging from the end—last fall's maple and cypress leaves, pine straw, grasses, all the usual components of a Carolina Wren's nest. Clearly, a raccoon had yanked out the nest, probably looking for eggs. Poor wrens. They had to search out every single blade of grass, every single pine straw, every single leaf. Each blade, straw, and leaf was a separate trip to the nest site. Each was woven in place, one at a time. So many trips. So much work. Now all is lost. I'd love to trap the rascal raccoons and relocate them, but I fear I'll trap a skunk. We have an abundance of both.

March 19

Catching a Cooper's Image

The Carolina Wrens are already at work rebuilding. I spotted one, I think the paler female, carrying pine straw toward a spot where I have several cavities for her choosing: a gourd, an open-faced platform, and a closed house. The area is out of sight from all rooms in the house, so I'll have to watch from outside to know if she's picked one of them.

Yesterday, we also mounted on the pergola something I call a bottle nest, a handmade pottery piece that attaches vertically, its mouth the perfect-size opening for wrens. Four holes in the bottle's side (bottom, as

A Carolina Wren pokes about looking for overwintering larvae or eggs that will offer a protein-rich meal.

mounted) drain any moisture that might blow in. Since the clay is unglazed, it's breathable. Supposedly wrens love these vintage colonial nest cavities. We'll see.

This afternoon a rain-soaked Cooper's Hawk sashayed into the yard. For maybe 3 minutes, it perched on the feeder's T-post, apparently oblivious of the steady rain. Other birds, however, were certainly not oblivious of the Cooper's presence: Every songbird vanished. While the Cooper's stretched its neck, eyeing every cranny in search of movement, I had time to cap- ture several digital images. Only when I uploaded the photos to my desktop did I get a clear view of its talons and beak—

A Cooper's Hawk shows evidence of its recent predation of another bird, the hapless victim's feathers stuck on the hawk's talons and beak.

both of which had numerous little feathers stuck to their surfaces. This greedy bird had obviously just finished off some poor songbird for lunch and was looking for more. Fortu- nately for our yard birds, the Cooper's was unsuccessful—this time. Of course, that meant the Cooper's went hungry.

March 20

Marking the Vernal Equinox

Today marks the vernal equinox, the meteorological first day of spring, the point halfway between the longest day of the year and the longest night of the year. Really? While the sun, moon, and earth may be aligned today in the pattern that designates the earth's tilt toward summer, Old Man Winter isn't through with us. In spite of the date, he blew in a surprising 2 inches of heavy, wet snow this afternoon. Since roads were relatively warm, snow didn't stick there, but it certainly did stick everywhere else. Birds fed as if they feared the worst, and a little flock of Red-winged Blackbirds arrived in the yard without fanfare to garner a few sunflower seeds. Oddly enough, they rarely show up in numbers unless there's snow, so I guess I shouldn't have been surprised to find them at the feeders today. Their group behavior, though, entertained me for the 15 or 20 minutes they foraged, jockeying for

Birds Do *That*?

If Bald Eagles could read, they could read a newspaper from across the length of a football field. According to information from the National Eagle Center, eagles can spot a bunny hidden in the grass from about 3 miles away. That's a keen-eyed bird! Most birds of prey have similarly sharp eyesight. Except for owls. They rely more on their sense of sound than sense of sight to find a mouse under a foot of snow in the dark of night.

The female Red-winged Blackbird is said to be the most misidentified songbird in the United States.

An immature male Red-winged Blackbird looks somewhat like a female, but this one is now beginning to show red on it "shoulders."

Mature and immature male Red-winged Blackbirds in a near standoff as they feed together, the immature bird (foreground) showing submission while the adult displays his epaulettes in aggression.

A male Northern Cardinal perches in a snow-covered sweetbay magnolia tree, the semi-evergreen leaves offering protection from the elements.

position according to pecking order. One male, obviously the dominant bird of the group, displayed his alpha rank, strutting his stuff, puffing out his red epaulettes, thrusting his "shoulders" forward as he threw his head back to sing. Quite a showoff, he was. No doubt the presence of multiple females and the potential threat from multiple immature males in the group triggered his flaunting, but his persistence in displaying certainly interfered with his opportunities to feed. Gotta put priorities in place! In response to his display, the immature males remained on the ground, foraging in a submissive fashion, acknowledging the very real pecking order established here. The scene as it played out made me wonder, however, if the twelve of them made up an extended family or if they just happened to be hanging out together. Since it's common for a single male to entertain and protect a harem, he could well have been the mate to the females and the sire to the immature birds. Given this first day of spring and the adult male's raging hormones, no matter the relationship between the males, I'm betting this alpha won't tolerate the youngsters much longer.

Because I absolutely can't resist photographing brilliant red male Northern Cardinals in the snow, I'm admitting up front that I took way too many images this afternoon—over one hundred, but I'm sharing just one. What stunning birds, these cardinals. How drab the winter yard would be without them!

March 21

Checking Junco Records

During the night the scratchy, thumping noise of scrabbling on aluminum awakened me, instantly suspecting that a raccoon was once again robbing the feeder hanging under the living room window awning. Drat! I'd forgotten to bring it in for the night. Since the March 6 episode when I caught a raccoon in the act of vandalizing that same feeder, and since I'd found the feeder on the ground on two occasions following, bringing it in for the night became my newly adopted routine, my effort to prevent the raccoon from destroying it. But I'd forgotten last night.

Padding to the door in my slippers, I flipped on the porch light. Ah, the feeder was still in place, swaying gently. Had the raccoon heard me coming, escaped, but left the feeder swinging? Or was the wind giving play to the movement? I watched. The feeder continued its gentle swing, an ongoing motion that had to have some additional impetus. Wind, I was sure. Relieved, my hand on the doorknob, I started out, even at this late hour, to bring the feeder to safety, anticipating a raccoon's later arrival.

I stopped short, though, when something bright caught my eye. Where the awning meets the supporting strut, in that little corner of protection, a male Northern Cardinal sat eyeing the door. Odds are he's the same bird that endured the raccoon's threat two weeks earlier. What a statement about this bird's behavior. Such a creature of habit—even after what was surely a night of horror and what I know to have been at least two additional nights of similar disturbance. The security of his roost, having protected him during those close encounters of a furry kind, means he's found the perfect place, protected from wind, rain, and snow—and predatory attacks. Now, after another night's disturbance, this morning he's singing a steady, "purdy, purdy, purdy; cheerah, cheerah, purdy, purdy, purdy."

This afternoon, with yesterday's 2-inch snow now history, twenty-six Dark-eyed Juncos foraged across the yard, pecking with seeming frenzy at nyjer seed fallen from feeders and sipping at an adjoining water feature. The number represents a high for the year, so the obvious question is why, on this first full day of spring, would more juncos populate the

A Dark-eyed Junco takes a drink at a water feature equipped with a recirculating pump that provides always-moving water.

yard than during the entire winter season? They are, after all, commonly called snow birds, birds that come for the winter. Folklore would have it, in fact, that when juncos arrive, snow comes with them. Well, okay, we had snow yesterday, but folklore aside, there's no doubt more to the story of their behavior.

Photo records show my personal latest spring junco images were captured March 23. That's not to say I've seen no juncos in the yard after that date, only that I've not taken photos of them after that date. Given the proximity to that date now, however, to have this large population of the species in the yard suggests one likely behavior: Juncos are moving north. The individuals currently feeding with such frenzy in the yard right now are likely new arrivals, birds that spent the winter farther south and have only now arrived here on their way home. Perhaps they'll hang out here, fattening up, readying themselves for the next 100 miles or so of their journey. Most will venture well into Canada to breed in the boreal forests.

Data on eBird.org—the premier website for bird sightings, hot spots, and species population statistics—verify that Dark-eyed Junco numbers in my county peak in March but remain relatively high through most of April. The population counts suggest interesting behavior: a prolonged migration of tens of thousands of juncos. Birds are creatures of instinct, their internal hardwired clocks telling them when to go and when to stay. The farther a bird has to go, the earlier it starts its travels, and not every junco heads for the same destination. In fact, their breeding range stretches coast to coast across Canada and throughout most of the western United States.

March 22

Visiting a Refuge

During this first really bright, sunny day in some weeks, we decided to visit an area national refuge to look for ducks. Seldom do I get really good looks at ducks. They're generally skittish, secretive, and distant. Especially distant. Given it's late March, their days here are limited as they follow their centuries-old migratory routes to Canada and the north-central states to nest. Because floodwaters closed much of the refuge area until this week, we feared we might miss the migrating waterfowl this year. Alas, the floodwaters are both a curse (roads closed and viewing sites inaccessible) and a blessing (waterfowl favor feeding opportunities in flooded fields), but today we had a bit of both. Yes, a couple of roads were closed and some were rather soft (almost all are unpaved), but other roads that opened earlier this week had already been cleared and graded. The result? We had decent views of American Wigeon, Gadwall, Northern Shoveler, Northern Pintail, Hooded Mergansers, and of course Mallards and abundant American Coots.

Generally, drab female shovelers, now in breeding attire, sport bright pink legs and matching pink shovel-shaped bills. Foraging alongside their multicolored mates, they pose a striking contrast. Male pintails always give me the anthropomorphic impression that they're in formal attire. I'm especially taken, though, with Wood Ducks because I'm of the strong opinion that they're our most beautiful waterfowl. Only the male Harlequin Duck—a diving duck that prefers rough waters along rocky coastlines and fast, powerful currents on inland streams in the Northwest and into Alaska—can begin to compete with the Wood Duck in any kind of feathery beauty contest. Still, my money is on the Wood Duck. Fortunately, we found numerous woodies today engaged in their typical behavior: secreting in scattered protected waters, mostly near woods. Because breeding season is upon us and because woodies nest in tree cavities (one of only a few ducks that do so), it's easy to guess where to search for them. Obviously they're in water, and logically they're near woods. But the woods must support wood-peckers. Really? Yep, here's why: Since the structure of Wood Ducks' bills makes them unable to excavate their own nest sites, they rely primarily on former wood-

The American Coot, a duck-like water bird, is usually found in huge numbers during winter months.

pecker cavities. The Wood Ducks' size, however, necessitates not just any woodpecker's old nest, but a large woodpecker's hole. Think Pileated Woodpecker. So woodies face a serious challenge finding a suitable nest site. Nowadays, some folks with the right habitat erect nest boxes especially for Wood Ducks. In fact, given our neighbor's farm pond and the adjoining woodland, we've shared that experience and enjoyed the excitement.

A few Ring-billed Gulls mixed with today's waterfowl on the mudflats, and in the distance I thought I could make out several Bonaparte's Gulls.

Lots of raptors soared in the wind today, including about a dozen Red-tailed Hawks and a single Northern Harrier. Given the waterfowl populations, hawks sense a feeding opportunity and regularly soar across the area. In addition, we found an American Kestrel perched on a road sign and a Bald Eagle on the nest, a nest the pair—or at least some pair—has occupied every year for about six years. It's part of our routine to check on the site.

All in all, we had thirty-five bird species—and one mink!

Wood Ducks (drake left; hen right) are one of the few ducks to nest in "found" tree cavities, usually but not always near water.

March 23

Tracking Hawks in the Yard

Carolina Wrens set off a barrage of scolding this afternoon—fast, frenzied, intense, as if seriously threatened by some monster in their midst. At the window, I looked for a marauding cat or some equally disturbing threat to the birds. Nothing. Then I saw it. A Red-shouldered Hawk flew from somewhere above the house, across the driveway, into the garden, landing on the now-empty shepherd's hook. The scolding stopped. While the hawk was obviously the target of the wrens' scolding, Northern Cardinals, American Goldfinches, Dark-eyed Juncos, White-throated Sparrows, and a lone Downy Woodpecker continued feeding in the front yard as if the monster was only imaginary. Mostly, they were right. Red-shouldered Hawks prefer larger prey than half-ounce-size songbirds, and they especially prefer prey easier to catch than songbirds. A Red-shouldered would likely exert more calories in the chase than it would gain from lunching on a songbird. What set off the wrens, I don't know. Perhaps the hawk perched precariously near their new nest. Since I'm not sure where they've chosen to re-nest or where the hawk had paused, I'll likely never solve that mystery. Nevertheless, the wrens were satisfied that they'd scared off the boogeyman.

Although rarely do our yard birds pay much attention to a Red-shouldered or Red-tailed Hawk in the surrounds, a Cooper's or, in winter, a Sharp-shinned Hawk, however, terrorizes the yard and sends birds instantly into hiding or into "freeze" mode. I've seen birds caught away from the safety of dense shelter choose to remain motionless in their spots rather than risk a flight to a too-distant spot. On occasion some birds will remain "frozen," even unblinking, for as much as 20 minutes, awaiting a secure opportunity to zip to safety. Sometimes they simply remain "frozen" until they deem the area safe once more and then comfortably continue feeding. They know! The behavior always amazes me. I've tried to remain motionless and unblinking for the same duration. Did not succeed.

An immature Red-shouldered Hawk surveys the garden for potential prey.

Finding nothing of interest in the yard—no mice, no voles, no frogs, no snakes, no baby bunnies or young squirrels—the Red-shouldered moved on without further disturbance. The wrens went quietly about their business, now settled down, perhaps assured that their fearsome scolds saved the day. Of course, it's unlikely their behavior actually drove off the hawk.

This brief, only minutes-long scenario brings to mind a point of curiosity: How do birds know the difference between non-threatening mammals like squirrels or rabbits and a death-threatening one like a cat? They all have four legs; they're all furry; they can be of similar color; and they're all typically on the ground when feeding. But even young birds seem innately to know the difference (and if they don't, they probably won't survive long). So how do they know?

March 24

Explaining Molt

American Goldfinches, still here in multitudes, look really scrappy now. Males are molting from their winter olive plumage into breeding gold, but since they can't shed and replace all their feathers simultaneously and survive, they take on a splotchy look during the process. Right now, we're talking seriously splotchy— and not at all attractive. None would win even honorable mention in a finch beauty pageant.

A molting American Goldfinch looks less than lovely here, but will appear in handsome breeding plumage within a few weeks.

Having said that, I'm always chagrined remembering the woman who told me she brought in all her nyjer-seed feeders in winter (when finches most need the high-fat seed) because her goldfinches all left. She did not understand that goldfinches change color for the winter, so she didn't recognize them in her wintertime yard. Of course, while all birds molt, some of them twice a year, only a few change color completely from season to season. In fact, the most dramatic color changes occur in birds that migrate to distant parts, returning here in spring decked out in gorgeous breeding plumage. When we see those same birds in the fall, returning to the distant south, we may not recognize them either.

Meanwhile, reports are coming from neighbors about the arrival of more Purple Martins. They've found their way, joining the early birds.

March 25

Praising Brown Thrashers

I heard a Brown Thrasher singing this morning! Gray Catbirds, Northern Mockingbirds, and Brown Thrashers are all fabulous mimics, but researcher Donald Kroodsma of the Rockefeller University Field Research Center in Millbrook, New York, found that Brown Thrashers hold the world's record for varied repertoire. Using a sound analyzer, Kroodsma

A Brown Thrasher approaches the bubble rock to take a sip and a splash.

recorded a single male. Within two hours the Brown Thrasher sang 2,400 distinctly differ-ent songs. Whew! So why would a thrasher make the effort to sing so many melodies? That behavior earns him a mate! Female thrashers apparently measure the quality of a potential mate by his singing versatility. What a trick!

The old rule of thumb for distinguishing which mimic is singing goes like this: Catbirds say everything once; thrashers say everything twice; and mockingbirds say everything over and over. So I had to stop, be quiet, and listen carefully to be sure this singer was saying everything twice. He was.

While the Brown Thrasher popped by off and on all winter, he was silent then. Why sing when there's no reason—no battle for territory or nest sites and no sweetie to impress? So hearing him this morning made me stop and look for his rufous-colored form. Maybe he'll find a willing female that will join him to nest here again this year. Then I can hear him sing all summer!

Birds Do *That*?

Birds eat rocks. In fact, birds choose not just any rocks to eat but sharp rocks. Of course, they don't "eat" rocks in the sense of digesting them. Instead they swallow them for digestive purposes. According to a University of California, Berkeley Museum of Paleontology research report, many animals that have no teeth need help grinding the food they must swallow whole. By swallowing sharp rocks that they then hold in their gizzards (the muscular part of the stom-ach), birds, especially those that survive mostly on plant matter, can better grind their food. Once the rocks wear down after all that grinding, the birds vomit them up and replace them. Just for the record, those upchucked rocks then take on a special name: gastroliths.

March 26

Measuring Nyjer Seed

For convenience sake I use an old gallon milk jug for filling nyjer feeders. In recent weeks, American Goldfinches and Pine Siskins along with a very few House Finches have fed so heavily that I've needed a full gallon of nyjer seed daily to fill the two tube feeders. There's cause for their behaviors: Siskins have been gorging themselves, putting on fat to prepare for their upcoming journey. Goldfinches have needed a robust, calorie-filled menu to replace a full body of feathers. And some of them, of course, are preparing to go north as well. In the past two days, however, things changed. I've seen only two siskins and about half the number of goldfinches—down to about twenty or twenty-five. Numbers are down because, as expected, both species have begun to disperse. On the other hand, Dark-eyed Juncos and White-throated Sparrows continue to feed heavily under the nyjer-seed feeders (both migrate a bit later). While neither can feed at the nyjer-seed ports, they manage quite nicely cleaning up spilled seed that escaped the siskins and goldfinches. With the now-splotchy molting goldfinches assuming a near monopoly at the feeders, however, I can rest easier, confident that my bird-feed budget will survive the winter season intact.

March 27

Anticipating a Wave

Radar images tonight show a wide band of storms training across the United States from central Texas through northeastern Pennsylvania and raging right over the top of us. From the south and southeast, radar also shows a major movement of migrating birds, heading north and northwest, hitting the storm band, and forced to stop. When the storm finally moves on, I'm guessing we'll see a huge wave of birds. Since they've been held up for so long, though, they could leapfrog over us in their rush to move north. It's a behavior I've seen before. The usual early migrants, the ones that are typically singing here by now—

Eastern Phoebe, Yellow-throated Warbler, Northern Parula, and Blue-gray Gnatcatcher—have yet to sound a peep. I'm probably getting as antsy to know they're back as they are to be back. But they mustn't out-fly their food source. If they do, they'll perish. For that reason I worry about the Purple Martins, knowing that they eat only bugs in flight. While I've seen bugs when I've been out and about, these chilly, rainy days aren't very conducive to flying insects. It's life on the edge for these birds, instinctively pushing to arrive early to find rich nest spots but risking a too-early arrival that leaves them hungry—or worse.

The Yellow-throated Warbler is usually one of four early arriving migrants to the yard, joining Eastern Phoebe, Northern Parula, and Blue-gray Gnatcatcher.

March 28

Noting a Diet Change

With a short break in the rain this afternoon, I made my way across the saturated yard, around the edge of the garden, and stood quietly watching the woods along the south edge of our property. The woods actually extends well into three adjoining neighbors' properties, so only a slim strip actually belongs to us. Still, with a binocular, I can see well into the interior now, when trees are still bare.

Several birds displayed behavior that caught my eye. White-throated Sparrows and a lone Northern Cardinal sat in a young gum tree eating leaf buds from the twigs. Birds are desperate this time of year with no seeds and no berries available. So they eat the next best thing: buds.

On the other hand, in the old sycamore tree, American Goldfinches and several cardinals sat plucking tidbits from the sycamore balls, seed heads that still cling to the branches. Regularly I see goldfinches, siskins, and House Finches foraging among the sycamores, but tonight was the first time I've seen cardinals yanking out the minuscule seeds from the hard seed heads. They're desperate, too. Desperation affects behavior. The more adaptable a bird is to desperate situations, the more likely it will survive.

Mostly, though, I was listening, hoping to hear something new, some migrant that had just arrived, perhaps a phoebe or a Northern Parula. Neither came within my earshot this time, but the evening serenade revealed a change in the winter-weak melodies. Now I heard a newly vigorous chorus of song, louder, more aggressive, more attention-getting, verifying the beginning of breeding behavior, hormones revving up. Among the many songsters were Tufted Titmice calling "peter, peter, peter," Carolina Chickadees giving their three-note phoebe-like call, Northern Cardinals whistling "cheer-cheer, purdy, purdy, purdy," and a Red-bellied Woodpecker sounding its "querr, querr, querr" calls. Off toward the west, I heard a Carolina Wren's loud, ringing "teacher, teacher, teacher," and several Dark-eyed Juncos' bell-like mechanical song. White-throated Sparrows, having turned up, now sang on-key, "Oh, Sam Peabody, Peabody, Peabody." European Starlings gurgled from the neighbor's barn lot; several American Crows cawed their way across the sky from the northeast to the southwest; and a Red-headed Woodpecker chirred from the center of the woods.

Among the many scolds, songs, chips, and chirrs, however, was another call, something like "kik-kik-kik-kik-kik-kik." It was coming from the woods, but not always from the same spot. Yes, from the same general area, but not from the same tree. I could see nothing moving nor anything perched. Trying to recall which species made that sound, I considered Sharp-shinned Hawk. But no, it's already gone, headed north toward its breeding range some weeks ago. Maybe, then, a Cooper's Hawk? I wasn't sure.

Pulling out my cell phone, I checked my favorite birdsong app for Cooper's Hawk. Played it. It sounded about right. I studied the app list to consider any other possibility. While I was distracted checking the list, eyes on the cell phone screen, "Whoosh!" Something flew within feet of my head. The wind whistled through the wings and stirred the hair on my hatless head. Wow! What was that? All I saw was the back end of a fairly decent-size bird flying away from me. It never veered, so I had no sense of species, and I lost sight of it as it dipped over the roof of the house. Then I heard the "kik-kik-kik-kik-kik-kik" from the backyard. Really? Within minutes, I saw a Cooper's Hawk coming from the direction of the house, flying about 30 feet high and off just to the east of where I stood, sailing back to the woods where I'd first heard it.

Mystery solved! The "kik-kik" definitely emanated from a Cooper's Hawk, and this bird was on territory. If the bird weren't on territory, my playing its call on my cell phone would have evoked no reaction. Instead, the recording obviously put the bird in defense mode—dare I say attack mode?—ready to chase out an intruder, to guard its chosen territory. Birds can pin down the source of a call or song to the inch, and while the Cooper's obviously didn't see another Cooper's, it knew exactly the spot from which the app call came. It responded instantly. The bird's startlingly speedy defense made me study the bird's behavior more carefully. Was that really the beginning of a nest in that large tree just past the old broken sycamore? With my binocular, I scanned as best I could through the tangle of tree branches, moving a step or two in each direction, trying for the best view.

A Cooper's Hawk hunts for songbirds for lunch.

The bird had landed near what looked like a few sticks collected in a high-canopy aerie, surely arranged more carefully than would be naturally fallen twigs. Hmmm. Could be a coincidence that the bird landed there. Could be the remains of a squirrel's nest. Could be nothing. Still, it bears watching over the next several days.

Cooper's Hawks are no strangers to the yard. In fact, on the fifteenth of this month, one took up a perch in the front yard, giving the area a once-over, hoping for lunch. I'm fairly sure a pair nested here last summer, too—although I never found the nest. She was just here. All the time. Every day. Persistently. Now, given this bird's behavior, I'm ready to say it's a female (she was large, and as with most raptors, females are larger than males). I'm also ready to stick my neck out and say, as a result of the apparent attack mode, she has established a territory. Whether the little mess of twigs is the beginning of this year's nest remains to be seen, but I'm betting she'll nest either there or somewhere nearby. Of course, once the trees leaf out, I'll not be able to spy into the tree without trespassing on the neighbor's property, which is probably not a good idea.

March 29

Analyzing Seed Cakes

A seed cake outside the front window attracts an unusual array of birds. At the moment, I'm watching a Northern Cardinal snack on one side of the cake while a Downy Woodpecker picks on the other side and a Tufted Titmouse awaits its turn, perched in a nearby

A Chipping Sparrow in fresh spring plumage forages in its usual manner on the ground.

shrub. While the cake is marketed for woodpeckers, in my yard it has hosted everything from the intended woodpeckers to Carolina Wrens and Yellow-throated Warblers—neither of which eats seeds! What evokes their behavior? Something in the cake attracts the little birds' relish, and I'm fairly certain it's the gelatin that holds the cake together.

This morning, another little bird enjoying nibbles was a Chipping Sparrow, making its first-of-the-year appearance in the yard. While during many winters, chippers stay around, this winter's cold and snow apparently sent them south, albeit probably not too far south. So this morning, at least one is back. I seriously doubt it was eating seeds from the cake, although of course sparrows eat primarily seeds. The morsels in this so-called woodpecker cake, however, are quite large, and the chipper seemed to be foraging between the seeds, not on the seeds. Perhaps, like the wrens and warblers, it was dining on the gelatin, and probably for good reason. Here's why: Gelatin is a natural protein made from processing animal collagen. Contrary to popular belief, collagen comes not from animal hooves and horns, which are made of keratin, but from animal hide and bones. The result: Gelatin is 90 percent protein.

Chippers always look as if they've dressed in a freshly washed, starched, and ironed outfit. The delineations between colors are crisp; the whites are glaringly bright; the browns are rich, maybe safely called chestnut; and overall the trim, neatly attired birds look gentile. Surely chippers are the prettiest of the little brown sparrows! Well, okay, the immatures and winter-plumaged chippers lack the pizzazz, but I know they'll change.

1 Chipping Sparrow
Species: 49 total in the yard to date for the year.

March 30

Exploring a Wildlife Area

I haven't seen a Pine Siskin in three days now, so I'm guessing they're gone. A few may pop by if they've been farther south and haven't yet passed through here, but I shouldn't expect many.

Likewise, the American Goldfinch numbers have settled down. They had piled up here, numbering as many as seventy to seventy-five, waiting for the weather fronts to align and give them tailwinds north. Over the past few days, they've had a break or two in the weather. Now a motley bunch of about twenty feeds at the nyjer-seed tube feeder. Some are as drab as they've been all winter; some look almost fully molted, in nearly perfect breeding plumage; and some wear such splotchy feathery coats that they appear not to be well. Such an array! Now a mere half gallon of nyjer seed fills the feeders, a sure sign of the population changes.

Given pretty weather this afternoon, we ventured an hour or so to our northeast to a fish and wildlife area to see what we might find. We anticipated that most of the ducks would be gone, and they were, but we found an unimpressive twenty-nine species, mostly expected, with one surprise. Among the usuals, raptors included Red-shouldered and Red-tailed Hawks, Northern Harrier, and American Kestrel. The Bald Eagle was on its nest, its white head visible even at a distance. Tree Swallows have returned in abundance,

A Great Blue Heron stands motionless atop a log, watching for passing fish.

necessarily dispersing soon to find adequate nesting cavities. Killdeer, Horned Lark, and twelve Wild Turkeys grazed the grasslands and fallow fields. A Belted Kingfisher rattled its way along a stream, and a Great Blue Heron fished from atop a fallen log.

In the water we found several Common Loons, changing into breeding plumage and preparing for the remainder of their journey, perhaps to Michigan's Upper Peninsula; at least a bazillion American Coots, on their way toward the US-Canada border; a few Canada Geese, probably non-migratory residents; several pairs of Mallards that may nest here; and dozens of Pied-billed Grebes, some of which will stay to nest while others will necessarily find other, less crowded territory. Then, wait. Something else. A grebe popped up, its silhouette different entirely from the usual Pied-billed Grebe. Definitely a grebe, but less squatty and longer necked than a Pied-billed. What? We studied it with our binoculars and tried for photos, but the glare on the water was unrelenting, no matter the direction we tried. Eventually, though, we zeroed in on the ID: Horned Grebe. Why is it here? These birds winter on both the Atlantic and Pacific Coasts and breed in northern Canada into Alaska, so they only migrate through the Midwest. During a few short days in spring and again in the fall, we might catch them resting and feeding here. They lack their full breeding plumage, but the promise is clear enough to give us a thrill.

A day watching the behavior of diving loons, nesting eagles, strutting turkeys, and a surprise migrating Horned Grebe surely refreshes the soul! And the intermingled songs of spring peepers, tree frogs, and American toads certainly added to the refreshment. A lovely afternoon.

This evening I caught sight of one of the Barred Owl pair perched at the edge of our woods. We made eye contact, and it stretched its head this way and that, a behavior that lets the owl get the perfect bead on me, bobbing to establish my exact location. So I averted my eyes and turned slightly to my left, avoiding the front-on confrontational gaze that animals find disconcerting and threatening. Out of the corner of my eye, I could see the owl doing likewise, rotating its head, checking right and left. But when I turned my head its way again, the stretching behavior resumed. Because several branches crossed between it and me, I did not have an unobstructed view of the bird, but I knew full well it could see me far better than I could see it. I'd bet it could tell not only the color of my eyes but how many hairs I have in my eyelashes! We kept up this eye-to-eye hide-and-seek game for a good 20 minutes before I wandered off. When I returned about a half hour later, it was gone. Well, it was gone from the spot where I'd seen it, and I couldn't spot it anywhere else. I'd lose money on a bet that it couldn't see me.

The unbelievably brave Northern Cardinal that stuck to its roost the night the raccoon raided the nearby feeder (see photo on March 6) continues to remain a nightly resident, tucked under the awning in the same spot. Having just peered through the door's window, light from my office in the next room faintly illuminating him, I can vouch for his presence as I'm writing this. I'd love to get a photo, but to do so I'd have to use flash. I fear that would disturb the bird—of course it would—and he might fly into the black night, fairly well ensuring his demise. So only my word can make the case.

March 31

Checking Grebes

After a Saturday morning breakfast at our favorite local mom-and-pop restaurant, we decided to make a quick stop at a little hot spot nearby. It's a relatively small lake, probably five acres, next to the interstate, behind a restaurant chain and two hotels—nothing that suggests a hot spot for birds. For whatever reason, though, some really prize water birds regularly show up there, and birders have learned it's worth a swing-by just to check. This morning was one of those intended few-minutes' swing-bys that instead lasted about an hour, because among the fifty or so American Coots and several dozen Pied-billed Grebes were six unusual grebes. They turned out to be the same species we'd puzzled over yesterday: Horned Grebes. What fascinated me most, however, was that each of the six was in a slightly different stage of molting from winter plumage into breeding (or, more properly, alternate) plumage. The sexes look alike, so I had no way of knowing if the various stages were representative of male versus female, or of age, with first-spring birds perhaps taking longer than mature birds to achieve full breeding plumage. By studying the photos this evening, I've enjoyed a lesson in molt.

I'm in awe of what's happening with the behavior of these birds. They're obviously molting. Their plumage does not resemble the bird's common black-and-white winter appearance. Nor does it resemble the strikingly beautiful breeding appearance illustrated in bird

Horned Grebes show a mix of winter and breeding plumage during a rare southwestern Indiana stopover along their thousand-mile migratory path.

guides. Their overall look is a bit ragged, feathers poking out with irregularity, an almost rough appearance to areas that should look smooth and sleek, like the back, neck, and wings.

Birds exert tremendous energy to grow new feathers, and these birds look to be undergoing a partial body molt. At the same time, however—and this is the part that puts me in awe—they're migrating. Flying long distances, in this case probably about a thousand miles, requires astonishing energy. These birds appear to be undergoing both— although they're obviously not molting wing and tail feathers. If they were, they couldn't fly now. Like ducks, these water birds do experience a short period in which they are flightless, as they molt wing feathers, but that occurs during the time their hatchlings are also flightless.

The question remains, however, how can they molt during migration? Where do they find the energy to survive both a marathon flight and a partial body molt? Some references claim that birds never molt during migration, but that seems an erroneous claim in this case. Oh my, how awesome, this bird.

April

A male Chestnut-sided Warbler sings during the early spring dawn chorus.

*I never for a day gave up listening to the songs
of our birds, or watching their peculiar habits,
or delineating them in the best way I could.*

—John James Audubon (1785–1851)

April 1

Spotting Sparrows

For April 1 the morning dawned unseasonably cool at 48 degrees, windy but sunny. The prediction, however, is for a low tonight of 35 degrees and snow, maybe an inch. The roller-coaster weather has affected migration big time, so almost none of the birds that should be here by now have made an appearance, neither in the yard nor in the area.

Today did prove to be a decent sparrow day with an unusual five species in the yard simultaneously: Chipping Sparrow, Field Sparrow, White-throated Sparrow, and Song Sparrow, along with our largest sparrow, Eastern Towhee.

Song Sparrows and Eastern Towhees hang out here year-round. Although I don't necessarily see them every day, I usually see or hear them at least every week. Both nest in the yard, and I find the Song Sparrow's nest regularly while weeding in the garden, where it's on or very near the ground, wedged in among dense stalks. While the towhee also nests on or very near the ground, she's more secretive, usually tucking in among the brambles. I watch carefully to spot the general location of her nest, but I never try to locate it specifically, fearing I'd step on it. I'm always amazed that different bird species, even those in the same family, have surprisingly different nesting behaviors!

White-throated Sparrows, of course, spend only the winter with us, arriving in late September or early October from their breeding grounds in northern Michigan, Wisconsin, Minnesota, or Canada. Their numbers in the yard grew to three or four dozen during the heart of winter but are now slowly diminishing. As they complete molting, they leave, heading to their ancestral breeding grounds. As with most species, the White-throats with the farthest to go leave the earliest. Those that wintered farther south, maybe as far south as the Gulf Coast, have only now arrived here, many still molting. So they look a little fuzzy, their lovely head pattern still not clearly defined. Those that molted earlier, showing off spiffy plumage a week or so back, have since disappeared, doubtless already nearing home. For those that remain, though, it's obvious that their hormones are stirring.

A Chipping Sparrow in breeding plumage may get the vote for prettiest sparrow, this one singing on territory.

In spite of what the range maps show, Chipping Sparrows sometimes stay year-round here in southern Indiana, but nasty winters like this past one drive them south, just not far. Because they don't go any farther south than necessary, they're back ASAP during the earliest days of spring. So indeed they're back now, their song so similar to that of the Dark-eyed Junco that I rarely know which is singing unless I can spot the source. Arguably, chippers in breeding plumage may be the prettiest of the little brown sparrows, their russet caps giving them a really spiffy look, males and females indiscernible. As always, though, beauty is in the eye of the beholder. Prettiest or not, chippers will set up housekeeping here, somewhere in open woodlands or along the woodland edges with grassy understory. It's their usual nesting behavior.

The assembly of five was rounded out today with a Field Sparrow. We're within the species' year-round range, but I have to be clear: I certainly don't see it year-round in the yard. Their populations are declining, perhaps because they like overgrown fields that include scattered bushes, saplings, and especially hedgerows, while farmers as well as others often prefer neat and tidy, much to the birds' detriment. Of course, our little three-acre patch doesn't offer the extended space Field Sparrows need, even for a single-pair territory. I'm pleased, though, that they wander through now and then, this morning being one of those day-brightener times.

Given their respective seasonal fluctuations and habitat differences, seeing all five of these sparrows simultaneously was a nice little treat. Cute April Fool's trick!

April 2

Making Memories

Sometimes a day with birds brings some really cool memories. Today was such a day.

Before breakfast this morning, my husband called out, "There's a Wild Turkey in the hayfield!" and off I darted to the window. During the past two years, we've had a little flock of eleven turkeys, hens, and their offspring wandering about, following a loose circle through the neighborhood. We learned to expect the routine behavior, and we periodically photographed them and their offspring. Last August a hen wandered alone across the hayfield with a single weeks-old chick, revealing a unique breeding behavior among turkeys. She'd obviously had early nest failure but, since hens can hold live sperm for about seventy days, she produced (probably) another clutch of eggs, managing to raise the single poult. It was a sobering but simultaneously rewarding sight, watching her watching her single offspring; we took photos. For whatever reason, she never joined the rest.

Birds Do *That*?

It's true. Robins get drunk. Oh, not intentionally, of course. It's just that they and other birds that eat fruits sometimes indulge in an abundance of overripe fruits. In late fall into early spring, fruits like crab apple and mountain ash have rotted. Their sugars have fermented. Hungry birds, though, don't know the difference, so they eat. And eat. Finally, if they eat enough of the berries, they get drunk or sometimes even die. Tipsy frugivores like American Robins and Cedar Waxwings lose their quick motor coordination and fly about wobbling, crashing into windows or vehicular traffic, often with disastrous results. According to field ornithologist Christopher W. Leahy, although some folks see humor in the birds' erratic movements, intoxication seriously threatens a bird's life.

Seeing the first Wild Turkey tom of the season in full strut is cause for excitement, understanding that he's here because he knows where the hens are hiding.

Then by early September, we missed seeing the flock. Nor did we any longer see the hen with her single poult. We watched more carefully, assuming they had wandered via a different route or perhaps on a different schedule. No sightings. We asked the neighbors, all of whom also kept track of the birds' comings and goings. No sightings. We asked the neighbor who offered corn to the flock. No sightings.

So the single bird this morning, emerging from the woods, was cause for excitement. A handsome tom turkey, his head a lovely breeding blue and his wattle flaming red, thrust his head forward each time he gobbled. He behaved as if he owned the place. He crossed the hayfield, following the crest of the rise, walking, stopping, gobbling, starting a partial strut, then as if changing his mind, refolded his feathers and resumed the walking-stopping-gobbling behavior. In my vivid imagination, I was betting his thoughts were something like this: "I know I'm in the right place. I remember every detail of the landscape—the woods, the hayfield, the farm pond, the next woods. Those girls were the finest—the whole flock of them. They were my harem. What's happened to them? They don't answer my calls. They don't show their faces. They don't seem to know I'm here. Where are they hiding?" I hope he finds his harem.

By afternoon, with temperatures still unseasonably cool, a high of only 48 degrees, further action in the yard seemed unlikely. Still, out of habit, I stood at the kitchen window, teacup in hand, idly watching all the usual birds, when something bright caught my eye. Oh my! A Red-headed Woodpecker landed in the top of the snag! Red-heads routinely hang out in our woods, readily visible from the yard and garden, but this was the first on the snag! They love dead trees.

This bird's arrival, however, ranked as a special occasion for another reason. Over the fifty-plus years we've lived here and worked on habitat restoration, Red-headed Woodpeckers have only rarely visited close to the house. Whatever visits there had been were mostly fly-bys. Now here it was, perched, looking over the yard, surveying the situation. Then, as if this were routinely repeated behavior, it flew directly to the platform feeder, snatched up a couple of peanut splits, and dashed off, up over the house. I blinked twice, almost in denial of what I'd seen. My camera, however, doesn't lie, and there it was in the photo, bold and bright, perched on the snag. Its behavior seemed practiced, so I wondered if this bird had been scoring a daily dietary home run without my noticing, maybe even making daily forays into the yard at the same time we typically go for our walk. Interesting.

Now it was time to call to hubby to grab his camera. Maybe, just maybe, the woodpecker would return—especially if I added another handful of peanut splits to the nearly depleted supply. I'm stingy with split peanuts, parceling out a single cupful each morning. Now, late in the afternoon, only a few pieces remained. Another one-third cup surely seemed in order, so I dashed out with an additional offering.

Within minutes, however, a Red-bellied Woodpecker caught sight of the delicacies and zipped in to partake. The Red-headed arrived almost simultaneously, but took offense at the company. Bill-to-bill battle ensued. The Red-bellied reconsidered and departed. The Red-headed grabbed two peanuts and left. Wow, that was fast. Maybe less than 2 minutes altogether?

Within the next 2 minutes, though, the Red-headed Woodpecker returned. This time, however, the bird behaved differently, seemed more timid, flying into the protection of the evergreen hemlock, hiding while it checked the surroundings. Finally, it dropped toward

A Red-bellied Woodpecker arrives at the peanut feeder almost simultaneously with a Red-headed Woodpecker, and a bill-to-bill battle ensues.

the feeder but swooped up at the last minute. Only a Northern Cardinal was feeding there, so I was surprised at the woodpecker's timidity. Again it swooped. A third time it swooped. Finally, it landed, grabbed one peanut, and fled. As we watched, I suggested to hubby that this might have been a second bird, because its demeanor seemed quite different from that of the first bird. Since the sexes look alike, I had little else to go on, but I also thought perhaps the second bird looked slightly smaller. Of course, that impression could have resulted from its timidity, sleeking its feathers flat against its body. There was no way to be sure.

I couldn't be sure—at least not until one returned, zipping in via a perch on the snag and down to the feeder. While that bird took its time filling its beak with at least three peanut pieces, the second returned to the protection of the hemlock. Aha! Two birds! Two patterns of behavior. So it went, each snatching a peanut or two before fleeing over the top of the house.

Then the puzzle added another dimension. What were they doing with the peanuts? Where were they going? Surely they weren't feeding babies, and if they were, they surely weren't feeding their babies peanuts. Really? So what was happening? What was this behavior all about? I decided to go outside, make myself somewhat invisible, and spy on them.

Outside, binocular and camera in hand, I moved into the front garden, tucked myself under the small trellis covered by semi-evergreen native crossvine, and faced the woods where I knew the red-headeds frequently hung out. Standing stock still, watching and listening, within minutes I was rewarded with the sight of one of the woodpeckers flying right over me and into the woods. It landed on a dead branch, but before I could get my binocular on it and focused, it moved to another branch. Each time the bird moved, I followed it, trying to fathom its behavior. That bird flew back over the house, presumably to the snag in the backyard, more or less simultaneously as another red-headed flew into the woods. The two of them continued the back-and-forth behavior for at least 20 minutes, but neither ever landed on the same branch nor, in some cases, even in the same tree. They seemed to hammer, as if breaking the peanut splits into smaller pieces, suitable for swallowing. Or were they hammering the peanuts into a hiding place, caching the pieces for feeding themselves when they were busy with babies? I really couldn't be sure, but it seemed all wrong for birds to be caching morsels in spring. That's an autumn behavior. Strange. I'd have to keep an eye out for what's happening.

A male Eastern Bluebird gathers dropped suet crumbles from an unseen feeder above.

When the flyovers ceased and my chilled hands had turned numb, I went back inside—and saw why the birds had stopped their to-and-fro activity: The peanut splits were gone!

With the afternoon waning into evening, surely little activity remained, but then the male Eastern Bluebird arrived on the backyard snag. He comes to check the suet feeder almost every late afternoon. Well, more specifically, he comes to check for crumbles beneath the suet feeder. Because I'd scattered a few spoons full of crumbled suet at just the spot he expected, he dropped down, ate a few pieces for himself, and then chose the largest piece and flew off with it. The female came shortly after and repeated the behavior. The male returned for the same routine. Oh, my, what telling behavior! They're feeding babies! Like almost all songbirds, bluebirds feed their babies bugs, but on a cold, wet day like today, bugs are in truly short supply. The suet provides a dandy substitute for mom, dad, and the hatchlings, to keep them going until the crazy weather settles down.

> 1 Wild Turkey, tom
> **Species:** 50 total in the
> yard to date for the year.

All in all, what great memories!

April 3

Seeing Purple

Eastern Phoebes were singing this morning, two of them! I find their hissy-spitty name-calling song amusing: "FEE-bee." They sound grumpy and cross, ticked off at the world. In seeming contradiction, however, I welcome the sound, a song that, to me, confirms spring. After all, the birds know for sure!

Since phoebes' winter range extends as far north as Tennessee, they migrate only short distances. Maybe the ones we see during some winters aren't "our" phoebes, but rather ones that normally breed well to our north. They may have migrated here for the winter while "ours" actually migrated a bit farther south. Without banding studies, we can only guess at the behavior.

Because it doesn't migrate far, the Eastern Phoebe is among the first to return in spring, this one flycatching in the yard today. Bristles at the base of the beak are feather adaptations believed to be nerve extensions allowing birds to "feel" a bug as they zoom in on the catch.

Later in the morning, a Red-headed Woodpecker returned. Twice, in quick order, red-headeds visited the suet feeder that hangs against the trunk of the snag. Maybe the same bird visited twice; maybe two birds each visited once. Oddly enough, in light of their behavior yesterday, this morning they ignored the ample peanut supply. Again, the direct flight to the suet feeder seemed practiced, as if they knew the way, as if they need not study the surroundings to see what was where, as if they need not explore to find our offerings. Rather, they flew onto the snag, dove directly to the feeder, drilled out a few chunks—seemingly satisfying their appetites—and left.

About the same time, I caught sight of an unusually rosy-colored finch, not quite the right color for a House Finch. Unfortunately, I missed the photo, and did not see the bird clearly enough to know for sure if it was a Purple Finch. In spring and fall, female/immature Purple Finches occasionally cruise through, usually only two or three, never a crowd, and rarely any males. So the glimpse of what I thought to be a male Purple Finch built anticipation.

A male Purple Finch wings in, perhaps foretelling an irruption, a phenomenon that occurs when Canada's mast crop fails and winter finches move south in search of food.

Waiting for its return led to nothing, so I went on about my business. Within a half hour, however, hubby announced the bird's return and managed a few photos. Oooo, yes! A handsome male Purple Finch. Good thing for the photos, because the speedy little guy was gone again by the time I dashed to the window. Later in the day, however, I finally managed to catch sight of him, satisfying my anticipation.

Distinguishing House Finches from Purple Finches can be a bit tricky, but basically the Purple Finch looks as if he's been dipped in raspberry juice. The streaks on his breast and flanks are rosy, not brown like the House Finch. He has deep rose on his head, not brown like the House Finch. And his wings and back look as if they've been painted over with rose, not brown like the House Finch. Yes, male House Finches can be really bright, but they're red, not rosy. Since Purple Finches show up only when their food sources grow limited in the north, we don't see them with any regularity. Sometimes in spring and fall. Sometimes in winter. Never in summer. Not here.

2 Eastern Phoebe
Species: 51 total in the yard to date for the year.

April 4

Unraveling a Mystery

Ice on the birdbath this morning!

The return of two Red-headed Woodpeckers this morning gave me pause. Two days ago, on their first visit, I was certain that two individuals had visited the yard. Photos, however, showed only a single individual. I knew that for a somewhat unsettling reason: Every photo showed a bird with an upper mandible slightly longer than its lower mandible. Surely, I reasoned, no two birds would be in the yard simultaneously with the same abnormality.

This morning, however, two birds appeared simultaneously, perched together at the peanut feeder. A single photo clarified the mystery. Only one had an exceptionally long upper mandible. The other, the more shy bird, the one that came and went with speedy purpose, the one that hid in the hemlock tree, zipped to the feeder, and zipped away with equal haste—that bird had distinctive markings. It had a few brownish feathers on what should be an otherwise entirely scarlet-red head; it had some brownish splotches on its back where it should be shiny black; and it had some black marks on its wings where it should be entirely white. Bingo! This was a first-spring bird, a bird that hatched last summer and had not yet completed its breeding-plumage molt.

I have to wonder: Are they a pair? Given the sexual monomorphism, or look-alike plumages, of male and female Red-headed Woodpeckers, I really can't tell whether one is male and the other female. If they are a pair, is the first-spring bird unable to find the perfect mate and has settled for a bird with an abnormality? Or maybe they aren't a pair. Maybe the first-spring bird is the offspring of the other, not having yet "flown the coop," not having yet headed out on its own. Still, that seems unlikely,

A Red-headed Woodpecker, having just visited the suet feeder, displays an unnaturally long upper mandible, an abnormality of unknown cause that ultimately renders the bird unable to preen, leaving it in dire straits.

A first-spring Red-headed Woodpecker lacks the adult's pure-white wing bars, sleek all-black back, and silky smooth solid red hood.

given this first week of April. Ah, the mysteries of the bird world, the clues that make me wonder about the drama playing out right out the window.

After last night's violent winds and nearby tornado, I was relieved to find the male Northern Cardinal tucked back on his weeks-long roost site under the front awning. He wasn't there last night and I feared the worst, but apparently, for whatever reason, he chose to roost elsewhere. Glad he found safe lodgings and survived the wicked weather.

What interesting behaviors to watch today!

April 5

Spying on the Roost

Sunset occurred at 7:17 p.m., and I was determined to catch the Northern Cardinal in the act of settling in on his now-regular perch under the front awning. With a cloud-free sky tonight, once the sun went down, the daylight faded quickly. Settled in my recliner at the front window with a view of the little corner where the bird tucks in, I kept my eyes trained on the spot. Good thing! At 7:29 p.m. the bird flew in, landed on the strut about 18 inches from the corner, jumped to the corner, flipped his body 180 degrees, and sat motionless. No fidgeting, no feather fluffing, no getting situated. Landed, turned, and stopped. The whole process took no more than 3 seconds. Had I not kept my eyes glued to the spot, had I blinked at the wrong time, I would have missed it all.

In part, the instant between landing and settling probably has something to do with practice. After all, he's been perching in this spot for at least a month now, almost every night. (I've found him absent only twice.) So, yes, he knows the way, the exact spot, the most efficient approach, the quickest way to situate himself. Why the rush? My best guess: The less commotion, the less attention he draws to himself, the safer his perch. He probably doesn't think that process through or intentionally analyze those steps; it's more likely instinctive behavior.

Why do our nightly movements inside a well-lit house, our shadows passing across the windows, our reading lights shining on his perch, and the noises that he surely hears from our television or our voices not disturb him? One thought: He's become accustomed to our ways. He's learned that the lights and sounds are harmless, and he's willing to tolerate them in order to feel protected in his safe place. Still, how did he become accustomed to it all in the first place? Why didn't he flee from the beginning at whatever disturbances we unwittingly created? Ah, more mysteries. More drama.

April 6

Sounding the News

A male Hairy Woodpecker hammers on the old tulip-tree snag, sounding a courtship call.

This morning the neighborhood resonated with woodpeckers hammering. Each species hammers with its own rhythm, so savvy birders (though not I) can recognize the woodpecker by its hammer. The noisy behavior is all about territory and attracting a female, and females have a critical ear. They want to breed with the strongest mate, so the louder the hammer the better the guy—at least in their minds. I remember well the year one male Downy Woodpecker chose our metal downspout for his hammering display. Metal makes for amazing resonance. Since he liked to advertise early in the morning and since the downspout was just outside our bedroom window, I have to admit the hammering didn't charm me nearly as much as it charmed the female Downy. Fortunately, he must have won her over quickly, because after just over a week, he abandoned the downspout. I hope the pair found bliss! I certainly did.

But I digress.

Song is a huge part of breeding birds' behavior, especially, of course, for males. So another song this morning made me pause, wondering if I really heard what I thought I heard: a buzzy, spitty song I hadn't heard in nine months. Every spring I have to retrain myself, relearn the songs and calls of the birds that spend only a few months with us or the birds that only migrate through. Of course, the best way to learn the songs is to watch the birds that sing them. The visual image somehow, at least in my feeble brain, reinforces the notes and helps me remember who says what.

A male Blue-gray Gnatcatcher, his facial "bridle" denoting his sex, has arrived, singing on territory, aiming to attract a female.

This morning's song made me comb through the cobwebs in my brain. Then I saw the source: Blue-gray Gnatcatcher. They're back! They wintered in Mexico and Cuba, perhaps Haiti or the Dominican Republic. Now they're here, in southwestern Indiana, ready to nest, hunting and catching bugs for their babies all summer. Since we never use insecticides, native bugs live in our native garden and draw birds in like a magnet. The gnatcatchers, little guys, sport white eye rings and white outer tail feathers. The male's facial "bridle" pattern distinguishes him from his mate. I love watching their hunting behavior: darting, ducking, bouncing, even hanging upside down, gleaning bugs.

Bluebirds have been active this morning, too, mating near their chosen nest box. A bit of a stir happened earlier, with a second male making an apparent play to intrude, a behavior that tested the pair's strength. Apparently they passed! The love triangle was defeated! In all fairness, the third bird may not have been an intruder, rather only one of last year's offspring, still needing a nudge on his way to independence.

A pair of Mallards flew over, on their way, no doubt, to a neighbor's woodland lake.

2 Mallard
1 Blue-gray Gnatcatcher
Species: 53 total in the yard to date for the year.

April 7

Watching Woodies in the Woods

Wood Ducks in the woods this morning! A first for our property!

Yes, on occasion I've seen Wood Ducks in trees, including female woodies going to and from their nest cavities. We've also had the privilege of photographing them, both males and females, perched in trees, but not on property, not even in our county. Certainly, too, we've enjoyed over the years the pleasure of woodies using our own handmade nest boxes mounted at the edges of the neighbor's field pond. The handsome drake sports unbelievable color! His chestnut brown, indigo blue, iridescent green, stark white, pure black,

A Wood Duck drake patrols the pond, protecting his mate and his nest cavity from intruders.

clear orange, subtle pink, and cherry red colors should surely clash, even jangle the nerves. Instead, the bird seems to boast an extraordinary burst of brilliant highlights.

Seeing the pair fly into our woods this morning, then, made my day, but I have to wonder about their behavior: Did they leave so quickly because they saw nothing suitable? Do they know on such a quick tour that the Barred Owls and Red-headed Woodpeckers have nesting sites there? Or did they tour through quickly only as part of a wider tour, in the process of narrowing the possibilities, and maybe still have our little patch on their top ten list? Wouldn't it be amazing if they returned, if we not only made the top ten but won the final! Of course, because they're so stealthy, they could very easily nest in a chosen cavity in our woods and I'd never know. That, of course, would be their plan, their instinct, their preferred mode of operation. I only saw them this morning because I happened to glance up from my morning's crossword puzzle at the perfect moment to see their movement, catch the identity, and see the direction of the tour's flight.

And speaking of catching the moment, I also caught sight of a pair of Purple Finches at the safflower feeder in the garden's east end. It's the farthest feeder from the house, so I don't give it the attention I give the close-up feeders—but I should. They're on their way to Canada to breed. According to range maps, we're in the heart of their winter territory, but the reality is that we see them almost exclusively only during spring and fall migration.

2 Wood Ducks
Species: 54 total in the yard to date for the year.

April 8

Watching Waders

Reports of migrant activity sent us out and about today, checking areas flooded by the just-crested river. Floodwaters, as devastating as they can be, often draw waterfowl and shorebirds that might otherwise overfly the area. We didn't hit the jackpot by any means, but among the abundant American Robins, we did enjoy watching the behavior of a group of Lesser Yellowlegs and a pair of Wilson's Snipe.

A Lesser Yellowlegs, a migrating shorebird on its way to the Arctic, forages in the mud for insect larvae, crustaceans, and worms.

A Wilson's Snipe forages in typical habitat, using its long flexible bill to poke in the mud in search of invertebrates.

Lesser Yellowlegs winter along the coasts—Pacific, Gulf, and Atlantic—and breed well to the north, mid-Canada up through Alaska, so they make appearances here in south-western Indiana only during migration. Fortunately, the migration window for them seems rather broad, so we typically enjoy multiple views of them both seasons. They're in a bigger hurry in spring, of course, than in fall, so these days they're pushing to get to their breed-ing grounds as early as possible. This unusually cold and prolonged, seemingly everlasting winter has significantly slowed their journey north. Since they dine on aquatic and terres-trial invertebrates like beetles, most of which they probe for in shallow-water mud bottoms or pluck from atop the water, frozen shallows hamper their feeding. Fortunately, last night's untimely subfreezing temps rose to the mid-40s by noon, so by then the birds were actively feeding in the shallows of the floodwaters.

On the other hand, Wilson's Snipes spend the winter with us, so seeing them isn't quite so rare as seeing most other shorebirds. To me, these plump little guys always look healthy, primarily because of their huge breast muscles. The musculature makes them super-duper fliers, able to reach speeds of 60 mph during extended flights. They, too, probe for their food—worms, insect larvae, and other invertebrates—but unlike yellowlegs, they probe in mud but not necessarily underwater. Their remarkable bills are flexible; they can open the tip to slurp up morsels without opening the remainder of the beak, a situation that enables them to eat prey without pulling it up first from the mud. They sport another uncanny characteristic that I find a remarkable adaptation: Their eyes are set so far back on their heads that they can see behind themselves about as well as they can see in front. Remember your elementary schoolteacher who you thought had eyes in the back of her head? She was absolutely no comparison to snipes! No predator will likely slip up on a snipe while it's drilling into the mud for lunch.

April 9

Passing a Milestone

We've passed a milestone today. For the first time since last October, I neither saw nor heard a Dark-eyed Junco. Yesterday I spotted one, foraging under the nyjer-seed feeder, and maybe there will be another stray sometime this spring. Or maybe not. I'll miss their bell-like single-tone song. It's a rite of passage, this migration thing. While a dozen or so White-throated Sparrows remain, they'll be gone soon, too. Every year I wake up some morning and realize they're gone, these visitors from the north, and struggle to remember when I last saw one. They go without an announcement, without celebration, without even a good-bye. They lift up on a south wind and go quietly in the night.

Back on March 30, I was relieved that I needed only a half-gallon jug of nyjer seed to fill the feeders, but the populations have fluctuated again. For the past three days, American Goldfinches have gobbled down a gallon each day. They're a motley crew, so splotchy that they appear seriously weather-beaten. Of course they are quite well—just desperately in need of rich nutrition to survive the physical ordeal of growing new feathers. Two con-ditions are at play with their behavior. First, the goldfinches, along with millions of other avian creatures, continue to move north, dispersing to their breeding territories, some moving only another state away and some moving as far as Canada's most northerly reach.

A Dark-eyed Junco forages for spilled seed under the nyjer-seed feeder.

Second, and more importantly, the unseasonably cold weather—the ongoing freezes and snow—has delayed buds and bugs, so the double-whammy issues of molt and migration are compounded by food shortages. That crisis helps explain the birds' behavior: Goldfinches are piling up here again, waiting for their food sources to allow them to move on. And what are their food sources? Goldfinches are 100 percent vegetarian, so they eat seeds. Given the current absence of seeds, they turn of course to buds. Leaf buds, flower buds, even flowers themselves offer the nutrition essential to their survival. Now, however, given the absence of buds, they've halted their progress northward and settled in here for the wait. I'm back to a budget-busting gallon of nyjer seed a day! Every backyard bird host I know is complaining. In spite of the cost, however, I'm enjoying the many behaviors, watching the varying plumages, noting the progress of molt, and catching occasional sight of a goldfinch so bright he competes with the daffodils!

At this very moment, however, the yard is empty save for a single Carolina Wren tucked tightly in the corner of a hopper feeder. The Cooper's Hawk just flew through and scared everything into hiding. She seems to have taken up residence in the woods to our south, nesting there, so she'll be terrorizing the yard all summer. While it's always disturbing to see a songbird meet its demise, the necessity for being on the alert is part of survival in the animal world. The old "eat or be eaten" mantra applies every day, every minute. Looking at the hawk situation from that perspective, the Cooper's is keeping the songbird gene pool strong. Only the fittest, the smartest, the healthiest, the most alert survive, passing their strong genes on to the next generation. Still, it's hard to see a hawk plucking the feathers of a Northern Cardinal and stay stoic.

Late this afternoon while tidying up the garden, I heard what I thought was a kinglet. After following the movement and the scold for almost 20 minutes, I finally saw the little guy out in the open. I managed one out-of-focus photo before it flew out of sight. Enlarging the photo on my desktop, I confirmed my suspicion: Golden-crowned Kinglet.

The two kinglets, Golden-crowned and Ruby-crowned, come here for the winter. Indeed, the Ruby-crowned Kinglet visited regularly all winter, usually somewhere near a suet feeder, sometimes feeding on suet crumbles. But I hadn't seen the Golden-crowned Kinglet at all. Now, probably migrating through, making our native habitat one of its migratory stopovers, it finally made an appearance.

> 1 Golden-crowned Kinglet
> **Species:** 55 total in the yard to date for the year.

A Golden-crowned Kinglet takes a drink and a bath at the bubble rock.

April 10

Surveying the Garden

Since yesterday's garden cleanup, bird activity there has changed. I'm not a compulsively tidy tender of this 100-foot by 40-foot garden, and in the fall I leave the garden for the birds. After all, I've planted the space to include food and shelter for as many winter species as this relatively little space allows. Come spring, though, it's essential to clean out last year's remains to give room for this year's regrowth. That was yesterday's goal. I broke off and hauled away the spent stalks of aster, goldenrod, coneflower, and black-eyed Susan. My activity, of course, affected the birds' behavior, so this morning the birds that had become accustomed to hiding there were gone. That's the bad news. The good news is that in the process of clearing out, I disturbed the layer of mulch that keeps weeding to a minimum. Last autumn's remaining leaves were also disturbed, stirred up, scattered, or rearranged, apparently exposing good munchies under the litter. Cardinals and White-throated Sparrows

Birds Do *That*?

House Wrens kill off their neighbors. As a result, Eastern Bluebird hosts dread the arrival of frightfully devilish House Wrens, fearing that the wrens will attack bluebird nests, jab holes in the eggs, scatter the nest parts, and, possibly, kill the incubating female. The wren's intent is to take over every possible cavity to prevent any competition for food for his brood. With a far different personality from the relatively calm Carolina Wren, the House Wren comes on the wings of a warrior and wages battle on the entire neighborhood. According to *Birds of North America Online*, House Wrens make every effort to drive out other nesters—including phoebes, woodpeckers, warblers, sparrows, chickadees, swallows, and nuthatches—from its territory.

rummaged through the debris, and Eastern Towhees found cause to scratch in the remains. One female cardinal hefted leaves, one after another, apparently checking for the perfect one of the perfect size to add to the foundation of her nest. Because I left an abundance of tiny twigs as well, I'm betting more birds will be exploring the real estate. The mostly now-bare garden still yields fascinating glimpses into how birds behave!

Speaking of nesting, breeding behavior is cranking up. An Eastern Bluebird is incubating her eggs in a nest box situated at the bottom of the hill near the north property line. The Carolina Chickadees have eggs in the nest box at the east end of the garden. Carolina Wrens have a nest, probably with eggs, in a nest box under the family room window awning. Another bluebird pair has the start of a nest in a box at the west end of the garden. Hubby hasn't walked the rest of our eleven-box bluebird trail in a few days, so there could be other busy family nurseries as well.

Woodpeckers must be nesting, too, although I don't know where any of their nest cavities are hidden. I see the various species flying to and from general areas, but they're coy enough not to fly directly to a nest site on a regular basis. I did see, however, a female Downy Woodpecker whose white parts were tan. Poor girl! In all this rain, while ducking in and out of her nest cavity, she's been exposed to tannins from the tree bark that have stained her feathers. Although I don't know for sure, I suspect she'll be tan until her next molt. It's unlikely the tannins will wash off in a bath or even a soaking rain. Ah, the perils of motherhood!

April 11

Predicting the Seemingly Unpredictable
I'm growing restless. Migrants that usually arrive by mid- to late March remain AWOL. The BirdCast website, however, which predicts migration and shows real-time night flight activity, forecasts that tonight and tomorrow night will bring decent migration activity in this part of the country. We'll see.

April 12

Walking the Bluebird Trail
Hubby walked our little eleven-box bluebird trail and found three active bluebird nests and one active chickadee nest. Two other boxes have the beginnings of bluebird nests; however, the birds may have abandoned those nesting starts in favor of one of the others. No way to know. I'm thrilled, though, to know that at least three pairs survived the winter, especially given their desperate searches for suet crumbles during the worst of the weather.

With our area and the spacing of the nest boxes, I suspect that three pairs are the limit for the territory. A territory can support only so many of any one bird species. While most authorities suggest that bluebird boxes should be placed 100 yards apart, ours are much closer to one another. That means, though, that we could never expect to have every box occupied by bluebirds—but we could expect every box to be occupied by something. Our neighbor once had two boxes mounted on the same pole, back to back. Simultaneously

A male Eastern Bluebird investigates a possible nest cavity in a Peterson-style box.

he had chickadees in one box and bluebirds in the other. Because they don't compete for the same foods, they were compatible neighbors. Although we've not had a similar experience, we do have regularly nesting chickadees, house wrens, and tree swallows as well as occasional titmice in our bluebird boxes. As long as House Sparrows don't take up residence, we're okay with whoever finds the real estate to their liking.

The primary purpose of hubby's weekly bluebird-trail monitoring is to make sure all is well. In the course of monitoring, he eliminates House Sparrow nests, repairs loose predator guards, checks for ants and wasps, and keeps track of who's nesting where, removing used nests as soon as the nestlings fledge. Untended nest boxes invite nonnative birds like House Sparrows and European Starlings to move in and further multiply. The lesson is simple: As hosts, we must never mount bird boxes unless we're committed to regularly monitoring them.

April 13

Welcoming Migrants

Hooray! Last night's BirdCast prediction was right on target. Migrants arrived in the darkness and greeted me at dawn.

One step out the door this morning and I heard it: a House Wren singing. When I tracked him down, he was perched very near the bluebird box in which a House Wren nested last summer. Could he be the same bird? Could this little half-ounce guy have actually flown to the southern tier of states or even farther south into Mexico and then found his way back to this very spot in my yard? How can a bird so tiny—or a bird of any size for that matter—fly hundreds of miles and find its way back to this little spot of geography where a nest

A House Wren sings from a redbud tree, setting up an exclusive territory for himself.

A Yellow-throated Warbler is singing on territory but hiding high in the canopy. This photo was captured last spring as the songster paused from time to time to forage on poison ivy berries, few of which now remain.

box stands? How can we explain such awesome behavior? It's a phenomenon that I'll never quite get my mind wrapped around.

But there's more.

As I ventured farther from the back door, I heard another migrant, one I've been watching for since late March, the time he usually arrives on territory. Finally! Upon his return from the Caribbean, he's now singing from the top of one of our 80-foot pines, clearly silhouetted against the early morning sky: a Yellow-throated Warbler singing his unmistakable series of descending notes. With the dramatic decline of so many birds, I feared I might have a spring—and, alas, a summer, too—without his song, right out of Rachel Carson's *Silent Spring*. Already I feel better about the record cold and late snows we've had this spring. Not better for having had them, but better that the birds have held off migration until food sources opened the door for their journey. If all goes well, we'll enjoy the second period of song in late June or early July, a behavior that tells us the pair has finished one brood and is planning another.

A singing Ruby-crowned Kinglet caught my attention, too. He teased me all winter, popping by now and then for suet crumbles and then disappearing for several days. In the deep of winter, though, of course he didn't sing. Only now are hormones pumping him up to vocalize and strut his stuff. Too bad he will leave soon, perhaps traveling as far north as the Arctic Circle, to join his mate to breed. He's so tiny, minuscule really, the smallest bird in the yard, smaller than chickadees. And he's fidgety. Never still, almost impossible to photograph without a blur. And to think how far he's going! He may, in fact, go out on tonight's winds.

1 House Wren
1 Yellow-throated Warbler
Species: 57 total in the yard to date for the year.

April 14

Hanging Hummingbird Feeders

By tax day I know the time has come to put out my first feeder for the Ruby-throated Hummingbird. Some years the migration maps show early arrivals here, as early as the last week in March, but this year only now are area folks reporting their first hummers.

During the early weeks of hummingbird migration, two one-cup feeders more than meet their needs—even with each being only half filled. If it weren't for the fact that I hang a feeder on both the north and south sides of the house, one feeder would be more than adequate for now. Putting out two feeders, I know I will waste a little sugar, replacing the syrup every three or four days, but experience tells me that hummers have strange habits. Some habitually prefer to feed on one side of the house and others choose to feed on the opposite side. Who knows why they behave that way. Nevertheless, during the opening weeks of the season, I'll not have enough hummingbirds to consume a full cup of syrup in three or four days. The few that do come through early will move on, usually quickly, and there will be lag days when no hummers show.

Here's how that plays out: The males arrive first. They're driven to be on territory ASAP, some perhaps migrating as far as the southern rim of Canada. Where hummers go to nest depends on where they hatched. Hummers always return to their ancestral breeding grounds. Thus, these early guys feed here only long enough to beef up for the next 100-mile flight. Likewise, when females follow a few weeks later, they, too, will tank up and move on. "Our" hummingbirds, the ones that stay here to breed, usually arrive the first or second week of May. So while minimal amounts of syrup more than meet their needs now, by late August into early September, I'm usually filling multiple quart-size feeders several times a day.

Today, then, marks the first day of the season. And if I somehow forgot to hang feeders in time, the hummers would return to the spot where last year's feeders hung, buzzing the area, hovering at the feeding spot, remembering exactly where they had found a reliable food source in the past. Since hummers live up to seven or eight years, many of these tiny guys have passed this way before. They pull up to the same restaurants on each trip, both going and coming. I'd best be ready!

April 15

Catching It in the Act

Seeds of course are gone, eaten, dispersed by wind and rain, mudded in by snow, ice, and rain. Well, okay, a few seeds linger here and there, on trees and weeds tall enough and strong enough to have remained erect, out of the wet. So what do seed eaters eat when there are no seeds? They've turned to richly nutritious buds, and their foraging behavior has held my interest. Cedar Waxwings munch their way through clusters of apple and crabapple blossoms. Chickadees bounce through maple trees, dangling upside down, devouring tree blossoms. Tufted Titmice scramble through the pecan tree blossoms. Mockingbirds follow suit. When they finally arrive, warblers will do the same. Nevertheless, this evening, as I was studying white- and tan-striped morphs of the White-throated Sparrows still dallying in the yard, I drew up with a start as my eyes focused on one

A White-throated Sparrow (tan-striped morph) lunches on violet blossoms, substituting the rich nutrition of blossoms for the winter fare of seeds.

white-throated "grazing." It was plucking violets! Literally! It plucked off the petals to get to the heart of the blossom and then plucked and ate the nutritious center. As the little guy foraged across the yard, he found kidney-leafed buttercups and likewise chomped off entire blossoms and downed them. This evening was my first experience witnessing White-throated Sparrows in the act. We don't spray our yard with broadleaf killer, so we have ample natural herbivore food. In fact, we don't spray our yard with anything, so birds forage freely, habitually taking advantage of every single opportunity available. The more diversified the plants in the yard, the more diversified the foraging opportunities—and the more diversified the birds!

Birds Do *That*?

A vulture was spotted flying at 37,000 feet. A Ruppell's Griffon Vulture, a bird native to Africa, holds the known record for high-altitude flight, and a Bar-headed Goose flying over the Himalayas was spotted rowing along at 28,000 feet. Janaki Lenin, in her scientifically detailed discussion of how birds survive flying at high altitudes, notes that flying requires ten to twenty times more oxygen than resting. Given thin air at such high altitudes, birds must have something humans don't. We would suffer seriously from altitude sickness, perhaps even die at such heights. And that's without exertion! Indeed, these high-flying birds can endure well beyond human capability because—to be overly simplistic—they not only have comparatively larger lungs than do humans, but they're also more efficient at using oxygen from the air they breathe.

April 16

Feeling Winter Again

Today, with ice on the birdbaths, off-and-on heavy snow flurries, and a record-low high of 35 degrees, birds fed heavily. So even at this late date, mid-April, I'm worrying for the bug eaters, our precious avian friends that have migrated for thousands of miles to reach us only to find freezing, wet weather. Bluebirds, too, were hunting this morning, perched for long minutes surveying the garden for potential bugs, perhaps crawling among the frosty grasses. Then they'd fly to another perch for more long minutes. I never saw them swoop down to catch a meal. A few times I saw them revert to their wintertime behavior, checking under suet feeders for crumbles, so I added a half cup of crumbles to the few morsels the woodpeckers dropped.

Like many other birds, goldfinches mobbed the feeders, consuming almost a gallon of nyjer seed today. Desperate. Desperate behavior all.

The wind was so vicious and the cold so bitter that I didn't venture out to listen for possible migrants. Actually, I hope the remaining migrants stay south for a while. It seems to me there is very little here for them to eat, especially since most of them don't come to feeders, and the buds froze. It's bleak out there. We're told by ornithologists that bird migration is triggered by length of day, but we're also told they'll not out-fly their food source. How do they know? Folks are reporting new arrivals every day: Scarlet Tanager, Black-and-white Warbler, Sora, Virginia Rail, Black-throated Green Warbler. Today someone reported "dozens" of Yellow-rumped Warblers and Brown Creepers, surely a puzzling behavior, right? Both birds spend the winter here and parts south. Now, they're moving, piling up here, waiting to go farther north. But there's more than a foot of snow on the ground in the northern tier of states. Surely they can't go, at least not go and survive. But again I ask, how do they know?

In short, I'm perplexed and saddened watching birds struggle with this all-wrong weather, irregularities brought on by climate change. Bluebirds hunt, seemingly without success, and at least one pair is feeding hatchlings. Another pair is, I think, incubating. They need to be on the nest, all of them, either brooding young babies or incubating eggs. What a dilemma for them—needing to eat but in so doing risking the loss of their babies or eggs. And I'm saddened knowing that martins and swallows may die, given the cold and wet that keep bugs down, the birds coming up empty after their repeated swooping flights. This ongoing cold and wet depresses me, and I doubt I'm alone. It's bad for the soul, this climate change.

In spite of the bitter weather this afternoon, Turkey Tom exhibited his best courtship behavior. Off and on I've heard him gobbling, faintly, some distance to our west, since we first saw him two weeks ago. Today the tom was in full strut, stepping side to side, turning slightly, displaying atop a low ridge edging the neighbor's hayfield. At first I saw no reason for the display, but finally a female made a brief appearance, stepping just over the crest of the ridge. If anything could look more nonplussed in the presence of a full strut, I can't imagine how. But he persisted in the showoff until I, too, lost interest and went about my daily business. When I checked later, I could see neither of them. Maybe, though, he'll find not just this one girl but a full harem and draw the birds back to the neighborhood. We all find pleasure in their amblings across our properties.

Cattle Egrets in winter plumage make rare appearances here, just at the northern edge of their summer breeding range.

In another matter, on the way to join friends for lunch in the adjoining county today, nine birds lifted up from a well-protected deep ditch: Cattle Egrets! They'd most likely dropped in the ditch for protection against the wild winter-like wind, but perhaps my passing within 50 yards caused them to lift up. Cattle Egrets, for goodness sake! Wow. We rarely see them here, and I can count on one hand the number of sightings in either county. Range maps list them as "rare" here, but the same maps show their migration route nearby. Typically, they breed to our south, so seeing them north of their normal breeding range during spring migration seems all wrong. Perhaps the vicious winds have blown them off course. Another birder today posted a Cattle Egret sighting at least 50 miles farther north. Wrong way!

April 17

Counting White-throats and Others

Given that most of the winter migrants have dispersed to parts north, the White-throated Sparrows remain the usual exceptions. It's just their normal behavior to be among the last to depart their winter territories. During my afternoon tromp through the yard, I counted at least thirty, hesitant to add more to the tally for fear I'd be counting some twice. That's about the same number that have tucked in among the brambles and vines here most of the winter, although these are unlikely the original group of winter residents. Yes, they've molted, or at least most of them have, but the big difference is song. Theirs is the most prominent in the yard now, both during the morning chorus (such as it is at this point) and in the evening when birds sing their nighty-night lullabies. Knowing they'll be leaving soon, I'm trying to soak up the memories, both the visual images and their auditory charm.

Since the weather warmed this afternoon into the 50s, bird behavior grew more active. They fed in a frenzy, trying to catch up, no doubt, after yesterday's weather-imposed fast, at least for bug eaters. So I enjoyed following a Blue-gray Gnatcatcher gnatcatching, first near the pergola, then across the garden, into the cypress trees, and beyond, finally out of sight. A Golden-crowned Kinglet was equally intent on its foraging in the pines. Kinglets, both species, are fidgety and crazy-busy birds to begin with, but add to their usual manner the search for bugs among the needles, and you get a blur of a bird that's tricky to identify. The golden-crowneds are less frequent here than are the ruby-crowneds, and this was only my second sighting for the year.

A Purple Finch pair feed together on their way north to breeding grounds. Except for her facial pattern, the streaky female doesn't bear much resemblance to the handsome raspberry-colored male.

Each day for the past week, we've found at least one Purple Finch, sometimes a single female, sometimes a single male, but today a pair. The truth of the matter is that they don't look as if they go together, as if they're entirely different species. The female is not much to look at in the first place, mostly streaky brown, but she does have a pretty face. Considering the rarity in our yard of finding the pair, it's worth noting. Of course, they won't be here long. Maybe one-day wonders. They're just passing through.

This morning I noticed the Carolina Chickadees behaving with urgency, zipping to and from their nest box, their activity confirming that they're now feeding nestlings. What a tough job they have, especially given the cold. Even as we anticipate the next two warm days, we dread the current prediction for a return of the cold on the third day. Boo, hiss.

April 18

Sighting Two Migrants

For the past three years, the first Ruby-throated Hummingbird has sipped at the feeder outside the kitchen window on April 18. And today, bingo! Given this spring's weather, I could hardly believe my eyes. A male, of course, since males arrive first. This one, however, won't stay long. He'll sip syrup enough for the next night's flight and move on, ultimately perhaps as far as southern Canada. Given that he left Central America about the first of February, he's been on the wing for a long time—and still may have a long way to go. I can hardly get my head wrapped around the fact that this tiny bird, not much bigger than a big bug, has flown from Central America to the Yucatan, then some 700 miles across the Gulf of Mexico (I needn't say "nonstop," do I?), migrating from the Gulf Coast to my feeder, this pin-dot spot in the world, probably because he was here last year, too. Finding my way across town during a construction project is challenge enough for me, but he has no map, no GPS, no directional signs. How can this incredible journey even be possible? Such drama! What remarkable behavior!

He seems truly hungry, visiting both feeders regularly late this afternoon and evening until almost too dark to see. There's so little blooming, though, that I wonder what other choice he has. Red-buds have opened and crabapple trees are in bloom. Favorites, however, like native

On April 18, for four consecutive years, a male Ruby-throated Hummingbird has arrived at our feeder.

trumpet honeysuckle, red columbine, and coral bells, are still in tight bud, their heads barely above the vegetation. While experts don't agree on the percentages, hummingbirds also demand tiny bugs for protein—perhaps as much as half of their diet. Bugs seem in equally short supply, but somehow the birds are here. "Our" hummingbirds, the ones that stay here to breed, will likely arrive in three weeks or so.

This morning, during my early wandering through the yard, a song caught my attention, pulling me up short, causing me to listen carefully, just to be sure. Yep! White-eyed Vireo! He and his kin wintered in the Yucatan or on the islands of Cuba or Haiti, but it's possible he may have stayed closer to home, hanging out along the Gulf Coast. Either way, today he sang from the cedar tree, no doubt because he could find no leafy vegetation for

A White-eyed Vireo sings an announcement of his arrival on his breeding territory but remains camera shy.

Two tom Wild Turkeys parade through the neighbor's hayfield, one in full strut.

protection. White-eyed Vireos don't like to be exposed, preferring to hide low in something dense. He sang only briefly, perhaps a dozen times, with long pauses between phrases, but what a welcome sound. I love his "chick, per-wee-tee-o, chick," sometimes "translated" as "Spit and see if I care; spit!" The things we do to remember bird songs!

While I was following the vireo in hopes of the opportunity for a photo, out of habit I scanned the neighbor's hayfield. What a surprise! The entire turkey flock from eight months ago was ranging across the rolling field—all twelve of them! I was tickled to find them back but still wonder where they spent last fall, winter, and early spring. Three toms were among them (although of course I have no way of knowing if one of the three was the single tom sighted yesterday) and showed serious attitudes, frisky, chasing one another, strutting, gobbling, showing off, generally apparently establishing the proverbial pecking order.

1 White-eyed Vireo
1 Ruby-throated Hummingbird
Species: 59 total in the yard to date for the year.

April 19

Worrying about Chickadees

The Carolina Chickadee nest is empty.

This morning, the chickadees seemed frantic, flying around the base of their nest box, touching down on nearby stalks and twigs, approaching the box roof, and scolding. Neither of the pair ever landed on the nest box, however, and never ducked inside. Then I noticed a male bluebird, first sitting on top of the nest box and then clinging to the entrance, poking his head inside and then backing out. He never went inside either, but seemed really interested in whatever he saw. When he was atop the box, however, the chickadees darted at him, never touching him, but certainly threatening him. What strange behavior!

Shortly, the female bluebird arrived on the scene and joined the male atop the nest box. He dropped down to the entrance hole once again, fluttering, chattering, behaving in much the same way a pair behaves when checking out a potential nest site for themselves. Was he hoping to gain access to this nest cavity? Hadn't they already chosen the nest box to the west?

When I witnessed the renewed anxiety of the chickadees, I slowly approached the box. Of course, both pairs of birds flew off. I stood for just a moment, trying to decide if I should open the box to check on the chickadees' nestlings' safety. What if they were almost ready to fledge? If I opened the box, they could fledge prematurely and face almost certain death. But if there was something inside threatening them, perhaps I could save them somehow. Knowing chickadees take about seventeen days from hatch to fledge, I made a few mental calculations and decided they were certainly not ready to fledge—not even close.

Lightly tapping the box as a warning and removing the closure, I tilted open the front slowly. Since I could see no activity, I eased the front fully open and peered into the deep, perfectly shaped nest. Nothing. No nestlings. No disturbed nest material. No evidence of the nest ever having been used. What? I'd watched the chickadees feeding just two days ago. Or so I thought.

The nest box is mounted on a steel pole and fully protected with a predator guard. No raccoon or snake could access the nest. The babies obviously had not fledged. Nestlings old enough to fledge produce too much excrement for their parents to carry off the fecal sacs, so a fully used nest in its last days turns truly messy. No mess here. What happened?

Sorting through the clues, I was still left puzzled. Would a bluebird destroy the nestlings in order to take over? Would a bluebird eat the nestlings? I searched the ground under the nest box but found no evidence that the babies had been tossed out the way a House Sparrow would do, a behavior that makes me do a slow burn. Did the chickadees attack the bluebirds because they knew bluebirds to be the culprits? Or did the bluebirds happen to be in the area, as they have been in previous days—using the nest box as a perch from which to drop-hunt for bugs? But why would the bluebirds appear to be house hunting in an already occupied box? With another nest box nearby, there is open housing at the ready.

Frankly, I'm left with many questions and no answers. And I'm sad because most references say chickadees raise only one brood a year. I wonder, however, after this first nest failure, will they, like some other birds, attempt to re-nest? All that time, work, and effort for naught. The drama seems more like a horror story, or a really troubling murder mystery.

A properly mounted Peterson-style nest box is protected by a stovepipe-style predator guard. No snake or raccoon has ever ravaged a bird's nest in our yard with this recommended setup.

April 20

Witnessing War

A Red-tailed Hawk circled over the neighbor's hayfield and looped a lazy circle over the woods, a little patch of which is ours. The circle complete, the hawk wheeled a figure-eight and came beak to back with an American Crow. I don't know this, but I suspect the crows have a nest in the woods because I see them regularly fly to and from the area. Today, however, I think my suspicions were confirmed. When that hawk soared too close to the nest, I'm reasonably sure that's what caused the crow to behave as it did, coming after the hawk, flying above it, and pecking its back as often as it could, cawing the entire way. The chase was on! Across the hayfield they jetted, no lazy loops this time, just a straight speed-driven chase to the north, the crow within inches of the hawk until they fled out of sight.

Within a few minutes the crow returned, cawing, but cawing in a different tone of voice. From the woods I heard a response, a quieter, more gurgling caw, typical of a female on the nest, cawing as if the pair was confirming victory. Most likely the male ripped after the hawk, so his returning victory cry was loud and territorial. Hers was a contact call, perhaps of gratitude and comfort. Or so I interpreted it.

The war seemed short-lived, but now I wonder if this encounter was only one of many battles to come or if, indeed, the war had ended—won!

April 21

Noting a Straggler

A lone Dark-eyed Junco flitted about the yard today, seemingly too nervous to forage for any length of time in places where juncos have loitered all winter. Its behavior suggested it's a migrant, having come from farther south, wandering through well after "our" winter visitors departed. Hope it catches a tailwind tonight and hooks up with the crowd.

Fewer American Goldfinches hang out here now; instead of a gallon of nyjer seed this morning, I needed only a half gallon to fill the two feeders. Those that remain look beautiful, almost all of them in full breeding plumage. No wonder they're called "gold" finches!

April 22

Celebrating Earth Day

Last night's southerly winds brought three migrants and a new yard bird, so Earth Day was especially celebratory.

Of special note, however, was an interesting raptor that flew low across the hayfield, looping and then darting down into the grass. My first glimpse made me think "Cooper's" because they have a nest nearby, one of those identity-by-expectation calls. Certainly this bird's wing shape was not that of a buteo. So what else could it be? But, oops! A white rump patch. Really? Among raptors in this part of the country, only Northern Harriers sport a white rump patch. True, during breeding season, Cooper's sometimes fly with their white undertail coverts flared, but that isn't the same look as a full-width rump patch. She was behaving the way harriers behave, hunting low and feeding on the ground. Harriers typically migrate during the day, hunting as they go, so she was surely on her way. A new bird for the yard list—and likely, as is often the case during migration, a one-day wonder.

Sometime later, still wandering the yard, I glimpsed movement, some little something picking about along the fencerow. Too small for a White-throated Sparrow, it begged a closer look. Even given that the bird was no more than 30 feet away, its cryptic plumage demanded a binocular view to ID. And the view revealed a second surprise for the day: Swamp Sparrow! Not a first for the yard, but certainly not a regular here. As the name suggests, a Swamp Sparrow hangs out—well, yes—in or near water. This little guy was kicking among wet leaves, no doubt foraging for bugs. I'm always rewarded when I leave some leaves during fall cleanup, and I'm happy for all that those leaves serve up—bugs, bug eggs, and bug larvae for birds of all shapes and sizes, including migrants, all desperate for early spring protein. Apparently having sated its appetite, the swampie finally flew up atop an old wooden fence post, paused, and then sailed off toward the woodland edge and its vernal puddle. I'm pleased it found our habitat a suitable migratory stopover, proving once again the importance of avoiding insecticides. Always.

A Swamp Sparrow hops up on a fence post before sailing north, perhaps no farther than Michigan but possibly into central Canada.

By day's end, from my office window I caught sight of two more migrants: First, a Pine Warbler picked at the seed-cake feeder a dozen feet away. Really? A warbler eating seed? Yep, a Pine is the only warbler to regularly eat seed, including millet, cracked corn, sunflower seed, and

A Pine Warbler, the only warbler to regularly eat seeds, picks at a seed cake.

peanuts—all of which are melded together in the seed cake. The warbler was a satisfied camper.

Then, a second Ruby-throated Hummingbird chased the first from the feeder. Two little stinkers back from a 1,800-mile trip and they have to fight over two feeders. Typical behavior. The little warriors are ready for the breeding season—prime, perky, and feisty!

1 Northern Harrier
1 Pine Warbler
1 Swamp Sparrow
Species: 62 total in the yard to date for the year.

Birds Do *That*?

Swifts may live ten months in the air without landing. True! They eat by catching insects in flight, drink by skimming the water surface, and sleep by closing half their brain at a time. And, yes, they even mate on the wing. In fact, they land only to construct a nest, lay eggs, incubate, and feed nestlings, gathering a so-called food ball, a mass of hundreds of insects. They store the food ball in their throats until they return to feed nestlings. According to Wikipedia: "No other bird spends as much of its life in flight" as do Common Swifts.

April 23

Listening for Migrants

A dreary, misty morning after heavy rain in the night leaves birds hungry but not very vocal. Two songs seem to dominate: those of a single Eastern Towhee and several White-throated Sparrows. Amid their songs, though, was that puzzling song that could be a Dark-eyed Junco, a Chipping Sparrow, or a Pine Warbler. While I did see a straggler junco this morning, and while chippers now readily range the yard, this song came from the pine trees. Oh, and there was that Pine Warbler at the seed cake yesterday. Hmmm. A tantalizing situation. So binocular in hand, I stood in the drizzle, trying to pick out silhouettes and make some sense of them. Finally, seeing enough contrast to pick out the wing bars, I identified two Pine Warblers foraging among the branches. Guess that's why they're called Pine Warblers! In fact, the only Pine Warblers I've seen on breeding territory in Michigan's Upper Peninsula were also in pine trees. Late this afternoon they—or two others just like them—continued foraging among the branches of the same two pines.

Foraging in our migratory stopover, a Lincoln's Sparrow has traveled from its winter range across the Gulf states on its way to its breeding range across Canada.

A Lincoln's Sparrow made a migratory stopover appearance today as well. Given that it's the same size as the Swamp Sparrow that was here yesterday (they're cousins, after all), the Lincoln's is distinguished by a grayer head and smartly crisp dark streaking against a buffy background on its chest and sides. It was noticeable not only because of its small size (especially compared with White-throated Sparrows) but also because of its behavior: It moves differently than do other sparrows. It's more elusive, more secretive, its movements more purposeful and measured. Lincoln's Sparrows breed well to our north, but we usually see a few during both spring and fall migration, always on the ground, foraging for tiny bugs and seeds.

This afternoon the first Barn Swallows of the season zigzagged across the sky, darting to catch bugs. They're the most abundant and widespread swallows in the world. While they breed across the United States, they winter throughout the Southern Hemisphere, so I can't even guess how far they've flown to be here. I can say, however, that since they nest in the neighbor's barn, their local low-flying, water-skimming, bug-hunting behavior assures us the bug populations will be under control. In part, it's the neighbor's farm pond that gives the swallows the added perk for nesting here: They use mud from the water's edge to build their stuck-to-the-wall nests. Prior to human involvement, the swallows nested in caves throughout North America. Having discovered the convenience of man-made structures, however, Barn Swallows have moved indoors, so to speak, and as a result, their populations have increased.

1 Lincoln's Sparrow
3 Barn Swallow
Species: 64 total in the yard to date for the year.

April 24

Comparing Arrival Dates

Today brought the first female Ruby-throated Hummingbird to the feeder. Generally males arrive about ten days earlier than females, and such was the case this season. While I saw my first male on April 18, exactly a week ago, other area hummer hosts reported males at least a week prior to that. Since hummingbird migration is spread over a three-month period, we don't see "our" hummers arriving at a given time, but of course that's a good thing. The drawn-out migration process prevents a single catastrophic event, weather or otherwise, from wiping out the species.

Typical behavior has hummers moving north at a rate of about 20 miles per day, the earliest males following the earliest flower bloom. Truth to tell, hummers are amazing little creatures in more ways than their nearly miraculous migration. They're built to nectar and snag bugs, but their special adaptations for nectaring in long-throated flowers boggle the mind. Their tongues are long, extraordinarily long, so long that they don't fit inside the birds' mouths. Instead, their tongues curl up inside, over the tops of the birds' skulls. For years most experts thought hummers' tongues were somewhat like straws, and the birds sucked up nectar. Other authorities claimed that the tongues worked along the lines of capillary action, raising nectar into the mouth. In the past few years, however, a scientist in Colombia, South America, worked out a delicate means by which to video record a hummer as it nectared. What he discovered was that hummers' tongues are really more like mops, sopping up nectar and carrying it into the mouth. Of course, this mopping activity is a bit speedy—about thirteen times a second! So only by slowing the video recording could the researcher reveal the truth.

A hummingbird's heart makes up about 2.5 percent of its body weight, proportionately the largest of all vertebrates. Such a relatively large heart muscle gives hummers the strength they need to fly as fast as they do. With a normal body temperature of 105 degrees, hummers survive the night only by going into torpor, a sort of short-term hibernation. When they awake at daylight, 30 minutes may pass before they fully resume their 500-beats-per-minute heart rate and their 250 breaths per minute. Revved up, feeding, their heart rate can reach as much as 1,250 beats per minute, all to power their 50 to 200 wing beats per second, depending on what they're doing and under what conditions. They can't waste too much time resting, however, as some authorities believe a breeding adult nectars at 1,500 flowers per day, roughly the equivalent of an adult human consuming 15 gallons of nectar per day. In addition, hummers snag about 600 to 700 insects per day, the source of necessary protein.

Mind-boggling behavior, isn't it?

April 25

Tracking New Songs

Warm sunny weather today followed a mild migratory influx last night and made for a pleasant birding day. As an early morning fog burned off, migratory and breeding behaviors were evident everywhere. Another Ruby-crowned Kinglet and a couple of repeat Pine Warblers greeted me first, followed by a territorial singing Eastern Phoebe and at least four House Wrens. Traffic increased at the hummingbird feeders. The Swamp Sparrow reappeared—or maybe it was another one. A male Eastern Towhee sang from mid-level tree branches, no longer on the ground merely calling to his mate, but obviously in a robust territorial mood. Tom turkeys gobbled from opposites sides of the neighbor's field, apparently vying for dominance—and the harem.

But two new songs in the morning chorus gave me special pleasure. First, a Northern Parula sang from high in the canopy, over a month later than his usual arrival. He winters in the Caribbean and eastern parts of Mexico into the Yucatan, so he's come a bit of a distance. Since so many migrants are late this spring, the tardy parula is no surprise. Still, I'm relieved that he's finally here! I look forward to his summer song, renewed, like that of the Yellow-throated Warbler, when the birds begin their second broods. Here's hoping he finds a mate and nests in the woods as he usually does. Parulas are one of the good-news warblers, as their populations have increased by 60 percent or more since 1970. In some locales, however, their numbers have declined, mostly, scientists believe, because of poor air quality, clear-cutting, and the draining of bogs.

Second was a song I didn't know, a sort of "zoo-zoo-zoo-zeeeeeeeee," three notes of the same tone and then a rising-end buzz. Was a Black-throated Green Warbler, perhaps his hormones not quite in full force, singing off-key and off-rhythm? He usually says "zee-zee-zee-zoo-zee," all notes the same tone except the dropped "zoo." This newcomer didn't match the standard, but was he maybe a youngster who didn't yet have the song quite right? The ascending end note was reminiscent of the Northern Parula's song, but I could readily compare him with the Northern Parula singing nearby. Not the same. In my mind, then, there was no question that this was some new migrant, not one that comes through here regularly, not one that I recognized, but which one? I followed him. Well, actually I followed his song, quietly inching through the woods, searching mid-level from where the song seemed to emanate. Try as I might, I could not spot the singer. Finally, I was out of time and forced to give up the search.

As I headed back indoors, a pair of Canada geese flew over, talking to one another so profusely that they sounded like an entire flock rather than a pair. Given that some geese are already leading strings of goslings now, this pair apparently suffered nest failure. Their behavior reveals their plight: Geese with goslings don't fly.

Later this afternoon, time allowed my return to the search. I was startled to hear the mystery singer again, basically singing from the same location. Since warblers migrate at night, it made sense that the bird was still here, but it was a surprise that it was still in nearly the same location. So again, the search was on. After following my ears until I reached the edge of our property, I still had no success spotting the bird. All else having failed, I turned to my warbler app on my cell phone and began checking songs, skipping those I knew, listening to the song in real time while cross-checking with the songs on the app. Check after check, no match. Then, bingo! Wait, wasn't that it? I played the app's song again—and the song in real time went silent, perhaps threatened by "another" male. But I had my match, and a new bird for the year: Black-throated Blue Warbler. While I didn't catch sight of the lovely creature this time, I know him well from the joy I've had photographing him at Magee Marsh along Lake Erie in northern Ohio. Wintering in Cuba, Haiti, the Dominican Republic, and Puerto Rico, Black-throated Blues cruise through here on their way to the very northern fringe of the United States and into the

A migrating Black-throated Blue Warbler sang in our woods almost all day today, but it won't stay. He breeds in the upper elevations of the Appalachians and throughout the Northeast into the lower parts of Canada.

A relatively tame Northern Parula makes an up-close-and-personal visit to my native plant garden, pausing briefly on a plant-support stake, almost within my reach.

southern parts of eastern Canada. Maybe this one is on his way through Michigan to the very northern part of the Upper Peninsula.

Later in the afternoon, hubby and I enjoyed hearing the "zoo-zoo-zoo-zeeeeeee" back on location, mid-story in the brushy areas, following its usual behavior, concealed but foraging, preparing no doubt to further his journey tonight.

1 Northern Parula
1 Black-throated Blue Warbler
Species: 66 total in the yard
to date for the year.

April 26

Aching for My Error

Eliminating or at least containing invasive plant species is an ongoing—and sadly, mostly unsuccessful—task for us. Wintercreeper, Japanese honeysuckle, multiflora rose, the list goes on. This morning, we made an early spring effort to rein in widespread wintercreeper. Ultimately this waxy evergreen vine moves from ground level to vine up the trees, sometimes strangling the trees and using its high-level position to produce berries and thus reproduce its kind. To whack vines down, we cut them at ground level at the base of the tree and then yank hard in an effort to dislodge the vines from the bark. It really doesn't matter if we don't dislodge the full vine; it will die anyway, cut from its root.

Feeling energetic, hubby and I attacked the areas of concern, freeing saplings and larger trees of the invasive vines. One particularly dense growth around a mulberry sapling

included not only wintercreeper but also Japanese honeysuckle, intertwined and winding up the bark, nearly obscuring the tree itself. I'd worked almost halfway around the tree before I saw it. There, near the base of the tree, tucked into the dense twining, was a now fully exposed nest with a single egg.

My heart sank. Look what I'd done. I'd destroyed who knows how many days' work of some diligent bird that had carefully chosen, in her estimation at least, the perfectly concealed spot to raise her family. Now the cover was gone, the nest tilted, about to spill its contents. Indeed, she had concealed the nest so well that I hadn't spotted it until I'd yanked away most of the cover.

The nest was a rather casual, somewhat messy affair: a few large pieces of last fall's vegetation, some leaves, pieces of corn stalk, a few shreds of dried pokeweed and other weed stems, and some grasses to form a not-too-tidy cup—although maybe my disturbance contributed to the messiness. The nest's location, appearance, and egg markings all matched the reference book description and illustration for Song Sparrow.

While removing invasive plants, I disturbed a Song Sparrow's nest with its single egg. Now I'm haunted by my destruction of the bird's days of nest-building labors and the female's egg production.

Indeed, I've witnessed the Song Sparrow hanging out in the area where I destroyed the nest, so it all fits. I wish I could somehow apologize to her and make up for the error of my ways. I'm sad.

Usual nesting behavior among Song Sparrows sees them lay three to five eggs, so this female had only begun to produce her clutch. Depending on weather and location, she may produce up to seven broods in a single year. Here, where we live, she'll most likely manage four broods, maybe only three since this first nest has failed, thanks to my interference. Last year she—or one of her kind—nested on the ground in the garden under the cover of daylilies. I was mindful of her presence early on and protected her efforts, remaining at a distance, making sure I didn't leave my human scent to attract predators to the spot. To my knowledge, that was a successful nest. On an earlier attempt that year, however, either a snake, raccoon, or skunk robbed her eggs from a nest under the buttonbush. How ground-nesting birds ever manage to fledge a successful brood, given the apparent ease of predation, seems to me almost miraculous.

April 27

Sorting Songs

While the so-called morning chorus is not yet at its peak, the choir's production is hands-down sufficiently voluminous to fill a concert hall. The sopranos outnumber the altos, but a few tenors make up the balance. This morning, as I tried to pick out new members of the chorus, I faced a challenge, sorting out singers and their songs. Each species' song is unique, a specialized part of their breeding behavior, each recognizable by well-trained ears. For me, well, my auditory skills are barely mediocre. But I tried.

A single Yellow-throated Warbler sang a descending scale from the pines along the driveway, and while he was only a single singer, his song carried well amid the quieter or more distant melodies. Several Northern Cardinals sang, but cardinals have numerous songs, and the repertoire was well represented by three territorial males. Perhaps the still-lingering White-throated Sparrow took the spotlight on occasion, his clearly whistled, "Oh, Sam Peabody, Peabody, Peabody" louder than most other phrases. More subtly, a Mourning Dove contributed his low-pitched "coo-ah-coo, coo, coo." Farther away, and thus less noticeable, the repeated monotone song of a Chipping Sparrow—or perhaps the similarly sounding Pine Warbler—took a back seat to more lilting melodies. A nearby Carolina Chickadee whistled his "fee-bee, fee-bay" tune and, to my ear, competed with a Song Sparrow's three-note introductory whistle followed by a trill. Softly, an Eastern Towhee called, then burst into a crescendo of "Drink your tea-he-he-he-he."

The rhythm section was led by a woodpecker's hammering, adding a staccato beat in odd measures. Blue Jays contributed to the cadence if not the melody, calling out, "Jay, jay" repeatedly. A Red-bellied Woodpecker chirred regularly in the distance. A buzzy Blue-Gray Gnatcatcher contributed to the beat, somewhat like a snare drum, while a tom Wild Turkey gobbled from across the hayfield.

Amid the many choristers, I wanted to pick out the Northern Parula, just because he's the newest arrival. Finally, softly, I heard his ascending buzzy song with that sharp staccato snap at the end.

In spite of my careful sorting of songs, however, one eluded me. An ethereal song I didn't recognize seemed to float from just around the corner of the house. I eased that way, binocular in hand, ready to identify the singer. Just as I cleared the corner, something warbler size flew from the old crabapple tree—and the song stopped. The mystery remains.

Of course, mornings work best for identifying birdsong. It's part of the intentional behavior among birds to sing in the morning. Sound carries best in humid air, and birds know

that. Males can shout out their messages about love and war—always the only two purposes for birdsong—and instinctively understand that the stronger their voices, the more attractive they'll be to the girls. From my perspective, though, as the day progresses, competition for my sorting out song grows overwhelmingly. Roaring lawn mowers and weed whackers from neighbors near and far; tractors powering through adjoining agricultural fields; cars and trucks on the winding country road gearing down for the curves and revving up again afterward; dogs yipping and yowling for breakfast, lunch, or

A singing male Blackburnian Warbler, his squeaky high-pitched song missing from today's dawn chorus, may have been drowned out by more robust singers.

supper; distant train whistles brought closer by south winds—even the wind itself—all drown or distort the avian melodies. I'm not the only one who has trouble sorting out the competing sounds. Researchers share a serious concern that our human noise interferes with birds' ability to have their songs heard by their intended audience. In fact, those same researchers have found that some birds in city confines and in proximity to heavy traffic or industrial noise have altered their songs, especially the pitch, in order to be heard above the din. What daily lowballs we throw at birds, threatening their survival.

April 28

Catching the Quick Ones

Spring migration is all about speedy progress to breeding grounds and, once there, garnering the best food-laden territory and attracting the best mate. So birds that breed to our north won't tarry here. As weather permits, they spend a day or maybe two gleaning bugs, and then move on, migrating at night. Other birds, "our" summer-only residents, the ones that come here to breed, arrive with a splash, usually males first, and immediately begin singing to stake out territories, and then singing more to attract mates. Sometimes the little guys that are merely flying through don't add much to the spring chorus. After all, they aren't laying claim to a territory here and they aren't seeking mates here. Those are the ones we have to watch for on a daily basis. We may never hear them, so we have to hope to see them. Often a single day makes up their entire spring visit with us.

Such was likely the case this morning with the Palm Warbler, often described as a warbler that doesn't behave like one. Obviously concentrating on feeding, it hopped along the edge of the driveway, moving steadily toward me, bobbing its tail, clearly oblivious to my presence. It was one hungry bird! So how many warblers hop along the ground and bob their tails! Then, as it drew closer, it eyed me critically, scooted into low cover, apparently found the cover ill-suited, and lifted up into a nearby shrub, pausing to check once more for safety before it flew, disappearing into the distance. It was likely a one-day wonder because this bird has far to go. In fact, it breeds farther north than any other warbler except the Blackpoll, and 98 percent of Palms breed in the boreal forest, the vast forest nicknamed "North America's Bird Nursery."

A Palm Warbler, having wintered in the Southeast and West Indies, pauses to forage and rest until evening, when it will lift off and fly all night on the next leg of its long journey to central Canada to nest.

On the other hand, the Orchard Oriole will breed here, so even though he stopped ever so briefly at the front-yard water feature this morning, I'm guessing I'll see him (and her) at a later date. The White-eyed Vireo that sang directly over my head falls in the same category: He's here to breed. In past summers he, or one of his kind, made this neighborhood home. A full-breeding-plumaged male Indigo Bunting that flitted about the yard and

A male Indigo Bunting returns to the yard after his winter respite, perhaps as far south as northern Central America. He and his mate will nest in the area, maybe in a weedy tangle in the garden.

slipped in for a nibble at the nyjer-seed feeder will also breed here, sometimes in the densest part of the garden and sometimes along the forest edge, in the shrubby vegetation there. Ditto with the Northern Parula, Blue-gray Gnatcatcher, and House Wren, all present and accounted for during this morning's chorus.

It's always a thrill to see the one-day wonders but a real joy to welcome back old favorites for the summer. It's taken me years to come to understand how they all behave, who visits and who stays. And now, oh how I appreciate them for who they are!

1 Palm Warbler
1 Indigo Bunting
1 Orchard Oriole
Species: 69 total in the yard to date for the year.

Birds Do *That?*

Owls can't move their eyeballs—because they don't have eyeballs. According to NationalGeographic.org, owls' eyes are tubular, not ball-shaped, held firmly in place by bony structures. Since owls can't move their eyes as humans do, they must compensate by moving their heads, bobbing and weaving, in order to see clearly and judge distance. They're further prepared to make up for their immovable eyes by being able to turn their heads about 270 degrees in either direction (but not 360 degrees as some myths proclaim) and move their heads vertically 90 degrees up and down—all without moving their shoulders. And unlike most other birds, owls' eyes are front-facing, thus giving them binocular vision.

April 29

Tallying Migrants

I tallied thirty-eight species in the yard today, moving closer to the average of forty typical here during spring migration. It's a crazy-busy, crazy-fast time and oh so much crazy fun! A little flock of Pine Siskins surprised me, especially since I haven't seen any since the late wanderers on May 12. Probably at least a dozen foraged among tree buds while at least three stopped at a feeder. They've been in the Deep South, only now reaching this migratory stopover, still with miles to go.

Our little flock of seven Blue Jays mushroomed to twenty or maybe twenty-five today, so I was again witnessing migration. Jays move in flocks, but not in the sense in which we usually think of "flocks." They're not bunched together as flocks usually are when on the move. Instead, rarely can we see more than two or three jays at a time. It's a behavior that protects them, prevents their numbers from attracting attention. Today the continuous stream flowed north, one after another, two, then three, then one, then another. That went on for about 2 hours, typical of Blue Jay migration.

A Carolina Chickadee gathers nesting materials for its secure nursery site-to-be inside a nearby nest box.

White-throated Sparrows have completed their molts now and show stunningly crisp white stripes and bibs—except, of course, the tan-striped morphs. But even they look more spiffy than they have all winter. One woke me at dawn this morning, singing just outside the bedroom window, a loud, clear, perfectly tuned song. This behavior suggests, of course, that they won't be here much longer. They're prime for breeding, hormones raging. Some may breed as near as northern Michigan, while others may migrate as far as the Arctic Circle. With about thirty in the yard now, I suspect those numbers will drop like a rock over the next week.

The Carolina Chickadee pair is adding nest materials to their newly chosen box at the opposite end of the garden from their first choice. I still don't understand what happened with the first attempt, but the bluebirds decided against the chickadees nesting there. Now the original nest is flattened and shapeless, obviously abandoned.

This afternoon I also caught sight of a woodchuck drinking from the backyard bubble rock, proving once again that everything comes to water! A single female Monarch butterfly also visited the front garden today, my first sighting of the year.

April 30

Awaking to Color

My furry four-footed alarm clock went off, as usual, at 6:15 a.m., begging for her morning treats. And as usual, when I swung my feet to the floor, my eyes traveled out the window to check for birds. The window looks out on our little water feature, a pond about 10 feet by 8 feet with exposed rocks and shallow waters that provide birds ample places to stand at water's edge to drink, or to stand in shallow water to bathe. It was on the exposed stone that a male Rose-breasted Grosbeak landed just as I cast my first glance out the window. What a way to become fully awake! Male rosies are probably the best-known of the migrants, mostly because they visit feeders. And this fancy-dressed migrant actually breeds within 100 miles or so from here. Someday, maybe a pair will actually stay the summer, but climate change is causing me to lose hope. Their breeding range will likely be pushed farther north, not south.

Next, though, after the grosbeak drank its fill and was about to lift off, a male Baltimore Oriole lit along the water's edge. What a splash of color: the black-and-white body of the grosbeak accented by its beautiful rosy bib in close proximity to the brilliant orange and black of the oriole! Woo-whee! It was a wake-me-upper!

The day continued to add more birds to the yard's year list. I suppose I needn't explain that after seeing a grosbeak and an oriole no sooner than my feet hit the floor, I was compelled to scurry outside ASAP. There, a Yellow-rumped Warbler, a male not quite fully

A Yellow-rumped Warbler has not quite finished molting into breeding plumage. By the time it migrates to its breeding grounds across most of Canada, however, it will be in full glory.

A male Rose-breasted Grosbeak is one of few migrants that visit feeders, here in brilliant spring plumage boasting his namesake rose-colored bib. See the female grosbeak on October 10.

molted into breeding plumage, foraged in the front-yard sugar maple. Another, brighter one roamed the yard later in the day. A Great Crested Flycatcher made its first appearance of the year, this time at woods' edge, calling his signature ascending "whuuup" from mid-high in the canopy. Here's hoping he stays to nest as he has in the past. In the early evening I heard and finally saw a male Summer Tanager, his "pikki-tuk-tuk" call alerting me to his whereabouts. While I thought I heard a Scarlet Tanager singing earlier in the afternoon, I suspect I was fooled and was really hearing not the Scarlet but the Summer Tanager's song. Both tanagers sing robin-like melodies, but experts explain that the Scarlet's song is more raspy, like a robin with a sore throat, while the Summer's is like a robin that's had singing lessons. Hmmm.

One fascinating note about these newly arrived birds' behavior: None of them, except the Rose-breasted Grosbeak, will visit a feeder. Some folks have luck drawing Baltimore Orioles to nectar feeders or to orange halves. In my yard, however, spring orioles come to tulip tree blossoms. Unfortunately, given this spring's unusually cold weather, the tulip trees are not yet in bloom, and orioles must certainly be searching for food.

Since I spent most of the day outside puttering in the garden and helping the landscaper plant five new cedars and six inkberry shrubs, I had an eye and an ear out for bird activity much of the time. A male Brown Thrasher sang from the dogwood tree. A female cardinal was working hard to yank off shreds of a dead vine winding among the brambles below the garden, obviously in the midst of nest building. She made trip after trip after trip to the cedar tree on the west fence line. Even though I know now where she's building, I'll not be poking around looking. It's enough to know she's there.

About 11 a.m. I heard the Barred Owl pair discussing something that couldn't wait until dark, his voice slightly deeper than hers, the two of them sounding not far apart.

Only a handful of White-throated Sparrows remain. The bulk of them left last night. According to the migration forecast, millions of wings will fly tonight's skies. The weather conditions are right, the wind from the south, and birds are ready to move. I'm already anticipating tomorrow's yard population! Migratory behavior is surely the most dramatic of all bird behaviors.

1 Great Crested Flycatcher
2 Yellow-rumped Warbler
1 Summer Tanager
1 Rose-breasted Grosbeak
1 Baltimore Oriole
Species: 74 total in the yard to date for the year.

May

The elusive, rarely sighted Mourning Warbler adds glamour among the array of spring migrants as it forages in dense, dark tangles.

You can know the name of a bird in all the languages of the world, but when you're finished, you'll know absolutely nothing whatever about the bird. . . . So let's look at the bird and see what it's doing— that's what counts. I learned very early the difference between knowing the name of something and knowing something.

—Richard P. Feynman (1918–1988), American theoretical physicist

May 1

Explaining Some of the Mystery

Given last night's massive migration, the fifty-six species tallied in the yard today have made me dizzy with excitement. And the prediction for similar migrations tonight and tomorrow night leave me giddy with expectation. Ah, yes, there's no eye candy sweeter than mature male tropical migrants in all their glorious colors—red, yellow, blue, orange, rose—flitting about the yard eating bugs. Which ones will show their pretty faces next?

Indeed, most, but certainly not all, migrants are tropical birds. In any case, migrants come north only to breed. As soon as their babies are fledged and independent, they all scurry right back to the tropics, sometimes remaining here no more than a couple of months. That's where another, larger mystery looms. Why do they do what they do? Surely we have to wonder why birds migrate, how they began migrating in the first place. And surely we have to wonder why some birds migrate and others don't. Ornithologists have theories, some of which make more sense than others, but unfortunately no one can prove beyond a doubt, these thousands of years later, any given theory.

In a nutshell, birds migrate not to keep warm but to eat. Birds with beaks designed to eat bugs do not have beaks designed to crack seeds. As a rule, then, bug-eating birds return to the tropics where bugs are in season year-round. That's a long flight, though, even on a passenger jet. The mystery grows exponentially, however, when we consider the same trip propelled only by tiny wings flapping long enough to travel sometimes more than 1,000 miles.

Well, wait. If bugs are in season in the tropics year-round, why don't birds just stay there? Explain that behavior! Okay, here's the problem: The tropics are filled with thousands of bird species. Colombia alone claims 1,900 species; Ecuador 1,200. By comparison, only about 900 species roam North America. So competition in the tropics for all those bugs runs fiercely high. Migration, however, is about more than bugs; it's partly about daylight. In the tropics, especially along the equator, every day is 12 hours of daylight and 12 hours of darkness, year-round. On the other hand, in the northern United States, birds enjoy perhaps as much as 18 to 20 hours of daylight at summer's peak—maybe 24 hours if they breed in the high Arctic. Given all those additional hours of daylight every day to feed babies all those nutritious bugs, birds can raise larger broods and still feed them well. More daylight. More bugs. More babies. Still, it's a long commute. But if the benefits outweigh the risks, then the birds may benefit. So they migrate.

How did they begin migrating in the first place? They didn't wake up one day and decide to make an arduous journey from the tropics to the Arctic just to breed. Of course not. The explanation for that behavior gets a bit sticky, but most authorities believe migration began at the end of the last ice age. At that time, ice drew down the ocean levels enough to form the Isthmus of Panama, giving birds a land route north. Ever resourceful, birds explored the emergent land, always on the search for good habitat. Then, as ice receded, opening more land beyond the isthmus, some birds followed the melt and discovered rich resources. The farther north the ice receded, the farther those birds flew to take advantage of bugs and daylight to raise their families, scurrying back to the tropics when winter set in. Okay, this is simplified way too much, but that's the general idea.

Fast-forward to today. When I see the migrants in my yard now, knowing where they've come from, how long they've been en route to get here (sometimes two months or more), how intense their instincts to breed are, and how long they'll be en route to return home (another two months or more), I feel I've been granted some sort of special privileges just to see these amazing creatures. A few will even nest in my native-plant-filled yard. How exciting. How humbling.

Today, more tropical birds joined earlier arrivals right here at home. With the colorful likes of an all-over-red Summer Tanager, orange-and-black Baltimore Oriole, black-and-white red-bibbed Rose-breasted Grosbeak, appropriately named Yellow-throated Warbler, and brilliant blue Indigo Bunting already on the spring's roster, colorful additions today included the mostly yellow Prairie Warbler and silky Gray Catbird—well, it's enough to spark a sense of hallucination, as if these vivid colors couldn't possibly be real.

A Yellow-breasted Chat sings its crazy song from a high perch.

The morning hours were so active that within 20 minutes of stepping outside, I'd identified twenty-four species. Number 25 was a Wood Thrush, a rarity in our yard, behaving as if on territory, singing from perch to perch, announcing his arrival from one end of the property to the other. Maybe he was testing the waters, so to speak, checking to see if a female might join him.

Later in the morning, a Yellow-breasted Chat arrived, another rarity. Gotta love that goofy song he sings, a cascade of chuckles, whistles, gurgles, and cackles. While it breeds across much of the United States, this elusive skulker is seldom seen, so his morning performance from a prominent perch will likely be my only chance. At one time considered the largest of our warblers, DNA tests have prompted ornithologists to now put it in a family all its own.

A first-of-the-season Tennessee Warbler joined the chorus, a bird we see more often in fall than in spring, but here he was, lovely to look at. In spite of its name, it breeds no closer to Tennessee than southern Michigan. Eastern Kingbirds, three of them, and a couple of Chimney Swifts were new but quick additions. They'll breed here, so I'll have better looks later.

A majority of the White-throated Sparrows left night before last, but most of the ones remaining are tan-striped morphs. I have no idea why that

A Tennessee Warbler forages through shrubs and trees for bugs, eggs, and larvae during its migration stopover on its way across Canada.

A fledgling White-breasted Nuthatch, calling today to be fed, means the adults started nest-building in early March.

quirky little behavior occurs. I was also startled—really startled—to find a pair of White-breasted Nuthatches feeding two rumpled-looking fuzzy-headed fledglings. Already!

That's some mighty early breeding behavior. Seeing a turkey taking a big-time dust bath was a first for me, and she really kicked up a cloud. Dust bathing is a common behavior among birds. The action helps eliminate parasites and, counterintuitively, keeps feathers clean and healthy.

In another 10 minutes, by 7 a.m., my count was at thirty-five. I had yet to step beyond the driveway. Why so many migrants in the yard? Most activity can be attributed to the hundreds of native plants that support the native bugs that feed the tropical birds. Add moving water, and the effect is magical.

2 Chimney Swift
3 Eastern Kingbird
1 Wood Thrush
1 Gray Catbird
1 Tennessee Warbler
1 Prairie Warbler
1 Yellow-breasted Chat
Species: 81 total in the yard to date for the year.

May 2

Relishing the Count

After two consecutive major migrations over the past two nights, today's yard count hit sixty-one species, including six new species for this year's roster. While the sixty-one total is only five more than yesterday, some of the birds that were here yesterday were unaccounted for today—and vice-versa. Some perhaps I simply didn't find, even though they were here. Others perhaps went out in last night's wave, availing themselves of strong tailwinds. For the two days, at least sixty-six species foraged on the property. Who knows how many I missed: the ones that didn't sing, the ones that foraged somewhere besides where I was at the moment, the ones that stayed only briefly or perhaps flew through without stopping, the ones that skulked so cleverly that they never even wiggled a leaf to reveal their presence. Whatever the case, migration challenges me to wrap my head around the

On April 13, 2008, "our" Blue Grosbeak was a state-record early arrival, but the record was broken the following year. Today, one finally appears in the yard again, nearly a month late.

mind-boggling behavior. So many birds. So many miles. So many weeks and months. So many dangers. So many risks.

I have to wonder, though, as I relish the flood of migrants enjoying our habitat: How do our year-round residents feel about this influx of competition for food? Okay, "feel" is a bit too anthropomorphic, but I'm at a loss to find another word. All of a sudden, our "regulars" are faced with a crowd of strangers. Do the regulars find the habitat growing a tad too crowded for comfort? Sure, most of the migrants won't be staying, but some will. They'll not only stay, but they'll take up nest sites and compete for bugs to feed their babies. Whatever are our residents thinking? Maybe something like: Who are these interlopers? Where did they come from? And what are they doing here? Or do birds even have such thought processes? Somehow, they seem to work out the details.

Several of our year-round species have already fledged babies. In addition to the White-breasted Nuthatches that I discovered feeding their recently fledged babies yesterday, Carolina Wrens called their babies out the day before, and one box of Eastern Bluebirds fledged today. Seeing these locals already with babies provides an interesting juxtaposition to the migrants moving through, only now on their way to breeding ranges where they'll eventually start their families. Some will need at least another week to reach their preferred territories, some perhaps longer. Once there, their respective unique breeding behaviors will require their establishing a territory, finding a mate, building a nest, breeding, laying eggs, incubating, feeding nestlings, calling out fledglings, and continuing to feed them until they get the hang of feeding on their own. That has to happen quickly enough that the fledglings will be sufficiently mature to migrate back to the tropics before food sources disappear here. No wonder they're in such a hurry!

Amid all the hubbub of migration, one constant remains: The male Northern Cardinal continues to roost every night under the awning at the front door. Ah, yes, and now no one can use the front door after 7:30 p.m.

1 Red-eyed Vireo
1 Chestnut-sided Warbler
1 Black-throated Green Warbler
1 Black-and-white Warbler
1 American Redstart
1 Blue Grosbeak
Species: 87 total in the yard to date for the year.

May 3

Watching Habitat Preferences

As I discovered four more new migrants in the yard today, I took special note of where I found them. Habitat is everything for birds. Always. During migration the right habitat means surviving the seemingly insurmountable rigors of long-distance travel. When birds can't find suitable stopover habitat, they can't build strength enough for the next flight. By the time they reach our little plot in southwestern Indiana, some have reached their destination. Others are almost there; some, only halfway.

Wilson's Warbler is one of those for which our area is about the halfway point. They winter in Central America and breed northward from the US border into Canada. So when I saw this charming little bird this morning, I was reminded of its preferred habitat: low shrubby tangles, perhaps at forest edge, especially along streams. Well, we don't have a stream, but I saw him (or her—the sexes are indistinguishable) in the tangles alongside the little pine grove. He flitted from there to the apple tree to the next apple tree and to the next and was gone. Wilson's are fast movers! Interestingly enough, I first thought I was watching one of the House Wrens scampering about to claim territory. Small. Same habitat. But busy. Its behavior was a little too busy for a House Wren. When my binocular gave me a full view of his bright yellow form topped by his little black cap, it was instant identification. His is a different appearance and behavior than most other warblers in that mid-canopy habitat.

All birds have habitat preferences. Some like high; some like low. Some like open; some like dense and shady. The huge old red cedar tree along the garden edge shelters oodles of birds, and I know to watch for certain ones there. This afternoon, a handsome male

A Wilson's Warbler makes a migratory stopover here on its travels from Panama to central Canada, filling up on bugs plucked from the undersides of leaves.

Magnolia Warbler spent at least a half hour foraging there. Like the Wilson's, he's also about halfway along his journey. While his song first attracted my attention, it was so abbreviated that I couldn't identify it. Finally, both male and female slipped out in the open as they picked tiny bugs, or perhaps bug eggs and/or larvae, from the cedar's bark and branches. He sang as they foraged, methodically moving through the mid-level parts of the tree. Gotta love warblers that seek lower-level habitat! Watching them is easy on the neck.

Common Yellowthroats, on the other hand, habitually occupy low, dense, watery places. Being notoriously secretive, they hide amid the tangles. Of course, journeying migrants may not find their perfect habitat preferences at every stopover site, so they must adapt. This yard bird exhibited the adaptive behavior necessary for survival. No swamp here, but he found adequate dense brambles—and bugs. Unlike the Wilson's and Magnolia, however, this little warbler may have reached his destination. Common Yellowthroats breed here, in the area, but they also breed way north and way south. Who knows where he will finally stake out breeding territory. But not here, not in our yard. The habitat here is only half right for him.

This afternoon, hummingbirds entertained me, their numbers having mushroomed in the past two days. Far more hummers buzz about now than I can ever remember seeing so early in the season. They're draining just over a cup of syrup per day, battles raging when all the ports are occupied and others, mostly males, vie for a spot. As with the orioles, the hummingbirds can't yet find their native-food preferences: The blossoms have not yet opened. Only native red columbine is ready for their dining pleasure.

1 Purple Martin
1 Magnolia Warbler
1 Wilson's Warbler
1 Common Yellowthroat
Species: 91 total in the yard to date for the year.

May 4

Recognizing Personalities

Tufted Titmice have claimed one of the bluebird nest boxes for their nursery, and Carolina Chickadees have claimed another. Both behave quite differently from bluebirds. While bluebirds allow us to walk up to their box to check for problems (ants, parasites, wasps, leakage, buffalo gnats, etc.) and flee only as we begin to open the box, chickadees and titmice flee the moment they hear us approaching, usually from at least 10 feet away. This morning, without my knowing the titmice had moved in, I followed my usual path through the yard, passing the nest box. I'm not sure which of us startled the other more, but the titmouse definitely startled me as she fled the nest box, darting toward my face before veering sharply away. While bluebirds will come and go from their nest while we're working nearby, either changing guard or feeding nestlings, neither chickadees nor titmice will venture near if we're within sight. It's a behavioral difference we must remember.

House Wrens will soon have to sort out their differences. As near as I can count, at least a dozen are yelling at one another in the yard, chasing, fighting over who occupies the four available boxes, an aggressive behavior unusual among same-species songbirds. Two boxes on the garden shed have entrance holes specifically sized for wrens, but House Wrens commandeer any cavity they can find. Some years ago we were thrilled to hear the song of a single House Wren. Now I honestly wish they'd get their differences sorted out sooner than later so that some will, by necessity, leave. Each tries to sing louder than the other, a behavior aimed to lay territorial claims, but after daylight-to-dark singing from every corner of the yard, the repetition becomes annoying. I have to admit up front, however, that I already have a love-hate relationship with these birds. While I think they're cute and their song is a pretty, bubbly, jaunty melody, I can barely stomach their most repulsive behavior: They'll toss bluebird eggs from a cavity and attack the female bluebird, sometimes killing her, in order to take over a nest box. That's why we put up additional boxes, hoping to assuage the robber instinct. So now, instead of having solved the nesting availability mess, it appears we've merely attracted more House Wrens. In the end, of course, they'll have to figure out who goes and who stays. I can't imagine the hubbub when the females arrive.

There was more evidence today of birds' foraging behaviors, especially where they forage. Some foraged at ground level. Another Palm Warbler walked through the St. John's wort and sweetspire, bobbing its tail as it picked up breakfast, reminding me that another of its kind waddled through a week ago, that one surely long gone. I know that if an Ovenbird shows up, he'll be walking, too, not hopping. Mid-high birds included Magnolia Warblers foraging again in the red cedar tree at about eye level. The Bay-breasted Warbler was at least mid-level in vegetation shrubby and dense enough that he never showed his face. Thank goodness for his distinctive song that let me know he was there. Up high, however, a Northern Parula and Tennessee Warbler foraged in their usual manner.

Baltimore and Orchard Orioles both foraged in maple trees, a change from a few days ago when they gobbled down the apple blossoms. We've had several days of seasonally warm temperatures, so buds have burst, bugs have hatched, and favorite foods have become more readily available. Those changes have also changed bird behavior, especially where they are feeding. Ah, yes, each species has its own preference for what and where it eats. Who knew their behaviors could be so different!

A male Orchard Oriole pauses in the mulberry tree, finds nothing, and wings on to the maple tree, foraging for buds and bugs.

Among other pleasures of the day was the return of the Wood Thrush. No birdsong is lovelier than the flute duet that the Wood Thrush sings with himself, thanks to his double larynx. Do I dare hope he will stay here to breed? I'm not sure the woods is large enough or dense enough to meet his needs. He and his kind are particular. And their numbers are declining dramatically, in part because of cowbird parasitism encouraged by fragmented habitat and in part because of acid rain destroying the invertebrates that they eat.

A bit of eye candy appeared in the form of two male Orchard Orioles, one a hatch-year male still wearing a distinctive black bib and the other a mature male in all his russet glory. When the Baltimore Oriole showed up to forage in the same tree, my eyes feasted on the lovely juxtaposition!

Multiple vireos showed up today, but I could identify only the Red-eyed Vireo with certainty. Since I could never catch sight of the little guys amid the now-thickening foliage, I can't add them to my list of sightings. Sigh.

A thunderstorm ended the day early, my yard count at fifty-nine species.

1 Green Heron, flyover
1 Blue-winged Teal, flyover
1 Blackpoll Warbler, female
1 Bay-breasted Warbler
Species: 95 total in the yard to date for the year.

May 5

Witnessing Migration

Migration, of course, isn't unique to birds. Creatures from whales to wildebeests and salmon to locusts engage in sometimes dramatic journeys. Among feathered creatures, however, migration becomes a mind-boggling affair, a behavior almost beyond my capacity to understand. No other animal so tiny migrates so far as do some birds. Okay, some merely wander from low elevation to high, but others travel staggering distances, enduring months-long flights, occasionally traveling an astounding number of miles without stopping for rest or food. An Arctic Tern, for instance, migrates from the Arctic to Antarctica and back every year, taking months to make the trip. Each species follows a migratory pattern unique to its kind, but within that pattern every individual bird makes its own trek, usually alone. Different distances. Different destinations. Different routes to get there. Different times to come and go. To this observer, birds' migratory behavior is surely the most incredible and nearly miraculous of any other activity birds pursue. Watching now-daily evidence of migratory behavior play out in my own yard simply sweeps me away.

Last night's forecast predicted high migration intensity, and once again the bird population changed in the yard. This time, however, more birds left than arrived. Over the course of the day, for instance, I never saw more than one White-throated Sparrow at a time. The sparrows no doubt left riding south winds in the night, following the cold front north. Other birds left, too, including most of the warblers. Among those passing through, only one Tennessee Warbler and one Magnolia Warbler remained today, at least that I saw. On the other hand, at least a dozen Rose-breasted Grosbeaks dotted the yard, probably a few new ones replacing a few that moved on. More males today were in incomplete molt than those that foraged here earlier. And a Yellow-throated Vireo finally made himself visible. Perhaps he was one of the vireos I heard yesterday that refused to show himself, leaving me puzzling over his identity. This morning's cool temps and drippy wet foliage from last

A male Common Yellowthroat forages in the native garden. He may nest here, or at least in the area, but he may also continue as far as central Canada.

night's rain brought the bugs down, which, in turn, brought the birds down. The vireo was among them, foraging steadily low in the maple tree. I find it interesting that this year, birds spend a high percentage of their time foraging in maple, cedar, and apple trees. In previous years, oaks, wild black cherry, and cypress trees ranked as the number-one attractions. This spring's late budding changed birds' behavior—out of necessity, for survival. Those that adapt will survive climate change.

Other migrants in the yard today were those that will stay here to nest—not necessarily "here" as in our yard, but "here" as in the area. One of those was the Common Yellowthroat, back again this afternoon. Usually secretive, he came into the garden, foraged among the densest parts, and sang periodically, just to remind everyone he was taking his place among the territorial battlers. House Wrens took note and gave way.

The day ended with my having identified forty-eight species.

1 Yellow-throated Vireo
Species: 96 total in the yard to date for the year.

May 6

Listening to Music

Since I spent most of the day doing yard and garden work, I found pleasure in the vast range of birdsong. In my mind, as I shoveled mulch around plants, I could "see" birds traveling from one part of the yard to another as their songs emanated from alternating locations. Most songs were those of birds that will nest in the area, both our year-round residents and recently arrived migrants. To my listening pleasure, the songs soared from early morning until late afternoon, telling me who's here and where. Much to my surprise, however, Pine Siskins buzzed from the maple tree and then flitted to the feeder—three of them. They're late compared to their compatriots, most of which left here months ago. I have to wonder about their behavior—where they wintered that they're so late moving toward their breeding grounds.

In short, today there was no need for ear buds to listen to music. It was live! At full volume! And without commercials!

May 7

Watching Evening Skies

At 7:45 p.m. today, I waited to hear if the Barred Owls would call, wondering if perhaps the youngsters had fledged so that I might also hear an immature screeching, begging. At that moment, however, I was distracted by another call from directly above me, a sort of nasal, raspy, frog-like "peent." I hadn't heard that sound since last August. Common Nighthawk! It's back!

Not that the call will ever compete with the likes of, say, a Northern Mockingbird for a music award, but the bird, in spite of its name, is not very common at all. Nor is it a hawk. Members of the same family as whip-poor-wills, they're nightjars, possibly so-named because their song, such as it is, "jars" the stillness of the night. But whatever we think of their song, musical or not, these 2-ounce birds consume far more mosquitoes in a single night's feeding than most other insect-eaters do in a lifetime. Bugging for its supper, the bird, mouth open, literally sweeps the air, feeding on the wing. In flight the nighthawk's slender, 22-inch swept-back wings sport a white vertical band near the tip, and with my binocular I could readily see the band, a dead-positive ID field mark. Later in the summer its aerial acrobatics rival those of the swifts as it wheels and darts, tipsy-like, but its long tail and twice-larger size set it apart from the so-called flying cigar swift. Indeed, it stands out in the dusky sky. Tonight, however, it was high, heading on an arrow-straight course due north, leading me to believe it was migrating, still on its way to its ancestral breeding grounds from its home in South America, somewhere on the east side of the Andes Mountains from Ecuador to Argentina. Now I'm seeing it here in southwestern Indiana. What stunning migratory behavior!

Birds Do *That*?

For bug control, look to hummingbirds. Really! Most folks think hummingbirds only sip nectar, either from flowers or feeders. Of course, they do sip nectar. But they would starve to death if that's all they ate. Their relying 100 percent on nectar would be like your kids or grandkids drinking nothing but soda for life's nutrition. So what else do hummers need? Like other critters, they need protein. Think bugs. Cornell University's Lab of Ornithology claims hummingbirds likely eat about 2,000 tiny bugs per day. Every day. In fact, one group of researchers followed a nesting female for two weeks and never saw her take a drop of nectar. But oh, my, the bugs she ate. Great protein for an incubating mom.

A Common Nighthawk, as the name suggests, feeds at dusk (and dawn), catching bugs on the wing. By day, it perches parallel to a branch, camouflaged by its cryptic plumage.

Nighthawks also exhibit unusual breeding behavior. They don't build a nest, preferring instead to lay their eggs on a tarred-and-graveled rooftop, attracted by nightlights—such as streetlights or athletic-field lights—that draw swarms of bugs for reliable every-evening buffets. Since they feed at night, they sleep during the day; masters of disguise that they are, I've startled them off day roosts without knowing they were anywhere near, perching length-wise on limbs, blending perfectly with the bark.

Unfortunately, nighthawks face declining numbers, most likely from changes in land use and from pesticide use that kills bugs and thus destroys the birds' food supply.

Oh, by the way, the owls called, but no fledglings screeched. Only a Green Heron called from the watery lowland in the neighbor's woods.

> 1 Common Nighthawk
> **Species:** 97 total in the yard to date for the year.

May 8

Hitting One Hundred

How I enjoy a leisurely early morning ramble through the yard, listening and looking for what's here. This morning dawned a cool 54 degrees, and the grass was soppy with dew. In spite of clear skies, boots seemed appropriate. And a light jacket.

At first I heard only the regulars, even from the woods to the south. One interesting behavior in the lower patch of tangles was that of the Eastern Towhees calling, calling, calling, surely trying to lure nestlings out and turn them into fledglings. Although I never saw the nest (mostly because I didn't try, not wanting to disturb them), I know it was in the area where they called this morning. They've scooted about in that area for some weeks now, obviously on guard.

As I continued my ramblings, I heard the Belted Kingfisher's flight call from some distance and watched the sky as the calls came nearer. Then, there! He flew right over my head, on course, I'm sure, to a fishy four-acre lake to our east. Every summer I hear kingfishers travel to and from that direction, although given their breeding behavior, I can't be at all sure they're nesting there. It seems to me the banks of the lake may not be high enough to accommodate a kingfisher's nest hole. They dig a tunnel in the dirt bank of a lake or stream and raise their family in a little compartment at tunnel's end. How I'd love to watch them at work, but I've never had the privilege.

The excitement of the flyover quickly behind me, I caught a sound I couldn't quite identify. Yes, I'd heard it before, but what was it? Short, two syllables. Dry and hoarse. Was it a call or a song? Tracking the sound wasn't easy because the bird wasn't sitting still, but finally I caught up with it among the blossoms of the wild black cherry tree. Aha! Grayish olive. Two wing bars. Clear, bold eye ring. And the song, now that I was closer, a pronounced "che-BIK," repeated rapidly. Bingo. Least Flycatcher. Two of them. No, three! They're only migrating through, visiting briefly on their way to the northern tier of states and southern Canada, so I was eager to watch them, foraging among the wild black cherry blossoms for the abundant small insects there. I have so little chance to see them, to study their busy behavior, to listen to their song—such as it is. What a treat!

Farther along my usual path, I watched the Tufted Titmouse going to and from the bluebird box the pair has commandeered, obviously now feeding new hatchlings. Likewise, bluebirds, in a box 100 yards away, were racing the clock to feed nestlings. They must have a box full of babies about to fledge, judging by their behavior—the frequency with which the adult pair is carrying bugs and caterpillars to keep the fast-growing beggars fed. A third box, situated between the neighbor's hayfield and grain field, hosted a surprise: a Tree Swallow perched atop, singing his little heart out. If I were a betting person, I'd bet he'll find a mate who agrees with him that this is the perfect real estate for their nursery. Although Tree Swallows arrived in the area at least by March 3, today's was the first I've seen around the yard. However, their arrival reflects their typical behavior. I have no idea what takes them so long to move

A male Tree Swallow arrives on territory, staking out his claim, watching for interlopers.

onto our property. Named for their affinity for nesting in tree cavities, Tree Swallows will readily accept man-made construction. In previous years the adults demonstrated their unique foraging behavior, sweeping over the hayfield like little aerial vacuum cleaners, bunching up fifteen to twenty tiny insects into a BB-size ball, called a bolus, for a single delivery to the nest.

How we love these acrobatic aerialists, iridescent dark blue on their backs, tuxedo-like, snow white on their fronts, the female slightly duller than the male. While they're amazing to watch, darting on the wing, their bug consumption ranks even more amazing. Two adults feeding young for fifteen to twenty days will consume about 300,000 insects. Since they snag insects only on the wing and fly low—under 40 feet—they consume the bugs most annoying to humans. This year, given our mosquitoes, I'm seriously hoping they decide to stay.

My husband, chief bluebird-box supervisor, keeps our precious bluebirds safe, protected from ants and wasps, by "running the trail" weekly, checking his twelve boxes, monitoring and cleaning out old nests. Bluebirds seem to take the checks in stride, perhaps burbling a note or two about the intrusion but bearing no ill will. Not so with tree swallows. Highly territorial, they take the whole affair personally, and their behavior demonstrates their offense. Over time, hubby has been buzzed and dive-bombed by little swallows that look surprisingly large when aimed toward one's eyes. Although none have actually made contact with his bare head, he's become really good at ducking—and wearing hats.

Adults and fledglings will hang around the area until early fall. Then they'll join hundreds of their fellows, roosting together, usually near marshes. The hundreds will join thousands and ultimately lift off for parts south, some migrating as far as central South America.

A lovely 2-hour walk this morning! Well, to be honest, more standing than walking, but a lovely 2 hours. The end of the morning count, however, has brought a milestone: I've passed one hundred species identified in the yard since January 1. Maybe our hard work, still ongoing, landscaping for birds, planting more and more native plants, is paying off. The joy of watching not only so many species but so many individuals of those species gives me great satisfaction. Some days the yard hosts an amazing number of birds—not at feeders but in the vegetation, foraging for bugs, berries, nectar, and seeds.

This evening, the call of the Eastern Wood-pewee announced his arrival, the first for the season. They say their name with such seeming pride that "pewee" becomes three syllables, "pee-a-WEE," with sort of a southern drawl. Welcome back! I know I'll be hearing more from him.

> 1 Belted Kingfisher, flyover
> 2 Least Flycatcher
> 1 Eastern Wood-pewee
> 1 Tree Swallow, staking out nest box
> **Species:** 101 total in the yard to date for the year.

May 9

Puzzling over a Waxwing Flock

A flock of Cedar Waxwings garnered my attention this morning. Well, actually, they drew my attention off and on all day with their varying numbers. My first count was twelve. Then I saw thirty-two. Nice little flock, I thought, singing that in-flight high-pitched whistle for which they're famous. Then I saw about seventy. (Who can count exact numbers with a flock that large?) By late afternoon the numbers had more than doubled, perhaps as many as 175. I've puzzled over why the flock was so large. But especially I've puzzled over the flock's behavior: Why was it here, roaming the yard, mostly flying to and from the maple trees? Strange, I thought.

In winter and during migration, according to reliable sources, it's not uncommon to see large waxwing flocks, often several hundred. Amazingly, flocks numbering in the thousands have been reported during spring and fall migrations. Okay, since winter is long past, the remaining likely option is that these birds were migrating. While we have Cedar Waxwings here year-round, being situated as we are near the southern edge of their year-round range, we may not have the same birds year-round. These particular birds could have spent the winter in the far south, perhaps as far as the Gulf Coast or even farther south, as far as Costa Rica. Now, whether these birds spent the winter with us or with our neighbors to the far south, they could be moving northward into their breeding range that stretches to central Canada. Without banding studies, there would be no way to know.

Still, why did they hang out here for the day, especially rummaging through the upper branches of the maple tree? True, I've had large winter flocks rustle through the native American holly trees, relishing the berries. In fact, waxwings prefer fruit for their diet and eat more fruit than any other North American bird species. But not now, not in May when vegetation has barely greened and bloomed and certainly no fruit has set. Substituting for the fruit, waxwings will eat flowers in spring. In fact, I've watched them munching apple blossoms in previous springs. All right, they'll eat flowers, but the maples have long since finished blooming—as have the apple trees. If the birds had been hanging out in the wild black cherry trees now in full bloom, I could understand. But I never saw them going to or leaving from the direction of those trees. Sometimes they forage for bugs on vegetation, and maples host a decent supply of bugs—but so do oaks and cherries and pines. The birds never varied from their focus on the maples. A true puzzle.

As happens when I see striking behavior I can't explain, I hit the books. What do the authorities say? Rooting through the research reports, the most definitive being in the *Birds of North America Online*, I read page after page. Then, bingo! In a single sentence, this:

A Cedar Waxwing, preferring berries but finding none this early in the season, turns to apple blossoms for nourishment.

A Warbling Vireo sings an extraordinarily lovely song for such an otherwise drab, almost nondescript bird.

"In spring, feeds on sap drips created by water freezing in small cracks of smaller branches of maples (Acer sp.); hangs from branches to feed on suspended drops of sap." Given this year's late spring freezes, I have a real gut feeling that this sentence precisely describes today's behavior.

Other busyness today included a pair of Summer Tanagers having a serious disagreement with another pair. Who knows which pair first claimed our yard as territory, but they were having none of the interlopers. By afternoon the ruckus was settled, and all was calm. Wish I knew who won—and why.

Likewise, the House Wrens have dispersed, having somehow settled the dispute over who stays and who goes. Of course, the males are still singing at their respective chosen nest-cavity sites, but the yelling and fighting seem to have drawn mostly to a close.

1 Warbling Vireo
Species: 102 total in the yard to date for the year.

A newly arrived Warbling Vireo caught my attention this morning as it sang at the woods' edge. These vireos tend to hang out in almost any sizable deciduous forest, foraging slowly across the high canopy. For being such nondescript little guys, their real claim to fame is the lovely song for which they're named.

May 10

Welcoming Nesters

Only two days ago a Tree Swallow perched 5 feet from one of our nest boxes, on a post with a 360-degree view of the nest-box neighborhood. He sang, hopped to and from the nest box, and finally, later in the day, abandoned the concert. Of course, typical behavior of most birds is to belt out their courting calls early in the day and feed and explore later. This morning, early, he again sang his come-hither song and was joined by a female, apparently pleased to have found a strong singer with good territorial real estate situated in the heart of a good bug supply. The two of them ducked in and out of the box and flew circles around the area, feeling out the location and security of the facility. Although I observed no further activity throughout the afternoon and evening, I'm betting they've made the serious decision to call this nest box home for the nursery.

Other songs tell me males of numerous species are defending territory, I assume with females accompanying them. The Yellow-throated Warbler sings daily, sometimes much of the morning and early afternoon, almost always from the towering pines at the end of the driveway. The White-eyed Vireo sings daily, too, but his behavior is different. Often called a singing machine, he roams dense, shrubby areas—north, south, and east (but not west where there is open pasture)—either not having settled on a territory or not having attracted a mate. Summer Tanagers talk to each other from our little patch of woods to the south, so I think they've settled on a site. House Wrens have staked out their respective nest cavities and begun stuffing them full of sticks, so they've settled into a this-is-mine-and-that-is-yours routine.

Strangely, three Pine Siskins roamed the yard again this morning, checking every feeder and announcing their presence in the tallest trees with their buzzy little calls. Hemlock cones attracted their attention, but mostly they fed on sunflower and nyjer seeds. The little guys need to get going. They're late for an important date! With the southern edge of their normal breeding range reaching only northern Michigan, they have a distance yet to go.

As we were out and about today, we drove along a narrow rock lane to a group of summer cottages along the river, hoping to say hello to friends. An out-of-place stake had been driven along the edge of the lane, almost into the tire track of the single-lane road. As we eased around, aiming to avoid scraping our vehicle against the stake, I looked out the window, studying the arrangement, wondering about the stake. Then I saw something! A killdeer had laid her eggs among the rocks, blending perfectly with the surroundings. Had she not looked up at me, allowing me to catch the glint in her eye, I would never have noticed her, much less her eggs, hidden in plain view. As we slowed, she stood up beside her nest, and we moved on, knowing she would go into her "broken wing" act if we disturbed her or seemed to threaten her nest. What clever defensive behavior for a ground-nesting bird! We understood, then, that the out-of-place stake was there to protect her from unknowing traffic—and we would have been one of the unknowing, probably destroying her eggs. Thanks to the residents along the lane, she will likely remain safe.

A Killdeer guards her "nest" (lower right, with four eggs visible), which is nothing more than a shallow spot among rocks, the eggs camouflaged by their splotchy markings.

May 11

Worrying about Impact

After the second-coldest April on record, we're now experiencing record-breaking highs in the midsummer-like 90s. I'm left to wonder how birds react to wild fluctuations in weather. This spring they suffered from temperature swings that affected their food sources: late freezes that halted plant development and therefore the development of bugs that those plants support; late freezes that killed fruit production and destroyed not only summer fruits but autumn berries important for migration; long-lasting cold that delayed spring migration (birds can't out-fly their food sources) and therefore threw breeding off schedule. Birds won't construct nests without camouflage, so bare or only budding vegetation—trees, shrubs, vines, even perennials—offer too little protection for successful breeding sites. Since birds won't construct their nests in poor sites, they must adapt, choosing Plan B, perhaps selecting nest sites among conifers. If birds wait for fully leafed vegetation, they miss the bug "bloom" to feed their babies, but too few coniferous building sites leave birds little choice but to delay nesting.

Undue heat, however, also impacts nesting birds, especially those that nest in cavities, creating stifling conditions for both the incubator and the incubated. Heat combined with dry affects bug production and reduces both the size and number of caterpillars, prime baby-bird food. Further, drought hampers or even halts seed production necessary for summer, fall, and winter survival, further impacting fall migration. And those are only the generalities. The specifics paint the demise of hundreds of birds.

Weather wreaks havoc in other ways as well. Strong winds rip nests from their anchors and heavy rain dissolves some nests (think American Robin's nest "glued" together with mud) or drowns nestlings (think shore-edge nesters like Common Loons). Last night's hailstorm that produced golf ball–size hail likely destroyed nests, crushed eggs, and perhaps killed birds. After all, a golf ball–size hunk of ice weighs more than most small songbirds, so being hit by such a hailstone is likely fatal, or at least seriously debilitating.

Still, birds have survived over thousands of years through all kinds of weather conditions. Granted, some weather events have been devastating for some species, but mostly they've recovered, mostly regaining populations over time. Now, however, we make it harder. We use pesticides to kill their food sources; we plant nonnative and invasive plants that turn yards into bird-food deserts; we keep tidy lawns perfected by pesticides and frequent mowing that basically create toxic dumps for birds; we bulldoze and pave vast acres that once offered rich migratory stopovers for millions of birds; we pollute the air, water, and soil without considering the impact on birds trying to raise nestlings; we create noise pollution that prevents birds from hearing a potential mate's song; we create light pollution that confuses day with night and throws birds out of sync.

As weather changes grow more and more wild as we endure climate change, I fear for all of us—humans and birds alike. In short, history points toward a simple homily: Those that can adapt will be those that survive. It's not a pretty picture.

May 12

Adding Native Plants

For the last many years, spring planting time involved adding not petunias, marigolds, geraniums, and other annuals, but instead a variety of native plants—perennials, vines, shrubs, grasses, an occasional tree—that support birds one way or another. Some plants add blossoms, nectar, berries, or seed for the birds. Some serve primarily as hosts for butterflies and moths, thus providing a fine protein source for birds and their babies. Some function primarily as shelter, especially in winter. Some provide a great combination of advantages for birds. The ultimate goal: to eliminate nonnatives and replace them with diverse natives. Here's why: The more diverse the native vegetation in the yard, the more diverse the bird species that come to dine and find shelter in the yard.

A male Indigo Bunting (top center), female American Goldfinch (center), male American Goldfinch (left), another female goldfinch (right), and Pine Siskin (bottom center) feed together on a nyjer-seed feeder, these few weeks being the only time of year when these three species can be seen simultaneously.

Today also let me savor a special combo. This is the only time of year when I'll ever see these three birds in the yard together: American Goldfinch, a mostly year-round resident; Pine Siskin, a lingering winter visitor; and Indigo Bunting, a just-arrived tropical migrant. How special to know where they've been and where they're going. Amazing, indeed, this miracle of migratory behavior, that only now, in mid-May, can I ever see these three birds together.

1 Great Blue Heron, flyover
Species: 103 total in the yard to date for the year.

May 13

Celebrating International Migratory Bird Day

In 1894 school superintendent Charles Almanzo Babcock of Oil City, Pennsylvania, set aside May 4 as Bird Day. It became the first US holiday designated specifically to celebrate birds. Babcock's intent was "to advance bird conservation as a moral value." While the "holiday" remained on calendars as a day to celebrate birds and all they stand for, not until about twenty-five years ago did the event really garner attention. At that point, the Smithsonian Migratory Bird Center reimagined the celebration and established the second Saturday in May as the day of celebration (and named the second Saturday in October for the same celebration in the Southern Hemisphere). Nowadays the project is coordinated by Environment for the Americas. In 2018, the Year of the Bird, the theme expanded globally, becoming World Migratory Bird Day (WMBD). According to MigratoryBirdDay.org, on this occasion, "We celebrate the ways we can help to protect birds every day of the year through actions, stories, and art."

Because birds fascinate me and have for years been part of my daily life, WMBD is hardly a blip on my radar, but I'm always excited to see how others acknowledge the day—today—mostly by participating in bird counts at home and away. The WMBD Counts, Christmas Bird Counts, and Breeding Bird Surveys plus the more recent eBird.org website combine to provide citizen-science input into international databases for access by anyone who can benefit. It's a small but important contribution to the world of ornithology.

May 14

Watching Migration Wind Down

For the first time since April 30, Rose-breasted Grosbeaks were absent from the yard. Maybe a straggler or two will venture through over the next few days, but although I'd certainly enjoy seeing them, they need to be on the way to their breeding grounds if they're to be successful parents. Unlike people, birds have only one purpose in life: to reproduce. So tardy birds may miss the mark for success.

Among the last migrants to arrive in our yard are usually cuckoos. Today, the Black-billed Cuckoo called from the woods, announcing he's joined the Yellow-billed Cuckoo in the hunt for caterpillars.

> 1 Black-billed Cuckoo, calling in woods
> **Species:** 104 total in the yard to date for the year.

The Black-billed Cuckoo is among the last of the migrants arriving here, waiting until caterpillars—its favorite food—are available in abundance. This one is foraging in a willow tree, a species known to support moths and their caterpillars.

May 15

Journeying to Join the Migration

Many years during May we've made the pilgrimage to northern Ohio, to the Lake Erie Shore, to hang out among the flocks of warblers and other migrants that pile up along the lakeshore, joining, too, the flocks of bird lovers who relish the up-close-and-personal views of the tropical migrants. A prime week there might draw 50,000 birders and photographers—and who knows how many birds. And no wonder! A 35-mile stretch of road accesses adjacent wildlife areas that attract and support birds as well as bird watchers.

What makes this isolated but concentrated geographic area such a bird magnet? For birds, it's pure logistics. Some birds, those that migrate up through the central United States on track toward parts of Canada, reach the Erie shore and find themselves at the edge of a body of water too big to see across. That gives them pause. But they're hardwired to continue, to reach their breeding range as quickly as possible. Instinctively, though, they understand the necessary preparation for a long flight across water. They drop down to feed. And they feed heavily. Because the migrants are so tightly tuned to finding food, especially those diminutive green caterpillars that richly nourish them, they're almost oblivious to the presence of people gawking, pointing big-eyed binoculars and cameras at them. The birds seem to understand that we bird watchers are confined to the strip of boardwalk that winds through their rich feeding grounds, seemingly comfortable snapping up bugs in our presence, sometimes startlingly close by. Of course, many of these incredible tropical birds may never have seen humans and thus have no fear of us—although you'd think instinctively they'd fear anything that much bigger than them.

Since the lakeshore is about 450 miles north of our yard, a trip there translates into a second spring. The old rule of thumb says that for roughly every 150 miles north, count on a week's delay in the season. So the lakeshore is about three weeks behind us.

May 16

Inching along the Boardwalk

Joining the human crowds on the boardwalk this morning also meant joining the avian crowds foraging from the ground up—Ovenbirds on the ground, Tennessee Warblers mid-level, Blackburnians high up. Early morning and late evening birding typically offer better viewing because birds, almost all of them, drop down to feed. And they drop down for good reason: The bugs have dropped down. Birds follow bugs. Sometimes strong winds will also bring birds lower, probably for the same reason. Whatever the conditions, elbow to elbow we inched along the mile-long boardwalk, needing the entire day to bird the distance, recording bird sighting after sighting, taking thousands of photos.

This place has something no other birding hot spot can claim. It shoulders against Lake Erie, protected on the east by a low ridge of dunes and on the north by a dense ribbon of shrubs and trees. Due north across Lake Erie lies Canada and its rich boreal forest, the destination of almost everything foraging here now. Prime breeding territory, thousands of undisturbed acres, the forest is the richest bird nursery in the world.

Birds Do *That*?

Blackpoll Warblers would log 720,000 miles to the gallon—if they flew on gasoline instead of fat. So explains ornithologist Miyoko Chu. You see, Blackpolls breed mostly in Alaska, but they winter in South America. It's just that in getting to their destination, Blackpolls choose to travel over open water much of the way. In fact, after flying from Alaska across the continent to the Atlantic coast, they cut out across the ocean to fly nonstop for 36 hours to reach Venezuela or Colombia. To accomplish this three-day feat, they pack on the fat, doubling their weight, before departing.

By day's end, exhausted from the strain of locating elusive birds amid the vegetation, arms aching from holding binoculars and long-lens cameras, and neck sore from looking up, up, up, we flopped into a restaurant booth to recount the sightings. We had seen a mind-boggling array of birds engaged in an equally mind-boggling array of behaviors: Cedar Waxwings plucking tree buds, Tree Swallows stuffing nest materials into tree cavities, Bald Eagles feeding young, Solitary Sandpipers poking in the mud, White-crowned Sparrows foraging in willows, Yellow Warblers building nests, Common Yellowthroats wiggling through swampy underbrush, Chestnut-sided Warblers plucking tiny somethings from under leaves, Tennessee Warblers foraging only feet away, Black-throated Green Warblers displaying various molts, American Redstarts flicking colorful tails, Warbling Vireos singing mid-level, Cape May Warblers bugging in box elders, Blackburnian Warblers showing off fiery-red throats, Lincoln's Sparrows walking through the leaf litter, Magnolia Warblers displaying breeding plumage, Northern Parulas searching spiderwebs, Wilson's Warblers checking bark crevices, Scarlet Tanagers boasting full red, Gray Catbirds nesting early, Red-eyed Vireos singing on territory, Swainson's Thrushes flipping leaves, Yellow-billed Cuckoos hunting caterpillars, Marsh Wrens skittering under logs, Blue-gray Gnatcatchers building hidden nests, Black-throated Blue Warblers eating spiders, and on and on. I was breathless. Tomorrow will bring even more! Migratory behavior changes the scenery every day. And the foraging behavior varies as widely as the birds foraging.

A male Cape May Warbler forages among the blossoms of American black currant.

A male Magnolia Warbler in breeding plumage forages for tiny arthropods in a maple tree.

May 17

Moving Our Search

Transporting ourselves from the boardwalk, a 7-mile auto drive gave us respite, inching along dike roads, stopping when birds beckoned but moving on to the nearest pullout for longer looks. To bird with any degree of care requires most of a day. Open water, marshes, streams, and meadows bump against shrubs and little patches of woodland, making for highly varied habitat resulting in highly varied bird life. Again today we found fascinating birds engaged in fascinating behavior: Common Gallinule foraging for crustaceans in shallow waters; Osprey nesting atop provided nest poles and fishing across the many ponds; Trumpeter Swans congregating in familial flocks and beginning to pair off for nesting; Black-crowned Night-heron perching inconspicuously for the day amid shrubs at water's edge; Pied-billed Grebes popping up from long dives for fish; White Pelicans rowing by overhead, eyeing the water but moving on; and scattered ducks, including Scaup and Green-winged Teal. Foraging among the shrubs were Yellow-rumped Warblers, Alder and Willow Flycatchers, Field Sparrows, Northern Rough-winged and Barn Swallows, Great Crested and Least Flycatchers, and a single Philadelphia Vireo, among others.

Given the time of year, everything was either proclaiming territory, seeking nest materials, already nesting, or still migrating toward a more northerly breeding site. How exciting to see the many stages of breeding behaviors all in one spot.

A Common Gallinule paddles alongside last winter's cattail debris, possibly looking for an appropriate nest site at water's edge.

Trumpeter Swans , their heads and necks stained from tannins in the water, reestablish their pair-bond relationship prior to the beginning of nest building.

A Pied-billed Grebe displays, wings spread, making a to-do over his search for a mate.

May 18

Searching for the Missing

Mourning Warblers, Connecticut Warblers, and Kentucky Warblers have always hung like albatrosses around my neck: They're hard for me to find. I've seen Mourning Warblers twice in the yard, the first a record for our county, but I've seen only one Kentucky Warbler at a distant sanctuary, and I've heard but never seen a Connecticut. Back on the boardwalk today, in spite of my efforts, the albatrosses remain in place. But finding the Mourning Warbler secreting its way through the dense, dark, shadowy underbrush at least made the albatross feel lighter! (See photo for May chapter opener.)

A Blackpoll Warbler stretches to snag a morsel as it forages for bugs, showing its orange legs, an identifying field mark.

A male Bay-breasted Warbler in breeding plumage forages for bugs, eggs, or larva hidden in bark crevices or amid spring vegetation.

Other birds, however, also showed their faces, doing what they do naturally. Blackpoll Warblers plucked bugs from bark and the undersides of elderberry leaves, singing Bay-breasted Warblers startled me with their breeding loveliness, Eastern Phoebes repeatedly called their own names, Ruby-crowned Kinglets reminded us of those that spent the winter with us, House Wrens staked out cavities for their nurseries, Indigo Buntings proved that some of them nest well beyond our claim to them at home, a Black-billed Cuckoo joined its Yellow-billed cousin, a Hermit Thrush sang on territory, and Green Herons and Wood Ducks made themselves at home in the marsh.

We had yet another exhausting but somehow simultaneously invigorating day, racking up a bird list of seventy-two species for the two days. I'm sure other folks saw far more, but we dawdle, watching how birds behave, how they feed, how Chestnut-sided Warblers hang upside down from leaves, how Black-and-white Warblers ratchet like nuthatches along tree bark, how redstarts flick their tails while snaring tiny spiders unseen by human eyes. It becomes predictable what feeds low, flipping leaves, foraging under logs and piles of brush: Ovenbirds, all the thrushes, catbirds, most sparrows, Common Yellowthroats, Marsh and Winter Wrens, American Woodcocks, and Hooded, Mourning, Connecticut, and Kentucky Warblers. It's likewise predictable what feeds mid-level to high, giving us literal pains in the neck from straining to see them. In short, it's the majority of warblers. Of course, some birds always hang out

A male Prothonotary Warbler sings to attract a mate and to defend his swampy territory, illustrating that birdsong is not about happiness but about love and war.

near water, but not just shorebirds and waterfowl. Catbirds like wet as do Common Yellowthroats, Yellow Warblers, and especially Prothonotary Warblers, the only eastern warbler that nests in cavities, particularly cavities in wetlands.

May 19

Exploring New Wetlands

A newly opened mitigated wetland, once farmland that has been reconstructed as marsh, now functions not only to filter runoff contaminants before waters flow into Lake Erie but also to provide much-needed migratory stopover habitat for many bird species, albeit mostly shorebirds. Among the variety foraging in the waters today were several hundred Dunlins, nicely decked out in breeding plumage. Additionally, Herring Gulls, Bonaparte's

During migration a Dunlin stops at a newly built wetlands, a mitigation project now attracting hundreds of shorebirds, proof that if we build it, they will come.

A Sora forages amid cattails and mud at wetlands edge, searching for invertebrates that provide protein for spring breeding, its long toes providing support across aquatic vegetation.

Amid last year's cattail stalks, a Marsh Wren sings to attract a mate and defend its watery territory.

Gulls, Ruddy Turnstones, Caspian Terns, and Semi-palmated Sandpipers foraged among grasses, poked in the mud, and floated throughout the area, mostly sheltered behind wind-protecting banks. A Whimbrel flew in for a brief look-see, causing every birder to gasp in surprise. It's one of the most wide-ranging shorebirds in the world and known to make a 2,500-mile nonstop flight from South America to southern Canada, so this one, in northern Ohio, had stopped short. It will venture to the far reaches of the Arctic to breed.

As rewarding as it was to see the variety of water birds, it's even more satisfying to know that if enough people care, habitat can be restored. And if we build it, they will come. That should become a mantra for bird lovers everywhere.

Just to prove the case, we drove on to visit yet another restored wetland. The absence of playgrounds and picnic areas also means an absence of people in this somewhat remote park, so we had the birds to ourselves. The most excitement came from a calling Sora that finally wandered out from the cattails, giving us an out-in-the-open view of an often elusive bird. Across the parking lot from the Sora's habitat, we heard a Marsh Wren calling from another broad, dense stand of cattails. The effort required patience, but we finally spotted the tiny, perky creature grasping a stalk about halfway up, proclaiming his territory. Even when humans build the habitat, desperate birds take to it in an instant. Such is the scarcity of habitat.

May 20

Running from the Wind

It was called a seiche (strong winds and changing atmospheric pressure forming a so-called standing wave in the lake, causing water to pile up against the windward shore). It sent us fleeing, the parking lot flooding, the road closing. We got out just in time as waters piled up, spilling over the low dunes, wind-whipped into massive waves that roiled against the beaches and crashed against trees. Once we and the 400 or so others who had been on the boardwalk were free of danger, TV newsmen wanted to hear our stories. Predictably, the birds were the least affected by the seiche. They simply tucked in, took cover as they would in any storm, and weathered it out. Just another day in the park for them. By late afternoon the winds had died, but flooding had closed roads—some because they were washed out, others because they were damaged.

Birds Do *That*?

Some birds have iron in their brains. Scientists have always marveled that certain avian species are so exact in their migratory paths that they return from South America to the exact nest site in Canada year after year. How can birds manage such travel precision—minus road maps or GPS? Turns out that beyond following geographic features, like rivers and mountain ranges, and tuning into astronomical guidelines, like the moon and stars, many birds, perhaps all of them, sense the magnetic field of the earth. According to world-renowned BBC commentator David Attenborough, the explanation has merit. In a sophisticated experiment, birds were fitted with slender rods of iron. Some rods were magnetized so that they impeded the earth's magnetism. Birds fitted with those rods got lost. Eventually, Attenborough writes, scientists discovered microscopic grains of iron oxide—magnetite—in the brains of some birds, perhaps enabling them to sense some sort of internal "compass" that aids their travel.

Both species in breeding plumage, a Great Egret (left), with its black legs and feet, yellow bill, and patch of bright neon-green facial skin, stands in dramatic contrast to a Snowy Egret (right), with its black legs, gold feet (not visible here), black bill, and reddish-orange facial skin patch.

Late that afternoon in a flooded field, we found a feeding group of Snowy Egrets poking their black bills in the mud, some showing evidence of breeding plumage: yellow lores, reddish skin patch, black legs, yellow feet, lacy plumes on their tails. Perhaps they had found a safe haven along the field's edge, tucking in out of the wind. In any case they ignored us, and we photographed them at our leisure. But Snowy Egrets in northern Ohio? Most range maps designate Snowy Egret breeding areas well to the south, but a small flock of breeding birds returns annually to the western end of Lake Erie. The birds we studied were obviously part of that group, but certainly unusual for northern Ohio.

By visit's end we had tallied 109 species in a wide variety of habitats.

May 21

Signaling the End of Migration

After a long day's drive, we returned home just in time to enjoy a few hours of daylight and a few birds.

Typically, when I hear the first Yellow-billed Cuckoo of the season, I make a mental note that migration is all but over. This evening two called, one from our little patch of woods and one from the neighbor's woods to the east. Grandma called them "rain crows" because, she said, when they call, it's going to rain.

So why are cuckoos so late to arrive? What does their tardiness say about their behavior? In reality cuckoos arrive in what seems to be a slow time simply because they follow the caterpillar emergence. As our best bet against invasive tent caterpillars, cuckoos have a special affinity for dining on them and are adept at ripping

Like its cousin the Black-billed Cuckoo, this Yellow-billed Cuckoo signifies the near-end of migration, typically the last migrant to arrive here. This one captured a bug as it foraged in the sweetgum.

open the webs to get at the goodies. Thus, until eggs hatch into caterpillars, cuckoo food supplies are all but absent. In our yard I see cuckoos foraging for caterpillars particularly in gum, oak, and sycamore trees. Since I hear them call most of the summer, I'm sure they nest somewhere nearby, but only once have I discovered a nest. Amazing behavior, isn't it, that some birds have already nested and fledged a brood while other birds are only now arriving on territory!

According to sightings reported on eBird.org, Yellow-billed Cuckoos, now listed as "threatened," spend their winters in Mexico, Central America, and the northern parts of South America.

2 Yellow-billed Cuckoo
Species: 105 total in the yard to date for the year.

May 22

Calculating Population Changes

American Goldfinches stay here year-round, but they're not the same individuals year-round. As a result, their roller-coaster behavior confounds backyard birders. Where do the birds go? Right now the answer is "north." The goldfinches that spent the winter with us most likely came down from the far north, escaping the seriously severe winter there. They'll not move south any farther than necessary, however, so come spring, their return to their breeding territories is as speedy as possible. So, for instance, while goldfinches roam the southern tier of states all winter, they don't breed there; and while they breed as far north as central-latitude Canada, they don't winter there. In places in between, though, such as where I live, they're found the entire year—just not necessarily the same individuals.

As the birds that wintered in the southern tier of states begin moving north, they may move no farther than, say, the central-latitude states. On the other hand, birds that wintered in the central-latitude states may move all the way to Canada. Some may leapfrog over others to gain quick access to their preferred breeding spots. All this movement is not necessarily coordinated, so populations can vary wildly, from abundant to scarce, within days. All it takes is a strong night wind from the south to send birds winging north, riding the benefit of tailwinds.

Right now, few goldfinches populate the yard, and the nyjer-seed feeders hang mostly empty. I'm watching for south winds—and change.

Something similar happens with Ruby-throated Hummingbirds. This spring in particular, weather delayed hummingbirds. Finally, when the time was right, however, they flooded north—in abundance. I had more hummingbirds earlier than I've ever had at that time before. Now, though, the numbers are few. The bulk of the multitudes that arrived early were intent on going farther north. In fact, the first hummers to arrive typically have the farthest to go. They're not the ones that will stay with us to breed.

In late May, however, the hummers arriving are "our" hummers. They've been slow to make their mark at local feeders in part because now that spring has sprung, the lush vegetation is producing a crazy profusion of flowers. Nectar is abundant. And bugs are equally abundant. While backyard hummer hosts may miss "their" birds, the hummers simply don't need our handouts. I know I need only wait (and keep syrup fresh) because nesting hummers like the quick convenience of ready feeders. The feeders will get busy soon enough.

May 23

Knowing Nesters

The behavior is clear: Any birds singing now are carving out or already defending territories. They're not practicing; these are serious performances. The noisiest among them

A Great Crested Flycatcher nested in this sycamore cavity last year.

this morning was the Great Crested Flycatcher. He has a series of calls, chatters, and songs that make him conspicuous enough, but when he moves across a multi-acre circle proclaiming his large domain, he becomes truly conspicuous. Unique among flycatchers, the Great Crested Flycatcher chooses a tree cavity for its nest site, a challenge given that competition for tree cavities is at a premium. The old sycamore tree at the edge of the front yard boasts a couple of decent cavities, and the storm-ravaged trees along the north property line include several as well. In the woods, more sycamores and a few dead and decaying trees add to the availability. Trouble is, many other birds depend on tree cavities for their nests, and only members of the woodpecker family can hammer out their own.

Adjoining woodlands surely include a few cavity trees as well, so I'm hoping the Great Crested Flycatcher will find one that meets his (and her) needs. They're great bug eaters!

May 24

Listening for Summer Residents

This morning a Gray Catbird "mewed" from the woodland edge and later launched into his mockingbird-like song, softer than a mocker, singing each phrase only once. Stopping to listen, I was lured into thinking he may have chosen a nest site nearby, perhaps on our property, and that would be a first. Mostly catbirds prefer places wetter than our habitat, perhaps even marsh-like. Maybe this guy thinks marsh isn't necessary; maybe he's been crowded away from his ideal spot; maybe he's decided after all that this area is ideal; or maybe he's not staying here at all, only

A Gray Catbird shows its russet undertail patch, believed by some authorities to play a role in seduction.

making overtures toward an unseen female, planning to lure her to the perfect marshy spot. Still, wouldn't it be pleasurable if he—and his mate—decided to stay and make our area their nursery! Well, I can dream.

May 25

Watching Berry Pickers

Every year when the native black mulberries ripen—and sometimes before they're truly ripe—all the berry lovers swoop in for breakfast, lunch, and dinner. This year the berries are about a week late, but most of the regulars are showing up for the feast, Cedar Waxwings in particular. They come in whistling their high-pitched call, announcing to one and all that the banquet is set. Sometimes the tree quivers with their activity.

This year for the first time, we also have an abundant crop of native serviceberries.

A Cedar Waxwing forages for just-right mulberries among the ripening fruits.

Cardinals and waxwings seem to divide their time evenly between the two, but my personal guess is that mulberries are an easier take. Since serviceberries hang on little 2-inch stems, they're set swinging by the bird's hopping along the twig. As a result, birds must perform a little flight-attack motion to capture the berries. Mulberries, on the other hand, have such stubby little stems that they're easy pickings from almost any direction.

Surely we'll see some thrushes now. They tend to show up for mulberries if nothing else!

May 26

Noting Berry Specialists

After spending additional hours watching the mulberry and serviceberry trees today, I'm surmising that the apparent widespread abundance of berries may be keeping yard crowds in check. Yes, the cardinals, waxwings, titmice, chickadees, goldfinches, indigos, bluebirds,

A male first-spring Summer Tanager forages in a mulberry tree, his splotchy plumage indicating his molt into breeding-adult plumage.

A stunning all-red breeding-plumaged male Summer Tanager approaches the bubble rock, watching cautiously before descending.

red-bellies, robins, downys, and jays presented themselves as acknowledged berry pickers, but the overall numbers seemed lower than usual. On the other hand, three special sightings gave me pleasure. A pair of adult Eastern Bluebirds fed serviceberries to their recent fledglings; a pair of Carolina Chickadees plucked mulberries for their fledglings; and—surprise!—a bright male Summer Tanager came calling, literally, sounding his distinctive "pic-y-tuk" as he lit, plucked a mulberry, and dashed to a nearby branch to finish it off. Then an even bigger surprise! A first-spring male Summer Tanager flew in to check out the berries as well. It's rare for me—or most anyone else, I suspect—to see first-spring male Summer Tanagers. There's a simple reason: Any given individual will wear this unique plumage for only a matter of weeks. Only males, and only once in their lifetimes—during the first spring of their lives. How cool is that!?

Disappointed that I missed the photo of the bright breeding male Summer Tanager when he visited the mulberry tree, I was rewarded when later this afternoon he came to the backyard bubble rock. How striking that he perched in plain view. I am grateful that the brushy woods-edge habitat makes these tanagers happy and keeps them here for the breeding season.

When it comes to diet, Summer Tanagers are famous bee and wasp specialists. Nevertheless, they do like a few berries for a fully rounded diet—mulberries among their favorites. It's part of their usual behavior.

May 27

Sorting the Evidence

It's my pleasure to begin the day about 6:15 a.m. or so watching birds. Sometimes the watch takes place while I'm standing at the kitchen window or, more leisurely, sitting in my recliner. Some days, like today, however, the outdoors calls and I situate myself in one of several vantage points to try to keep tabs on who's here and what's going on, which habitat draws which species, and what in my native habitat feeds birds. This morning was one of those outdoors times.

The watch started with more or less routine observations of birds and their particular behaviors. Across the hayfield, tom turkeys strutted and gobbled, touting their respective dominant positions among members of the harems. Crows picked in the newly planted field, probably devouring whatever type of grain the neighbor had just planted. A Red-shouldered Hawk hunted along the edge where the pasture meets the woodlot, dropping to the ground before swooping off, no doubt with breakfast in her talons. Her big size told me she's a she.

Then I saw something amiss with a nest box. Last week I watched Tree Swallows feed nestlings cozied in the box. Now, though, from its opening, a suspiciously long strand of grass hung down, a telltale sign suggesting something had been carrying additional nesting materials into this box. Had House Sparrows invaded? Did they kill the nestlings and try to move in to raise their own brood? It's one nasty behavior of House Sparrows, those nonnative birds that threaten the very existence of our native cavity nesters. Or was I being too harsh? Had the nestlings fledged and the adults were no longer tending them? Catching bugs on the wing in the manner in which all Tree Swallows feed takes skill, practice, and coordination. Until such muscular development is complete, fledglings need continuing food supplies from their parents. Fledglings don't go from nest box to independence in a day or so. This didn't bode well. What happened?

That question will not likely ever be answered with total assurance, but launching into my detective mode, I started putting pieces together.

As I watched, one Tree Swallow sat for a long 12 minutes on a post within a half dozen feet of the nest box. Eventually, a Tree Swallow face appeared in the nest box opening. The two sat motionless for some minutes before the female flew out and into the willow tree within yards of the box. The male followed. Within minutes, fluttering activity gave away the secret. The swallows were mating! After a figure-eight nuptial flight across the field, they returned to their respective positions, the presumed female entering the nest box and disappearing.

Okay, they're re-nesting. They're using the same nest box. That doesn't bode well, either. Typically a cavity that has housed a brood through fledging is way too messy for adults

A male Tree Swallow perches on an old fence post near the pair's chosen nest box, protecting his territory as well as his mate nesting inside.

to consider it suitable for another brood. Until it's almost time for fledging, Tree Swallows, as well as certain other songbirds, will carry away fecal sacks—sort of an avian version of dirty diapers—to prevent odors from attracting predators. Only during the last few days do nestlings defecate so much that parents can't keep up with housekeeping efforts. Thus, by the time the babies actually fledge, the nest is soiled beyond reuse. I made the trek across the hayfield to see. A quick check verified what I feared: This box hadn't housed fledged birds. It was still clean.

With their babies destroyed and the season still early, these swallows decided—instinctively, no doubt—that they had time to re-nest, raise a family, feed them to maturity, and have them ready to migrate south, perhaps, come fall, as far as southern Mexico. I'm pleased that we've been able to offer them suitable housing, but I absolutely despise the fact that House Sparrows have almost certainly caused them so much futile work—up to a week or so of rigorous nest building, up to a week of egg laying, eleven to twenty days of egg incubating, and fifteen to twenty days of nestling feeding—for naught. The female laid up to seven eggs, equaling almost as much as her own body weight, only to have House Sparrows, by extension, deplete her energy resources. Of course, the babies apparently didn't fledge successfully, so the feeding time was reduced. Still, we humans have done some mighty mean stuff to our birds, in this case by introducing foreign species into our birds' native habitats.

My job now is—as it's always been—to prevent House Sparrows from breeding on our property. I can't make much of a dent in the world's population of birds that are indirectly killing our native birds, but I can keep them from expanding their populations here. My ire motivates me.

Birds Do *That*?

Hummingbirds can't walk. While this tiny agile bird can hover, fly backward, even fly upside down, it cannot walk or hop. Its very short legs and muscular structure prevent it from doing anything more than a bit of a shuffle. According to hummingbirdcentral.com, if a hummer lands on a twig and wants to position itself 6 inches farther to the left or right, it must lift up, fly over, and land. No bouncing along the way!

May 28

Noting a First

Birds never cease to amaze me. Okay, that's a cliché, but this morning I witnessed something that gave me pause and made me want to share my amazement.

Depending on whose reference one consults, authorities believe hummingbirds obtain essential protein by snaring bugs on the fly, with bugs being between 50 and 80 percent of their diet. It's well-documented behavior. One research team, in fact, tracked a single female hummingbird for two weeks during nesting season and never saw the bird nectar. She ate only tiny bugs.

Most hummingbird hosts have likely witnessed the behavior, a hummer doing a little flycatching—perching on an open branch, darting out after a bug, and returning to the perch to await another passing bug—not an especially uncommon sight. This morning, however, I caught sight of a male hummer, his gorget glistening in the just-after-dawn light, hovering. Oddly, however, there were no flowers or even any vegetation near where he hovered. Why would he waste energy hovering in a single spot, turning side to side, moving a few inches right or left, up or down, but hanging almost as if suspended in that one spot? What could possibly attract his attention in the middle of vacant space?

I raised my binocular to spy on him, to sort out the purpose of his behavior. Because I was about 100 feet away, the magnified view let me see in detail the hummer's behavior—and its cause. A swarm of gnats encompassing a space about the size of a large dinner plate was amassed at the spot, and the hummer was moving around and within the horde, plucking bugs at will. Because the little throng remained compact and continued to hover in the same spot, the hummer needed only to waltz around the throng's edges, gliding in and out among the mass. He and the gnats continued their dance for some minutes until, I suspect, the hummer's little belly was filled.

What a sight! A first for me.

What if I'd used insecticides in the yard?

May 29

Taking a Census

A leisurely 2-hour morning yard-sit helped zero in on what's here. Now that migration has mostly ended, with a few flycatchers and thrushes still missing in action, the nesters have by and large taken their places amid the habitat, merging finally with our year-round residents in what seems a relatively peaceful coexistence.

By 6:15 a.m. I'd settled into a metal lawn chair under the shade of a fifty-year-old dogwood tree, my back to the rising sun and my eyes on the distance, our west property line fencerow immediately in front and the neighbor's hayfield, pasture, and agricultural fields stretching toward the even more distant fields to the horizon. Woodlots dot the expanse, mostly areas too wet to farm, left to the wild and leaving me to wonder how long the habitat will remain before greed calls for cutting the trees and tilling the land to expand crop production.

An Acadian Flycatcher hunts from a vantage point. The bird, similar to many other flycatchers in its family, is best identified by its "pizza!" song.

A male Eastern Bluebird feeds a soft, ripe mulberry to his fledgling. Since bluebirds swallow berries whole, they look for relatively small fruits.

But this morning I left those worries and concentrated instead on what I could identify among the birds—who's doing what and why?

Tom turkeys, strutting across the newly planted corn field, gobbled their usual calls to their harems. Barn Swallows, Tree Swallows, Chimney Swifts, and Purple Martins made passes over the hayfield, snaring bugs on the wing. Flycatchers have finally all arrived and are singing on territory, including Eastern Phoebe, Eastern Wood-pewee, and Great Crested Flycatcher. A new flycatcher joined the family this morning as I heard three Acadian Flycatchers call simultaneously from our little woodland patch and from the neighbor's woods to the east. Blue-gray Gnatcatchers, foraging heavily in the native bald cypress trees, are feeding a brood, probably about ready to fledge. Beyond the flycatchers, the Yellow-throated Warbler sings daily from his high perches, moving around the perimeter of his territory. Waxwings feed in the serviceberry. Bluebirds, singing, corralled their fledglings first at the serviceberry and then at the mulberry tree, feeding them nutritious fruits. Yellow-billed Cuckoos called back and forth, probably competing for territory. One even took up a song perch in the front yard, just yards from where I sat.

Eventually I heard all six of the woodpeckers, including a fair amount of hammering. While I saw a good many cardinals, they were almost all males—a sure indication that females are on the nest. One late bloomer, though, was gathering grasses, pulling off just the right length to fit that perfect spot she obviously had in mind. Chipping Sparrows maintained a monotone staccato from three points in the yard. White-breasted Nuthatches gave their nasal "yank" calls, probably keeping track of their fledglings. The House Wren nesting in the garden continues his nearly nonstop singing. Indigo Buntings sang their say-everything-twice songs from various shrubs. Doves cooed in the distance, but scolding Blue Jays mostly drowned them out. Since they fledged their brood some weeks ago, Carolina Wrens have moved to the woods, distancing themselves from the interlopers. I suspect they've fled our yard to avoid the mean-spirited House Wrens. The Song Sparrow moved silently along the fencerow where I know the pair nested, but the absence of song suggested they're into another brood now.

In short, everything that's going to stay for the summer has likely arrived—finally. Breeding behavior has peaked. Some species have already set up housekeeping, many already incubating, some feeding nestlings. Our regulars are well along with their breeding cycles, too, some already tending a second brood. So it's one giant nursery out there! Everything is in a family way.

3 Acadian Flycatcher
Species: 106 total in the yard to date for the year.

May 30

Accounting for Big Hummer Increase

With remnants of a tropical storm pouring buckets in our part of the country, this morning proved a challenge for hummingbirds. Their behavior reflected the crisis. All-night and early morning rains washed nectar from blossoms and downed bugs, so by mid-morning hummers faced a serious plight. At any given moment they're already living on the edge, their high metabolism feeding their frenetic lifestyle requiring sustenance about every 20 minutes. Without nourishment in a timely fashion, they face trouble. As a result, the four one-cup feeders that have been hanging nearly unattended outside my kitchen and office windows during the past weeks were suddenly the hot spots in the yard. For that dramatic and somewhat unsettling reason, I saw more hummers today than I've seen so far this season. Sometimes six at a time dashed after one another around a single feeder, one occasionally taking a quick sip before being chased off by another. Both males and females have now joined the frenzy, so if the rain continues, I'll need to add more feeders to let more birds feed simultaneously. Once females begin nesting, having a reliable food source nearby often means the difference between nesting success and failure.

May 31

Loving the Symphony

I spent much of the morning tending flowerbeds while keeping an eye and an ear open to the birds around me. Bluebirds and robins scolded me for working too near the serviceberry tree, disturbing their forays for food. The usual birds sang from their usual territories, clearly defining boundaries with invisible lines. How important this singing, a behavior unique to birds!

One soloist, however, doesn't sing as regularly as his colleagues, so hearing the Warbling Vireo in the old oak tree at the edge of the neighbor's hayfield made me stop to listen. No weed pulling or branch snipping should interfere with that distinctive namesake song. As luck would have it, while he sang a Purple Martin flew zigzag across the hayfield, gleaning bugs on the wing, singing his sweet burbling song. How he can sing and eat at the same time makes no sense to me, but he has the system perfected. For me, though, the duet of the Warbling Vireo and the Purple Martin was a first. Who would ever have considered the two together, how their warbles and burbles might mingle into such a lovely song? Surely some composer somewhere has put that combination on paper, played by a symphony, awarded rich applause.

June

A female Yellow Warbler weaves the foundation for her nest, tucking strands of seed fluff in place.

Really great products, like a nest, have the design built into them from the beginning, instead of slapped on at the end."

—John Maeda (1966–), American designer and technologist

June 1

Adding to the Census

My May 29 census was missing a few birds that obviously have taken up summer residence here, including the Red-eyed Vireo that sang almost nonstop for a couple of hours this morning. The Northern Parula continues to serenade his mate somewhere among the pine trees. Nuthatches and towhees have both fledged their young, and perhaps they'll both try for a second brood. Somewhere in our little patch of woods, the Acadian Flycatcher added his two cents, talking about "pizza," or at least that's what his otherwise unremarkable song sounds like to me. Barn Swallows hunted behind the house, sweeping the air for bugs. More than the usual number gathered for the hunt, so some kind of bugs must have hatched and lifted with air currents to a comfortable cruising altitude for the birds. I love watching them swoop and dive. So, in spite of their absence from the original tally, these six regulars are still regular, behaving like the breeding birds they are, sometimes tucked quietly away, taking care of family matters.

The coldest April was followed by the hottest May on record, breaking the record established in 1934. What will June hold for us? Scientists with The Nature Conservancy say that in our area going forward, we'll have heavier precipitation in winter and spring, hotter year-round weather with droughts in summer and fall, and more severe weather events throughout the year. How will the changes affect the birds? I'll be watching.

June 2

Remembering Green Herons

I heard it before I saw it, calling out its sharp "skeow," and it's become a regular flyover most mornings. A single Green Heron winged south to north about 7:30 a.m., and I have to wonder where it's headed—or where it's been. Granted, there are some sizable lakes in the area, but none seem wooded enough or marshy enough to offer a Green Heron its ideal nest site. Obviously, however, I'm not privy to its preferences!

Each time it flies over, though, I'm reminded of a pair that five years ago nested among the cattails alongside our neighbor's cattle pond. Yes, the pond was stocked with

Birds Do *That*?

Crow families work together. Ornithologist Lawrence Kilham was the first to describe cooperative American Crows back in the 1970s after he observed helpers bringing nesting materials to a female—too much nesting material, it seemed. Over two weeks, however, the female used the overabundance of materials to construct her nest while the helpers backed off and waited. When the eggs hatched, the helpers started delivering food to the babies and continued helping with feeding chores two weeks after the babies fledged. Scientists now know this scenario is common among crows. The largest extended crow family recorded included fifteen members.

Green Herons nest throughout our area, usually alongside a lake or stream. This one forages at our water feature, snatching little fish suitable for nestlings' small gullets.

fish—sizable, skillet-size fish. In our yard, however, designed to welcome drinking and bathing songbirds, our little yard-feature puddle was—and still is—stocked with small native fish. That summer we puzzled over the fish's decline. They seemed to be disappearing, but no dead fish floated to the surface. Strange, we thought. Whatever could be wrong? Then, mystery solved! Hubby caught the heron in the act as it lifted off, a fish in its beak, to feed its young, the little fish the perfect size for babies.

June 3

Seeing More House Finches

While the numbers of House Finches have remained constant over the winter and into the spring, in the past two weeks, the numbers have more than doubled. It's a clue about their current behavior. While males continue to be in the minority, there's an even greater gap

The bright plumage of a male House Finch serves as standard measure for females evaluating his quality as a mate.

A nondescript drab female House Finch blends in with other streaky brown birds, but her drab plumage is especially beneficial for camouflage on the nest.

between the numbers of males and females. In fact, there's a significant influx of females. Or not. Here's the missing information: When fledglings arrive in the yard, they all look like females. In short, there's an influx of babies. It's certainly been a good nesting season for them, and I doubt that the season is over. They will surely re-nest.

June 4

Witnessing an Attack

As we were out and about today, we stopped for lunch in a shopping center where light poles punctuate the parking lot at regular intervals. Behavior ensued that makes a good story, which I'll share here.

A Northern Mockingbird took offense at an American Crow that landed on one of the poles and promptly chased the crow from its perch, following after it as it lit on another nearby pole. The crow landed on one side while the mockingbird landed on the other, their size difference amusing, the mockingbird dwarfed by a crow twice the mocker's length and outweighing the 2-ounce mocker by more than a pound! After a brief but surprising standoff, given the size difference, the mockingbird jabbed at the crow. After several such aggressive but generally ineffectual attacks, the crow, probably nothing more than mildly annoyed, finally lifted off. But the battle raged, and the mocker was right behind, pecking the crow's rump, following closely, continuing to close in, peck, drop back, close in, peck, and finally close in and peck the crow's head. It was a persistent, no-nonsense attack that surely said, "Get away from my nest." No, I didn't see a nest, but that's the only reasonable scenario that would prompt such an attack. And of course, it all had to do with a crow's common behavior. Crows love to steal eggs or nestlings, not necessarily to satisfy their own appetites but to provide a rich protein meal for their nestlings. Only strong and strong-willed smaller birds can fend off the larger crow, but obviously this mocker had the determination, guts, and agility to stem the onslaught and protect its family.

Of course, it's not unheard of for birds, not just mockingbirds, to wage war against impressive odds, behavior triggered by the birds' intense instinct to protect a nest and its contents. Indeed, mockingbirds will attack cats, dogs, and even people who stray too close to their nests, but other birds display a similar devil-may-care attitude toward defense. For instance, I've seen hummingbirds dive after hawks when the little guys perceive the raptors threaten their territory. I've seen Brown Thrashers take on a king snake, pecking it, leaving marks in its back, as it raided their nest. It's not that the birds know no fear; their instincts are to protect their nest, eggs, and offspring at all costs.

June 5

Noticing Chippers

Sitting quietly in the yard this evening, I watched a Chipping Sparrow working its way along the rock driveway. Vying for title of "Most Lovely Sparrow," it wears a crisp rusty cap atop an outfit that looks freshly washed and pressed. Since the sexes look alike, I can only guess who's who, but I like to think the one I watched this evening was a female. She

A female Northern Cardinal breaks off a length of vine stem to suit her exacting preference, the stem to be woven into a new nest, likely her second of the season.

was checking each blade of grass in the driveway, scattered there from recent mowing. Her behavior defined meticulous. As she eyed each grass blade, she made a quick decision whether to pick it up or move on. Occasionally, she actually picked up a blade, seeming to measure its heft. Each time she dropped it. Surely choosing just the right building blocks for her nest, exactly what was she checking? Was one blade too curved? Too thin? Too thick? Too long? Too short? She searched, scratched, hefted, dropped, moved ahead, and repeated the careful search. Eventually she moved beyond my line of sight, still searching for the perfect blade to suit her needs.

Earlier today I watched a female Northern Cardinal gather nest materials, too. Typical of her kind, she aimed to break tiny twigs from their sources rather than pluck seemingly suitable ones from the ground. I suspect twigs the birds break off themselves are more sturdy, less likely to have been softened by rain. She also found dried vines wound among the brambles and sought to tug those loose, too. Sometimes, though, the breaking-off process seemed a bit torturous as the female leaned back or twisted left or right in an effort to make a clean break. But she prevailed.

June 6

Ogling Hummingbirds

Hummingbird populations have probably quadrupled here in the past week. Maybe the rain a week ago that washed nectar from the flowers and drove bugs to the ground compelled hummers to expand their food search and ultimately led them to my feeders. Or maybe the last of the migrants have only now arrived. Whatever the situation, my four one-cup feeders don't last the day, so I've added three one-quart feeders. Given the spiffy appearance of all the birds, they're obviously prime. Some look small, maybe first-year birds, so perhaps they're visiting feeders more frequently than older birds that better know the flower patches. Authorities tell us that hummers remember the exact locations of specific flower patches, even after their arduous trip to Central America and back.

I know they remember feeder locations from one year to the next. In fact, it's an astonishing behavior I witnessed myself. My mother used to feed hummers, pouring out a gallon or more of nectar daily during peak season in late August. After she moved to an assisted-living facility and I cleaned out the house, I'd see hummers buzzing the spots where her feeders once hung. The rather heart-wrenching experience still tugs at me, knowing the birds may well have been counting on her handouts to support a successful nesting season, or maybe some migrants counted on her handouts to get them through the next leg of their migration home. I still tear up thinking about the ramifications . . .

This evening as I watered the outdoor flower pots, planted now with tropical blossoms attractive to hummingbirds, I heard the "varoom, varoom" of a male hummingbird displaying. When a male finds a female perched, he will perform a courtship flight that involves his flying high, swooping down almost to the ground and then back up again, following a U-shaped trajectory. A tiny notch on one feather of each wing causes male Ruby-throats to emit a distinct wing noise during flight. The intensified speed during courtship flight, however, exaggerates the sound so that "varoom, varoom" is noticeable to us mere humans even some distance away. The speed is designed, of course, to impress the female, as is the flashing of his gorget as light plays across his throat during the flight. This evening I never saw the female, no doubt tucked in quietly on a branch among protective vegetation. Whether she was impressed I don't know, but I was! It's an eye-popping behavior to watch.

June 7

Hearing Flutes

Oh my! How wonderful! I had the pleasure of listening to the lofty "ee-oh-lay" notes of a pair of flutes this evening! The melody emanated from our little patch of woods, and the behavior meant something special: The reclusive Wood Thrush is surely nesting somewhere nearby. He wouldn't be singing here this time of the season if that weren't the case. If it were earlier in the season, he could be singing to attract a mate, perhaps without success and then moving on. If it were later, he could be singing (but with less enthusiasm) as he wandered back to his winter home in Central America. Now, though, it's the perfect time for him to be on territory, serenading a mate on the nest. True, he could have already experienced nest failure and is attempting a second effort. Still, it means that he's nesting—or at least planning to nest—nearby. Wood Thrushes are becoming so rare that just to hear him this one evening lifts my heart. Sadly, their numbers are threatened by Brown-headed Cowbird parasitism.

Nothing else locally can match this king of song, although his cousin the Hermit Thrush, which breeds to our north, has a similar melody. Because thrushes have the human equivalent of a double voice box, they can produce two notes at the same time, essentially

My personal favorite singer, the bird I call the "king of song," a Wood Thrush sings to defend his woodland territory.

singing a duet with themselves. No wonder their songs are so lovely, so enchanting, reverberating through the woodland. What a great way to end the day, hearing his flute notes drifting with the breeze.

June 8

Understanding the Quiet

Stepping out the door for my usual 6:30 a.m. time-alone-in-the-yard wandering, the quiet surprised me. Perhaps it shouldn't have, but that old cliché about "deafening silence" came to mind. No, it wasn't truly silent, but the dawn chorus is no more. The birds that sang robustly each morning for almost two months now have either gone quiet or have softened the urgency of their melodies.

There's reason for that behavior. Likely without exception, any bird here now is breeding here. Most have chosen mates, defended a territory large or small, and advanced to the family stage. Early migrants, in fact, have already fledged a brood and most likely have re-nested, working on a second brood. Whether birds are still incubating a first or second set of eggs, the advanced breeding activities mean there's no reason for the male to sing his best and loudest to find a girl and mark his real estate. Sure, he still sings, but more quietly, less frequently, and closer to home turf, mostly defending territory and making soft talk to stay in touch with his mate.

A Northern Parula visits the bubble rock for a drink and a splash.

After about an hour, however, having chalked up thirty-eight species within my hearing, it's obvious the yard was anything but silent—just quiet. Not all the songs and calls came from the immediate yard, but all were well within earshot and readily identifiable. Given the variety of habitat both on and adjoining our little patch of property, each species has found its preferred comfort zone, some at ground level, some at mid-level, some high in the canopy, and some in cavities.

This evening, movement around the bubble rock in the backyard caught my eye. Something little. Something with yellow. Something fast. A binocular view revealed a Northern Parula hopping from branch to twig, approaching with caution, coming for a bath. This morning he was singing in the front yard, somewhere within the arms of the maple tree, but I could never see him, only enjoy his song. This evening, though, he made a bold, right-out-in-the-open appearance.

Once the weather turns hot and humid, as it has here already, birds love the opportunity to clean their feathers. It's a behavior that draws birds to the bubble rock with its flowing, recirculating water. Maybe the bath cools them. Maybe clean feathers are cool. Maybe birds just need a break from household chores. This was a fine-looking male, the mossy color on his back, in my opinion at least, being one of the most lovely field marks of the species. And this was a bird loving his bath. He splashed. He squatted in the water and fluttered, leaning side to side. He leaned forward and wallowed up to his neck. He soaked himself, his feathers finally getting so wet he was nearly unrecognizable. Then he flew a few feet to the sweetbay magnolia, shook himself free of droplets, preened briefly, and flew from the yard. Surely he felt better. And I enjoyed the little peek into his private life and his bathing behavior.

June 9

Talking Turkey

What a surprise! Early this morning three tom turkeys gobbled once or twice, one from the hayfield, one from the woods well to our west, and one from the woodlot just north of the hayfield. Since it's become a common occurrence to hear a few gobbles most mornings, I barely made the mental note that they were calling and went on with my gardening. By 8 a.m., ready to quit the garden, I turned to the lawn chairs under the dogwood for a cooldown, a spot that affords a 180-degree view of the hayfield and its environs. Three hen turkeys picked through the grasses nearby. Then two toms wandered into view from the north. Another popped up from just over the rise. Then another and another, and finally fourteen turkeys wandered toward an invisible central hub, gathering without seeming to gather, a couple of toms strutting, the rest feeding as they walked. A few clucks but no gobbles, the entire group at ease. Then as slowly as they came together, they separated, meandering back from where they came, the whole process taking about a leisurely hour.

The behavior left me puzzled. It's the second week of June. Nesting season. Around these parts, tom turkeys gather their harems by April. Egg laying follows for a two-week period in May, each hen laying one egg per day, slipping onto the scrape-on-the-ground nest only long enough to lay her egg and then quickly departing, hoping to avoid predators. When she's finished laying, perhaps up to a dozen eggs, she begins incubating, rarely leaving the nest even to eat for the twenty-eight days it takes for eggs to hatch. Within 12 to 24 hours of hatching, poults leave the nest with the hen and follow her wherever she goes, imitating her behavior, eating on their own from the get-go.

Last September 17, a Wild Turkey hen closely attended her young poult as the two wandered across the hayfield.

Okay, then, why were fourteen turkeys, a mixed flock of hens and toms, roaming the hayfield together, minus any poults? Last year we photographed hens with their several-weeks-old poults on June 30.

Granted, we've had a cold, wet spring. While length of day triggers turkeys' hormones to breed, cold, wet weather can retard the breeding process. So maybe hens are only now slipping away to lay their one egg a day, and incubation, delayed by weather, is yet to come.

Granted, the cold, wet spring could have other effects: Perhaps the subfreezing temps affected the viability of eggs, especially given the fact that hens lay eggs and desert them until they've laid the entire clutch. The eggs lie unprotected for as long as two weeks.

Granted, we have more predators than I care to think about, any of which could destroy a clutch of eggs: raccoons, foxes, coyotes, bobcats, skunks, opossums, dogs, and crows, for instance. Once eggs hatch, those same predators can take flightless poults, as can hawks. While young turkeys can fly to low roosts by two weeks of age, they are highly vulnerable during those first two weeks. So maybe every hen has lost her clutch or her brood, although it seems a bit preposterous to me that every hen could lose everything.

Granted, given nest failure, some turkeys will re-nest, thus bringing poults onto the scene as late as August. So maybe even if all or most of the hens lost everything, there's still hope. Last year we photographed a single hen with a single month-old poult on September 17.

Over the next week or so, I think we'll figure out what's what. I fervently hope I don't see the hens for several weeks. Their absence would mean they're just late with the nesting season, incubating late, and all is well in the turkey world.

June 10

Sorting Swallows

The behavior was telling: fifty to seventy-five swallows in a loose congregation, all of them swooping and darting in a feeding frenzy to snap up as many bugs as possible from a high-altitude bug swarm. After some minutes a few birds darted away, perhaps heading to a nearby nest to feed hungry nestlings. Simultaneously, more swallows joined the flock. With all the comings and goings, counting them became a matter of frustration. I quit trying.

The sizable throng consisted mostly of Barn Swallows, but readily identifiable within the group were also Tree Swallows and Purple Martins. Then I spotted a couple that were different. Brown. No forked tail. No flashy iridescence. Whitish undersides. Smaller than Barn Swallows, way smaller than Purple Martins, about the same size as Tree Swallows. They were Northern Rough-winged Swallows!

We've had them in the yard before, but they were never common, so it was a pleasure watching them navigate within the high-level feeding-frenzy mob.

They're called "northern" to separate them from their cousins, the Southern Rough-winged Swallows found in Central and South America. They're called "rough-winged" for small serrations on their outermost wing feathers—not that anyone could ever see those serrations without the bird in hand. They're mostly identified by their overall drabness—brown back, wings, tail, and head, and a dingy throat fading to a white belly. The description doesn't sound very fabulous—and it isn't. Still, they're bug-eating machines and wonderful to have as part of the habitat.

Given this mixed assembly of swallows today, I found myself curious about how they compare to one another and to the two additional swallows found in the area, although not in our yard. Among them, the ancestral chart places Bank Swallows as our oldest and most primitive. Like their burrowing ancestors, they excavate into mud banks and raise their families at the ends of the burrows.

Next on the ancestral chart come the swallows called "cavity adopters," the birds that adopt a "found" cavity, even man-made cavities, in which to nest, including Tree Swallows, Purple Martins, and Rough-winged Swallows. While mostly we think of adopted cavities as those we provide, we've spied Rough-winged Swallows evaluating cavities in flood-eroded mud banks. Those, too, would be "found" cavities. The birds didn't excavate the cavities themselves.

Barn Swallows and Cliff Swallows hold the most recent spots on the ancestral charts. Unlike the others, they build their own mud nests. Barn Swallows create cup-like nests with mud and sticks, usually pasting nests on the side of a building near the roof line, sometimes on porches, in carports, under decks, and, of course, in barns. The most advanced of the swallows, Cliff Swallows go fancy with a construction referred to as mud retort-shaped nests. The term "retort" refers to those glass chemistry-lab distilling containers that have a spherical shape with a long downward-pointing neck. It's a good description of the shape of the Cliff Swallow's nest. They're also colony nesters, constructing their amazing mud architecture under bridges and on other high structures that somehow, in their minds at least, seem like cliffs. Unique behaviors among unique birds!

A Northern Rough-winged Swallow perches in front of a "found" cavity, a hole in a creek's dirt bank.

A Cliff Swallow brings bugs to its nestlings snuggled in a retort-shaped mud cavity nest that is "glued" to the underside of a railroad bridge. At left, an incubating female is barely visible through the opening.

A Barn Swallow builds her cup-shaped nest under a deck, her mud-saliva combination "gluing" the nest in place.

6 Rough-winged Swallow
Species: 107 total in the yard to date for the year.

Birds Do *That?*

Crows use tools. In the *New Scientist Daily News Letter*, scientists at Lund University in Sweden observed a crow slip a thin wooden stick into a metal nut and fly off, carrying the tool and the object with it. While earlier research revealed crows using tools for such activities as removing otherwise inaccessible food items from a container, this experience involved a novel tool for a novel use. Scientists concluded, "This is typically seen as a hallmark of complex cognitive abilities." Smart birds.

June 11

Singling Out a Flycatcher

Flycatchers have a lot in common: A good many of them look very much alike with few if any field marks to single them out in a lineup, and a small number can be distinguished only by song. Think Eastern Phoebe and Eastern Wood-pewee and all the Empidonax members, including Least, Alder, Willow, Acadian, and Yellow-bellied Flycatchers. Without a careful look, then, maybe checking for wing bars or a view of the bill for different-colored upper and lower mandibles, and in some cases an ear for their songs, they're impossible to separate. The Great Crested Flycatcher, on the other hand, stands out in the crowd. It's bigger than most other flycatchers and has a bright yellow belly, the color rising well up onto its chest, and a russet-colored tail and wing feathers. In spite of its name, it doesn't really have all that much of a crest, but when agitated, the bird certainly makes its crest noticeable. The sexes look alike.

For a small bird—7 inches long and weighing only an ounce—the Great Crested is nevertheless considered aggressive. Well, aggressive behavior for a flycatcher, that is. During the past month it's been displaying that aggression around the yard during grand chases that involve two individuals flying almost in tandem, but not as any kind of loving pair! Such squawking and darting and diving! Now, though, their differences apparently having been settled, no doubt over who gets the girl and who gets which territory, they've become more gentle—and genteel! This evening, one came to our little homemade bubble rock for a bath—or more like a thorough soaking. Its behavior made me chuckle as it wiggled about in the half-inch water flow until its belly was wet, then flew to an adjoining perch to preen. The preening lasted only a few seconds before the bird was back splashing, wallowing, fluttering, fanning its tail, spreading its wings, giving the bath its all. Then back to the perch, this time to preen for several minutes. Birds like a sheltered perch near the bath so they can dry off a bit, fluff themselves, rearrange their feathers, and prepare for safer flight.

In spite of the fact that they're flycatchers, Great Cresteds show a penchant for fruit, so they've been hanging out in the mulberry tree, its fruit now likely less attractive given the end-of-season small size. Still, these flycatchers enjoy the morsels on a daily basis. Otherwise, though, they're high-canopy birds. I've never seen one on the ground. It never hops, never walks, but flies everywhere it goes, even short distances. Given their lofty preferences, it's special to have them down at eye level feeding on fruit or near the ground bathing.

A Great Crested Fly-catcher raises its crest in agitation, possibly because of my presence near its nest—although I never saw the cavity.

Now, here's hoping this guy or gal has found a cavity suitable for its nursery. As our only cavity-nesting flycatcher, the Great-cresteds face some difficulty these days because folks cut down every dead or dying tree and chop off every dead or dying branch that might otherwise offer a cavity. Competition is keen—even for an aggressive 1-ounce flycatcher.

June 12

Catching Up with Fledglings

Yesterday and today we had fledgling Downy and Hairy Woodpeckers in the yard. The female Hairy was at the suet feeder poking suet chunks into the gaping beak of her off-spring. The Downy fledgling was all eyes on the seed cake, looking for a quick meal, but he didn't quite "get it" and flew off without pecking at any of the seeds. Since he was alone, I surmised that one of the adults had brought him to the seed source earlier. Somehow he probably thought that if he sat there, food would make itself available. Sometimes I'm amused by the behavior, wondering if I'm interpreting their actions correctly. Surely these little guys are smarter than that, right? Otherwise, how would they ever survive?

Both Hairy and Downy male fledglings are recognizable by a quirky little field mark: They wear red on the tops of their heads, rather than on the backs of their heads as do adult males. Female fledglings can be identified by

A fledgling male Downy Woodpecker (as well as the fledgling male Hairy Woodpecker) wears red on the top of his head. Only when the fledgling molts into adult plumage does the red move from the top to the back of his head.

tails noticeably shorter than those of adults and by their crisp white plumage. White plumage on adults will look worn, almost dingy, as a result of their popping in and out of the nest cavity during frequent feedings. If adults have fed nestlings during rainy weather, they will look even more dingy since the tannic acid from wet tree bark at the cavity entrance will likely stain their white plumage into shades of tan.

June 13

Zeroing In on Dickcissels

While driving through a nearby agricultural area this afternoon, we heard Dickcissels singing and stopped to enjoy. They're here only for the summer, spending their winters primarily in northern South America. Birds of open grasslands, their typical behavior is to perch atop the tallest vegetation, maybe on nothing more than a stout weed or perhaps the upper branches of a low shrub, singing from the vantage point to mark their breeding territory. Their song, however, has such an insect-like quality that I sometimes fail to recognize it as a bird's. Some think he says his name, as in "dick dick dick ciss ciss ciss." Well, okay, maybe in a stretch.

Since they dine on seeds and insects, I was surprised to find them vocalizing from the shrubby bank of a ditch cutting through mostly sterile habitat. Agricultural fields are generally farmed to the road edges, sprayed heavily to eliminate insects, and completely cleared of growth along ditches, fencerows, or property lines. These farm practices have destroyed significant habitat for birds, including grassland birds like Dickcissels. The singing Dickcissels caused me to wonder, then, where these little guys were finding seeds and insects. Surely a ditch bank through an area of seemingly poor habitat wouldn't serve as a suitable nesting locale. Even if the habitat supported the adult pair, what would they feed their babies?

Perhaps part of the answer lay in what's across the road. There, a couple hundred acres of farmland was put into the Conservation Reserve Enhancement Program (CREP) and is reverting to forest, the emerging growth providing attractive habitat that, after only four short years, is proving to be rich habitat, brimming with birds. During winter bird counts, we find a wonderful array of White-crowned Sparrows, White-throated Sparrows,

A male Dickcissel, demonstrating habitual behavior, perches atop the tallest twig available.

Dark-eyed Juncos, and Northern Bobwhites. Now, as we listened, we heard not only Dickcissels but Indigo Buntings and, in the distance, an Eastern Meadowlark. I'm guessing the new habitat has filled so completely that birds are spilling over into less desirable habitat such as where we first spotted these Dickcissels singing. What a statement about the need for habitat for birds to survive! And what a tribute to the cliché: "Build it and they will come!" Restoration efforts everywhere are garnering the same results.

June 14

Offering Pet Hair

Tufted Titmice have a reputation for an amusing behavior: plucking hair from wherever they can find it, yanking it from sleeping dogs, grazing horses, shedding cats, even snoozing humans. Naturalists who have analyzed used titmouse nests have found all manner of fur and hair, including that from raccoons, opossums, dogs, fox squirrels, red squirrels, rabbits, horses, cows, cats, mice, woodchucks, and humans. Having learned about their penchant for gathering hair to line their nests, I've taken to gathering fur from our cat's brushings. Stuffing the fur in an old onion bag, I tie it top and bottom to strips on the trellis outside the kitchen window. Without anchoring the bag at both ends, it flaps in the wind and is tricky for birds' landing, clinging, and gathering. Hoping to call attention to the offering, I pull a few tufts through the bag's holes.

Late this afternoon I caught the titmouse hanging upside down, pulling and yanking and tugging and gathering so much cat fur that finally I could see only the bird's legs and feet. How could that poor creature see to fly?

Similarly, chickadees also appreciate the gift of hair or fur for lining their nests. Earlier today a Carolina Chickadee also visited the fur-hair combo bag and, in a much more mannerly and delicate fashion than the titmouse, gathered a beak full of hair, ultimately appearing as if it had a massive moustache. After the four trips that I managed to witness, the bird apparently had everything it needed for nest lining.

For both birds this behavior probably represents a re-nesting attempt. Both raise only a single brood per year, so at this mid-June date, I have to assume both birds had nest failure and are going for a second attempt.

For anyone planning to put out similar nesting materials, keep in mind that human hair, particularly more than an inch or two

A Carolina Chickadee finds proffered cat hair perfect for nest building and gathers it by the beakful, leaving me to wonder how it can then see to fly.

long, can entangle a baby bird and cause its death. Likewise, dryer lint is a no-no. It retains moisture, so in a rain it will collapse and destroy a nest's structure.

June 15

Comparing Geese

This evening thirty-four Canada Geese flew over, south to north, high enough to suggest they weren't locals on a lake-hopping escapade, rather they were moving a distance. The mere fact that they were in flight, however, is more significant than the altitude of that flight. Canada Geese, like other waterfowl, engage in an unusual molting behavior: They lose all their flight feathers simultaneously, rendering them—as one might guess—flightless until wing feathers re-grow. For most waterfowl, this period of flightlessness requires birds to stay mostly in the water, huddling in protective vegetation as far from threats (especially human) as they can. After all, other than swimming (they're not very fast), running (they're really awkward on land), or diving (not all waterfowl can dive), they have virtually no escape route during this period of molt.

As Mother Nature planned it, however, the flightless period coincides with the time during which their ducklings and goslings are small and also flightless. Parents protecting their young have no reason to be airborne. Then, about the time the young are ready to fly, the adults are also ready to fly. Even when adults complete the molt and can fly with ease, they never leave their young unattended. So they're earthbound by necessity.

This evening's flight, however, means these birds have completed their molt and are without progeny. They may have been unmated; they may have been infertile; they may have paired with an infertile mate; they may have lost their eggs to bad weather or predators; they may have lost their brood to predators like foxes, coyotes, raccoons, and especially, turtles. That the group was traveling, their altitude offering testimony to the length of their journey, verified their obvious release—for better or for worse—from any family responsibilities. They announced their approach long before I saw them, their typical in-flight communication in full effect. Pairs stay in touch with one another during flight, his honking deeper than hers. The multiple pairs and perhaps unpaired members of the flock certainly had lots to discuss during this journey. I have to wonder: What were they talking about?

A Canada Goose, honking in flight, keeps in touch with its mate during their travels.

June 16

Reaping Seeds

The garden is growing more colorful by the day now, beginning to absolutely burst with a showy array of coneflowers. Mine are not the ones with unusual colors, the hybrids that occupy shelves and shelves of nursery space, touted as the newest or brightest for the year. No, mine are the native coneflowers, both purple and prairie. I avoid the hybrids because, by definition, hybrids multiply only by cloning, and that means their seeds are infertile. Since I'm planting for the birds (and bees and butterflies) especially to provide nectar and seeds for them, why would I plant anything that offers infertile seed? There's no nutrition there for feathered friends! Actually, the tough natives have more to offer than just healthy nectar and seed for birds and pollinators: They offer me carefree maintenance. Native coneflowers need no fertilizer, no watering, no overwinter care, and they come back reliably year after year. Often they also multiply by seed, so once I have a few established plants, I'm set for the long haul.

Unlike purple coneflowers that maintain a fairly even height of about 3 feet, prairie coneflowers can easily top 8 feet tall. They're clustered at the far end of the garden, creating nice, bushy lower growth where Song Sparrows like to hide and sometimes nest. Above the bushy vegetation, those spectacularly tall, flower-topped, wave-in-the-breeze stalks shoot up. It's up there, on those flowers, that goldfinches in particular love to forage. Since male goldfinches are nearly the same color as the bright prairie coneflower petals, I sometimes have to stare a bit to pick out the active birds among the rustling stalks. With absolute certainty, I know they forage there frequently without my catching them. Today the birds were busy, busy, busy, mostly in the prairie coneflowers but also checking out the earliest of

A male American Goldfinch matches colors with the prairie coneflowers and their seed heads on which he feeds.

the purple coneflowers. It's a little slice of heaven watching bird behavior when it involves their hanging out several hours over the course of the day, feeding on what I've carefully tended for them.

As I sat watching the goldfinch activity from my window, a red fox trotted past the garden, cut across through the neighbor's hayfield, and disappeared into the woods. Glad to see it but also suspect it might have had something to do with the absence of turkey poults this spring.

June 17

Creating a Spa

A landscape makeover two years ago resulted in turning a bare spot in the yard to a shrub- and tree-packed area of shelter. Immature vegetation by necessity leaves blank spots for future growth, and the blanks have been mulched heavily with wood chips, now bleached light gray from two years' exposure to weather. In the midst of this new landscape sits a bubble rock, a true bird magnet, now many years in use.

This summer, perhaps because wood chips absorb the heat, the bubbler-mulch combo has created a situation surely akin to a spa for a whole range of birds, including blue jays, cardinals, robins, titmice, and doves—and maybe others that I've missed. The spa wasn't part of a conscious plan on my part, but I think that's the result. The "patrons" arrive in singles or pairs, splash and wallow about on the bubbler, getting a good soaking, then flit to the sun-soaked wood chips, align themselves for maximum sun exposure, facing away from it, wiggle down onto the heat of the chips, spread wings and tail, and raise their back feathers nearly straight up, exposing their black skin. Within 15 seconds or so, they're panting, beaks wide open.

They're sunning! They've taken a dip in the water, they've stretched out on the beach, and now they're soaking up the sun. Wait a minute. Really? The question, of course, is why would birds pursue such a day-at-the-beach-type behavior. They never do anything that wastes energy or puts them in danger. They always hang out near sheltered protection. Their purpose in life is to reproduce. But here's the kicker: To do so, they must keep themselves fed and healthy. Still, sunning doesn't seem to fit anywhere in that life pattern.

Wait, though. What about the need to stay healthy?

In winter, birds sun themselves, tucked into a protected wind-free spot, to help maintain body temperature. But recent 95-degree days hardly qualify for the need to stay warm. Several theories suggest their sunning really is all about health and safety. First, the sun helps convert preening oil into Vitamin D. Birds need it as much as we do. But second, heat from the sun causes any parasites on their feathers to go on the move. Then, by preening, birds can rid themselves of the annoying pests. The parasites cause feather damage, which, in turn, can affect flight, upcoming winter-necessary insulation, and appearance. Birds with a poor appearance are likely to be considered poor risks as mates and may find themselves alone. Indeed, the sunning birds in our yard preen during and especially after sunning. Rather like a massage after a steam bath!

Interesting, isn't it, that a habitat change so seemingly insignificant as adding a couple of wheelbarrow loads of wood chips gave birds a perfect spa and gave me an insight into their health needs as well as their personal lives. Gotta love habitat improvement!

A Blue Jay appears to have collapsed in exhaustion but instead is sunning. By fanning its tail and wings and lifting its body feathers, the bird allows the sun's rays to reach its skin, thus helping to control parasites.

The jay's behavior today, however, reminded me of another behavior I've witnessed among these birds: anting. Sounds a little uncomfortable, but a bird will wiggle itself into the top of an anthill. That makes the ants really mad and they come storming out to attack, crawling all over the bird. In so doing, they gobble up any bacteria they run across while at the same time emitting an antimicrobial quality that further protects the bird. Meanwhile, eating the feather bacteria makes the ants less bitter, so the bird then gobbles up a few ants. Whew! Fast-acting remedy, if you don't mind the process. Depends on if you're the ant or the bird.

Birds Do *That*?

Doves feed their babies milk. Pigeon or dove milk is actually chemically similar to human breast milk. Instead of its being a secretion of mammary glands, however, it is a secretion from the lining of the birds' crops—the crops of both males and females. The approaching hatch of their eggs triggers the secretion, usually about two days before hatchlings emerge. Described as looking a bit like cottage cheese, pigeon/dove milk serves as the nestlings' complete diet for about the first week outside the egg. According to ScienceAlert.com, after the first week, the secreted milk is supplemented by regurgitated seeds for another several days. Afterward, regurgitated seeds serve as the nestlings' complete diet.

June 18

Admiring the Garden

A pair of Eastern Kingbirds bugged in the garden this morning. How gratifying! They're handsome birds, black heads and backs, white throats, breasts, and bellies, and the trademark identifying field mark: white tips on their black tails. Since the sexes are alike, I can only assume that the two birds were a pair. After all, this is the height of breeding season, and these birds come from the forests of the western Amazon basin in South America to raise their babies here. They're nothing to shrug off, these long-distance travelers. While they're true flycatchers and rely on flying insects for their meals here, when they return home to the forests, they frequently dine on fruit. Because they feed their youngsters for almost seven weeks, however, they have time for only a single brood.

So why were they bugging in the garden, and what was special about that?

As sizable flycatchers, Eastern Kingbirds eat an abundance of bugs, this one hunting in the garden from a flycatching vantage point.

Let's start with the fact that while kingbirds have been in the neighborhood regularly over the years, they're mostly somewhere besides our yard. Oh, maybe they cruised through, stopped for a brief look-see, but they've never been regulars. Over the course of many years, however, I've persistently reworked the garden, replacing nonnative plants with natives, removing the likes of daffodils, daylilies, roses, chrysanthemums, barberry, and Japanese ferns and replacing them with natives such as inkberry, hyssop, rattlesnake master, mountain mint, monarda, purple coneflower, prairie milkweed, prairie dock, buttonbush, sweetspire, and ninebark. Sometimes I made the replacements because the exotics died and sometimes because I dug out the exotics and passed them on or threw them away. Now, given the pollinator plants and the seed- and berry-producing plants, birds have an almost year-round buffet of nectar, seeds, and berries, all visible out my front windows.

What brought the Eastern Kingbirds to the garden, however, was not the nectar, seeds, or berries. Being the flycatchers that they are, kingbirds want bugs. Flying bugs. Period. Obviously, I can't go out and buy a box of flying bugs to feed the flycatchers, but when I plant all those native plants, they in turn support native bugs—butterflies, moths, bees, beetles, and all their eggs and larvae. Those feed the birds. As the cliché goes: "To feed the birds, first feed the bugs."

That the kingbirds were behaving the way flycatchers do, flycatching in the garden, proves there were sufficient flying insects to make their dining experience worthwhile. For the first time, my garden met their needs. For me, that translates into success for the garden!

But let's address the elephant in the room here. Surely if I've planted all those natives that support all those bugs, the yard must be a nightmare of buzzing, biting bugs, right? Certainly one might expect so. Truth of the matter is, however, that being the outdoors folks we are, we regularly lounge in the yard without ever noticing an insect. Since we haven't used insecticides in the yard for over twenty-five years, I can say with certainty that the birds keep the bugs under control. And bugs bring birds to the yard like magnets! It's Mother Nature's intended balance. Eastern Kingbirds love it. And I love Eastern Kingbirds! Guess who wins? Hint: It's not the bugs.

June 19

Missing the Flickers

Every year about this time, I start missing the Northern Flickers. I don't see them; I don't hear them. It's a routine phenomenon, part of their regular behavior. They disappear at the beginning of nesting season, usually sometime in mid- to late May. They have to find a suitable spot to hammer out a cavity—no small challenge given the keen competition for the few dead trees remaining these days. The degree of decay makes all the difference to flickers, since the more rotten the tree, the easier the excavation. Next, of course, comes the excavation process, pecking out chip by chip until the cavity reaches a foot or more deep. That's a lot of tiny pieces of wood. By now, several weeks may have passed, depending on the challenges the birds face with nest competition and the quality of wood they're trying to excavate. Then the female lays her eggs, one each day for perhaps a week. Incubation lasts about ten days, and they feed their nestlings for about twenty-two days before the babies fledge. Now we're looking at as much as nine, maybe ten weeks—two and a half months. Given that time frame, they or their offspring tend to reappear in our yard sometime in late July. Meanwhile, I miss their "wicka wicka wicka" calls.

A female Northern Flicker is identifiable by her lack of a black moustache. Both males and females, however, have red chevrons on the backs of their heads.

As woodpeckers, they're a bit odd about their feeding behavior. They prefer to forage on the ground, especially given their penchant for ants and beetles. Last winter, of course, there was a record number of flickers in the yard, foraging at suet feeders, a behavior entirely out of character for them but witnessed by many of us backyard bird hosts. While flickers live here in southern Indiana year-round, part of the uptick in winter populations is no doubt the result of migration. Flickers breeding in Canada move south for the winter, some of them perhaps as far south as here. Still, it seems logical that the year-round population, the one that breeds here, should somehow make an appearance sometime during the months of June and July. But not in the yard.

Breeding, however, requires full-time attention on the pair's part. It's likely they nest farther from our yard than would be convenient for daily back-and-forth visitations. Since unlike most other woodpeckers flickers will reuse a cavity, and since they may live seven or eight years, and since they do show some nest-site fidelity, maybe flickers wander off to their preferred nest site without wishing us a good day and hang out there for the duration. Here's hoping that, when they return, some of their youngsters will come with them. Since they lay five to eight eggs, even with the loss of a few eggs or chicks from their single brood, they should return with a couple babies in tow. I'll be watching.

June 20

Interpreting Wren Behavior

Carolina Wrens have most likely begun their third broods, maybe even already feeding nestlings. The raggedy-looking adults show the wear-and-tear challenges of having completed two full rounds of kid-raising. After constructing a nest for each brood, the pair incubated each brood for just over two weeks and then fed the three to six nestlings in each brood for over another two weeks, not to mention the continued feeding after the chicks fledged. The way I figure, that's more than two months of nonstop work. They've had to forage, catch insects, zip back to the nest, duck in and out of whatever convenient tucked-away place they've chosen, and do that sunup to sundown. Somewhere along the line, they've had to feed themselves, too.

A Carolina Wren, plumage now a bit tattered from a busy nesting season, picks around the hopper feeder, most likely finding bugs, bug eggs, or larvae amid the cracks and crevices.

Now they're somewhere along the same process with the third round. Poor things, their feathers look worn, some missing. If birds can look tired, that's how I would describe them. But they're singing, both the male and the female, keeping track of one another, perhaps one saying where he's found the best bugs or the other saying when she's fed one or two of the brood. I don't know where they've hidden their nest (and they don't want me to know), but they've moved closer to the house than they were for the second round. Just after they fledged the first brood from a nest in a structure under the south awning, they moved the crew to the edge of the woods. And they stayed. Most times I heard them singing near the neighbor's backyard. But now they're back in the yard. Somewhere.

This morning, one (the sexes look alike, so I'll just choose the masculine) picked about in the backyard hopper feeder filled with safflower seed. That caught my attention, because wrens don't eat seeds. Their narrow sharp bills are designed for bugs, and they are unable to crack open seeds. So what was he picking at? He examined every nook and cranny of that feeder—every crack in the wood, every hinged joint, every spot where the glass sides slide into the slots, every roofline. He cocked his head at every angle, every corner, every edge. Aha! Smart little guy. We all know that wild birdseed, left in the heat, can readily—and sometimes quickly—get buggy. While my comparatively weak human eye can't see the evidence, the wren's eye can. I'm ready to bet money he was finding eggs or tiny larvae in those cracks and crevices. Without a reward he would never have tarried so long, never have scoured every inch of that feeder. At least that's the way I interpret his behavior.

June 21

Clocking Hummingbirds

On this longest day of the year, the sun set behind a heavy cloudbank, and the curtain of darkness dropped within 17 minutes after sunset. Hummingbirds remained at feeders, guzzling nectar, until the very last second of the last minute of dusk, too dark for me to see anything more than their movement. They lingered long and drank deeply, so much so that I began timing them. While one individual drank almost nonstop for almost 3 minutes, most clocked out at about a minute and 20 seconds. Surely their tiny crops were full to bursting with such long sips of syrup! But they were feeding against the clock. This last long drink must nourish them for the night—and that's for a bird that during daylight hours nectars about every 20 minutes.

Males can go into torpor overnight, a kind of short-term hibernation. Their metabolic rate drops by as much as 95 percent and, as a result, they use fifty times less energy during

A female Ruby-throated Hummingbird comes for nectar at a feeder, taking only seconds away from her nesting duties.

torpor than when they're awake. Their normal 105-degree body temperature drops to what scientists call a set point, loosely described as the minimum temperature at which the bird can stay alive. Hummers in torpor are so deeply asleep that they can be touched without their reacting. During torpor, then, hummers make exceedingly efficient use of the final food intake of the day.

Nesting females, on the other hand, can't afford to go into torpor. They have eggs to incubate, and if their body temperatures dropped, their eggs would spoil. The sad fact is that some females don't survive the nesting effort.

Knowing how on the edge these hummers live, it's with compassion that I watch them feeding until darkness settles in. They must find a safe perch for the night, one where owls won't pluck them for an appetizer, one where they're protected from summer storms, one where they're secure from strong winds. Tiny though they are, they're not fragile. Still, they have their limits. Here's hoping the feeders sufficiently supplement the tiny bugs and nectar in the garden to make their nighttime slumbers safe.

June 22

Courting Doves

Mourning Doves exhibit an amazing breeding behavior, reproducing nearly year-round, raising up to six broods a year, two chicks each time. The flimsy nest surely collapses from time to time, and maybe chicks even fall out—or fall through the cracks. But the incubating birds sit tight, unmoving and nearly unblinking, thus camouflaging the little pile of small twigs, their eggs, and finally, their youngsters.

While male and female Mourning Doves look mostly alike, during breeding season, males wear a pinkish "blush" that separates them from the slightly smaller females.

Today, a male seemed particularly insistent on mating with a seemingly uncaring female. He followed her within inches, mimicking her every move, as she scooted ahead or to the side and sometimes flitted ahead several feet. It's easy to recognize the male, puffed up, his pink neon neck patch glistening in the right light.

When the pair finally flew, their accelerating wing noise reminded me that some observers believe the takeoff wing sound is a flight alert to others. As strange as it seems, the sound results from undulating waves on the outer edges of flight feathers and says quite audibly, "I'm taking off. Check around to see why." Of course, not every flight is one of fear, but it's still an alert to the masses. And indeed, sometimes the masses take off, too.

June 23

Explaining a White-capped Hummingbird

In Central and South America white-capped hummingbirds, including one tiny little fellow called a Snowcap, nectar across a wide range of blossoms. But in the United States? No. But I saw a white-capped hummer at my feeder today. Yes, I really did. She zipped in for a good long sip at the feeder, perching while she drank, giving me an equally good long look at her before she darted to a nearby branch, pausing a few seconds before no doubt returning to her nest. And she definitely had a white cap atop her usually emerald-green head.

So if she was not some special species, something rare and unusual apart from our regular Ruby-throated Hummingbird, what was she? The answer is she was one busy gal, nectaring at everything available to her in the garden, including numerous tubular flowers, now in full bloom, that left their pollen on her head as she partook of the nectar! Cool evidence of cool behavior.

Mystery solved!

A female Ruby-throated Hummingbird appears to wear a white cap, but it's only a dusting of pollen left from when she nectared in tubular flowers.

June 24

Keeping an Eye on Bathers

Yesterday's puttering about the yard led me to clear a nonnative creeping vine that concealed my kitchen window view of a birdbath. Situated near the base of a massive old pine, the concrete bowl has long since lost its pedestal simply because I got rid of it. My logic for the ground-level placement was that a naturally situated bath, even one of concrete, would better attract birds than one on a pedestal. After all, no natural water source stands 3 feet off the ground. By using a crude foundation of flat stones on which to set it, I've kept the water level even and the bowl's rim aboveground. A few more flat stones on the downslope side make a sort of spillway for overflow to help maintain the bowl's position.

The bath, cleared now of the concealing vines, still remains barely visible from the kitchen window, its location in dense shade keeping it fairly well hidden. Today, as I expected, with the bath freshly filled, birds popped in and out all afternoon. Mostly Carolina Chickadees and Tufted Titmice splashed and bathed, darted away to shake off, and returned to repeat the splashing. A few soaked themselves so thoroughly they were nearly unrecognizable!

But one behavior seemed telling. Every single time a bird left the bath, it flew to vegetation within a few feet and perched. Each bird, no matter the species, always shook itself free of excess water droplets, and most times it also preened, even if briefly. The perches each bather chose were well-protected, safe spots for lingering, and the bath-perch combo provided safety. Although many birds seem attracted to the bubble rock for its moving water, there's no arguing birds also enjoy the natural still-water "puddle." I think sometimes the stillness of the water attracts them; sometimes it's likely the cool shade (and relatively cool water); sometimes it's possibly the location, tucked away from the openness of the yard. By late afternoon, hardly any water remained in the bowl, all splashed out by frequent bathers!

June 25

Admiring Smart Chickadees

Carolina chickadees forage with a busy intensity surpassed, in my yard at least, only by kinglets. As chickadees scoot about snatching up tiny bugs or bug eggs and larvae for their babies, they find themselves in all manner of positions. They hang upside down from the tips of leaves, checking the undersides for hidden gems other birds missed. They swing from the tiniest branch, checking the bark for anything tucked in the crevices. They flit from one leaf to the next with an abandon that seems at first reckless but is actually carefully intentioned.

Birds Do *That*?

Birds add medicinal herbs to their nests. Perhaps to protect against parasites or other nestling threats, some birds, mostly males, add fresh green aromatic herbs to their nests periodically during the egg-laying, incubation, and nestling periods. Two University of Bristol professors investigated the behavior among European Starlings, Tree Swallows, and Blue Tits, a European bird in the titmouse family. While their review of thirty years of research proved inconclusive, many nests garlanded with herbs contained fewer mites and other parasites than those without added greenery. Likewise, House Finch nests often include cigarette butts. Since tobacco plants contain smelly toxins, the butts may offer protection similar to that of other essential oils, bringing to the forefront the possibility that aromatic plants somehow strengthen chicks' immune system, helping them better survive once they leave the nest.

Today, however, I caught one in a smart maneuver, behavior that shows intelligence. As the chickadee explored the broad, foot-long leaves of pokeweed, moving in measured leaps along the edge, I noticed that the bird explored first the leaves that showed bug damage—leaves that sported large holes from having been eaten by some little creepy-crawly. Apparently the chickadee recognized the cause of the leaf damage and sought the culprit that would surely mean a delectable meal. As the chickadee foraged, it first scoured the edges of the damage and then explored the remaining edges of the leaf before flitting to another. Smart, huh?

June 26

Determining Titmouse's Age

Tufted Titmice fledged a few weeks ago, so now I'm having some difficulty recognizing which are adults and which are youngsters. Titmice mature fast. In the nest, by day ten a baby titmouse has a well-feathered body. Four days later it's fully feathered and very much looks like its parents—except for the shorter wing and tail feathers. But "shorter" is relative and tough to discern, especially when I see one without the other.

After youngsters fledge on about day sixteen, they depend on their parents for another six weeks or so before they're feeding themselves independently. Some juveniles even hang out with their parents for the remainder of the summer, all winter, and into next year's breeding season. Surely, they're learning the ropes of parenthood during this unusually long process, a bit of an odd behavior for songbirds.

A fledgling Tufted Titmouse wears a pale bill and plain facial pattern, thus differentiating it from adults.

So when a titmouse showed up in the yard today, giving me a grand look and an opportunity to photograph it, I took the up-close-and-personal opportunity to study the bird's age. While my photo did not capture the wing-feather length, two details declared it a youngster: This bird lacked the truly black bill of an adult (youngsters of many species wear a more lightly colored bill than do the adults), and the boldly black "bridle" pattern above the beak was too faint to be mature. Bingo! The kid was on his own.

An adult Tufted Titmouse (the sexes look alike) wears a black beak and black "bridle," thus differentiating it from youngsters.

June 27

Sorting Out Blue Jays

A little flock of Blue Jays continues to visit the yard on a regularly intermittent basis. Watching their behavior provides insights into their minds. Sometimes they come screaming into the yard several times a day; sometimes they yell out what seems like profanities only once a week; and sometimes they imitate Red-shouldered Hawks to clear the yard, thus feeding in singular peace! They're stinkers. But they're really smart. They and the other members of the Corvid family—like Gray Jays, Stellar Jays, Scrub Jays, American Crows, Ravens, and Magpies—are undoubtedly the smartest and most clever birds on the planet. They've even been documented using tools! Having them in the yard, then, always makes me pay attention, watching them to see evidence of their braininess.

Although all Blue Jays look alike, at least to us humans, they can be identified individually by their slightly different facial patterns. Compare this bird with the one in the next photo.

Recently I've read that ornithologists believe Blue Jays recognize each other as individuals by the black markings on their faces, some markings forming what could be called a necklace—except the black starts at the base of the crest, considerably too high to be called a "neck"lace. This afternoon I watched three individuals sailing back and forth from a seed cake to the maple tree while I tried to detect any differences in their markings. Sure enough, they weren't exactly alike. Variations in band width and length, variations in how the band joins the scant bib and how the band joins the crest, even variations in the design of the scant bib itself all indicate that these jays can be sorted out individually, named or numbered for identification. Perhaps the ready identification somehow plays into the fact that Corvids are truly family oriented. They support and look out for one another. They hang out together in extended-family units. The young often remain with the adults to raise the next brood. And they learn to recognize us, coming to understand which of us is helpful and which of us is not! How cool is that?

Compare this Blue Jay's facial pattern with that of the one in the previous photo.

June 28

Welcoming Juvenile Cardinals

Only a few fledgling Northern Cardinals have made appearances in the yard so far this season, and I've been puzzled by their tardiness. When I review photos, however, there's evidence that the females were also late this spring constructing their nests. With an abundance of male cardinals flitting regularly about the yard, I feel fairly certain, however, that females are on the nest. More fledglings to come!

Today, a young cardinal made a brief stop on a branch just outside the kitchen window. It's been out of the nest a few weeks already, long enough to show a molt pattern into its first adult plumage. New, short primary coverts show just at the top of the wing, and color is evident in the primaries. Feathers just behind the eye are missing, further evidence of the bird's molt. When first fledged, youngsters have dark gray, almost black beaks, so this bird is in transition, its pale yellow bill on the way to changing to the bright orange-red of adults.

A juvenile Northern Cardinal shows new wing-feather growth, bill color in transition, and overall molting.

I'm always amazed that birds can change their bill color. Made of keratin, like human fingernails and hair, the beaks of several bird species change dramatically, but perhaps the change is most dramatic in cardinals, from youth to adulthood, and in American Goldfinches, from winter to summer and back again, a change that occurs every season throughout the goldfinches' lives. How do they do that? Imagine changing the color of your fingernails without using nail polish!

June 29

Oiling Feathers—or Not

Preening takes up more time in a bird's day than anything other than feeding. By preening, birds align their feathers into the most aerodynamic shape, so well-preened feathers enable birds to fly more easily and with improved agility. Beyond that, however, preening helps keep feathers healthy as birds remove feather lice and parasites during the process. And while all this fussiness is going on, the behavior also makes the bird more attractive, thus more alluring to a mate. Birds aren't so different from humans in that respect—except we call it primping, not preening, and our lives don't depend on our primping well.

The Mourning Dove this afternoon was preening in such a position as to display its handsome array of undertail coverts—feathers we rarely see otherwise. The bird's behavior just before this guy—or gal—started preening, however, tells more of the story: It sat on the branch, its right wing spread wide open, soaking up rays of hot sun. After some minutes it folded its wing, sat up, and preened. Then it repeated the process with the left

Mourning Doves lack the preen glands that most songbirds have, so its feathers deteriorate into powder down, the powder substituting for oil. As this dove preens, it shows its undertail coverts, which we otherwise rarely see.

wing. No doubt taking a momentary break from nesting duties, this bird's preening most likely also protected its nest by ridding feathers of potential disease that could spread to the family.

Most birds come equipped with an oil gland or preen gland, properly called a uropygial gland, at the base of the tail. As those birds preen, they spread the oil from the gland across their feathers, making them waterproof. Doves and woodpeckers and some few other species, however, lack preen glands. Instead, they have special kinds of feathers that deteriorate into powder down, and the powder down substitutes for the oil—not for waterproofing but for all other purposes. As a result, this specialized feather protection also causes doves to behave somewhat differently from other birds. They rarely if ever immerse themselves at the birdbath. They'll come to drink, but not to bathe. Their feathers aren't waterproofed. Kind of strange, isn't it?

June 30

Empathizing about Heat

While I cower inside in the air conditioning to avoid the 105-degree heat index, birds must go about their regular business. How do they behave in the heat?

First, they don't sweat, but they do pant. Sometimes I've caught them, beaks open, breathing heavily through their mouths.

Second, and perhaps more readily observed, is their sleek appearance. No, I don't mean they're silky lovely after all these weeks of feeding babies, scooting in and out of nests, wearing feathers ragged. Rather, they've sleeked their feathers down as flat as they will go, holding them tight against their bodies, aiming to stay cool. Fluffed feathers hold heat (remember your down jacket?), so while wintertime sees

A female American Goldfinch holds her wings away from her body as a method of cooling herself during sweltering summer days.

birds look plump, even fat, they're merely fluffing feathers against the cold. Now, though, they're doing just the opposite, pressing out any heat-holding air.

And third, sometimes to allow cooling air to brush their skin, they hold their folded wings away from their bodies, rather the way we humans might hold our arms akimbo for the same purpose.

Still, it's just plain hot.

July

A male Bobolink, a bird in serious decline, carries caterpillars to his nestlings.

*Birds are indicators of the environment. If they are in trouble,
we know we'll soon be in trouble.*

—Roger Tory Peterson (1908–1996)

July 1

Venturing North

We're almost 800 miles north of our backyard habitat today, in northern Michigan along the border with Canada, here to find some of the birds that flew through our area this spring and have now taken up summer nesting residence. What astounding evidence of birds' mind-boggling migratory behavior! Already, we've found Magnolia Warblers, Northern Parulas, Yellow Warblers, and American Redstarts and nesting colonies of Common Terns, Double-crested Cormorants, and Ring-billed Gulls.

Most of the gulls that frequent areas in and around the Ohio River in winter are those that migrate south from the Great Lakes, mostly Ring-billed Gulls. We know them from their frequenting dumpsters near fast-food joints and still-to-be-covered garbage at the landfill. Between feasts, they bob along in the river's current. In winter they're mostly white with a soft pale gray mantle, yellow legs, black wing tips, pale eyes, and a namesake broad black ring near the bill's end. Now, though, as breeding adults, the white is more brightly white and the eyes boast an amazingly bright red ring around them, called, in the proper sense, an orbital ring. The same bright red also shows along the edge of the mouth between the face and the end of the beak, an area called the gape. Up close, then, the ordinary, omnipresent, sometimes-annoying Ring-billed Gulls show a strikingly stunning face. Gives them a bit of drama!

Gulls and terns look a bit alike, but while I find gulls interesting scavengers, terns are sleek acrobats. And among the terns, I'm especially pleased to watch Common Terns, perhaps because I don't get to see them very often. Although Common Terns aren't so common inland, they have maintained a fairly large breeding colony in the Upper Peninsula, one of the southernmost areas for them to breed. Because their preferred breeding behavior is to nest on rocky islands, they've found a suitable habitat along a rocky pier undisturbed by humans, cordoned off from public visits. The birds have set up housekeeping all

A Common Tern, a species in decline, carries a tiny fish to its nestlings at a protected refuge.

Birds Do *That*?

At age sixty-seven, the world's oldest bird had a baby. According to Christine Dell'Amore at National Geographic, a Laysan Albatross nicknamed Wisdom, now sixty-seven years old, is breeding—again—on Midway Atoll. Of course, an even older bird could well be present, just unknown. Most yard birds live two or three years, perhaps up to seven years. In general, however, the larger the bird the longer it lives. And Laysan Albatross tip the scale at up to a hefty 9.5 pounds. Red-tailed Hawks, weighing a comparatively paltry 3.2 pounds, have surpassed twenty-five years of age. The oldest known Northern Cardinal, a bird that typically weighs less than 2 ounces, made it to fifteen years, nine months. The oldest recorded Eastern Bluebird in the wild, barely tipping the scales at 1 ounce, lived ten years, five months. Similarly size Dark-eyed Juncos can live for ten years. A banded Ruby-throated Hummingbird, weighing a tenth of an ounce, survived nine years.

along the pier, disturbed only by an occasional Bald Eagle or Ring-billed Gull dropping in to snatch an egg or a chick to feed their own nestlings. It's hard to watch the carnage of such raids, but it's so often the rule with Mother Nature: Eat or be eaten.

Meanwhile, though, I'm amazed to watch how the terns behave, returning to the colony with beaks full of tiny fish. Finding their own nests among the hundreds jammed side by side seems an insurmountable challenge to us mere humans, but the birds fly as directly as an arrow to the spot where their respective chicks beg for attention. Catching terns in flight becomes a photographer's challenge, one that kept us occupied for hours. The Common Terns that nest in North America typically spend their winters along the tropical coasts of South America. Those that breed in Europe and Asia winter in Africa and Southeast Asia.

While photographing the terns, I also caught sight of Cliff Swallows picking up tiny pebbles from the parking lot. I'm guessing that, like Barn Swallows, they're adding the pebbles to their diet to better digest their food, but it's the first time I've witnessed that behavior among Cliff Swallows.

July 2

Driving Back Roads

Venturing along the perimeter of protected Department of Natural Resources (DNR) property, we enjoyed several hours of fine birding, idling in our vehicle along a 2-mile stretch of dirt road, acreage on both sides bustling with marvelous birds, many readily recognized merely by their behavior. The most abundant were Savannah Sparrows, perched atop weathered cedar fence posts. Their insect-like songs marked their respective territories, and every available territory seemed to have a singing male protecting it. Among them, however, Song Sparrows belted out their own territorial ownership while Common Yellowthroats held the densest damp spots for their own. Spiffy Clay-colored Sparrows, always looking extraordinarily well groomed, occupied a small section that looked no different to me than anywhere else within the hundreds of acres. Whatever was different, however, suited them best. They garnered those territories.

A few other sightings are worth a mention. Yellow-billed Cuckoos called from time to time, obviously having found abundant caterpillars. Caterpillar webs were everywhere, and most had holes poked into the sides, likely a telltale indication of cuckoo raids. A single Wilson's Snipe dropped down from its winnowing display and disappeared in the waist-high grasses. And a Sharp-shinned Hawk, like the one that picnicked last winter at our house, was now serving as a force to be reckoned with among nesting warblers at woods edge. Of course, I love singing White-throated Sparrows, those little songsters that spent the winter with us and were now singing on their breeding territories in northern Michigan. Indeed, the songs were sweeter and more melodious now than when those birds sang somewhat off-key and haltingly in our yard.

Then, a special song! Among the similarly sounding Savannahs, a single LeConte's Sparrow shared its brief buzzing, a barely discernible call. Actually spotting him across

the vast grasslands proved impossible for me, even after a binocular scan of every heavy weed and stick in the general area, triangulating my efforts to his song. Most likely his low perch was amid vegetation just tall enough to serve his version of king-of-the-mountain but just short enough to be obscured from my view by twigs or blades slightly taller. Still, knowing that this endangered bird was there, apparently breeding, gave a positive spin to the day.

A Swamp Sparrow, a species that made a migratory stopover in the yard, snaps up little orange-winged European skippers to feed its nestlings in northern Michigan.

Another experience, a first for me, gave both me and the birds reason for pleasure. Wildflowers alongside the road and spreading across the fallow fields hosted quite literally millions of skippers. Never have I seen so many tiny skippers, all of the same species, all feeding heavily. In fact, at one point the road grew so narrow that the car door brushed against roadside flowers, causing the skippers to rise in a cloud. A few would sometimes fly inside the car, hover a bit, and find their way back out, I suppose uncomfortable in the relative darkness.

And the birds, especially flycatchers and sparrows, were having a heyday, their behavior a response to the abundant prey. They plucked skippers from the air and from the flowers to feed themselves and their nestlings. Since tiny skippers, about thumbnail size, probably offer little nourishment compared to the effort of catching them, though, I suspect that only on days like today with its overwhelming profusion of the insects do birds take the time to snap them up. Still, when the pickin's are easy, it's a go!

One fallow field within the preserve now serves as perfect habitat for Bobolinks, ground nesters that prefer the grassy, shrubby lands near marshes. Once their families have left the nest, the birds return to their winter range fairly quickly. They do, after all, travel about 5,000 miles each way from Michigan to the fields of Argentina. Who can really understand the challenges they face over such a long journey, so even if they weren't absolutely gorgeous birds, I'd still watch them with a sense of awe.

Another pair of migrants shared their family with us—although probably not willingly. We spotted a young bird perched atop a weathered cedar fence post, but even at first glance, we thought it seemed a bit unsure of itself and whatever lay beyond the post. That behavior was immediately followed by a second head appearing just above the post's rim. And then an adult Eastern Kingbird landed on the post with a dandy-size dragonfly in its beak. Turns out the two youngsters were emerging from a hollow post that held the

Color variations in male Bobolinks mean some individuals wear lemon-colored patches on the backs of their heads while others wear off-white. Compare this male with that in this chapter's opening photo.

family nursery. These were babies in a nest! As soon as the adult poked the dragonfly down one nestling's throat, it must have issued the command, "Get down." Like magic the two youngsters melted down inside the post, and the adult stood guard until we inched away, hoping to limit any perceived threat. An hour later, as we retraced our steps, the adults remained actively flycatching in the area, the young still hidden from our prying eyes. How awesome to have witnessed the behavior of that magical moment!

An Eastern Kingbird brings a dragonfly for its two nestlings, now having nearly outgrown their nest space inside a deteriorated wooden fence post.

July 3

Finding Loons

I have a thing for Common Loons—love their yodels, love their plumage pattern, love their red eyes, love their long dives, love their breeding behavior. For years I've seen photos of loons carrying their babies on their backs and have always wanted to witness this unique parental protection. Sometimes seeing a photo just isn't enough. I've been on the mission for several years now.

Why does it take so much effort to catch loon chicks on an adult's back? It's only for the first couple of weeks that hatchlings hitch a ride, scrambling up on mom's or dad's back, but the free ride is anything but a playful game for youngsters. Loons nest at water's edge (they're terrible at walking), and as soon as chicks break out of the shell, the whole family takes to the water, the one or two chicks making the supreme effort to keep up with their parents. Of course being only an hour old, chicks tire quickly and chill rapidly in the often nippy northern waters in July. Tucked up on an adult's back, riding dry, or tucked under an adult's wing, riding warm, the chicks are safe, protected, and coddled against what must seem like brutal elements during the first few days out of the egg.

Within a week or so, the chicks can produce sufficient body warmth for their own well-being and no longer ride on adults' backs, but parents remain super protective to prevent eagles from picking off the youngsters to feed their own nestlings. So the time frame for witnessing riding-on-the-back chicks is short. Very short. Since hatch dates vary with the season, depending on when the lake ice melts, when the adults arrive on territory, and when the weather sends a clear message that nesting can begin, when we can witness chicks on their parents' backs varies as well. Every year that we've traveled north to watch the loons, we've been too early or too late. But this year we hit it just right.

Within a few minutes of arriving at our destination refuge, we spotted four adult Common Loons grouped together as if sharing a morning coffee break. They were socializing. Unfortunately, the four had nothing else to do since both pairs had lost their clutches. The male of one pair is known to be thirty-one years old, banded as a chick on what is now his territory, verifying a remarkable behavior: A loon returns to the lake on which it fledged to establish its own adult territory. His mate was banded as an adult, so she's older than her banding date suggests, but of course no one knows her exact age. The two have produced dozens of chicks, but for the first time, this year they were unsuccessful. The other pair, their bands concealed and therefore their identities unknown, showed no aggression, merely paddled about, yodeling, diving, dining, socializing. After watching their leisurely behavior for a half hour or so, we moved on.

That's when we came upon a pair of loons with a single chick, just a tiny black fluff ball, no more than three days old—riding on an adult's back! Finally, I was witnessing the behavior I'd longed to see. Here they were, a family reasonably close to the shore, perhaps no more than 40 feet out, huddling close together, tending their chick. As we watched, the chick slid into the water and bobbed about, always within inches of an adult. Within no more than 15 minutes, however, the chick clambered back up on the adult's back, situated itself under the adult's partially raised wing, and snuggled in to dry out and warm up. We watched the unencumbered adult dive and come up with tiny fish, some so small they were barely visible at the tip of the loon's beak. As the adult offered fish to the chick, the little one

A newly hatched Common Loon chick rides on the parent's back, partly shielded under the adult's wing, a behavior that keeps the tiny chick warm in frigid northern waters.

needed encouragement to take the nourishment, apparently unsure what it was supposed to do with the wiggly offering. For almost an hour, we watched the care and attention the adults heaped on this tiny babe, a heart-warming experience of the sweetest kind. Ultimately, all three went to sleep, the chick completely concealed under an adult's wing. We wandered off, knowing all was well.

Having finally seen what I'd waited years to see, I was a bit giddy. We'd taken hundreds of photos, recording every family scenario we witnessed, but knew our presence had not disturbed the loons. They were accustomed to auto traffic along the wildlife drive, and by remaining in our car, the birds saw nothing out of the ordinary, nothing to cause them alarm. It just couldn't get any better than that.

And then it did!

By late afternoon, no more than 50 feet from the road, we spied another loon pair with not one but two chicks, riding together on a parent's back. With the car again as our blind, we stopped to watch their behavior. Double chicks meant double scenarios and double our watching pleasure. The chicks looked to be several days older than the single chick we'd seen in the morning, but the two of them together were still only about fist size. So tiny. So vulnerable. And so coddled. Sometimes the chicks took turns, one riding with one adult and the other with the second adult. At one point, though, an adult emitted a short yodel, and the two puff balls dove! Gone! I was startled to see them disappear so fast and even more startled to see them do so apparently on command. But why? Had we somehow disturbed the family? Then we saw: A Bald Eagle, returning to its nearby nest, flew past, directly overhead. Ever on the lookout for lunch for their own babies, eagles notoriously take anything small enough and weak enough for their talons. In fact, eagles, we were told,

Common Loons feed and protect their 5- or 6-day-old chicks.

accounted for the near-total absence of baby swans, or cygnets, at the refuge this year. The loons understood. The babies reacted on command, the behavior untaught, unlearned, instinctive.

So the day ended even better than I could have dreamed. Sure, over the course of our drive through the refuge, we saw other loons feeding other chicks, but they were weeks older, way too big to ride piggyback. We were thrilled to see other adults diving for morsels for the chicks, watching the chicks dart to the just-surfaced parents, eager to grab another beak-fed nibble. But the tiniest chicks won my heart ten times over. What an experience!

A Bald Eagle, ever on the alert for an opportunity to steal fish from an Osprey, flies across the wetlands.

July 4

Ogling Eagles

Appropriately, we spent part of the Fourth of July watching Bald Eagles at and near their nest site, feeding their chicks. Carnivorous opportunists, they will take roadkill or clean up hunters' discarded deer carcasses, but they especially love fish. Sometimes, though, it's easier to steal fish than to catch them. With that theme in mind, we watched a Bald Eagle harass an Osprey until the Osprey dropped its catch. Then, for the eagle, snatching the falling fish midair made for quick success, and off it went toward its nest. Poor Osprey. Off on another fishing trip.

A Bald Eagle perches in a dead tree near its massive nest. Did the eagles break off these branches to reinforce this year's nest?

July 5

Beholding Abodes

Driving the back roads and byways in Michigan's Upper Peninsula this morning, we focused on the vast grasslands and fallow fields common in these parts. Some, being DNR or otherwise protected, have grown shrubby, ideal for a variety of sparrows, including Savannah, Clay-colored, and Song Sparrows as well as Bobolink, Indigo Bunting, and Eastern Kingbird. Hayfields predominate within active agricultural farms, and it's mowing season now. As a result of the early mowing, birds that unwittingly chose the fields for their nurseries have almost certainly lost their broods. Other birds, having built their abodes in fallow fields, continue to defend their territories, singing robustly, chasing any perceived threats.

Having heard Clay-colored Sparrows doing their double-buzz song (can a buzz really be called a song?), we stopped, hoping to catch a better look and maybe even a photo or two. At home in southwestern Indiana, I've never seen a Clay-colored Sparrow, although a few dedicated birders have, but only during migration and only rarely. So, parked along the side of a dirt road, we were enjoying the experience of watching their behavior and listening to their song. Patience being the guiding word when awaiting a closer view or a better angle, we'd not only stopped the car but turned off the engine. This is remarkably quiet countryside here, away from traffic, far from an airport, sparsely populated. (The whole of the Upper Peninsula boasts a population of just over 300,000, smaller than many small cities.)

We waited. Meanwhile, looking for anything else of interest, hubby spotted a Bald Eagle land in the tallest of three trees atop a slight ridge. No sooner had it landed, however, than another bird dove, talons out, attacking the eagle, reaching for the big bird's back. The eagle lifted up in defense and flew, but time after time, as we watched, the littler bird attacked the giant. The "little bird" turned out to be a male Northern Harrier. Brave creature! What would explain his behavior? Best guess: Since harriers nest on the ground, the tree surely provided a fantastic vantage point for an eagle looking for lunch—or more likely looking for a high-protein meal for its own young. The harrier, bent on protecting his own young, went all out to save his nest and send the eagle on its way. The harrier won. Wow.

Continuing to listen for the Clay-colored Sparrow with one ear but simultaneously tuning into other activity around us, we turned out attention to a ramshackle homestead some distance down the road, the house collapsing on itself, but the sagging roof still intact and the chimneys on either end crumbling but still standing. On each chimney sat a Turkey Vulture. Northern Michigan marks the northern edge of their range, so populations are sparse. Thus, seeing the pair struck us as fortuitous. Indeed, one of the curious behaviors of Turkey Vultures is that they love to nest in old buildings, those generally undisturbed by any regular human visitation. How I would have loved to peek inside the house to maybe spot their nest, probably on the attic floor, perhaps in a corner. The risk of annoying them, however, should cause anyone pause. When disturbed, these rascals exhibit yet another curious—and not so nice—behavior: They spit at intruders, but the "spit" is actually vomit, highly acidic and nauseating, and their aim at intruders' eyes is famously accurate. Well, maybe that's more than you wanted to know. Also fearing reprisal from the landowner for trespassing, I gave only fleeting thought to the idea. The likely nest site went unchecked.

A Turkey Vulture pair roosts atop a dilapidated house, most likely the site of their nest.

Later, as we drove slowly past, we heard one of them croak its disapproval. Wait, what? From a bird that's usually silent except for occasional hissing, clucking, or whining, the call was entirely new to me. We stopped. Did we hear what we thought we heard? And again, "Croak." Hmmm. Another curious vulture behavior. And another first experience for me.

Meanwhile, yes, the Clay-colored Sparrow finally made an up-close-and-personal appearance. He even sang for us, virtually just outside our open car window. Gotta love the quiet moments that are rewarded with sweet connections.

A Clay-colored Sparrow defends its territory that harbors its camouflaged nest.

July 6

Understanding the Need for Bugs

After watching Bobolinks, Song Sparrows, Great Crested Flycatchers, Red-eyed Vireos, and Eastern Kingbirds feeding their babies fat, juicy bugs and caterpillars today, I'm reminded once again of the old mantra for bird watchers: To feed the birds, we must first feed the bugs.

As a young woman, I remember driving on any summer night, cringing, knowing for certain that the windshield, grill, and in fact the entire front of the car would be plastered with bugs. Now the plastering rarely occurs. We have very few bugs. The farmers spray their fields to eliminate bugs. They plant genetically modified crops that kill bugs that eat any part of the plant, including the nectar. Homeowners spray their yards to eliminate bugs around the house. Gardeners spray to eliminate bugs from their favored plants. Studies have shown a direct connection between the resulting dramatic decline of bugs and the equally dramatic decline of birds.

A Song Sparrow snags an insect that it will feed its nestlings. Native plants support these native bugs that native birds need to survive.

Feeding babies, a female Bobolink carries an insect back to her hidden grassland nest.

A Red-eyed Vireo carries bugs back to its nestlings.

Our week in Michigan's Upper Peninsula confirmed the veracity of the study. Our car, after having been driven only during daylight hours (darkness falls in summer there well after 10 p.m.), has been thoroughly plastered by bugs. Every vehicle we saw was equally plastered. There are lots and lots and lots of bugs. And of equal interest, when we pulled into little roadside parks for a break, we found lots and lots and lots of birds. At a single pull-through roadside park today, I found a family of Red-breasted Nuthatches, Yellow-rumped Warbler, Cedar Waxwing, Ruby-crowned Kinglet, and at least a half dozen American Redstarts. Had I spent more than 20 minutes looking, who knows how many more species would have revealed themselves. By comparison, at home, where we're more and more bug free, I would never find an array of birds at a little roadside park—except perhaps some nonnative House Sparrows or European Starlings. How scary. The canary in the coal mine has collapsed.

July 7

Surveying Swainson's

Most springs, Swainson's Thrushes linger a day or so in our yard, plucking mulberries, before continuing their journey north. This spring, however, with mulberries ripening about a month later than usual, I never saw a Swainson's in the yard. Made me sad, and uncomfortable, worried that somehow their absence had to do with more than the absence of ready-to-eat mulberries.

This morning, then, was a real treat. Birding along the St. Mary River in a mixed alder-willow-aspen forest abutting some open meadow-like areas, I stopped in my tracks at the ethereal, flute-like song of the Swainson's Thrush. The melody, like that of most of the brown-colored thrushes, always seems to drift across the forest, the music like a flute duet. Wood Thrush, Hermit Thrush, Gray-cheeked Thrush, and Veery all sing flute-like repertoires.

This morning's song, however, was more than a single bird singing a duet with itself. There were four singers within close range of my position, and I could hear another just across the river. Since these birds were obviously already on territory, already nesting, perhaps already feeding young, my lack of experience with their behavior in their breeding range left me puzzled by their close proximity to one another. References, however, shed light on the mysterious behavior: Because their territories are small and the birds are abundant, during the breeding season they often create their own singing chorus, morning and evening. And so they did.

They're secretive birds, far more often heard than seen, and such was the case this morning. While I did get an identifying look at one, enough to be sure the singers were indeed Swainson's Thrushes and not another of its cousins, that little guy—or gal—ducked quickly into dense underbrush and disappeared. Not another rustle. Such is their behavior. Furtive ground dwellers, they breed in the north, mostly amid coniferous forests, but on occasion they choose deciduous, riparian forest, where I found them this morning, nesting in shady thickets.

Amazing travelers, Swainson's Thrushes spend their winters in Central and South America, mostly in the Amazon Basin and well into Argentina.

Last year during spring migration, Swainson's Thrushes frequently fed at our mulberry tree.

In March they begin their long journey north to breed, flying up the western Gulf Coast and then fanning out across the Mississippi Valley and north, some of them through our yard. By late May or June, they've reached their breeding grounds. While males arrive on the breeding territory first, the females insist on nesting where they were born, so males finally give way and accept the persistent females' demands for their nursery locations.

Swainson's Thrushes, like most songbirds, migrate at night, and folks who listen on cloudless nights can hear the flutes in the sky. What an awe-inspiring experience, hearing them travel, knowing they've come thousands of miles to breed where they can find lots of bugs to feed their babies—and have an abundance of daylight to get the job done effectively. Quite a family commitment, wouldn't you say? And quite a behavior to witness.

July 8

Marking Tragedy

On our daylong journey home from Michigan's Upper Peninsula today, I was saddened that, over the course of nearly 800 miles, five road-killed hawks lay crumpled alongside the interstate highway. Two were too badly mangled to recognize at 70 mph, but three were clearly Red-shouldered Hawks. Collisions with vehicles, especially semis with their enormous surface area, have been recognized as the primary cause of death for hawks. There's good reason. We've created the perfect hunting habitat for raptors. Highways, especially interstate highways, typically have broad mowed areas between the shoulder and the often-fenced boundary separating highway from forest or field. In addition, the median in open country is usually broad and frequently mowed. These mowed borders and medians create easy hunting for raptors, the short grass offering little or no protection for mice and other rodents that make up much of hawks' menus. But there's more. We've also created the perfect hunting perches with the fence posts and, in many cases, the utility poles that often parallel highway rights-of-way. As hawks survey vast hunting grounds from atop a perfectly sited perch, the birds focus on potential prey, not on approaching vehicles. Thus, at the perfect moment to snare prey, hawks dive, sometimes directly into the path of an oncoming vehicle.

Birds Do *That*?

Nesting chickadees feed on more than 400 caterpillars per day. Yep, that's a bunch of caterpillars! Since native plants host native bugs (including the caterpillar form), the more native plants in the yard, the more food birds can find. In fact, according to Audubon.org, a yard without native plants creates a "food desert" for birds. For instance, researchers at the Smithsonian Conservation Biology Institute found that Carolina Chickadees require a landscape with 70 percent native plants to keep their population steady. "For other birds, such as warblers, vireos, and flycatchers, the percentage rises significantly. In short, native plants determine whether a yard is "boom or bust" for bird populations. But don't chickadees come to seed feeders? Of course, but they—like 96 percent of all songbirds—feed their babies only bugs, and only native plants host native bugs. In short, every plant in the yard should be evaluated as a bird feeder. Does it offer native seed, berries, or nectar, or is it a host plant for native bugs in egg, larval, or adult form? What's in your yard?

To further exacerbate the situation, we sometimes thoughtlessly create a roadside lure. Some folks toss bits of food from the window, thinking there's no harm. After all, some critter will eat the scraps. Thus, folks reason, they're not really littering, not tossing out wrappers or cups or cans. Indeed, just as folks have reasoned, the food scraps are attractive to scavengers, including mice and other rodents. As the morsels lure the rodents, the rodents lure the hawks. The hawks swoop down and collide with a vehicle. The food tossed out the window ultimately lured the birds to their deaths.

It's inevitable: High-speed driving on crowded roadways renders drivers and birds vulnerable. Most likely the damage is mutual, perhaps a shattered windshield or dented vehicle, perhaps worse. The ramifications for the hawks, however, are deadly, even if the birds don't die instantly. A hawk with a broken wing is soon a dead hawk.

Unfortunately, the collateral damage exceeds the demise of the hawk, especially this time of year, during the nesting season. The loss of one of a nesting pair most likely means the loss of the nestlings. Rarely would a single parent be able to capture sufficient prey to feed itself and a couple of offspring, especially as the offspring near maturity and exhibit enormous appetites. Most adults finding themselves alone simply give up, desert the nest, and let nature have its way. Perhaps an eagle finds the struggling youngsters and snaps them up for its own nestlings. Mother Nature can show a truly brutal side.

Our behavior affects their behavior.

July 9

Indicating Age

Having been away from the yard for over a week, I looked for what's changed. This afternoon, four American Robins gathered at the bubble rock: two adults, bright yellow bills confirming their maturity; one youngster, speckled fledgling plumage declaring its youth;

An adult Mourning Dove (foreground) perches with its recent fledgling, the scaly-looking plumage and short tail indicative of its youth.

and one adult, its dark bill contradicting its mature plumage. Since breeding robins have bright yellow beaks, sometimes with dark tips, an otherwise adult-looking bird with a dark beak is a puzzle. Does the dark beak make it a hatch-year bird? Nope. In fact, given the post-mid-season breeding period now, adult birds no longer have reason to impress the opposite sex. So robins, like European Starlings and American Goldfinches, begin to show post-season signs of bill darkening.

Nearby, three Mourning Doves picked about in the pine-straw mulch, their scaly-looking plumage giving them away as having only recently left the nest. Indeed, they look more trim, lacking the fully developed bodies of adults. Still, without careful observation, they could easily be overlooked for what they are: pre-teenaged kids. The youngsters look so oddly different from the adults that I've had folks insist that the fledglings were not Mourning Doves at all, that they had to be another, although similar, species.

Changing appearances give real clues to a bird's age, another one of those behaviors that make these creatures so fascinating.

July 10

Seeing Old Friends

Now that we're back home from visiting about 800 miles to our north, I was reminded of how many of my common year-round yard birds are not at all common there. How I missed Northern Cardinals, possibly the most abundant birds in my yard, listed in Michigan's Upper Peninsula as "rare." Likewise, Blue-gray Gnatcatchers, those busy, buzzy little birds that flycatch in my garden on a daily basis during breeding season, didn't show their

A Great Egret, shown here flying with fish in its beak, is somewhat common in our area, especially during fall dispersal.

faces there. Rarely do UP residents see Summer Tanagers, the melodic singers that call from our woods most mornings and evenings. UP wetlands rarely host a Great Egret, even though the handsome long-legged showy birds breed not far to their south. By comparison, I remember counting over 600 of them coming in to roost one evening in a wetland not far from our house. In the UP there are no American Coots, no Northern Bobwhites, and only sparse sightings of Indigo Buntings or Eastern Towhees. Yellow-billed Cuckoos are also considered rare, although Black-billed Cuckoos make appearances often enough to make themselves known.

On the other hand, the handsome Purple Finch breeds in the UP and shows up fairly regularly. Here, we're lucky to see one or two, especially during tough northern winters—if at all. The chickadees up north are Black-capped Chickadees, not our Carolina Chickadees. Although the two look very much alike, their songs differ. Where their ranges overlap, they're known to interbreed. And Scarlet Tanagers are regulars in northern forests, while I've been watching to see one in my yard all year with no luck so far.

So it goes. It's a fascinating chapter of bird behavior. Birds have their often very specific preferences for varying winter ranges, breeding ranges, and migratory routes. Just because a Northern Cardinal, for instance, lives in my yard doesn't mean it lives in everyone's yard. Some birds find living conditions more to their liking in one place versus another. You have to wonder why, right? Much of their decision making is based on the availability of the food they prefer and the evolutionary means by which they've learned to gather that food. Food types—bugs, berries, seeds, nectar, whatever—are almost always determined by bill structure. So a bird that needs bugs to feed its babies looks for a place with high bug density, most likely in wetlands or grasslands. Or a bird that prefers the kinds of bugs found in tree bark to feed itself and its babies will look for forest with dead and decaying trees.

The rest is about the availability of nest sites, nest-building materials, shelter, and water. In short, each species has evolved to prefer a specific lifestyle. Only those that can adapt will survive climate change and the ongoing loss of many of their preferred habitats.

July 11

Following Bluebirds

Of the thirteen bluebird nest boxes hubby has around our property and on two neighboring lands, only two are currently active. The box closest to the house, at the west end of the garden, has a little pile of bluebird babies, probably four, that the adults are faithfully feeding. Another, the one alongside the hayfield, holds four bluebird eggs. Five boxes have recently gone empty—the Tree Swallows, House Wrens, and three boxes of Eastern Bluebirds having fledged—and we've removed the old, soiled nests. While the remaining boxes have been empty all season, two of those hold completed nests but show no signs of activity. Those unused-nest situations always signal odd behavior for us: After the bluebirds went to all the work of completing the nest, did they find something unsatisfactory about

the box or its location? Did wasps or bees bother them? Did something threaten their safety? We see no signs of insect infestation and no signs of predation.

So here's what we think the situation says about their strange behavior: Probably the birds have met up with some unsatisfactory breeding condition, and when the conditions are right, they'll get on with a family. And what might cause birds to wait to breed? Many things: bad weather (maybe too hot or too cold), weakness (one or the other infertile), poor bug supply (too little food for adults to

A female Eastern Bluebird smacks a caterpillar on the tree branch until dead before taking it to her nestlings.

feed themselves and a brood), or changing conditions in the habitat (maybe vegetation grew too tall for the birds to feel safe or maybe some other critter moved in nearby). We mere humans will likely never fully understand what caused the birds to abandon a perfectly fine nest, but we can bet they had a clear, specific reason. After all, building a nest takes about a week's work—steady, day-after-day work. No bird builds a nest for practice or fun.

Still, given the mid-July time frame, aren't the bluebirds waiting too late to nest? Not really. Since they don't migrate, they have ample time to raise another brood and bring it to maturity before cold weather sets in. By then the little family will be hanging out together as a unit, foraging together for delectable winter morsels. Migrants, on the other hand, probably can't start new broods at this late date. Fledglings wouldn't be ready to migrate in a timely fashion.

Meanwhile, though, those two bluebird nests are ready, and when the time is right, the birds will likely begin their broods. That seems to have been the case with the box in the garden now. The nest sat empty for weeks before any egg laying began.

July 12

Wondering about Wanderers

For at least two months now, no Red-headed Woodpecker has come into my view. Perhaps they're here somewhere, roaming the woods and other parts of the neighborhood, but not where I've been watching. While red-headeds to the south will often attempt a second brood, I suspect our more northerly pairs aim for a successful single brood—meaning that they may attempt a second nest only if the first fails. So maybe our earlier visiting red-headeds were taking advantage of our handouts to make life easier while feeding a couple of nestlings. Since then, perhaps they've dispersed, as birds often do, roaming farther afield to check other habitats and foraging spots. I just hope they'll return later, perhaps for the winter or for another breeding season. Typically, though, they'll hammer out a new winter roost and a new nest site each season. It's called keeping a clean house, a behavior that earns them their reputation as hard workers.

July 13

Loving the Song—and the Songster

According to the all-inclusive authoritative *Birds of North America Online*, the Wood Thrush has become "a symbol of declining Neotropical migrant birds," noting further that the bird has become "increasingly rare over much of its range since the late 1970s." While the songster has been silent here since mid-June, this afternoon it sang briefly but loudly from the woods.

The Wood Thrush, a bird of woodlands, typically forages on the forest floor.

Typical Wood Thrush behavior sees them departing the Yucatan in time to arrive along the Gulf Coast in early April, then fanning out to breeding grounds as far north as Canada and from the central plains to the Atlantic Coast. They nest primarily along the Appalachians and the Mid-Atlantic. It's a day-brightener, then, to hear them in southwestern Indiana, especially now, in mid-July. Singing. But on territory?

Typically a female Wood Thrush raises two broods, but she may make three or four nesting attempts to achieve her goal. She likes deciduous or mixed forests with an understory of shrubs giving ample shade, holding the moisture in deep leaf litter—a perfect description of the woods where the male sang this afternoon and again early this evening. The smaller the forest footprint, however, the more likely the nest will meet its demise from predation—from Brown-headed Cowbirds. And we have plenty of these parasitic birds. I remember well the hundreds that crowded the yard this past winter. Ugh.

Fingers crossed, then, I wish her well, knowing that a singing (that is, a male) Wood Thrush most likely is here because his female is nesting. Wood Thrushes face myriad obstacles—reduced habitat, forest destruction and fragmentation, cowbird parasitism, and tropical forest destruction—trying to survive. I hear so few of them now compared with thirty years ago that I'm keenly aware of their population's dramatic decline. They'll be gone by early September, on their return to Mexico and parts south to Panama. I hope they'll be taking a few offspring with them.

July 14

Observing the Bathers

This afternoon an American Robin spent almost 15 minutes hunkered directly over the bubble of the bubbling rock. He made me laugh, thinking about how the water spout must surely feel against his now-wet belly. From time to time he wallowed deeper in the water, splashing like some maniac. And from time to time he hopped just beyond the spout, preened a bit, ruffled his feathers, only to return to hunker over the bubble. Meanwhile, House Finches, Goldfinches, Northern Cardinals, Carolina Chickadees, Tufted Titmice, and a lone female/immature Indigo Bunting approached for a drink or a bath, only to be the target of the robin's attempted sharp jab. Given the chunky bird's bulk and formidable beak size, no little critter like a chickadee would brave the robin's barrage to try for a drink. So a dozen or more fluttered about, flitting from one

A bathing American Robin squats down over the rising bubble of water at our homemade bubble rock.

nearby branch to another, landing close, trying every approach they could muster to gain access to the water. When the robin left for a few minutes, they scampered in, took quick drinks, and cleared out—just in time for the robin's return.

Since bathing helps clean feathers and control parasites, most birds seem to strive for a good soaking on hot days like today. This bird's behavior, however, told me more. As an adult male, he obviously had no current nesting duties and no babies to feed. His leisurely pace suggested he had time to spare. Maybe he and his mate are between broods; maybe she's taking her turn incubating a new clutch while he takes a break; maybe they've finished their final brood for the season; maybe he's unmated. Whatever the situation, he obviously had no reason to get out of the bath and on to more pressing matters.

July 15

Rising before Sunrise

Shortly after 5 a.m., in the gray before dawn, I sat quietly, mostly motionless, on the front step, listening. Which birds get up earliest? Which sleep in a bit? What do they do? And why?

At 5:05 a.m. a Northern Cardinal broke the silence, first somewhat timidly, quietly, then louder, more robust, and finally full blast. Meantime, two others added their song, and another, then another, and the chorus of varied cardinal songs blended into one. Given their different locations, I should have been able to count the individuals, but they sang on top of one another, their songs running together, some of those nearer drowning out others more distant. As a result, I don't know how many sang, but at least six females scurried about, foraging the little patch of native perennials in front of me, the only spot I could clearly see in the pre-dawn gloom.

Two House Wrens tuned in within minutes, from opposite ends of the house. They have clearly delineated territories, and their songs marked the general boundaries. Each has a nest underway, so each male was testifying to his strength in protecting his mate and his territory. A lusty Carolina Wren, no friend of the House Wren, sang from the neighbor's woods. A dog barked sporadically in the distance to the east.

Closer in, near our east property line, a single Mourning Dove cooed intermittently. And Ruby-throated Hummingbirds buzzed me as I sat within 6 feet of one of their feeders. Their wing whirs and twitters sounded loud in the morning air. Females are incubating second clutches now.

At 5:27 a.m. the neighbor's rooster crowed. Twice. Whoever said roosters awoke first?

By 5:30 a.m. the sky chittered with the calls of zigzagging Chimney Swifts. I know they settle overnight into chimneys nearby, but I've never been able to identify the exact spot or spots. Odd little birds, Chimney Swifts live on the wing, eat on the wing, bathe on the wing, mate on the wing (yes), and sleep on the wing. But at night, they will cling to the sides of a chimney or similar vertical surface. Because of their foot structure, they cannot perch as other birds do. So they either fly or cling. Period.

As I watched the swifts' antics, an Indigo Bunting whistled his say-everything-twice song. Two Carolina Chickadees dropped into the hemlock to forage briefly. The Carolina Wren moved from the woods to the backyard. They, like I, will likely be relieved when the House Wrens go back home and they can once again have their territory to themselves. At the edge of our woods, another chickadee gave his "phoebe" call, persistently, probably trying to make contact with the rest of his family. A Downy Woodpecker called nearby.

At 5:33 a.m. an American Robin went "tut-tutting" as he hopped across tree-tops—probably the same one that hogged the bubble rock yesterday. The cardinals went quiet, only one or two making occasional song from distant shrubs. As they grew quiet, the doves filled in, at least four of them serenading. Goldfinches flew overhead, sounding their "po-ta-to-chip" flight song. Hummer activity increased. A bullfrog grumped a single call from our little yard pond.

Two minutes later, at 5:35 a.m., American Crows flew over, cawing. More Chimney Swifts joined the insect-hunting flight, at least eight of them. Darting birds are hard to count. Wing whirs of Mourning Doves made me look up to catch sight of their landing nearby to forage in the garden.

At 5:37 a.m. a Song Sparrow announced the day. A few cardinals joined briefly. Then I noticed, seemingly out of nowhere, a flock of perhaps thirty Barn Swallows had filled the air above me, swooping, forked tails and swept-back wings serving as perfect identifying silhouettes. What a

House Wrens stuff every available cavity full of twigs, including this nest box in my native garden. The behavior prevents other cavity nesters from taking up residence, thus staving off competition for food.

lot of them! By now, only one House Wren continued to sing, perhaps the other now busy foraging for hungry nestlings. A leopard frog barked once from the pond.

Then, at 5:39 a.m., official sunrise!

By 5:41 a.m. more goldfinches joined the overhead flights. Two Eastern Bluebirds perched on the utility wires, silent, watching, hunting juicy bugs for their nestlings, now nearly filling the nest box at the west end of the garden. An Eastern Wood-pewee called from the woods. House Finches arrived at feeders in multiples, mostly fledglings looking for a ready meal.

At 5:45 a.m. a Red-bellied Woodpecker chirred from the woods.

At 5:52 a.m. an airplane, quite high, a silver bullet with the sun's reflection making it shine like a moving star, emitted a slight drone after it was nearly past.

The leopard frog called one last time at 5:54 a.m. A Hairy Woodpecker's "pik-pik" call seemed to come from the backyard, along with a Tufted Titmouse's "peter, peter, peter."

By 5:56 a.m. the morning song was falling quiet. A neighbor's truck went dieseling out the lane, a working man heading off to the job. From the distance an approaching train whistle marked every crossroad along the way. And only the House Wren sang.

At 6 a.m. the distant church bell rang the hour. Then a second bell joined in a joyous greeting to the day.

As I reflect on the morning sounds, it's obvious what was missing: No Yellow-throated Warbler, no Northern Parula, no Blue-gray Gnatcatcher, no Purple Martin. Their absence means either they're busy with nesting duties, maybe feeding a second brood, and have no need to sing (just like the silent bluebirds). Or maybe their absence means they've finished nesting duties and have grown silent, perhaps already heading south.

That's the tricky thing about the behavior of southbound migrants: I never know for sure when they leave. Usually it just dawns on me one day that I haven't seen them recently, so they must be gone. Or at least I think they're gone. Then, days or weeks later, I may see a single individual, or maybe two, and then I think, okay, they didn't leave after all. Ah, but maybe they did. Maybe the single individual is another of its kind, just passing through from parts farther north. "Our" birds, the ones that nested in and around the yard, may indeed have left earlier.

The absence of some of our summer birds this morning, however, may have been just a momentary miscue. But by now, in mid-July, birds that manage only a single brood may well be heading home. I'll keep watching.

July 16

Donating Cat Hair

As I mentioned earlier, our three always-indoor, slightly spoiled cats get regular brushings, and I save the hair, wads of it. Using an old onion bag, I offer it for the taking, hoping birds will enjoy it for lining their nests. Indeed, I've watched Carolina Chickadees and Tufted Titmice pulling so much cat hair from the bag, stuffing their beaks, that I feared for their ability to see well enough to fly.

Late this afternoon, however, I caught sight of a new user of the offering: a female American Goldfinch. Goldfinches are one of only a few birds that are 100 percent vegetarian and feed their babies not bugs but partially digested seeds that adults regurgitate for their nestlings. They also prefer to build their nests of native thistle down. Combined, those two behaviors require goldfinches to nest late in the season, sometimes well after other birds have finished, perhaps even finished a second brood. So this afternoon's tim-

A female American Goldfinch tugs cat hair from an old onion bag. She's a late nester, just now building, lining her nest with the soft hairs.

ing for gathering hair to line her nest was right in keeping with the species' routine. She took her time, poking into the mesh to clamp onto another beakful of hair, repeating the effort for several minutes, each time adding to the "whiskers" that formed on either side of her face. And then she was gone. How I'd love to know where she's building her tight little nest, so carefully structured that it's firm to the touch, tight enough to hold water—a unique goldfinch nest-building behavior. In fact, the brood can drown in a heavy rainstorm if parents don't adequately cover the nest.

Birds Do *That*?

A robin cocks its head not to hear but to see. Like most other birds, a robin's eyes sit on the sides of its head. Thus, while it lacks binocular vision, it has about a 340-degree (but not a 360-degree) peripheral vision, aiding it in spotting predators on the approach. So with fixed eyes on the sides of its head, a robin must tilt its head to look down to the ground. But if a robin tilts its head to look down, the other eye must be looking up, right? Right! Birds' brains sort that all out, the one side of the brain able to focus on the "down" view while the other side focuses up. Thus, while robin-redbreast is catching the early worm, it keeps the other half of its brain on the situation skyward in case a hawk soars past or a cat stalks nearby. Now that's multitasking!

July 17

Threatening Bluebirds

After supper this evening, I wandered outside to enjoy the sunset amid somewhat cooler temperatures but was immediately distracted by scolding Eastern Bluebirds. Their nest is tucked safely in a Peterson-style nest box that hubby built, mounted at the west end of the garden, a predator nest guard in place. He monitors it, as well as all the others, religiously. Inside, a brood nears fledging, is almost fully feathered, and tended by a devoted pair of parents who bring bugs nearly nonstop these days. The chatter first made me think the adults were calling the nestlings out, that indeed they were ready to fledge. As hubby joined me in the yard, he firmly denied the babies were ready for the outside world: He had checked the box the previous day.

Unable to see anything amiss and unable to spot the two adults that continued their scolding, I edged closer to the box, slowly, watching carefully. I feared causing the brood to erupt prematurely from the nest. At the same time, I feared the birds may have already erupted and the little ones were in danger. Then something moderately large flew into the hemlock that towers 30 feet from the box. It was just a flash out of the corner of my eye, something with white but indiscernible at a glance. I stopped and watched, but saw no further movement, no trembling limbs, no indication of what may have dashed past. Then it called. Unmistakable. And troubling. It was the call of a Cooper's Hawk. I hadn't seen a Cooper's in some time, nesting activity having come to an end, for better or worse, at least a month ago. I had seen no evidence either way whether the Cooper's young survived and fledged, or fell victim to an owl (the Barred Owl nested in the adjoining woods), a hawk (the Red-shouldered Hawk nested nearby), a crow (a pair chased a hawk from the woods), or even a climbing mammal like a raccoon. Any one of these potential predators would have been eager to chow down on Cooper's nestlings themselves or to offer them as dinner to their own babies.

Now, though, a mature Cooper's was hanging around, upsetting the bluebirds, obviously looking for supper for itself. My presence sent it flying, and for that I'm glad. Yes, hawks have to eat, too, and for having interrupted its chance at a meal, I should feel penitent. But

Much to my chagrin, a Cooper's Hawk hunts our backyard for tasty songbirds.

please, not the bluebirds. Some would argue it's not my right to choose among favorites in the yard, that nature takes its own course. Only the strong and smart survive while the slow, witless, and weak do not. In all likelihood the bluebirds would have been just fine, and even without my presence, their babies would continue to rest comfortably in the predator-proof nest box. Still, as the scenario played out, the bluebirds had just a little longer this evening to bug hunt and feed their growing brood. My interference may not have been Mother Nature's way, but I'm still glad.

July 18

Spotting Clues

This morning a male Ruby-throated Hummingbird sat idle for some minutes, perched near the array of nectar feeders, apparently eyeing them but showing no interest in feeding. Odd behavior, but I suspect his tummy was already full, and he merely hoped to guard the ready food supply against the dozens of other males that frequent the feeders. Of course, there's no shortage of nectar now, given the abundance of blossoms in the garden and yard. Really, then, hummers need not go full blast at territorial disputes. But they do. It's just instinct. The tiny little jewels of the air that some folks call "cute" are really vicious warriors, sometimes fighting to the ground in territorial disputes. Share and share alike are not within their realm of behavior.

So I was amused that this little handsome bundle of testosterone could sit so quietly, viewing the domain as if he hadn't a care in the world. Perhaps his sitting quietly reflected nothing more than his unwillingness to flit about. In any case, his ruby-red namesake gorget flashed with the sunlight—black when no light struck it and blindingly bright when light reflected perfectly, showing varying shades of brown, rust, and red in between. Just for the record, though, the feathers themselves have no color—it's only reflected light that lets us (and presumably the females) see red. As he sat facing me, his forked tail showed prominently. Only males have forked tails, and only females and youngsters have white dots on the tip of each tail feather. Nothing distinguishes the male more beautifully, however, than that dramatically changing gorget, especially when he tosses his head about, purposely flashing the color, showing off his prowess to any female within sight. Talk about strutting his stuff! What a courtship behavior!

Male Ruby-throated Hummingbirds flash their red gorgets by moving their throats in the sunshine. Without light, the gorget is black.

As I considered this little guy's quiet demeanor, seemingly demonstrating his nonchalance, I realized I needed to consider the calendar clues. He is, indeed, close to having not a care in the world. While hummers well to the north have time for only a single brood, local hummers generally pull off two broods. Given the usual chronology of events, the females have by now fledged their first broods, have built their second nests, and may well have a second clutch of two eggs, incubating them with their usual near-religious fervor. They're surely the world's most independent single moms. Yes, single. Male hummingbirds serve only one purpose, and having completed that task within seconds, they move on to seek any other partner with whom to spend a few seconds. Males never help build nests, never help incubate eggs, never help feed nestlings, never help protect fledglings, and perhaps never again see the females with which they've bred. How's that for paternal behavior?

Compare this photo with the previous hummingbird photo. The two images are of the same bird on the same perch but with their heads in different positions to catch the light on their gorgets.

But back to that chronology. Given that it's late July, with most females likely having produced their second clutches, the males have no further purpose. Without purpose, the birds' hormones and all they trigger now slow. It's time for these males to give up the battles, gain weight, and head south. After all, they've had an exhausting summer. Some folks would say, "Hey, wait a minute. We see male hummingbirds here in southwestern Indiana even in late August. What do you mean, they're leaving now, in July?"

True. Those August and even early September male hummers, however, are most likely males that finished their work to our north, fattened up on territory, and have begun the long flight home, moving measure by measure south toward the Gulf of Mexico, across the vast waters to the Yucatan, and venturing as far south as Costa Rica. On that journey, they've made a migratory stopover here, fattening up for the next leg, flying perhaps as much as 100 miles per night. In short, the males here now are not the males here a month from now, or even a week from now. What an astonishing life these tiny birds live! What amazing behavior they demonstrate!

July 19

Identifying Hummingbirds

In early spring, distinguishing male from female Ruby-throated Hummingbirds is a snap. The males have dark throats—red, brown, or black, depending on the light—and females have white or light-gray throats. Males have forked tails while females have straight tails. His tail feathers are emerald green, almost black, but her tail feathers sport white dots on the ends. Then the youngsters fledge, and all confusion breaks loose.

When nestlings leave the nest, they're the size of adults. Thus, there's no such thing as a baby hummingbird outside the nest—at least not naturally. Anything that suggests "baby hummer" flitting about the garden is most assuredly one of the sphinx moths, usually the one often called hummingbird moth or a similar one called Snowberry Clear-wing moth. And just because a hummer looks small doesn't identify it as a youngster, either, since adult males are smaller than adult females, sometimes quite dramatically so.

How then, can we recognize who's who among just-out-of-the-nest hummingbirds? Beyond the fact that fledglings' back and head feathers show buffy edges, all juveniles, both males and females, look like adult females, a fairly typical phenomenon in the bird world. So all fledglings, like adult females, have white dots on their tails and whitish throats, sometimes with throat speckles in varying degrees of density. Typically, the more throat speckles, the more likely the bird is a male. But not necessarily. In short, sometimes positive identification can be made only with the bird in hand, something legal only among licensed hummingbird banders.

A nectaring, day-flying Snowberry Clear-wing moth, nicknamed hummingbird moth, is often mistaken for a "baby" hummingbird. By the time a hummingbird fledges, however, it's as large as the adults.

July 20

Logging Change

For nearly two months the yard population has remained static, the same species flitting in and around the area, only youngsters adding to the count. Still, their behaviors are telling—who's had a good breeding season, who's still nesting, who's preparing to leave. And behaviors are beginning to change.

Northern Cardinals, House Finches, Mourning Doves, American Robins—all have had good years in the nest. Some year-round residents that made themselves readily visible in winter have disappeared from view, not because they migrated but because they've hidden themselves away in some discrete nest area, away from my prying eyes. Red-headed Woodpeckers, Pileated Woodpeckers, Red-bellied Woodpeckers, and Northern Flickers have all abandoned the yard for private nurseries. Among woodpeckers, I see almost exclusively Downy and Hairy Woodpeckers. Blue Jays hid out for a time but have since returned. A few rather thin and scraggly looking individuals are no doubt hatch-year birds that otherwise look just like their parents. A pair of Eastern Towhees has reappeared occasionally, picking about under the nyjer-seed feeder, their single youngster popping in and out but always alone, making its identification a bit of a head-scratcher. Its almost nondescript plumage offers few clues. Carolina Wrens, chased off by too many House Wrens, are edging back into the yard, making headway toward regaining their usual habitat even though two House Wren pairs still have active nest sites in the yard. Eastern Bluebirds have remained constants, and hubby tells me we still have three active nests, all with nestlings, one box about to fledge.

Yesterday and again today, a pair of Indigo Buntings visited the bubble rock, he taking a quick bath while she lingered, chasing away anything that disturbed her leisure. I've not seen them since late spring, before they chose their territory and nested, I hope successfully. The challenge for me, of course, is identifying her, separating her from her offspring. In short, I can't. Not with any certainty. Again, like so many birds, her fledglings closely resemble her, though sometimes with a bit more streaking on their breasts. Their plumage, however, drab as it is, changes quickly when they're young, growing sleek and silky looking and simultaneously less streaky. In her own quiet way, however, the female is elegant, showing just a tinge of blue, although the tinge is sometimes indiscernible in poor light.

A female Indigo Bunting shows only a tinge of blue, but even that tinge can be indiscernible in poor light.

All in all, then, things are beginning to change, a sure indication that breeding season is nearing its end for a good many birds (although American Goldfinches, the last to breed, are only now setting up housekeeping). The summer doldrums of the bird world—at least from a bird watcher's perspective—are about to end. And I'm loving it! Every day offers more clues about what happened in the nurseries.

July 21

Questioning Baldness

Young Northern Cardinals—some just out of the nest, some a month old, some pushing two months old—bring an array of plumages to the yard. Separating hatch-year birds from adults is fairly simple: Although cardinals are dimorphic (males and females wear different identifiable plumages), regardless of sex, all adult cardinals have look-alike bright orangey-red beaks. On the other hand, hatch-year cardinals can have beaks ranging from almost entirely black to yellow to pale orange, and their plumages also vary dramatically, from overall gray brown with little or no reddish tinges to splotchy but bright all-over red.

Occasionally, though, a brightly beaked cardinal with brightly colored overall red plumage shows up wearing a black head and face. That happened today. He's a strange-looking critter, actually rather freaky, but he's common enough to have a recognized nickname: lizard head. Despite his appearance, however, he's not a rare tropical migrant, not a hybrid species. He's just a regular guy—sort of. The black head and face are simply featherless skin. The poor guy has gone bald.

A male "lizard-head" Northern Cardinal, his head bare of feathers, revealing his black skin, likely suffers from an infestation of feather mites.

Balding among birds, especially cardinals and Blue Jays, seems to be the result of one of two causes: First, some authorities believe the baldness is the result of an unusual molt in which the bird loses all its head feathers at once. Indeed, the most common time to see baldness in cardinals is after the end of breeding season, the time when most songbirds molt. Typically when birds molt, however, they lose only a few feathers at once, like a single flight feather on each wing, the symmetry of loss allowing them to continue flying safely. But sometimes this quirky "bald" molt occurs during which the so-called capital ring of feathers falls out simultaneously. Second, other authorities claim the baldness is the result of feather mites or lice. Because the birds cannot effectively groom their heads while preening, perhaps the mites accumulate there and destroy the feathers, resulting in baldness.

Given that breeding season is still well underway here among cardinals, and given that I see no evidence of molting among other adult cardinals, I'm inclined to believe that the bird I saw today is suffering from mites. Fortunately, in spite of the bird's rather unsettling appearance, the infestation is not life-threatening. It unlikely causes pain. Surely, however, a mite infestation would cause itching, resulting in the bird scratching frequently—perhaps exacerbating the feather loss. The big problem he faces, however, is the effect of his appearance on his ability to breed. Since female cardinals are known to choose mates based on the quality and brightness of their plumage—her best visual clue to the male's health and well-being—he will remain lonely, at least until he recovers and re-grows the missing plumage. But I do pause to consider: Having a full head of pinfeathers must surely be an uncomfortable, itchy situation. Poor guy! Here's wishing him better days within the next few weeks.

July 22

Birding after the Rain

After a short but moderately heavy rain late this afternoon, bird activity increased this evening. There's a logical explanation for birds' busy behavior. Because they lose foraging time during rainstorms, a time when they seek shelter from the elements, they make up for lost time afterward by increasing their feeding frenzy. Especially close to sunset, birds are instinctively driven to stock up, fill their bellies for the night, helping them make it through the dark hours alive. Their little bodies, all running on incredibly high metabolisms, need constant energy replenishment.

As a result, this evening's short amble through the yard gave me twenty-two species and almost one hundred individuals. Even the Blue-gray Gnatcatcher, which seemed earlier to have disappeared, presumably on its way back home, showed up, silent now, dashing into the eastern red cedar trees, probably to settle in for its overnight roost. Hummingbirds, of course, buzzed feeders even more frantically than usual, multiple birds feeding simultaneously at all feeders, sipping steadily for a full hour before and just at dark. They, too, must guzzle down enough syrup to make it through the night, a truly critical activity for them this evening given that the rain washed away the garden flowers' nectar. Barn Swallows swept the hayfield like little machines on hyperdrive, gathering bugs galore. Chimney Swifts did the same at a higher altitude. Busy, busy, busy, all of them.

Thus it went with goldfinches, chickadees, titmice, Song Sparrows, Indigo Buntings, Chipping Sparrows, woodpeckers, cardinals, wrens, doves, and all the rest.

One bird, however, gained my attention above all the others. The Eastern Wood-pewee arrived in the garden to flycatch, aiming to fill his tummy while coincidentally reducing the garden bugs. Gotta love that combo! Pewees are sit-and-wait hunters, teed up on an open, sometimes high perch, watching, dashing out to grab a bug and flying back, usually to the same perch, to dine at leisure. But what really drew my attention was not the flycatching effort, but another behavior: the battle it had with another pewee. For little guys weighing less than half an ounce, what fierce fighters they are! As war raged, I could hear their beaks clicking as they snapped at one another, their wings smacking in some sort of boxing match, their feet extended in attack mode. The combat lasted only 10 to 15 seconds, but it seemed as if they had engaged in a full-fledged battle. Within 20 minutes or so, just as I thought all peace had been restored, one apparently approached the other's feeding spot too closely, and the battle scenario replayed. I never saw feathers fly, but thank goodness the apparent

An Eastern Wood-pewee flycatches from a vantage point, gleaning dozens of insects.

loser departed quickly. Otherwise I fear things could have gotten deadly. Of course, two questions linger: Who were the two fighters? Adults? Hatch-year birds? One of each? And second, why were they battling? Over feeding rights? Surely there's no reason this late to argue over breeding territory. Puzzling behavior.

Birds Do *That*?

Winged pirates steal food for a living. A behavior called kleptoparasitism, practiced by a surprising number of birds, deserves jail time. After hunting for hours and risking its life diving for fish, an Osprey finally struggles into flight, carrying its hard-caught fish back to shore. Enter a Bald Eagle. It dive-bombs the Osprey, forcing it to drop the hard-earned prey. In turn, the eagle readily snatches the dropped prey from midair and carries if off for a grand meal. The Osprey is left empty "handed" and hungry. Gulls, ravens, crows, and pelicans have all been documented engaged in similar behavior. In research summarized in AllAbout Birds.org, scientists have concluded that only the smartest birds engage in the skullduggery.

Aside from their warrior ways, pewees are odd little flycatchers. They resemble Eastern Phoebes in many ways, but their behaviors differ. While migrating phoebes typically arrive first in my yard in spring, pewees usually arrive last. At least they're the last ones I hear adding spring song to the chorus, sometimes even after the cuckoos arrive. But pewees have good reason to be tardy: They've come a long way. Every spring they trek their way here from South America, wintering deep into Brazil, even as far as Bolivia. While they're forest birds, they really don't need much of a wood patch to be at home. Our little patch works for them. Even though they're regular nesters here, I've never found a nest, but I've read that it's so small, seemingly too small for the bird, and so carefully lichen-covered that it looks like a knot on a branch. Clever behavior, that nest building.

July 23

Monitoring Nest Boxes

Because good hosts clear nest boxes as soon as nestlings fledge, this morning I checked boxes I knew were active on the last check but could be empty now. One box that had the makings of a tidy little pine-straw bluebird nest during my last check now sounded active, little peeps coming from inside. How good to know another batch of bluebirds was on the way! Or so I thought, until, as I approached, I saw a House Wren flee the box. What? As I cautiously opened the box, I found the bluebird nest still intact, but an additional lining of feathers made a nursery for a little brood of babies. My blood did a slow boil. Only one possible scenario here, a behavior distinctive to the species: The House Wren robbed the bluebird of its nest, took over the box, and was raising her own brood here. She didn't even take time to redecorate by adding the typical clutter of sticks to the nest. She just moved in. My fervent hope is that she didn't kill the female bluebird in the course of the take-over. And I have to wonder: Did the bluebird build elsewhere, choosing another of our ready boxes for her brood? Why couldn't the House Wren have chosen one of those other boxes? It's such a cruel world out there. I wish House Wrens (along with House Sparrows) would play nice. But nice isn't survival of the fittest.

$$July\ 24$$

Verifying Raptors

Taking advantage of superior weather conditions, we journeyed south to the Land Between the Lakes (LBL), where the dams forming the two lakes and the accompanying hydroelectric plants make great birding sites. Great Blue Herons, Great Egrets, Ring-billed and occasional other gulls, Black-crowned Night-herons, American Pelicans, Ospreys, and Bald Eagles all hang out there, attracted by the fish. Sometimes fish that are sucked through the power-generating turbines are stunned, even killed, and that makes for easy pickin's for fisher-birds.

Today, with fewer than the usual multitudes of birds, we concentrated on fishing Ospreys. Eight adults circled above the turbulent waters gushing from the turbines, each bird looking for quick picks for their near-ready-to-fledge youngsters. Since these raptors discovered the rows of power transmission-line towers in the area, they've chosen them as nest spots, great substitutes for the natural snag, treetop, or cliff side. Their acceptance of these and similar man-made structures for nest sites has been key to their recovery after the pesticide DDT caused their disappearance in some areas. Since the birds' typical behavior sees them return to the same nests each year, increasing the bulk of sticks as they make annual improvements, some nests reach 10 to 12 feet across and 3 to 5 feet deep, big enough for a human to sit in. And yes, some of the nests in the LBL area equal these dimensions.

Osprey fishing behavior is a sight to behold. They catch fish by diving, talons outstretched, beady eyes focused straight down their legs as they aim for their prey. Research reports that they have a 70 percent success rate and hunt only an average of 12 minutes before making a catch. Impressive! What makes them such successful fishers? Unlike their hawk cousins, they have a reversible outer toe that allows them to grasp objects with two toes in front and two toes in back. Given the slipperiness of wet fish, they need some added grip, and they get that from barbed pads on the soles of their feet. In short, they don't often have a story to tell about the one that got away.

Watching them carry fish back to the nest—or off to a dining perch—also shows their masterful behavior. They arrange their captured fish vertical to their flight path, head first, making the sometimes sizable catch more aerodynamic. Clever, huh?

So we spent a couple of hours watching these amazing anglers, tying to photograph them flying and making a catch. It turned into an entertaining venture. At one point, in fact, a screeching Bald Eagle caught my attention. As is the eagle's peculiar habitual behavior, it was chasing an Osprey that had a nice-size fish in its talons, trying to force the Osprey to drop its prey. Dropped prey is eagle lunch. Diving and darting, the two put on an aerial performance that would challenge the Blue Angels fighter-jet pilots in any air show they might perform. Sometimes the Osprey dropped below the eagle, sometimes it veered sharply left or right, sometimes it lifted up and away, outmaneuvering the eagle even while carrying a sizable fish. The eagle finally abandoned the chase. Good! Thieves shouldn't win the war.

After another 20 minutes or so passed while we continued aiming our cameras on the fishing Osprey, a sound other than an Osprey's call caught my attention. Although I knew the call was that of a bird, I couldn't pull the name from the recesses of my brain. Nor could I find the source of the call. Again, though, an aerial confrontation caught my eye, but the

A juvenile Peregrine Falcon pauses from its hunting, perching on the superstructure of a hydroelectric dam.

An Osprey flies back to its nest with a fish, aligning the catch aerodynamically, a behavior that helps the bird fly efficiently.

An Osprey flies with its eye on the waters below, hunting fish close enough to the surface to snatch.

two birds in battle were new to the scene. Long, sharply pointed wings, slender tail, flying like jet-propelled acrobats, they obviously disagreed about whose space was whose, and the one was having none of the other's presence. As the obvious loser in this little war fled the battle, it jetted to the top of the dam's superstructure. My eyes popped. And so did my camera—even given the long distance. Could it be? Really? I studied the image on my camera's monitor and confirmed my surprise: juvenile Peregrine Falcon. Well, of course, no other bird behaves like a Peregrine. They're the absolute flight masters!

Who knows where this one came from. Reintroduced in the area after extirpation by the pesticide DDT, Peregrines have adapted their nesting behavior. Nowadays, they choose architectural ledges or purposely installed nest boxes on tall city buildings, reminiscent of their preferred cliff-side dwellings. Indianapolis and Fort Wayne, Indiana, and Louisville, Kentucky, host Peregrines in proffered nest boxes. Some pairs nest on tall bridge structures, including the double-decker bridge spanning the Ohio River at Louisville. Given that Peregrines disperse after the breeding season ends, often following waterways, perhaps this youngster found its way here from Louisville. Or maybe it fledged from a nest much closer to today's sighting. Was the juvenile related to the other Peregrine? Maybe the battle-champion Peregrine was an adult teaching the juvenile to find its own way, a sort of kicking-it-out-of-the-house kind of maneuver. An ample supply of pigeons roost in and around the dam, and they're a favored food among Peregrines. Maybe the adult was forcing the kid to learn to hunt on its own. In any case, I was ecstatic to witness the behavior, even if I can't be sure exactly what was happening.

July 25

Grinning over Grasshoppers

Watching for the little flock of Wild Turkeys to wander across the hayfield or through the pasture has again become a daily routine. Oh, it's not that I sit waiting and watching, but each time I'm near a window, I glance out, scanning the area, checking on their presence. This morning I was pleased to see six hens foraging from the crest of the rise, moving my way. I stood patiently watching. Then I began wondering: What in the world are they doing? One would dart to the right 8 or 10 feet. Another would charge forward a few feet. Still another might circle around, ending where she began. Their erratic behavior seemed senseless. Focusing my binocular on the sextet, I studied them. Dart here. Jump there. Circle around. Scamper back. Run forward. Sometimes, they looked toward the ground. And finally I saw. They were chasing grasshoppers!

While turkeys feast on acorns by preference, the mast crop is a long way from falling this early in the season. Thus, turkeys turn to insects. The hayfield offers a wide variety of bugs, but apparently this morning the real feast was on grasshoppers. Without understanding what the turkeys were doing, surely a person could think they were a bit goofy. A little comedy in the bird world! Well, comic to me, perhaps, but certainly not to serious food hunters like the turkeys. Survival behavior is rarely comic.

July 26

Checking for the Dead

This morning I had to stop and consider: Do I have a pulse? When the Turkey Vultures soar closer and closer to where I stand, knowing they smell out dead stuff for their dining pleasure, it's cause for pause. Maybe they're watching to see if I move. Maybe they're watching for some other blob on the landscape that could be a carcass. In either case, it's a bit unnerving when they come close—close enough to see their bare red heads and pale hooked beaks.

Although I've never gone inside to investigate, I'm fairly sure the vultures nest regularly in a dilapidated barn several miles from here, a building now nearly collapsing from structural demise. It's the perfect spot for these carrion eaters, inside something as spooky as a Halloween haunted house where nobody cares how putrid it smells. Now that breeding season is over for them, they've dispersed, soaring around the larger neighborhood. This evening, four of them soared just over the treetops, across the garden, swooping down even lower near where I stood watching, behaving just the way Turkey Vultures always behave. They're magnificent fliers, sometimes soaring for hours without ever flapping a wing. In fact, because of their lazy preference for soaring rather than flying, they get a late start to the day, loafing until the warm air currents give them the lift they need to drift across the skies. Who knew some birds were lazy?

Turkey Vultures have such a strong sense of smell that engineers rely on the birds as leak detectors along distant and mostly inaccessible gas pipelines. By adding a carrion-like scent to the gas, they can count on vultures to circle with pinpoint accuracy over any leaks along ever-so-remote locations. In spite of their strong sense of smell, however, Turkey

A Turkey Vulture soars in search of carrion, usually smelling its prey before seeing it.

Vultures tend to find carrion only after it thoroughly ripens. In fact, Black Vultures, which also roam in these parts, typically rely on Turkey Vultures to find the day's meal. Blacks don't have the superb olfactory sensory perception that Turkeys do. Both vultures, though, lack the ability to rip open hides and so must wait for a carcass to burst. Okay, that was more than you wanted to know, but the details help explain their master behavioral plan for survival. In fact, their preference for carrion also explains their feather-free heads. They would have no way to clean head feathers after poking about inside a carcass, so vultures evolved to meet the needs of their trade. Yes, you're absolutely correct that this whole scenario is sickening, but imagine what conditions would be like if there were no vultures. We'd be knee-deep in carrion. That's even worse!

And by the way, yes, vultures are what some folks call buzzards. True buzzards, however, live mostly in Africa and some parts of Europe and Asia. No true buzzards fly across North America—no matter what folks call them!

July 27

Spying on Fledglings

Carolina Wrens fledged today from one of our bluebird boxes, and I managed to spy on the family behavior. Adults were noisy, scolding, making a general fuss of things. I'm not sure how much of the scolding was aimed at the youngsters, directing them where to go and how to be safe, and how much was directed my way as I did some pruning nearby. Two fledglings flew across the path, their stubby little tails offering little by way of a necessary rudder, and crash-landed in their target tree. It's hard to refer to the end of that flight as a "landing." In fact, they just quit flying and fell onto a branch, uprighted themselves, and

A just-fledged Carolina Wren finds itself being soaked in an afternoon rain shower, probably preferring its cavity nest to the wet weather.

clung for balance. At least they didn't crash to the ground! Within a few days, however, they will have mastered the art, making graceful landings on their branch of choice.

July 28

Recognizing Clues

Goldfinches have been clinging to purple coneflower seed heads, plucking lunch. Some folks would have deadheaded the plants, aiming to rid the garden of anything spent or "ugly." Since I plant for birds (and bugs and, therefore, butterflies), certainly I wouldn't want to deprive birds of the purpose of my efforts: food!

A Yellow-billed Cuckoo called from the woods this morning. His "cloke, cloke, cloke" message means he's found food here, too—and he loves caterpillars. Of course, when folks spray to kill caterpillars, they risk killing the cuckoos as well, not only because of the toxicity of the dying caterpillars but also because of the resulting shortage of food.

The echo of hammering Pileated Woodpeckers made me realize they're at work, each in its own territory, preparing for another season. Rarely do woodpeckers, especially Pileateds, use the same nest hole for raising their young and then for sheltering during winter. Now they are testing out wintering sites, looking for the perfect cold-season protection. I'll be glad when they return to the yard on a regular basis. I've missed their big, brassy presence!

A Red-eyed Vireo sang briefly this morning from the neighbor's woods. Like most other migrants—and year-round residents for that matter—birds' vocal behaviors change now, and they sing more softly. Without the need to blast out their territorial defense, instead merely keeping track of the family, the softer, shorter, more intimate songs and calls make for a quieter woodland. Even if the pair managed a second brood this summer, I suspect they won't stay much longer, heading south, deep into South America, as far as Argentina. When birds have a long way to go, they must allow time, leaving as soon as they can to make a leisurely trip home.

A Killdeer forages for bugs, head slightly cocked, looking and listening.

A Killdeer called from the pasture. After nesting and raising their families, they're dispersing now. While they were silent most of the summer, they're once again making their presence known as they begin seeking out fall foraging areas. While some will hang out with us all year, weather permitting, others head south into Central America. Maybe the ones that nested farther north are already moving through here on their way to a more comfortable winter range.

An Eastern Wood-pewee perched on the utility wire running alongside our driveway. It never made a sound—no calls, no songs—although I did hear an occasional bill snap as it snagged bugs on the wing. They're fattening up, readying themselves for a long journey as well, into Central America and, for some, to Bolivia.

So the clues are in place. Bird behavior is changing daily, especially among those birds that have finished breeding.

Birds Do *That*?

A Brown Thrasher sang 2,400 distinctly different songs in 2 hours. Using a continuous spectrum analyzer, zoologist Donald E. Kroodsma of the Rockefeller University Field Research Center in Millbrook, New York, proved that Brown Thrashers outperform Northern Mockingbirds. During a 30-minute span, the mocker sang 465 songs, but only 93 were distinctly different. Wonder how many the mocker would have performed if the study had lasted 2 hours? And how would the thrasher have fared if studied for more than 2 hours? Did he sing every song he knew in those 2 hours? Or did he forget a few? In any case, Brown Thrashers hold the record for most songs sung.

July 29

Enjoying Night Birds

We found our way to the riverfront this evening to enjoy the pleasant (and unseasonably) cool weather. Atop the riverbank, there's always a breeze, and some birds hunt along the course of the river, especially just at dusk. Others take advantage of the streetlights to snag bugs in the air. A half hour before sunset, we began to think the Chimney Swifts had departed way sooner than usual, but within another 10 minutes, bingo! The sky above us fluttered with at least thirty swifts, diving, darting, snatching bugs in their wide-open gapes, enjoying a feast. Chimney Swifts are such crazy little creatures, unable to perch, only to cling, so we always try to figure out where they go for the evening, in whose chimney they drop into for the night.

A Common Nighthawk also soared among the swifts, making its readily identifiable call, a nasal "pent." While the white vertical band across each wing also identifies the bird in flight, it's the call that makes me look up, hoping to see the bird. Common Nighthawks are declining, and the fact that I heard only one calling this evening causes me concern. Now, at the end of nesting season, I should hear at least three, maybe four—the pair and their offspring. So it was with mixed emotion I listened to the one, knowing that it will soon head to deep parts of South America, returning home, apparently alone.

July 30

Recording a First

Today marks the first record of known breeding Black-bellied Whistling Ducks in Indiana, discovered in a private golf-course pond in southwestern Indiana. The birding world is all abuzz! These distinctive ducks are hard to misidentify, but they are, after all, primarily mid-South American ducks with small populations along the coasts up through Central America and now into the United States, especially in Texas and Louisiana. Only in the past twenty years or so have breeding Black-bellies taken up residence in Florida. So now they've bred successfully in Indiana, albeit in the farthest southern corner of the state, a spot farther south than Louisville, Kentucky. Surely climate change has caused these birds to wander so far north.

Even in profile, Black-bellies would be hard to mistake. Sexes are identical, so it's a straightforward ID. They look a bit gooselike with long legs, long necks, and an erect stance. Mostly chestnut brown with namesake black bellies, they're truly dark ducks—except for that wide white wing stripe. Oh, and don't forget the bright pink bill and legs.

Then there's the unmistakable face. Pete Dunne, widely published master birder, describes Black-bellied Whistling Ducks as having an "overpainted harlot-like face, showing too much gray pancake makeup, an oversize lipstick-colored bill, and an exaggerated pale ring around the eye." Well, that should say it all!

We've photographed Black-bellies in Florida and Texas, including some with youngsters. And we've also clicked off occasional photos of them here in southwestern Indiana. The local photos, though, were of birds visiting on a momentary basis, stopping by for a

A female Black-bellied Whistling Duck keeps a close eye on her two ducklings.

few days to rest, feed, wander about, and then move on. Last year in June, we photographed five, a little flock of one-day wonders.

What makes them such rarities here? According to the North American Breeding Bird Survey, Black-belly populations have been growing at an estimated rate of over 6 percent per year for the past fifty or so years. Maybe, then, these critters are searching for new territory, and perhaps because of climate change, they're wandering, following the rivers northward. As the Cornell Lab of Ornithology notes on its website, "They seem to readily adopt human-altered habitats, and this has helped them move north." Golf courses count as human-altered.

The current eBird map, an online international record of what's where, shows Black-bellies as far north as Minnesota, Maine, and Nova Scotia, all east of the Rockies and most east of the Mississippi River. It's certainly mounting evidence that the ducks are expanding their territory. And now a breeding record in Indiana!

Generally, though, Black-bellies don't migrate. They mate for life, find a happy home, and settle down. I really don't think that can happen here, given the winters. Since they prefer nesting in cavities, usually tree snags, and build no nest, I also have to wonder where they incubated their eggs at the golf course. True, if given no other choice, they will lay eggs in a scrape on the ground, surely knowing that such a location exposes their eggs and ducklings to predation. So maybe that happened here. In parts of the deep south, a few Black-bellies have adapted, accepting man-made nest boxes. As a result of their preferred tree-nesting behavior, they're often seen roosting in trees or on logs over water and are particularly adept at perching on precarious spots. They've even been known to perch on corn stubble.

Black-bellies also display an odd daily-routine behavior. They loaf all day in or along shallow freshwater ponds, leave at sunset (giving their squealing-whistling call as they fly), and forage all night in grain fields, in short grass (like the golf course), and especially in flooded rice fields. Near dawn, they return to a shallow freshwater pond where they can stand around and pick at aquatic vegetation. Their behavior earns them another title for their oddity: They're the least aquatic of all waterfowl. Maybe that accounts for the small size of the pond on which they're hanging out now as a family of sixteen.

July 31

Discovering Beheaded Bunnies

This afternoon I found a beheaded bunny in the yard, probably 40 feet from the house and 15 feet from the garden shed. It's a sheltered area, heavily shaded by dogwood, wild cherry, mulberry, and red cedar trees and edged along the side by a fencerow, pruned but dense. With the crime scene engrained in my mind, the search was on. What would behead a bunny, take the head but leave the body, only two tufts of fur within a foot of the carcass but with otherwise no sign of struggle or mess. Okay, it's hard to say a beheading isn't messy, but my point is that the severed head was cleanly cut without the mess of ragged flesh or innards.

No, it's not the result of some sick cult behavior. Although I can't be 100 percent certain of the culprit, by process of elimination, I can find enough evidence to take the suspect to trial. And maybe convict.

Here's what I know. Large raptors are known for beheading, admittedly a strange behavior. Sometimes they behead in order to eat that part first, crushing the skull, and then later consuming the rest. Sometimes, raptors behead in order to take the head back to the nest, especially, according to some reports, to retrieve the brain, the only part of bunnies—and some other critters—that contains fat. Maybe that's more than you want to consider, so let's pose one other, perhaps more suitable possibility: Large raptors may consume the head, or plan to consume the head, and before they can finish the meal, they're startled, forced to flee their catch. They take off with the head and abandon the rest.

Maybe that's what happened. Maybe not. What we'd really like to know, of course, is which large raptor did the deed? Possible suspects: Great Horned Owl, Barred Owl, Red-tailed Hawk, and Red-shouldered Hawk. That's not to say there are no other suspects, but here, in southwestern Indiana, these are the prime candidates. So how do we sort through the possibilities? Think about behaviors.

Great Horned Owls and Barred Owls don't like each other for one simple reason: Great Horned Owls will eat Barred Owls for lunch. They never occupy the same territory, but if the Great Horned decides to move in, it's his move to make. The Barred Owl understands who rules. While Barred Owls nested in the adjoining woods this spring and the female has maintained her territory here for a couple of years, it's possible, I suppose, that a Great Horned may have moved in. On the other hand, I've not heard a Great Horned call all summer. Recently, however, I've not heard the Barred Owl, either. But it's August, so nothing unusual about owls being quiet now. Another consideration in this mystery, too, is that owls hunt strictly at night. Of course, I can't say when the bunny met its demise. And finally, the location of the carcass suggests something swooped into a rather protected area to make the kill. Would a large owl take the risk of diving into a confined place to make a kill? Maybe. Why not? Hunger drives many strange behaviors.

Red-tailed Hawks and Red-shouldered Hawks don't like each other, either. While Red-taileds don't eat Red-shoulders for lunch, they do take on one another in some rather spectacular aerial fights. The Red-shouldered Hawks nested in the woods to our south, and I saw the pair regularly during the nesting season. Lately, however, I've not seen or heard them, except at a distance. On the other hand, a Red-tailed called this morning three or four times from the pines along the east property line. Then, shortly after lunch today, probably around 2 p.m., I heard the scream again, that hair-raising call of the Red-tailed coming from near the site where I'd found the beheaded bunny. Had the big raptor come back after the rest of the carcass? I went out to look, but the carcass remained. Given the hot weather, I suspect the raptors may well forfeit the carcass at this point, leaving it for scavengers like raccoons and opossums.

Given the clues, which bird is, in my opinion, the likely suspect? If I were on the jury, I'd vote to convict the Red-tailed Hawk. Maybe it's too much circumstantial evidence, but it's the only one of the four large raptors whose presence I can verify at the scene of the crime. But I'll spare you the photo of this event.

August

A female Ruby-throated Hummingbird fans her tail, showing aggression toward other hummingbirds that may try to invade her territory.

May my heart always be open to little birds
who are the secret to living.

—e. e. cummings (1894–1962)

August 1

Celebrating the Snag

This month marks the three-year anniversary of the creation of the tulip-tree snag. Because the tree was leaning, threatening the house, we made a reluctant decision to have it downed. I could barely stand the thought of losing such a bird magnet. As a native tree it offered sweet nectar in early spring, treating Baltimore Orioles to nourishment in those lovely tulip-shaped namesake flowers. Throughout spring, summer, and fall, it hosted hundreds of moth and butterfly species, producing prolific populations of tiny caterpillars for migrating warblers and all the summer nesters' babies. In winter the seed heads fed jays, cardinals, titmice, and chickadees. Yikes. What would happen to the birds when we lost this tree? We'd likely lose who knows how many species and face the decline of more. While I ultimately agreed to the decision, I'm not ashamed to say that I felt teary-eyed for days after.

The compromise, such as it was, called for the tree guys to leave a snag. Following my hand signals from his cherry-picker bucket, the sawyer cut the heavy limbs, many the size of my body, well out from the trunk, dropping them by cable and pulley. As he moved around the tree's circumference, he cut the tree's "arms" more or less symmetrically, quickly tuning in to my preferences and understanding my intent. I'm not saying he thought I was sane, but he was gracious and cooperative.

What we had in the end was the skeleton of a once-grand tree. Then we girdled the trunk, cutting several inches into the bark just above ground level, enough to prevent the

The old tulip tree snag serves as a sculpture-like attraction for dozens of birds. At my instruction, tree trimmers cut the massive branches and girdled the tree trunk to prevent sprouting, saving the house from the tree's likely collapse but simultaneously saving Mother Nature's nursery and grocery store.

tree from sprouting. In time the snag would begin to rot and the bugs would move in, feeding under the bark and into the heart, serving as Mother Nature's nursery and food pantry. We assumed that when the bugs moved in, the woodpeckers would follow.

Since then, three years after the heartache, I've re-landscaped the backyard, aiming to improve the habitat for birds. The new natives join the old to offer birds nectar, berries, seeds, and shelter, and they all host bugs and butterflies. Of course, in ten years the snag will rot, begin falling around itself, and perhaps open cavities for nesting chickadees, titmice, bluebirds, flycatchers, woodpeckers, and maybe even owls. It's become the centerpiece for my backyard bird watching and a natural "sculpture" attractive to the eye. Above all, contrary to my fears, over the past three years, bird populations have grown and the species are more diverse because the habitat is now more diverse. Woodpeckers and nuthatches visit daily.

August 2

Marking Nectaring Memory

Hummingbirds show an affinity for foraging among native plants, but they will visit anything that offers beneficial nectar. Since they migrate vast distances, from Canada at the northern extreme and Costa Rica at the southern extreme, "native" has little meaning for them. Okay, Asian doesn't fit their "native" needs, but they demonstrate broad behavior when it comes to choosing nectar sources. While some gardening magazines like to say the little jewels are attracted to red (and indeed they are), they're not blind to any color that offers food. This morning, I watched one female (or perhaps a juvenile, since all juvies look like females) methodically poke her bill into almost every native nodding onion blossom in the garden. They're white. Simultaneously today, hummers nectared on hyssop, a nonnative butterfly bush,

A Ruby-throated Hummingbird nectars in my native garden, here feeding on hyssop blossoms. Later, other species will feed on hyssop seeds.

and Virginia mountain mint, all blooming white. Of course, given mountain mint's reputation as an astounding pollinator plant, hummers could have been plucking bugs there.

Earlier, when the deep pink crepe myrtle hung its head in heavy blossom, hummers nectared there. They also visit native Joe-pye weed (pinkish lavender), nonnative Russian sage (powder blue), nonnative abelia shrub (pink), native American wisteria (lavender), and even common milkweed blossoms (pinkish white). In short, hummers visit oodles of flowers. I plant native salvias (deep blue and pale blue) for them and pot nonnative firecrackers and lantanas (orange). Their favorite perennials earn my favored treatment. I even insist on a no-mow zone to protect the sprawling patch of native jewelweed (yellow orange) that grows along the woodland edge. Across the eastern United States, jewelweed blossoms are hummer's favorite fall-migration food source.

Hummer behavior boggles my mind when it comes to their nectaring habits. They remember, among the hundreds of blossoms visited, precisely which flowers they've already visited, thus wasting no energy revisiting them. They also remember from year to year where they've found rich sources of nectar and return to those gardens, including those

visited during spring and, especially, fall migrations. I find those memory skills absolutely astonishing behavior, but researchers have verified the findings. Something to keep in mind when we plan our gardens, right?

And by the way, hummingbirds are the only birds that truly hover. You've watched that behavior, their hovering while nectaring at both flowers and feeders. While kingfishers and kestrels hover briefly, neither can sustain the hovering activity that hummingbirds can. Another remarkable hummingbird behavior!

A female Belted Kingfisher perches, hunting at water's edge, watching for a fishing opportunity.

August 3

Taking on a Challenge

A Blue-gray Gnatcatcher spent about 10 minutes this evening foraging in the nearly bloomed-out crepe myrtle, obviously plucking little bugs not only from spent blossoms but also from maturing seed heads and the leaves themselves. Since I'd not seen a gnatcatcher in some weeks, I assumed they'd already gone, heading back home to Central America. Well, "ours" may indeed have gone, but perhaps one from farther north forages now, our yard its migratory stopover rather than its nesting territory.

As I trained my binocular on this mature male, watching his behavior, a hummingbird flew through my line of view, landing within a few feet of the gnatcatcher. Nothing unusual about a hummer in the crepe myrtle. Hummers actually nectar there from time to time on a schedule I'd call regularly irregular. Now, though, few blossoms remain, and the hummer perched well away from any viable blossoms. As the gnatcatcher continued foraging, I noticed the hummer edging toward him more and more closely, moving in tandem with the gnatcatcher. When the gnatcatcher flew to the left, the hummer flew to the left; when the gnatcatcher flew up, the hummer flew up, landing finally within inches of the gnatcatcher. Strange behavior, I thought. After the next tandem move, however, the hummer didn't land and instead flew left and right, back and forth, a distance of about 12 inches, zoom, zoom, buzzing remarkably close, probably within 4 or 5 inches of the gnatcatcher. After the third repetition of this scenario, the gnatcatcher dropped down to an adjoining Virginia mountain mint, presumably to forage in peace and pluck a few tantalizing bugs from the blossoms. The hummingbird, however, had other ideas, and dove down, poking the gnatcatcher with its saber-like bill, landing a glancing blow on the gnatcatcher's back. As the gnatcatcher retreated to the depths of the crepe myrtle, the hummer pursued, continuing its aggressive behavior. Hmmm. Was this a female hummer defending her late nest, perhaps tucked securely in the crepe myrtle branches?

In the dim early evening light, I kept watching, awaiting an angle that showed the hummer's throat, white if a female, red if a male. Finally, I saw it. Red. A male. Wow. That blew my theory of a female defending her nest, and male hummers have nothing to do with nest building, incubating, or tending nestlings. So, not a late nest. What, then, could explain this behavior? Given a male, given early

A male Blue-gray Gnatcatcher is distinguished from his mate by his distinctive "bridle."

August, the only remaining option was territorial defense. Oddly, males never seem to let go of territorial defense behavior, even in migration when "territory" translates into a spot for only a few days' visit. Even hatch-year males demonstrate the instinctive behavior, chasing fellow juveniles from a feeder or other nectar sources. In any case, this evening's hummer eventually drove the gnatcatcher away. Who says size doesn't matter? Not with these little warriors!

Since that hostile episode, goldfinches, cardinals, and a chickadee have all landed in the crepe myrtle, not to forage but to check for safety before approaching nearby feeders. I saw no further evidence of the hummer's aggression. Instead, he perched near the top, on a bare twig, apparently proclaiming himself king of the mountain surveying his domain. Perhaps the goldfinches, cardinals, and chickadee were allowed to visit in peace because none of these seed eaters competed for nectar or bugs.

August 4

Catching the Rays

The hot, humid afternoon with its direct blistering sun brought a few seconds of "What in the world . . .?" to this backyard. Watching the plethora of Ruby-throated Hummingbirds dart to and from feeders, I noticed one foraging in the native American beautyberry bush. Typical to form, the shrub is still blooming while having already set a voluminous number of berries, some fully developed, some only beginning to fill out. As a result of the ongoing blooms, hummers are attracted to the tiny bugs that almost constantly feed on the shrub's tiny flowers.

This particular hummer, though, worked its way down, dropping below the blossoms, finally to the ground. He lay there as if injured, breathing his last. His eyes were open, his breast feathers fluffed so that the dark bases of the feathers showed. One wing drooped. He looked for all the world as if he were dead, or at least dying. Today's episode marks the second time I've witnessed this behavior among hummers. At the first sighting, I had concluded it was a fluke, some weird craziness that defied logic. This time, however, there was no mistaking the behavior. I'd had my eye on him from the beginning, and his lying

At first glance, a sunbathing male Ruby-throated Hummingbird appears to have expired, but his position was only momentary as he sweltered in the heat, attempting to rid himself of parasites.

in the pine straw, stretching his neck back, was a purposeful behavior with intent. This hummingbird was sunbathing!

While it's not uncommon to catch doves, robins, cardinals, jays, and other species stretching out a wing, fanning a tail, and fluffing back and breast feathers to gain full exposure to the sun, catching hummers in the act is rare. Perhaps that's because his sunbathing effort was exactly like the rest of his life—fast. Although I didn't have presence of mind to check a timer, I'm certain his sunbath lasted no more than 10 seconds. With the afternoon's intense sun, the accumulated heat in the pine straw, and his dark colors absorbing heat, he probably needed no further rising temperatures to achieve his purpose: setting any tiny mites or other parasitic insects on the run. Then he could preen, cleaning his feathers. I'm betting that when the preening was finished, he found someplace to bathe. It's routine behavior among sunbathers.

Birds Do *That*?

Hummingbirds are the avian world's best single moms. According to conventional wisdom, as spelled out in a University of Maine extension bulletin, male and female hummingbirds associate with one another only during the breeding season. Each has its own territory; after breeding, females retreat to their already-constructed nests, lay and incubate their two eggs, and then raise their young alone. Males, on the other hand, will breed with multiple females and then, mating opportunities over, return to Costa Rica to recuperate, leaving the females and young behind to migrate on their own, alone.

August 5

Monitoring Early

Early out of bed this morning, I planned to spy on the hummingbirds' crack-of-dawn behavior. How soon would they arrive to feed? They're famously early risers, primarily because they live on the edge and need morning sustenance ASAP. Nesting females, especially, face a critical need.

So at 5:30 a.m. I stood in the dark at the kitchen window. I could distinguish almost nothing outside. By 5:40, I could pick out features like bushes, tree trunks, and the backyard fence. At 5:41, when I first sensed movement outside the window, I had to watch carefully to be sure the ghostly images were, in fact, hummers. And indeed they were, arriving at the feeders by the dozens, flying at their usual rip-roaring speeds, causing me to wonder how they avoided crashing into stuff—and each other—in the darkness. I've always known cardinals to give the first calls of the day, but this morning their silence seemed out of character, given the craziness at the feeders. Finally, at 5:46 a.m., a full 5 minutes after the first hummer mobs arrived, I heard the weak first call of a cardinal. The songs cranked up quickly in both volume and number, but this morning at least, cardinals were the Johnny-come-latelies to the feeding frenzy. By 5:52 a.m. I could no longer pretend to count the numbers of hummers nectaring at feeders. It was still 4 minutes before official sunrise.

The ready, reliable availability of these feeders makes a huge difference for these birds. Awakening routinely in a state of near starvation, these birds depend on a quick pick-me-up before moving on to forage through the yard and garden. At pre-dawn and post-dusk, hummers swarm feeders en masse. It's survival behavior.

August 6

Taking Morning Stock

Puttering around outside early this morning to do a bit of gardening before the blistering sun made the heat unbearable, I enjoyed a quiet morning with only a handful of migrant birds welcoming the day, a clue to the status of breeding behavior. Two caught my particular attention.

The "picky-tuck" call of the Summer Tanager, very close but out of my line of sight, sounded only twice, typical of mid-August behavior. Breeding season is over for the pair, so they're only making contact out of curiosity: a sort of "Are you still here?" or "Are you leaving soon?" They'll not migrate together, these families, and length of day will determine general departure dates while weather conditions will dictate the specifics.

As the sun slipped above the treetops, warming the bugs and triggering them to fly up from the vegetation, Barn Swallows showed up, zigzagging across the openings between the trees, over the garden, yard, and house, ducking and diving, obviously finding a bountiful breakfast. While nearly impossible to count as they swooped and swerved, the feeding flock surely numbered at least thirty. They're beginning to "stage," a term that refers to birds of a species gathering together in big, sometimes massive, flocks before departing on migration. While migration takes on the semblance of "mass migration," birds manage quite well flying alone. Somehow, though, by staging, they seem to know as a flock when

A male Barn Swallow pauses before continuing his sweep across the hayfield.

it's time to head south. When they go, they all go, any stragglers only remaining for a day or so, perhaps gaining a bit more fat before joining the exodus. Eventually, by midwinter, Barn Swallows range across almost all of South America, including into the deep southern parts of Brazil.

August 7

Studying Bachelors

While I never saw any young Wild Turkeys this year, presumably done in by any number of possible predators, I have watched two groups of turkeys wander the neighbor's hayfield. Sometimes, usually early morning or late evening, I'll catch sight of a group of five to

Six out of a group of eight Wild Turkey hens wander the neighbor's hayfield.

eight hens. Such was the case yesterday when seven hens and a single tom ambled across the field, chasing grasshoppers and other bugs, always raising their heads between chases, always on the alert for trouble. Turkeys usually display a skittish behavior, sly, weighing their options in light of potential danger. Yes, they can fly and fly well, but they'd rather not. At dusk they fly into trees to roost, but at dawn they come down and forage at ground level for the day. Given their lack of responsibility in the absence of poults, I suppose they could be considered a carefree lot—at least as carefree as they can be, given the need to find food every day and protect themselves from potential predators 24/7.

Today, however, the flock of eight was all toms, their "beards" giving away their sex. Of course, now, in early August, none are strutting, fanning those magnificent tails. No females to impress now. No, these are the bachelors, the toms that didn't win the favor of the females. Surely they envy the single tom in yesterday's flock, the "king" and his harem. Someday, though, he'll lose a challenge from some young tom who will dethrone him and become the new reigning monarch, then to be admired by all the females in his realm. So it goes among Wild Turkeys. All or none. It's their usual behavior.

August 8

Accounting for Survival Skills

Having seen not a glimpse of the Red-shouldered Hawk whose territory over the past several years has included our little patch of woodland, I've speculated about her nesting success. The male, of course, is long gone, no longer welcome in her territory. But the youngster—or possibly youngsters—should be somewhere in the neighborhood. But I've not seen them either. Not until today.

Young hawks are slow to learn the tricky coordinated eye-foot behavior required to snare prey on the fly, coming down lightning fast, talons extended, to capture a meal. Prey varies by the circumstances and most likely by the birds' hunting prowess, but references say they'll take lizards, snakes, crayfish, amphibians like toads and frogs, and mammals like voles, moles, chipmunks, young rabbits, and squirrels. Our yard boasts an abundance of toads and frogs, oodles of young rabbits and squirrels, and, of course, a plethora of birds. But Red-shouldereds don't often take songbirds. Songbirds are so small with so little meat on their bones that the big Red-shouldered (or Red-tailed, for that matter) would exert more energy catching it than the hawk would gain from eating it.

It was with interest, then, that I watched the juvenile Red-shouldered cruise around the yard today, landing in the garden and yard, apparently watching movement, anything giving a clue to prey. Cardinals and chickadees continued to feed nearby, knowing somehow that the big bird was unlikely to bother them, but it was obvious by their body posture that the hawk was on their radar—just in case. While I've seen the inexperienced hunter drop several times onto what I suspect was supposed to be lunch, only once did I see it eat. Even then, the meal—probably a toad—was gone in two bites. A young hawk's poor success rate is, indeed, the primary cause of its demise. Unsuccessful hunters soon become too malnourished to hunt with the speed and dexterity necessary to snare a meal. The worse the malnourishment, of course, the worse the hunting success, and the downward spiral has a certain end.

An immature Red-shouldered Hawk perches in the garden, apparently still learning to hunt. Immature hawks will meet their demise if they're slow to become agile hunters.

Even youngsters who resort to grasshoppers and young toads, however, may be able to garner enough food to have time to improve their hunting skills. I suspect that will be the case with the juvenile now wandering the yard and beyond. I'm sure the bird's success rate, or lack thereof, will become evident over the next weeks. I'll be watching.

August 9

Feeding the Young

Yesterday I worried about the underdeveloped hunting skills of the immature Red-shouldered Hawk in the garden. There's cause for my concern: Once hawks survive all the threats in the nest and successfully fledge, their inability to hunt productively becomes the number-one cause of death. It was with some relief, then, that I coincidentally heard from my neighbor that she had watched two big hawks yesterday, both about the same size, one feeding the other.

After her answers to my grilling (she probably thought I was a tad goofy with my nosiness about what she considered only a mildly curious experience), I have surmised the following: The adult Red-shouldered Hawk is still feeding her offspring. Yes, the youngster is making an effort to find its own food, most likely because the adult is not feeding her fledgling the high volume of food it became accustomed to in the nest. Mom has a method to her madness! Gotta get the kid to fend for itself!

What my neighbor witnessed, however, made me a bit jealous of her experience. The adult hawk brought the fledgling a snake! Because my neighbor watched at some distance, perhaps from about 50 yards, she could only say the snake hung from the fledgling's talons about 6 inches. So this wasn't a monster snake, but probably 10 to 12 inches long. The adult delivered the snake to the perched fledgling that in turn gripped the prey in its talons, biting off swallowing-size chunks, taking its time, feasting in leisure, learning about yet another food source readily available. Surely the youngster found more satisfaction eating the snake than it did eating the toad. I hope it gets the hang of this hunting business sooner rather than later.

August 10

Speculating on Behavior

An old crabapple tree near our west property line has come very near the end of its life. Having provided blossoms, fruit, and shade for over thirty-five years, it's dying back the way old trees do—a branch here, a limb there. Sagging limbs prematurely lose their leaves mid-season, causing us to think we should whack down the aging tree and replace it with something native and vigorous. Just when we think we're ready to cut it to the ground, another spring produces more blossoms and a full set of leaves. Then, once again, by mid-July its age shows. Recently, we've pruned several dead limbs, those about to crash onto the neighbor's fence.

Each time I think I'm ready to let the chain saw bite into the bark, however, the birds catch me off guard. Like this morning. A dozen birds of nine species foraged simultaneously among the dead and dying branches and twigs. Four cardinals flitted about, picking here and there without my being able to see what attracted their efforts. Two immature Chipping Sparrows skittered among the mid-level branches, picking mostly at loose bark. A House Wren, the only one of the dozen that sang while at work, checked the undersides of leaves. A Carolina Wren foraged carefully in the crevices, especially where one branch forked from another. A Downy Woodpecker worked his way methodically along the undersides of branches, reaching where the others missed. A titmouse explored the little cavities, places where limbs had rotted back, leaving a tantalizing hole that promised tasty morsels. Even a young robin explored the lowest branches

This crabapple tree sheds its leaves early every summer, making me believe it's in its last season, but the birds remain so active in the branches that I can't bring myself to have it removed.

for bugs, checking loose bark for anything of interest and dropping from time to time to the ground, perhaps to gather some morsel that fell as other birds foraged. Although a hummingbird paused in the upper branches, I think it was only to perch briefly, or maybe flycatch from the treetop. Tellingly, no bird chased another from the site, the loose bark, rotting cavities, and buggy leaves giving up something for everyone.

How could I give nod to the chain saw's work, given this apparent fabulous buffet?

August 11*

Mowing for Bugs

While it's a common behavior, I haven't noticed it recently, so when I saw Barn Swallows swooping behind the neighbor's lawnmower, I was reminded of the many times I've chuckled at the scenario.

Barn Swallows catch their food on the wing. Always. And their sole diet, of course, is flying bugs. Sometimes in summer, however, bugs don't fly as high as swallows like to feed. When bugs don't go up, swallows must come down, sometimes swooping only a foot or so above the ground. When folks run their lawnmowers, the whirling blades scare the bugs up, allowing for a feeding frenzy among the birds. The comedy comes from the daring approaches of the swallows, soaring within inches of an oncoming mower, going vertical at the last minute, immediately diving back to within feet of the ground, directly behind the mower, zigging and zagging across the just-mowed grass. Of course, the feeding frenzy happens only behind those lawnmowers mowing untreated grass. When folks choose—unwisely, in my opinion—to have their lawns treated or perhaps treat it themselves to kill insects, they kill the birds' food supply. Mother Nature intended for there to be a happy balance between bugs and birds. An abundance of bugs means an abundance of food for birds and their babies. Watching the swallows' behavior this afternoon, following the lawnmower, tells me that the yard is a perfect spot for feeding birds. Hooray for the balance of nature.

August 12

Hooting from the Woods

This afternoon and again this evening, a Barred Owl called from the woods, first in a wooded area at a distance and then closer. Because of the oppressive heat, I've not been outside much, to listen for birds or to do much of anything else. Today, however, the weather shifted, bringing a comfortably low-humidity day with temps in the upper 80s. So maybe I would have heard the owl earlier had I been out and about.

I'm guessing this is the female calling. It's her territory to defend and protect against intruders. It's her territory in which to allow prospective mates for the breeding season.

Birds Do *That*?

Common Loons can dive 250 feet deep and stay underwater for up to 5 minutes. As the Minnesota Department of Natural Resources website explains, most birds have lightweight hollow bones. Loons, on the other hand, have solid bones. The added weight enables them to dive more easily and fish waters at all depths. While their added weight helps them dive, it causes them difficulty when trying to lift up into flight. Depending on weather conditions, they may need 100 to 600 feet to become airborne. If they land on a too-small lake or mistake wet pavement for water, they may become stranded and suffer the consequences. Once in the air, however, they can fly at a remarkable 75 mph.

Now, though, in mid-August, she's wished the male good travels and sent him on his way. Soon she'll do the same for her offspring, readying her rather large territory for another breeding season. Depending on the territory's available food supply, female Barred Owls reign over an area that varies from one-third to as much as one and a half square miles. That's a wide cruising range!

August 13

Foraging in the Garden

Watching from my office window this afternoon, I witnessed the behavior of dozens of birds of a wide variety foraging in my approximately 100-foot by 40-foot native garden, now lush with blooming as well as gone-to-seed varieties. The most numerous, goldfinches plucked seeds from still-blooming 10-foot-tall prairie coneflowers as well as the seed heads of purple coneflowers and long-lasting spikes of liatris. For further rich nutrition, goldfinches also plucked petals from the black-eyed Susans, nipping off the still-developing seeds at the flower's heart. Even given their brilliant yellow, goldfinches can disappear among the blanket of blossoms, attracting my attention only by the wiggling stalks.

Hummingbirds nectared at the bright yellow prairie coneflowers, white spikes of hyssop, and tiny blossoms of short-toothed mountain mint, flowers that collectively give the appearance of a snow-dusted mound. They checked out the button liatris but seemed

generally uninterested in the pretty blossoms. Those blooms must lack the rich nectar of other choices. A favorite among hummers, however, are the frilly lavender-pink blossoms of Joe-pye weed. The tiny jewels of the sky make daily visits to the four shrubby plants arranged across the garden, each about chest high and each laden with multiple dinnerplate-size clusters of flowers.

A female Indigo Bunting flitted about among the rudbeckias but seemed more interested in the Joe-pye weed. Seed eaters extraordinaire, buntings forage for after-blossom goodies, not nectar.

Carolina Chickadees hung upside down plucking seeds from prairie dock, long since bloomed out but still poking up strong spikes of brown seed heads 3 or 4 inches tall on stalks reaching well over my head.

The branches shaking in the native ninebark shrub drew my attention to five cardinals, all males, foraging on the

A Ruby-throated Hummingbird nectars on native Joe-pye weed.

still-green berries. Significantly, berries provide the carotenoids that cardinals need to produce their namesake cardinal-red plumage. Given their current molt condition, I have to assume they simply can't wait for the berries to ripen. They need the nourishment now. Berries are late because blooms were late. And blooms were late because of late freezes this spring. It's a weather cycle that has impacted birds and their behaviors all year.

A Carolina Wren foraged twig by twig through a compact buttonbush. Since the seed heads hang on the outside perimeter of the shrub, the wren had to be hunting for bugs, scouring the vegetation top to bottom, front to back, side to side, wiggling every single twig but failing to show its face for a photo.

August 14

Feeding Big Babies

Although I've not personally experienced the phenomenon this year, I certainly have in the past. This week several folks posted photos on social media or sent emails with queries asking, "Why is this goldfinch (or Chipping Sparrow or Song Sparrow or whatever) feeding a baby that looks much bigger than itself?" And my heart sinks. It's obvious what's happened. The goldfinch or Chipping Sparrow or whatever has had its nest parasitized by a female Brown-headed Cowbird. The cowbird laid a surreptitious egg in the carefully built and well-tended nest of another bird. Since the cowbird egg hatches more quickly than other birds' eggs, the baby cowbird can crowd out any competition. On most occasions, the goldfinch or Chipping Sparrow eggs get shoved out of the nest before they hatch. Or, if the eggs actually hatch and the nestlings try to compete with the larger cowbird, they are destined to lose the battle, getting shoved from the nest to their deaths. The cowbird chick thus gets all the food, all the attention, and all the advantages of being the only mouth to feed.

When the cowbird fledges, the host bird continues to feed it until it's ready to be on its own. That's what folks are seeing now. At some point, the fledgling understands it's a cowbird and joins its biological family. All that work, all that nest building, all that egg laying, all that physical exertion, all that biological output, all that time—gone. Wasted. Used to raise another bird's offspring.

A male Brown-headed Cowbird shows iridescent plumage in the right light.

A female Brown-headed Cowbird, wet from a bath, lacks much of anything to recommend her. She never builds her own nest, parasitizing other birds' nests, causing the host birds' babies to die.

Cowbirds originally followed the buffalo herds and foraged for bugs stirred up by the bison's footsteps. Following the herds, however, precluded a cowbird spending enough time at a nest site to lay eggs, incubate, and feed nestlings. So for eons they have laid their eggs in host birds' nests and let the hosts do the dirty work while the cowbirds followed the herds. Now, of course, with the bison herds generally decimated, the cowbirds turned to a convenient human-provided alternative: cattle. Since cattle herds don't wander vast distances, the cowbirds remain localized, but they continue to raid other birds' nests to lay their own eggs—as many as forty per season. The impact now on local birds is greater than it was hundreds of years ago when cowbirds laid an egg here, moved on, laid an egg there, moved on, and laid another egg somewhere else. Today, more than 120 species of birds are parasitized by cowbirds, and some species' populations have significantly declined as a result. Humans have worsened the situation because we've also opened the forests, taking down trees to open land for building lots, roads, and power lines, creating all manner of forest fragmentation. The fragmentation, in turn, gives cowbirds direct access to nests that would otherwise have been protected by expansive tracts of contiguous forest.

It's yet another way our behavior has affected the birds' behavior, making life more and more tenuous for our feathered friends. In hindsight, we should have been better friends.

August 15

Griping about Peeping

It's happened. Goldfinches have brought the first of their babies to the yard. The fledglings, engaging in their usual behavior, incessantly begging "dah-deet, dah-deet, dah-deet" to be fed, calling attention to themselves in a world where the resulting attention may not be of

A female American Goldfinch gathers hyssop seeds for her vegetarian-fed babies. She will partially digest the seeds and then regurgitate them for the nestlings.

the healthy kind. After all, predators abound, and fledgling birds rarely own the dexterity to flee a determined hawk or other hungry watchers-of-young. But "dah-deet, dah-deet, dah-deet" they sing. While the results of their "dah-deet, dah-deet, dah-deet" tend to be of the safe kind—namely food—I have to admit the constant begging can grow annoying. Ever, ongoing, insistent "dah-deet, dah-deet, dah-deet." As more fledglings join the ranks, the "dah-deet" grows more insistent, more annoying. It lasts about a month. Set the clock.

August 16

Noting Juvenile Titmouse

Seeing a Tufted Titmouse pick a sunflower seed from the feeder, fly to a nearby perch, clamp the seed between its feet, and hammer open the hull makes for ho-hum bird viewing. That's the typical titmouse behavior, year in and year out. But today's titmouse attracted my attention not for its feeding behavior but for its appearance. First, it lacked the dark above-the-beak "bridle," a reliable field mark of mature titmice. Even though the hint of the bridle was clear, it was pale, almost like a shadow. Second, the "tufted" wasn't very tufted. The crest lacked the full head of feathers that give the perky little Tufted Titmouse its perkiness as well as its name. Third, the beak still showed a bit of a yellow gape. Nestlings of many species wear a yellow rim around their bills, Mother Nature's design to help adults find the mouths of babies tucked away in dark, camouflaged nests. After the birds fledge, they outgrow the yellow gape and take on the dark-rimmed beak of adults. This little one showed every sign of being a recent fledgling.

So what's attention-getting about a titmouse fledgling? Titmice raise only one brood a year, so producing young at this point, in mid-August, indicates a noteworthy behavior. Most likely the adult pair faced nest failure with the first brood. Needing about a week to build another nest, two weeks to incubate the eggs, and another two weeks or so to raise the babies to fledgling, the pair cut their timing close. Judging by its appearance, I'd guess this fledgling has probably been out of the nest a bare two weeks. Now, given mid-August, it was tricky timing for the pair to re-nest those seven weeks ago, risking whether their offspring would be ready to survive alone by winter. But today's proof means she was successful. I have to wonder: Did any of the rest of her usual three to nine eggs survive?

Seeing an immature Tufted Titmouse now surely means the adult pair lost its first brood and re-nested to produce this fledgling.

August 17

Marking Molt

Readily observable today was evidence of birds' molting behaviors, the usually twice-annual act of shedding and replacing feathers. A mature male American Goldfinch foraging among the black-eyed Susan seed heads today wore all the clues. This bright yellow bird with strikingly black wings and black cap will turn into an olive-drab bird for the winter.

Smart move! After all, a bright yellow bird perched amid bare branches would blare, "Eat me! Eat me!" to any predator within eyesight. For them, molting is a camouflage event, protecting them during the drab days of winter. Better to be drab than to be the target of a predator!

Today's view showed white pin feathers on the upper wing, a sure sign that he's growing the white wing bars that make even the drab winter males a striking sight at winter feeders. In addition, today's bird looked a tad on the rumpled side, yellow feathers no longer perfectly groomed or neatly aligned. He won't look scruffy for long, though, and feeding as heavily as he is in the garden, he'll pack on the protein he needs to reproduce all those feathers. Another sign of molt, though, bears witness to a remarkable behavior: His bill shows signs of dulling and will turn dark for the winter. The darkness is only a hint now, but it's there.

A mature male American Goldfinch, foraging among black-eyed Susans rich with seed, shows early signs of fall molt, its plumage now less than perfect.

An immature male Northern Cardinal is molting into adult plumage. Its bill is also beginning to lighten and will eventually change from fledgling black to adult reddish orange.

An immature cardinal displayed another kind of molt when he wandered through the backyard today. He's molting from juvenile plumage into adult plumage, and his bill is beginning to show a shift from nearly black to red orange, a color he will maintain throughout the remainder of his life. His bill-color switch differs from that of goldfinches, which change bill color twice each year.

Today's cardinal is a splotchy, ill-groomed specimen at the moment, but I can see that he is, indeed, a he—taking on the overall red plumage of an adult male. While his initial red plumage will carry a gray overcast, making him look a bit dirty and perhaps even unhealthy, as his feathers wear over the course of the winter, he will be brilliantly handsome come spring. That's routine molting behavior among male cardinals.

August 18

Tracking a Bugging Pewee

For the past several days, an Eastern Wood-pewee has been flycatching here—in the front yard, backyard, side yards, garden—obviously enjoying a bonanza. Every year, the two birds that cause me confusion because of their similar appearances ultimately show off

This Eastern Wood-pewee spends hours flycatching in the backyard, and its youthful improvement shows. It now succeeds more often than not when it sashays out for bugs.

their different behaviors come fall. The Eastern Phoebe is almost always the first migrant to sing its name each spring, and the Eastern Wood-pewee is among the last. Come fall the pewee sings from the woods long after the phoebe goes silent. In spite of this every-year phenomenon, it seems all wrong—and certainly counterintuitive. Here's why: Eastern Phoebes are loners, sometimes rarely even joining their mates on territory. I haven't heard it or seen it in weeks. But given its "loner" status, it could be quietly going about its foraging and I've simply missed it. I'm guessing it's around. Somewhere. After all, phoebes may actually stay the winter here, assuming a mild, ice-free season. Even if snow does blanket the ground, phoebes may find comfort where ice-free lakes or rivers offer adequate openness for bugging. These flycatchers winter farther north than any other flycatcher. In fact, rarely do they leave the United States, even in winter, and then only into Mexico, perhaps only into the central part of the country. I've seen phoebes around during some really winterish days. No wonder it's the first to arrive in spring; it hasn't far to return—if it ever goes in the first place.

Eastern Wood-pewees, on the other hand, while they breed across most of the eastern half of the United States, winter in South America, sometimes lingering in Central America, hanging out in wooded, partially cleared, and shrubby areas. Given that, I'd think they, like other songbirds that have a long way to go, would head south early. Every fall, though, I see them bugging late into the season. Even later, I hear their namesake song from the woods, almost as if they're reluctant to leave the good bugging here.

It's no surprise, then, that over recent days I've watched the pewee's acrobatic behavior, sallying forth from strategic perches to snap bugs from midair. What bug catchers they are!

August 19

Checking the Calendar

Historically, bird populations in the yard in mid-August remain fairly static, with prime-time migration not kicking into high gear until early September. While I don't see all species every day, I hear them or see them often enough to know they're around. The perky little Blue-gray Gnatcatcher—the female more often than the male—bugs in the garden, plucking lunch from the undersides of leaves and along the stems of buttonbush, ninebark, baptisia, and asters. Yellow-billed Cuckoos call, usually early or late, and sometimes I see them fly across the yard. I've not heard or seen the Yellow-throated Warbler or the Northern Parula for at least a month, but I usually catch them at the bubble rock during late August and September, engaged in a good splash. An Eastern Wood-pewee has been bugging with enthusiasm in the backyard, presumably because of satisfying buggy multitudes. House Wrens still sing in the mornings, albeit much more quietly now that breeding season is dragging to an end.

While populations also remain static among year-round residents, they're changing behavior, too. Cardinals, finished with nesting and defending territories, have returned to the yard. Youngsters are beginning to display their true adult colors, showing me finally whether they're male or female. Goldfinches feed heavily, sometimes at feeders but mostly in the garden, on the seed heads of black-eyed Susans, purple coneflowers, liatris, and hyssop. Most of them are molting into winter plumage, so they need lots of protein and nutritious, rich seeds. Chickadees and titmice roam through their usual places in the garden and at the bubble rock, some still recognizable as juveniles but other hatch-year birds now indistinguishable from adults. Robins rarely stay here after they've fledged their young, instead joining up with other families to begin forming winter flocks. I'll see the flocks, sometimes in the hundreds, when the holly berries rotate through sufficient freeze-thaw cycles to soften and become attractive for birds' dietary preferences. Doves have gathered in extended families to forage along agricultural field edges, sometimes picking grit from along roadsides to aid their digestion. In spite of their nearly year-round breeding efforts, I've not seen any recent evidence of courtship. Carolina Wrens call loudly from the woods, attempting from time to time to regain their in-the-yard territory from the rascal House Wrens. Like many other species, the Carolina Wrens' scroungy appearances verify they're in the midst of a full-body molt. Everything is gearing up for winter.

Given the usual mid-August behavior, I was startled today to find three migrants at the bubble rock. Two nest in the area, but the third nests some distance away.

True, Baltimore Orioles nest here, but they rarely show their face in the yard. Today, a breeding male checked out the territory, gawking at the bubble rock but too intimidated to drop down for a drink much less a bath. He left without even getting his feet wet. But two little warblers popped in with less timidity, drank, and bathed, giving me time to snap some identifying photos. Fall warblers, famous for their confusing back-to-basic plumage, often give me identification overload. While one was an easy Chestnut-sided Warbler, the other

A drab fall-plumaged Prairie Warbler makes a migratory stopover and bathes at the bubble rock.

A fall-plumaged Chestnut-sided Warbler, foraging in the pine-straw mulch, bears little resemblance to its stunning spring version. See the opening photo in the April chapter for a spring male.

first led me to think Magnolia Warbler. Still, with no wing bars and an all-white undertail, the field marks didn't match. Rethinking, checking the warbler app, and matching illustrations with my own photos, the ID finally came into focus: a drab, fall-plumaged Prairie Warbler. On only one other occasion, fourteen years ago, have I identified a Prairie Warbler in the yard in the fall. While we're situated along the northern fringe of its breeding range, the habitat in our area doesn't suit the bird's needs. So while I typically find one or two during spring migration, fall migration usually leaves us on the outs. Of course, it's possible the Prairie Warbler has come through the yard in the fall and I just plain missed it or didn't correctly identify it. Still, to have missed it every year for fourteen years seems a bit unlikely. Definitely, it's an unusual fall bird in the yard.

The Chestnut-sided Warbler, on the other hand, breeds well to our north, from Michigan through central Canada. Only during migration does it visit here. Spring visits are fast, which is usual behavior given their eagerness to reach breeding territory and get on with family responsibilities. Fall migration, on the other hand, is often a leisurely, lingering event. Now, birds have no reason to rush. The Chestnut-sided will winter in the Caribbean and throughout southern Central America, so our location in southern Indiana isn't even halfway home. Almost every fall I see at least one, sometimes several, over the course of a few weeks. Certainly there's no way to know if the individual I see one day is the same one I see a week later, but I'd guess probably not. Aside from that speculation, however, it's remarkable to have sighted one today. My previous early fall sighting was a few years back, on September 6. On average, however, sightings in the yard over the past twenty years have ranged between September 19 and 25.

Birds Do *That*?

Be nice to Northern Mockingbirds; they get the bad guys. In an experiment on the University of Florida campus, researchers confirmed that by annoying mockingbirds, folks could expect an eventual attack. According to a report in the *Proceedings of the National Academy of Sciences*, mockers learned to recognize individuals, even when they dressed each day in different clothing. In short, within four days the mockingbirds learned to distinguish between individuals who were "nice," never disturbing or approaching their nest, and individuals who were "naughty," appearing to threaten them or their nests. Smart, huh?

Why is this bird so early? What does the behavior mean? Does its arrival predict an early winter? I doubt it. Instead, I suspect this bird, already in winter (basic) plumage, suffered nest failure. With no responsibilities holding it on the breeding grounds, it headed home early. Given the travel distance, the bird would have no time to attempt a second brood, so why hang around? It's disconcerting to think this tiny creature will have flown about 9,000 miles round-trip apparently without achieving its life's goal to reproduce.

August 20

Enjoying a Return Visit

The Prairie Warbler was back today, visiting the bubble rock, this time without any hesitation, without any timidity, hopping directly into the water for a good splash. Maybe it's finding sufficient bugs so that it wants to hang out, fatten up, and refresh itself at our migratory stopover before journeying on to its winter range. It's not the dramatic long-distance flier that the Chestnut-sided Warbler is, however, with its winter range including Florida and not much farther south, usually no farther than Haiti, the Dominican Republic, and Cuba. Of course, today's visitor could easily be a different individual. And probably was.

August 21

Surveying Hummer Populations

Two days ago I noted that the number of bird species in the yard remains mostly static now. True, the number of species has been relatively static for the past two months. But the number of individuals is anything but static, especially if we're talking about Ruby-throated Hummingbirds. Typically, hummer populations peak in my yard the second week of September, although last year they peaked a week earlier. I can't be sure, but I suspect this year the peak population is occurring now. Either that, or the peak is going to bring outrageous numbers.

What are those numbers? Oh my, how does a person count hundreds of hummers? The backyard is consumed with such a swarm of hummers that with a bit of imagination, I could swear a plague of locusts infested the scene. The little guys pause for mere seconds in the trees, perch briefly in shrubs, pop by the bubble rock, bathe briefly, storm the feeders (two in particular that are their favorites), fight over air space, fight over perches, fight over feeding ports (can they ever quit fighting?), nectar at flowers throughout the garden, swoop the length of the backyard, and dive from branches to snatch a perch at a feeding port. It's breathtaking. So I can only "count" by figuring out how much nectar they lap up in a day's time. Using an online calculation formula (and who knows how accurate

the formula may be), here's a guesstimate: Hummers preparing for migration consume their weight in nectar each day. On average, Ruby-throated hummers preparing to migrate weigh a hefty 5 grams. If the hordes consume a gallon of nectar a day, based on that formula, there would be about 800 birds lapping it up. Since I've been using about a gallon and a half of nectar at a slightly richer proportion than usual, calculations take me up to over 1,200 birds. That seems an unreasonably high number, but I have no other means by which to take a census—or even make a guess. Let's just say the numbers are huge and the birds have been consuming pounds and pounds of sugar.

A migrating immature Ruby-throated Hummingbird shows a single ruby-colored feather in his gorget, a signal of a handsome male-to-be.

By the way, hummers don't sip nectar as if through a straw as we long believed.

Two hatch-year male Ruby-throated Hummingbirds engage in early practice of territorial defense.

Current research, including some amazing microscopic video from a South American researcher, shows instead that hummers lap up nectar the way a cat or a dog laps up water. Think of the hummer's tongue as something like a mop, soaking up nectar and drawing it into the mouth, and zipping the tongue back out past the long bill to mop up another measure. Okay, so not much nectar makes it to the mouth in a single lap, but given the bird's ability to flip its tongue in and out thirteen times per second, a hummer can drink its weight in a somewhat drawn-out feeding session. Sometimes I see the little guys lingering long minutes at a feeding port, their lapping evidenced by their quivering throats.

Here's hoping the fights soon subside. And then let's see how the numbers hold over the next week or so.

August 22

Predicting an Early Fall?

When I posted on social media three days ago the arrival of the Prairie Warbler and Chestnut-sided Warbler on the bubble rock, several friends wanted to know: Does this mean we're expecting an early fall? An early winter? A more severe winter than usual? I have no crystal ball (not that it would help me with this answer), but here's the deal with migrating birds: Migration is all about length of day.

When the days grow short in autumn, birds' inner clocks tell them it's time to head south. Since some birds travel much farther south than others, and since some start from more northerly points to begin with, the alarm clock doesn't sound at the same time for

A group of six Nashville and Tennessee Warblers congregates on the bubble rock to drink and bathe.

every migrant. Obviously, then, they don't all come swarming through on the same day or even during the same week.

There's more to the story, however, than length of day. If a migrant has experienced nest failure, it has no housekeeping responsibilities—no nest to tend, no mouths to feed, no off-spring to teach how to eat and survive. Thus, it can begin its journey back home early, per-haps wandering afield, dispersing off the usual beaten path, so to speak, enjoying the benefits of a slow-paced trip, including a two-day visit in my yard, perhaps enjoying the spa-like ben-efits of the bubble rock. With almost all songbirds, however, once the fledglings are out and on their own, the adult birds head south, leaving the youngsters to fend for themselves. In some instances, like with Tree Swallows, migration is a family affair, maybe even a monstrous extended family affair. For warblers, though, migration is a solo event. Youngsters only weeks out of the nest have inherited the internal clock that triggers their southward movements. They're also hardwired to know where and how to find food along the way—assuming, of course, we haven't destroyed the native habitat on which that hardwiring depends.

This evening as I stepped outside to bring in the hummingbird feeders overnight (a rascal raccoon has discovered the sticky sweetness of nectar and has destroyed three feed-ers this week), I heard an owl in the neighbor's woods to our east. Wait! What? I stopped to listen again. And again, just to be sure. The Great Horned Owl was calling its typical "Who? Who? Who? Who-hoo?" That's the first time I've heard him in over a year, so wel-come back to the party, big boy! He seems to have tested the territory to the east, knowing, I'm betting, that the Barred Owl has the territory to the south and west. I hope the two species can both remain and keep the peace, but I fear for the Barred Owl. She's had that territory for many years, so I hope she can keep it. I'd miss her questioning "Who cooks for you?" if she is chased out. On the other hand, she's no youngster any more. I wonder if the Great Horned Owl knows she's probably not the strong bully she used to be?

1 Great Horned Owl
Species: 108 total in the yard to date for the year.

August 23

Taking Another Census
With the coolest morning temps since the first week of May, I couldn't resist wandering the yard at my leisure, making a mental list of whatever behavior I saw and heard. For some minutes, I watched a White-breasted Nuthatch caching safflower seeds in loose bark on the tulip-tree snag. He would tuck the seed in, lean back, look the situation over, and often remove the seed, replace it elsewhere, and recheck the security of his work. Given the very loose bark on the old snag, I suspect most of his seeds will be lost, but he may have way more instinctive sense than I about the security of his caches. Either way, his caching is typical fall behavior.

Later this afternoon I caught sight of a yellow bird, smaller than a cardinal, more the size of a large warbler, edging its way toward the bubble rock. Long tail, sharply pointed black beak, distinct white wing bars and white wing-feather edges, sleek and trim. A bit skittish about the gurgling water but interested in a drink or a bath, she worked her way hop by hop down the photo-op branches we've "planted" in the ground nearby. Once I had her in full view and verified her field marks, I knew: female Orchard Oriole! Unfortunately, the many goldfinches on the bubbler were too much for her to challenge; after some long looks at the situation, she skittered off without a drink or a bath and, as far as I know, without returning. The male Orchard Oriole made an ever-so-brief appearance last spring, so seeing the female offers a clear possibility that they paired and perhaps nested somewhere nearby, choosing a tall tree near a lake or marshy spot. At least that's their common nesting behavior.

A female Orchard Oriole arrives to investigate the bubble rock.

August 24

Welcoming Back Woodpeckers

Now that breeding is all but over, our year-round resident birds are beginning to take up non-breeding habitats and resume routine behavior. Aside from the hummingbird explosion, the return of woodpeckers may be the most obvious change in populations. Red-bellied Woodpeckers are back at the seed cake, suet cake, and old tulip-tree snag. Pileated Woodpeckers are hammering again in our little patch of woods and occasionally in the woods to our east. Northern Flickers are calling from time to time, probably keeping track of one another. For most of the summer, only the Downy and Hairy Woodpeckers visited the yard with any sort of regularity. Both have taken to foraging up and down the tulip-tree snag on an almost daily basis.

Why did the woodpeckers wander off and where did they go? Likely their behavior is a clue to a breeding dilemma: In order to hammer out nesting cavities, woodpeckers need dead or dying trees at just the right stage of decay. Not decayed enough and the birds find the going too tough to excavate an adequate nest site. Too decayed and the birds risk the collapse of the tree at the site of their excavation—or as the result of a storm during a critical part of their nesting cycle. To find these specific and necessary nest sites, woodpeckers wander far and wide. Sometimes, in fact, they fail to find an appropriate tree. Given that, they don't breed. So the return of these woodpeckers at the end of the breeding period tells me they most likely raised families. That's good news!

Absent has been the Red-headed Woodpecker. I've neither seen nor heard it since early spring. Of course, its arrival last spring was a noteworthy occasion after years of absence, so maybe we had the pleasure of its presence only for those couple of months and we'll have to wait another span of years before it returns. I hope not, but Red-headed Woodpeckers insist on an unintentionally self-limiting behavior: They directly and irrevocably depend on old-forest habitat. Ours is such a tiny patch of woods, and not much surrounds the neighborhood that fits the definition of "old forest." Worse yet, the tree that the Red-headed Woodpecker favored early last spring crashed in a windstorm this past summer. I fear I know what that means. Habitat is everything for birds. We certainly enjoyed them, though, while they were here.

August 25

Taking "Note" of the Towhee

The Eastern Towhees, a male and female, have visited the yard with irregular regularity all summer—not daily, but probably weekly. Always a bit furtive, careful to stay near dense ground cover, they nevertheless foraged comfortably on seed, either spills from the commercial variety or offal from the native variety. Rarely, however, did I hear them sing. Call, yes, that questioning "Wheee?" that is their contact call, a sort of "I'm looking for you." I'd hear the two of them calling back and forth, sometimes from opposite sides of the yard, but more often from closer by, either in our little patch of woods or down the hill in the brambles, an ongoing behavior that suggests they consider our habitat their home.

This morning, though, I heard that sweet song that sounds like a command to "Drink your tea-he-he-he." Granted, it was somewhat quieter than the rousing springtime version, but wafting from our little patch of woods, it made me pause, face the direction of his song, and enjoy the tune. Although I did not hear the female call back (she calls but doesn't sing), I'm betting each knew where the other was. Why else would he sing? Sure, breeding season has long since ended for these early nesters, their one or two offspring from their single brood out and on their own. Since I've not seen any youngsters recently, however, I fear the one I spotted very early this summer may have met its fate before maturing. Ground-nesting birds have such a difficult way to go that I'm always amazed any of them

A fledgling Eastern Towhee is most easily identified by the company it keeps.

manage successful nests. But I know they do. Now, given his song, I'd like to think the pair will hang around for the winter—as they have for the past several winters. Experts say towhees mate for life and may be more loyal to each other than most any other songbird species. Since banded birds in the wild have been known to live over twelve years, it's possible that the pair I've seen here over the past many years are, indeed, the same individuals. Or perhaps at least one of the pair is a long-term resident here.

Surely towhees are our most beautiful sparrows! Sadly, however, since 1966, their populations have declined by almost half.

August 26

Judging Jumpy Birds

How do I know birds are on the move? Let me count the ways. Well, let's start with one way, and it always amuses me, this odd behavior.

Everything goes to water, of course, so the bubble rock attracts everything—birds, mammals, insects. Our bubbler is constructed so that the recycling pump pushes water up from the reservoir through a three-quarter-inch hole, then over and down across the rocks. The gurgling sound attracts anything looking for a drink or a bath. The bubble spot, where the tube reaches the top edge of the rock and water flows out, seems to hold special fascination for our regulars. I've seen robins sit atop the bubble, seemingly enjoying the rush of water across their tummies. I've seen cardinals stick their faces into the bubble, apparently engaging in a face washing. Sometimes bathing birds wallow around immediately atop the bubble, soaking their feathers front to back.

When the gurgling draws in birds new to the yard, though, they're timid, and their behavior gives them away. Today I saw a handsome male American Goldfinch hop down to the rock, peer over the edge, and jump back, startled by the flowing water. He edged forward again, jumped back again, then edged forward more slowly, studied the bubble, eased into the water for a drink, and eventually took a short bath. I knew, then, that this goldfinch was new to the yard, perhaps only migrating through, perhaps arriving to stay the winter.

Repeatedly I've seen that behavior among migrants and new arrivals, both summer nesters and winter visitors. But they need only one experience to be comfortable with the bubble rock and its beckoning call.

Birds Do *That*?

Hummingbirds are the only birds that can fly backward. This unique ability comes from the hummer's muscle structure. While most birds have a powerful downward wing stroke for flying forward, they rely on moving air to help raise the wing back to position. By contrast, hummingbirds move their wings in a figure-eight pattern, producing equal power on both the downstroke and the upstroke. Thus, according to an account in the *Journal of Experimental Biology*, hummers can fly backward purposely, at length, with agility and speed.

August 27

Tracking Early Hummer Migrants

Based on nectar volume consumed, daily hummingbird numbers have declined by about two-thirds. About a week and a half ago, up to a gallon and a half of nectar disappeared daily from the feeders, demanding my regular attention to keep feeders supplied. Today, I stirred up only a half gallon. That's not to say there won't be another wave or two as weather fronts bring birds south, but the peak seems to have come and gone. That's early. Too early. Consistently over past years, peak here has been the second week of September, with numbers declining fairly quickly after that. Last year, peak was several days earlier, starting midweek during the first week of September. But weeks earlier? Strange.

Because peak seems unusually early—by at least three weeks—to verify my observations, I checked with a bird banding station about 250 miles to our northeast. During a 3-hour banding session yesterday, they netted only thirteen hummingbirds. Typically on this date, they would have banded closer to eighty. Our birds arrive about three days later, so their low numbers easily predict our low numbers.

Surprisingly, given what was probably peak last week, three mature males hung out at feeders this afternoon. Since male hummers leave territories first, immediately after potential breeding opportunities have passed, by peak migration virtually all mature males have already passed through. Perhaps their presence indicates unusual behavior, the meaning of which I've been trying to piece together.

This spring's late freezes held migrants south. If birds out-fly their food sources, the results, obviously, are catastrophic. Generally, birds don't make that mistake. This spring, however, buds opened, bugs came out, and birds moved north, only to face yet another freeze, another wave of destruction of nectar and protein. I fear the outcome was not good. Those birds that waited or migrated later more likely survived and reached their ancestral breeding sites. But they were late. And late arrivals mean a reduced number of available breeding days.

So here's the deal: Hummingbirds (and other species as well) that reached breeding ranges several weeks late faced a time crunch that prevented their raising a second brood. Of course, birds that travel the farthest, such as those that range into southern Canada, for instance, have time for only a single brood even during good years. Maybe if they face nest failure early in the season, they may attempt a second brood, but for the most part, one brood is it. On the other hand, those that choose a less northerly range typically do raise two broods. The late arrivals, however, cut the nip-and-tuck schedule enough that many were restricted to a single nesting.

How do they know they've run out of time? Those incredible internal clocks synced to length of daylight tell birds when to migrate. They also tell females when they're out of time for another brood.

Putting the times together suggests that perhaps females left their breeding grounds early, knowing they couldn't raise a successful second brood. Shortly after their first broods fledged, they likely headed south. Males, finding that breeding opportunities had passed, also headed south. Youngsters hang out long enough to gain strength and fatten up, and then their inherited internal clocks tell them it's time to head south, too. For hordes of hummers, southern Indiana is on the path south, in some cases a midway point on their way to Costa Rica. We see all that complicated timing playing out at our feeders now.

August 28

Recording Early Warblers

Distracted by necessary chores, I missed my 3 p.m. start time for watching the backyard, and the clock had chimed 6 p.m. before I sat down. Immediately, activity caught my attention in the crepe myrtle just outside the kitchen window. Expecting to see more hummingbirds flouncing about, I was surprised by a warbler shape. Two white wing bars, white near the tip of the undertail. Oh, no, the light was so bad, and a backlit bird is neither readily identified nor satisfactorily photographed. It flew off. Figuring that everyone wins some and loses some, I accepted I'd missed this one. As it flew, though, I watched it land near the bubble rock, work its way across the landscape, and finally drop down for a full side view. Bingo! Bay-breasted Warbler! Even in its so-called drab fall plumage, it's a delicately pretty bird. The soft wash of pale rust on its sides helped identify it, but what a difference from its bright breeding plumage. No wonder the mantra is "confusing fall warblers." It's here on schedule, its migratory behavior perfectly timed.

Shortly, another warbler silhouette caught my eye. Hoping for a better look at the Bay-breasted, I turned my binocular to the flitting image. Tennessee Warbler! Such a pretty green bird when it wears fall plumage. In spring it's more gray than green, so I actually think the fall plumage is prettier. Tennessees are fairly common in our yard during migration, but seeing any migrant is always special. They're just early. Really early. Predictably, I see these two migrants in late September.

What accounts for the early behavior? It's likely that breeding thing again. These birds probably faced nest failure too late to retry. So they're heading home. Early.

A migrating fall-plumaged Bay-breasted Warbler makes a leisurely visit to our homemade bubble rock, giving me time to sort out his identity among the notoriously confusing fall warblers.

August 29

Forecasting Migration

A website called BirdCast.info, built by Cornell University's Lab of Ornithology, predicts migration based on weather radar and tracks bird movement live during the night. Radar predicts a significant migration tonight along a strong cold front to our northwest. Tomorrow night, the front will pass through here, perhaps bringing a little wavelet of migrants. If the prediction plays out, August 31 could be an interesting day.

August 30

Greeting Favorites

Lying awake just at dawn, deciding when to put my feet to the floor, I heard the singing Carolina Wrens. Since the arrival of the first House Wren on April 13, the Carolinas have abandoned their usual territory in the immediate yard, moving into the woodland edge. Although I've heard them in the distance, I've missed them in the yard, especially their cheerful "teakettle" song. They're perky, vibrant, busy, and nosey, and their behavior verifies their dedication to each other. Males and females are indistinguishable, but her song is quieter than his (yes, she does sing), and she more often calls than sings. Hearing his song and her answering call this morning made an otherwise partly cloudy morning a little brighter!

Did House Wrens behave so aggressively toward the Carolina Wrens that they drove the Carolinas away? Or did the Carolinas simply choose to avoid the forever-singing House Wrens, instead assuming a submissive behavior and taking up residence in a more secluded and protected spot? For whatever reason, the two seemed to avoid one another. Thus, since the House Wrens have gone quiet—and maybe gone, period—the Carolinas are back. I'm glad. Some scientists claim birds don't experience happiness (although other researchers show evidence to the contrary), so it's out of place to wonder if the birds are happy to be back in the familiar territory. So, instead, I'll wonder if the Carolinas find better foraging and better winter shelter being back.

Also, the Pileated Woodpecker boldly announced his return this morning. He called, and called, and called. I've never heard the ongoing call for such an extended time as this morning. I'm hoping that behavior means he's establishing winter territory in our little patch of woods—as he did last year. Each season they hammer out a new winter roost site, so I'm holding my breath that suitable trees offer him an option. This afternoon, he flew along the lane, then ducked into the neighbor's woods to the east. I think he's planning to winter with us, but perhaps he's not yet decided exactly where.

Late this afternoon I discovered a surprise visitor foraging in the sweetbay magnolia. Fortunately, I managed several photos, albeit some of really poor quality, even the best being less than perfect. Even crappy photos, however, can aid in identifying a mystery bird, ruling out some species while verifying others. Indeed, this bird's identity caused me some degree of puzzlement. My first reaction was to call it a Red-eyed Vireo. They breed here, so it's the most likely of the vireos to be hanging out in the backyard. A closer look at the photos, however, dashed my ID. In this case, the eyes have it. Red-eyed Vireos have a strong

A Philadelphia Vireo, uncommon in our yard, challenges my identification skills.

eyebrow and—bet you guessed it—red eyes. Well, except when they're young, before the eyes turn red. This bird, however, had no strong eyebrow. All told, this was no Red-eyed. So which was it? Warbling Vireo? Philadelphia Vireo? After a thorough search through the field guides lining my bookshelf and consulting birding apps on my phone, and given the time of year, I finally determined it was a fall-plumaged Philadelphia Vireo, not a common bird for my yard but also not a new bird to the yard—just new for the year.

Why are fall birds so hard to identify? It's all about their molting behavior—when they molt, how often they molt, sexual dimorphism (if any), and seasonal plumages, the current switch from alternate (or breeding) to basic. Vireos molt in the fall, so their plumage is now fresh and bright. But the molt may not be complete, thus revealing plumage variations that lead us astray when it comes to identification. Always a mystery. Always fun to solve! Don't you love a good puzzle? This mystery puzzle was free, right in my own backyard.

The presence of a first-fall male Baltimore Oriole testifies that the species likely nested somewhere nearby this summer.

Shortly after the vireo mystery unraveled itself, a first-fall male Baltimore Oriole arrived at the bubble rock for a drink and a bath. My, what a pretty bird! Again, it's all about the oriole's molting behavior that gives us this lovely bird—and then only in August and September. Isn't it truly amazing that we can see this bird in this plumage only during this brief time?

1 Philadelphia Vireo
Species: 109 total in the yard to date for the year.

August 31

Verifying Predictions

The cold front went through last night, and, just as predicted, a little wavelet of migrants showed up in the yard this afternoon and early evening. Keeping vigil at the kitchen window from 3:30 until 6:30 p.m., overlooking the backyard and our little bubble rock, I spotted seven warbler species. They included Nashville Warbler, a species that breeds from northern Michigan well into northern Canada; and Magnolia Warbler, Tennessee Warbler, and Black-throated Green Warbler, all three that breed in Canada but also in the upper elevations of the Appalachians. These little guys have come a distance already, heading to their southern winter ranges. A Black-and-white Warbler made multiple appearances (or multiple birds made single appearances?). According to range maps, they breed in our area, but I never see them except during migration. In addition, a Yellow-throated Warbler and a Northern Parula arrived, but those two breed here, right in our yard. Sure, these were unlikely the individuals that nested here, especially since I've not seen either of them for at least

A fall Nashville Warbler stops by the bubble rock, giving me a look at its drab plumage.

a month. That makes me strongly suspect these are not "our" birds. While the Yellow-throated's breeding range does not extend much farther north than central Indiana, the Northern Parula breeds well into northern Canada. Who knows how far they've come. It's that mind-boggling migratory behavior again, the one that absolutely astonishes me no matter how often I see evidence of the activities.

Most of these warblers also made appearances during spring migration. The Nashville Warbler, however, is new for the year this fall. Typically, we'll see many over the drawn-out autumn migration. In addition, two adult male Baltimore Orioles and one hatch-year male sashayed through the yard, and the Eastern Wood-pewee and Eastern Phoebe spent most of the late afternoon flycatching in the backyard. After all the hubbub of the Philadelphia Vireo during yesterday's vigil, the more mundane Red-eyed Vireo showed up today. Nice busy day, verifying the predictions about the migration pattern—amazingly predictable behavior of birds on the go. Once again, it's evident that weather dramatically affects bird behavior in almost every way!

1 Nashville Warbler
Species: 110 total in the yard to date for the year.

September

A Canada Warbler, one of our most beautiful migrants, stops at our homemade bubble rock to refresh itself before continuing its travels south to northern South America.

Even the smallest bird is a miracle that needs no further vindication or defense—which by its very existence demands our attention and respect.

—Scott Weidensaul (1959–), naturalist and author

September 1

Taking Time to Watch

Sometimes I'm absolutely certain I don't have good sense, and I'm fairly sure there are a number of folks who would agree. Who has time to spend hours sitting at the window,

A male Prairie Warbler, a rare one-day wonder in our yard, makes a migratory stopover before heading to Florida and the Caribbean.

A Wilson's Warbler, a northern Canada nester, makes our yard a stopover site to prepare for the next leg of its journey to Central America.

A Magnolia Warbler, still in mostly breeding plumage, makes a migratory stop in our yard on its way to southern Mexico and Central America.

looking out at the backyard? I have things to do! Laundry. Yard work. Housework. Meal preparation. Ironing. Bill paying. Yikes!

Later. Later. That stuff can wait. Migration occurs only twice a year. For me, migration behavior is the most dramatic and exciting observable behavior among the oodles of birds that visit our yard. So again this afternoon, I kept vigil from 3 p.m. until 6:30 p.m., hubby joining me most of that time. Birds have traveled perhaps several thousand miles—or more!—to nest, and they're now right here, right outside my window.

Today's list was as nicely rewarding as yesterday's. A female or look-alike immature American Redstart foraged through the beautyberry bush. The redstart's wide breeding range, from near the Gulf Coast all the way into northern Canada, means it could have nested in the area, or it could be on its way home from Canada or almost anywhere in between. A bright breeding male Prairie Warbler bugged through the sweetbay. We're nearly at the northern edge of his summer range, but the species never nests in our yard. Wrong habitat. An adult Wilson's Warbler treated us to his visit. He comes a long way, nesting almost exclusively in the mountains and forests of Canada but wintering in Central America. He splashed on the bubble rock alongside two Tennessee Warblers and, later, with an American Redstart. Talk about public baths!

Repeats from yesterday, including Nashville, Tennessee, Yellow-throated, Magnolia, and Black-and-white Warblers, could be the same individuals, but they could also be new arrivals. With fall migration following its leisurely pattern of behavior, sometimes individuals hang out in good stopover habitat for several days, foraging and putting on a few grams of fat. It's a behavior unlikely repeated in spring.

September 2

Spying First Winter Visitor

With warblers on the brain, I scanned the trees and shrubs for some of the most elusive. There! That's one! Misidentifications sometimes come on the heels of expectations—"seeing" what I think I'll see. So the plain, basic-plumaged Chestnut-sided Warbler in reality turned out to be a returning Ruby-crowned Kinglet. Maybe not this particular individual, but kinglets do spend the winter in the yard. And here it is already, way early. Is that a sign of things to come, this early arrival of a winter visitor? I don't know, of course, but I can verify that I was not popular with my friends this evening, having announced this sighting and speculating what it might mean.

Aside from that kinglet as a possible omen, I did keep an eye open for warblers. Although I finally spotted five repeats from the past two days (Yellow-throated, Nashville, Tennessee, and Black-and-white Warblers and several Northern Parulas), they were sparse, infrequent visitors. Still, the bubble rock remains the primary attraction for them, so that's where I watch most often. The lack of rain this fall has left the grass so brittle it crunches underfoot, so water keenly interests migrants—and everything else. Again, then, weather affects behavior.

Drought has also dramatically affected hummingbirds. Flowers have either bloomed out or died back. Nectar is scarce. As a result, hummers are relying heavily on feeders to the tune of about a gallon and a half of syrup a day. I thought peak hummer migration occurred a week or so ago, but today's flood of birds made me change my mind. They're here in droves. Hundreds. I have to rethink what the lull in last week's numbers means.

Birds Do *That*?

Migrants fly headlong into dangerous night skies. According to a *Journal of Field Biology* article, radar has adjusted what we understand about the altitude at which birds migrate. During typical migration most songbirds stay below 5,000 feet, and most of the smaller ones stay below 1,500 feet. Raptors usually stay below 3,000 feet to take advantage of thermals, while waterfowl may cruise at 4,000 feet. Of course, the higher the altitude, the cooler the temperatures, helping migrants to avoid dehydration and to escape obstacles. The obstacles that most seriously threaten migrating birds—power lines, wind turbines, communication towers, and buildings—unfortunately affect most dramatically birds migrating low, under 1,500 feet. According to famed researchers Paul R. Ehrlich, David S. Dobkin, and Darryl Wheye, however, birds "around home" fly quite differently than they do during migration, conserving energy, flying as new pilots are instructed: low and slow—and in daylight. Birds adjust their flight behavior to the times.

September 3

Grinning over Growing Numbers

While no new warbler species showed their pretty little faces today, several returned in multiples. What does that mean about their behaviors, notably their migratory behaviors? A handsome full-breeding-plumaged male American Redstart joined the females (and/or immatures) that have become semi-regulars over the past several days. Three Tennessee Warblers appeared together, so I know at least a trio is here. Likewise, three Northern Paru-

las splashed in the bubble rock together. The three were in such different plumages, however, that they stood out as individuals, one an adult, one a molting bird with only faint wing bars, and the third a hatch-year bird just gaining good markings. They will likely finish their molts before venturing south to their homes in Mexico and the Caribbean. As a group, then, these warblers all have the same goal: Hang out in a good migratory stopover to prepare for another flight. Maybe the multiples are extended family groups, or maybe—and more likely—they just happened to show up at the same place. They don't migrate together, instead only by themselves, each at its own pace.

A female or immature American Redstart (all immatures look like females) makes a foray into our yard, bugging its fill to prepare for another leg of its journey to Mexico, Central America, the Caribbean, or even as far as northern South America.

A male American Redstart shows a stark contrast to his pale mate.

Many hatch-year birds, only weeks out of the nest, are well along on their migratory journeys that will cover unbelievable distances. By contrast, the famously late-nesting American Goldfinches are only now producing fledglings, their behavior making backyard news. Today a youngster begged morsels from an adult and then flew a drunkard's path across the yard only to find its landing gear a bit off. Learning to fly an arrow's path and simultaneously land gracefully on a pinhead takes practice. And more practice! This little one was obviously still in the early practice stage. It's gotta be tough being a baby bird.

September 4

Ticking a New Yard Bird

Never in my wildest hallucinations would I have suggested that we might host a Lark Sparrow in our yard. They don't live here. Range maps don't show them here, not even during migration. Today, however, one splashed in the bubble rock and preened in the sweetbay. Photo files show we snapped images for over 6 minutes. Where it went from here remains a mystery, but I'm relatively sure it remained long enough to forage for seeds to fill its handsome little belly. While range maps put it about a hundred miles to our northwest, a local friend with similar native habitat typically catches sight of one or two during spring and fall migrations. It's not at all uncommon for birds to wander out of range in the fall, a behavior called post-breeding dispersal. Maybe dispersal brought the Lark Sparrow here. Still, one noticeable clue about this bird's behavior made me curious: It was certainly comfortable at the bubble rock, approaching confidently, directly, as if it had been here before. Hmmm. In spite of the many hours I spend watching, I know that all kinds of things likely happen when I'm not watching. In any case, this was my first sighting of a Lark Sparrow in the yard. Ever. Maybe I need a trail cam!

The crazy part about sighting this rarity brings to my attention once again a bird-viewing habit many of us have. We tend to see what we expect to see. My first glimpse of the Lark Sparrow made me think Song Sparrow. A sparrow with a black stickpin spot on its breast, dark moustache, sighted in September, is probably a Song Sparrow. That's what's here and what I'd expect to see. I barely paused for a second look but decided to snap a photo because the bird was in a nice pose. Then, bingo! I realized something was different, several somethings, in fact. The eyes looked funny. This bird had a broad white rim under its eyes, but Song Sparrows sport only a hint of an eye ring. True, this bird had a stickpin breast spot, but it was set against a clear breast. Song Sparrows have a stickpin surrounded by streaks. This bird had a black moustache and a rust-colored cheek patch; Song Sparrows wear a reddish-brown moustache and a gray cheek patch. It also seemed a bit large for a Song Sparrow, maybe longer. While Lark and Song Sparrow sizes can overlap, Songs can be considerably smaller, the smallest only 4.5 inches long, while the smallest Lark is typically at least 6 inches long. Weight varies by about the same proportions.

So finally, in spite of my see-what-I-expect-to-see mentality, I was jarred by the realization that this bird was definitely not a Song Sparrow. Then it clicked! Only once before have I seen a Lark Sparrow, but my foggy brain pulled up the possibility. A quick check of a birding app confirmed the new ID. The bird lacked the strong harlequin face pattern of an adult, but it also lacked the heavy breast streaking of a juvenile. Sorting through field

A young, out-of-range Lark Sparrow visits the bubble rock. There is some evidence that the bird's range may be expanding since area birding friends have had breeding Lark Sparrows on their properties.

guide photos and illustrations, I matched its plumage with that of a first-winter bird—just beyond the juvenile plumage but not yet in the full adult plumage it will wear come spring.

On a more amusing note, behavior observed this afternoon confirms that two Eastern Wood-pewees cannot hunt the same territory. Wow, are they ever fierce defenders of fly-catching space! Because I was sitting at an open window, I heard their chatter as they threatened one another, heard their bills click as they fought in midair, and heard their wings smack as they made full-battle contact. Little warriors! The defeated one left quickly (perhaps a juvenile, maybe the other bird's offspring?), and all was well, the remaining bird back to its feeding frenzy. As I watched it hunt, however, its head as if on a swivel, I was amused to see it eyeing hummingbirds jetting past. It seemed the flycatcher measured each hummer passing, considering whether it might be fair game, a good meal, or too big for flycatcher dining. The pewee never chased a hummer, at least not that I saw, but it also never missed watching one zoom past.

1 Lark Sparrow
Species: 111 total in the yard to date for the year.

September 5

Missing Color

Seeing all-white birds that aren't supposed to be white always causes a double take. White or partially white cardinals, robins, bluebirds, goldfinches, starlings, cowbirds—the list goes on—become the subjects of emails and social media posts. Sometimes, but rarely, the birds are truly all white—snow white, bright white—with pink eyes, pink bill, and pink legs and feet. Those are albinos. Mostly, though, the birds have a little color somewhere, although maybe the "color" is only an off-white or a beige tinge, but those birds lack pink eyes, bills, legs, and feet. A partially white cardinal, for instance, may have red wings or a red tail, or it may be such a splotchy affair that the bird looks moldy. A partially white goldfinch often has black flight feathers. A partially white bluebird may have just a hint of blue on its back or head.

An all-white hummingbird is a ghostly looking creature, and most of us have probably seen photos gone viral. So this afternoon's call about a white hummingbird caused me to change my plans from backyard window watching to white hummer watching.

Partially white birds—and other wildlife species—suffer from a genetic disorder called leucism and are referred to as leucistic individuals. While they often cause a stir among observers, their condition rarely foretells a long life. The unnatural appearance attracts predators. White feathers don't hold up well, especially in flight (thus most white birds like gulls and pelicans have black wing tips for durability). And migration is almost certainly an insurmountable challenge for these unusual creatures. But as we spent the early evening photographing this attractive bird, I forced those thoughts from my mind.

A Ruby-throated Hummingbird, in plumage called leucistic, visits a nearby feeder. To be an albino, the plumage would be pure white and the bird would have a pink bill, pink eyes, and pink legs and feet.

September 6

Adding Gold

Dry weather continues to draw birds to water. A birdbath bowl, minus the pedestal that came with it, sits on the ground under a little cluster of evergreens. Two bubble rocks, one in the front yard against the south wall of the house and one in the backyard among dense native plantings and a few yards from a wooden fence, seem to attract a fair amount of feathered traffic. Finally, our little yard pond, with its inch-deep "creek," also hosts occasional birds in the shallows. Conscious of the crackling dry conditions, each time I walked past a window this morning, I paused to check for any little birds at the water.

The usual array, less than newsworthy, has become routine, the same species as on previous days. Until one. Raising my binocular to double-check, I caught sight of something rare! Raising the window as quickly but quietly as I could and grabbing my camera, I snapped the first series of photos before I took a better look. Yep, true to my first suspicion, this was a rare Golden-winged Warbler, either a female or a hatch-year bird, the two typically inseparable among many warbler species. On only two previous occasions, once in the fall of 2013 and again in the fall of 2016, have we identified a Golden-winged Warbler in the yard. On those two occasions, the birds were males. In all three cases, water brought the birds within my view.

My heart skipped a beat when this rare female Golden-winged Warbler visited the backyard.

What is it, then, that makes Golden-winged Warblers rare? In fact, according to Cornell University's Lab of Ornithology, they have "suffered one of the steepest population declines of any songbird species in the past 45 years" and hold one of the smallest populations of any bird not already on the endangered species list. The problem? They've lost much of their breeding habitat, with about half of the global breeding population now confined to parts of Minnesota. According to AllAboutBirds.org: "Recent work with radio-transmitters [reveals that] the birds breed in shrubby, tangled thickets and other 'early successional' habitats. But after chicks fledge, the families move to mature forest habitats to continue raising their young." Mature forest habitats in the United States have disappeared at a rapid rate, as they have on the species' wintering grounds throughout Central America and into Colombia and Venezuela.

Seeing a bird with such a limited population is a sight to remember, and seeing it in one's own yard is a lifetime experience. I only hope whoever is living on this land fifty years from now will also see a Golden-winged Warbler from time to time.

By mid-afternoon, storm clouds gathered and the remnants of a hurricane began its predicted slow slog through the area. Heavy rain, welcome but lasting less than 10 minutes and totaling only four-tenths of an inch, nevertheless doused thirsty ground and thirsty plants. As a result, I expected to witness two behaviors among the birds: First, given the rainwater, birds would have less interest in the bubble rock. And second, given that the rain had washed away nectar from whatever flowers still bloomed, hummingbirds would inundate feeders. As late afternoon turned into late evening, the bubble rock stood empty, the entire backyard devoid of birds. Even our year-round residents had vacated the premises. But while hummers flocked to feeders, they did not show in the numbers I've seen in the past several days. As for the general absence of birds in the backyard, I think a hawk may have perched where

I couldn't see it, even though I walked through the little grove of evergreens studying branches for its hiding place. Hummers, of course, have no fear of hawks. After all, no sensible hawk would waste energy chasing a speed-demon hummer for a half-mouthful morsel.

> 1 Golden-winged Warbler
> **Species:** 112 total in the yard to date for the year.

September 7

Weathering the Changes

With hurricane remnants smacking up against a cold front, an all-day soaking not only broke the drought but caused flooding and in some places serious damage. The rain gauge here showed just a hair under 3 inches, so we had quite a wet-down. While there was little activity in the backyard this afternoon and early evening, I suspect that was mostly because of the ongoing rain. Hummingbirds, however, drained feeders quickly, requiring me to fill the little feeders several times today. Where else can they feed?

September 8

Counting Shades of Gold

American Goldfinches arrived today in hordes. Dramatic increases in the number of individuals make their migration obvious, but the amazing variety of plumages verifies their backgrounds—and says worlds about their breeding behavior.

Because goldfinches that bred well to our north operate on a different breeding and hormonal cycle than do those, for instance, that nested here, they are also in different stages of molt than "ours." Today's feeders hosted handsome full-breeding-plumaged males, spiffy mature females, many "dah-deet"-calling fledglings, and an array of partially molted, mostly molted, and fully molted birds. Their behavior is evidence that goldfinches from up north disperse to the south, perhaps only to here, to find more reliable feeding conditions. Rather than wait for conditions to become dire, they migrate now, probably leapfrogging over goldfinches only slightly farther to our north. Others will leapfrog over us to

American Goldfinches at a nyjer-seed feeder display multiple plumage variations, including breeding and partially molting males and females as well as one in immature plumage.

move deeper south. After all, they can't all pile up in one place, at the most northerly edge of a comfortable winter range. Further, the birds that have piled up here may not all stay. In fact, given the numbers, I know they can't stay. The habitat can't support so many.

September 9

Recognizing Effects of Migration

As migration continues, some expected sights occur, both in the yard and nearby, all indications of changing behavior. European Starlings gathered by the hundreds, even thousands, to perch in long lines on utility wires, and carpet fields and sometimes yards. Every time I see the massive flocks, I mentally calculate the number, divide by two, and know that all those pairs of invasive birds have robbed our native birds of nest cavities. By a quick calculation, about 800 congregated on the wires today—400 pairs, 400 nest cavities stolen from bluebirds, chickadees, titmice, and all the woodpeckers.

A single adult male hummingbird appeared among the flocks today. I wouldn't be surprised if he's the last one I see this season, and he's probably come a long way, maybe from as far as Canada. Following typical hummer behavior, his offspring will follow his route some weeks from now.

Only two warblers wandered through today, at least that I saw—a drab Magnolia Warbler and a female or hatch-year Black-and-white Warbler. In due time, more migrants will arrive. In fact, migratory behavior will play out for several more weeks. Each species tends to move through about the same time each year: some, like American Redstarts, zipping through habitually early, with others, like Orange-crowned Warblers, passing through

A female Black-and-white Warbler forages along tree branches much the way nuthatches do.

notably late. Logically, then, the later birds will mostly be different species than those seen to date.

Several circumstances affect the varied migratory behavior. All the breeding complexities like nest failure and multiple broods affect migration departure dates. Since hatch-year birds migrate last, breeding adults coming through now predict the later arrival of the youngsters. As always, weather patterns play a huge role in the timing of migration and migration waves. Finally, some migrants simply have a longer jaunt to get here than do others. Those with the longest journeys tend to show up earliest.

September 10

Birding Afield

Knowing that a decent migration was predicted for last night, I headed out early this morning with a birding friend to wander the mostly ill-kept and unmarked trails of an 800-acre forest. Of course, not all birds are forest birds. More accurately, few birds are forest birds. In fact, most birds prefer edges to deep forest. Nevertheless, birds that do love the forest abound in this spectacular hilly and diverse woodland.

Acadian Flycatchers greeted us immediately, even before we left the car, with their "pizza!" song, more an emphatic call than a song, but the best they can do. One after another after another we heard. Before we passed through one Acadian territory, we could hear the song of the next defender. Since the breeding season has ended, I was surprised to hear so much song.

Then the thrush "pit" calls took over. Wood Thrushes habitually nest in this vast forest, which is perfectly suited to their preferences, so it was no surprise to hear their now-subdued songs and calls. Swainson's Thrushes, on the other hand, are migrants. In fact, we watched nesting Swainson's Thrushes defend territory this summer while birding in northern Michigan, just this side of the Canadian border. Now, the thrushes are here, in southwestern Indiana, moving toward their winter homes, perhaps in Central America but more likely concentrated in South America along the west coast, through Colombia, Peru, and even into Bolivia, Chile, and parts of Argentina. We guesstimated that we heard between twenty-five and thirty, always seemingly nearby but only occasionally within sight, instead hidden in still-dense vegetation. They maintain their usual secretive behavior even in

Birds Do *That*?

Long-billed shorebirds suffer from rhynchokinesis. Well, not quite. They don't "suffer." That fancy word (try dropping it into your conversation at your next cocktail party) may sound like a dire disease, but instead it refers to a bird's ability to flex its upper bill independently of its lower bill. According to a Cornell Lab of Ornithology report, shorebirds and certain other long-billed birds use their flexible upper bills to better catch slippery items in sand or mud. Watch a shorebird poke its way like a sewing machine along a mudflat or sandy shore and you may catch a glimpse of rhynchokinesis in action.

A Yellow-throated Vireo, photographed in the yard last year at this time, may have been the vireo species glimpsed among the chickadee flock.

temporary habitat. Given the early morning dark woods, though, when we could manage a direct line of view, their spotted breasts and eye rings showed.

At one point we zeroed in on a little foraging flock including a trio of Carolina Chickadees. Chickadees seem the socialites of the wintering foraging flocks, and all manner of species often join chickadees, their flock-foraging behavior in full force. So what else foraged with them now? Craning our necks until our muscles ached to check the high canopy of a skinny maple tree, we could see multiple birds, all backlit against a bright sky. Arrrrgh! A little yellow, maybe? Something almost as small as the chickadees? Then we heard their calls and knew. Vireos. I won't guess how many because they were in and out of leaf cover, flitting from one cluster of greenery to another, never still enough to get a count. And the attraction? A massive grapevine twined throughout the canopy, and those birds were having a feast on the now-ripe wild grapes. Ah, yes, for birds it's always about habitat!

Back home this afternoon, I hoped to catch sight of a few more migrants, perhaps at the bubble rock. But no such luck today. Initially I wondered why the dearth of birds—all birds, not just migrants. Then I realized that three goldfinches were "frozen" in position on a feeder. They did not move their bodies. They did not move their heads. They did not blink their eyes. I checked the time. How long would they remain motionless? After 9 minutes, one of them flew. I can hardly imagine remaining motionless for 9 minutes. Even as I watched, I fidgeted, picked up my binocular and put it back down, checked my cell phone for time, considered photographs, took a few photographs, rechecked the time, watched them again through my binocular, fidgeted some more. And all this while, none of the three moved. They had good reason, of course, for their behavior. While I couldn't see it from my vantage point watching the goldfinches, I knew a hawk was somewhere near. Eventually, I opened the back door and stepped out. As I did, the shadow of a big bird moved over me from atop the cypress tree. Aha. A huge female Cooper's Hawk (females are larger than males) lifted up and away. Even though I thought the birds would now return to the yard within a few minutes, it took almost an hour before the first cardinal and the first goldfinch returned. They were skittish, watchful, eating quickly, and skittering off, back into the dense evergreens. Only the healthiest and smartest birds survive a resident hawk. While I understand perfectly that the hawk has to eat too, I really wish she'd move on to somewhere else and snare starlings and House Sparrows, not cardinals and goldfinches. I'm conflicted because, after all, I created a perfect feeding place for her by offering feeders to the songbirds.

September 11

Bringing Them In and Taking Them Out

Strong weather fronts that bring migrants in also take other migrants out, providing a tailwind to speed them along. So the historic pattern has repeated itself over the past few

weeks. Today, additional American Redstarts, a Least Flycatcher, and our first-of-the-year Swainson's Thrushes arrived. Photo-file dates indicate this is the week that fall-migrating Swainson's Thrushes have arrived every year for the past five years, an amazing statement about their migratory behavior. Since we were birding out of state during their usual spring arrival, we missed them then. So it was good to see them here today. Yes, true, I saw them yesterday in the forest, but somehow that isn't the same as seeing them in the yard.

A Swainson's Thrush forages among the fruits of the beautyberry shrub, its bold eye ring separating it from similar-looking thrushes.

Simultaneously, along with the new arrivals, hundreds of hummingbirds went out, the feeders emptying only about half as fast today as they have the previous two days. Whew! The bag I dumped into the canister yesterday marks 100 pounds of sugar fed this season. About now, when syrup making has grown tedious, I try to remember how excited I was when the first hummer arrived last spring. The more I understand about these tiny birds, the more in awe I am of their behavior, including their comings and goings. Right now, they're going—to Costa Rica.

A Least Flycatcher in the yard announces its presence by song, surprising me that it would sing so late in the season.

Beyond hummers, migrants of all kinds, still on the way, will roam the yard for the next several weeks, perhaps for a month. In general, birds arriving now stay short-term, maybe a few days, perhaps a week, and then continue their migration. Later, other migrants will arrive to stay the winter. Unfortunately, winter visitors lack the vibrant colors of tropical migrants, the lovely little creatures that are the avian epitome of eye candy! But, if you're wintering in a drab southwestern Indiana environment, you'll more likely survive predators if you're drab as well.

1 Swainson's Thrush
Species: 113 total in the yard to date for the year.

September 12

Reporting on War

Two Pileated Woodpeckers scolded on the wing. Their strong voices approaching the spot where I sat were both as loud as I've ever heard. If birds can yell, that's what they were doing. Looking up in anticipation of their flying through an opening in the canopy, I was startled to see instead a Red-shouldered Hawk sail quietly past. Close on its tail were the two screaming woodpeckers. Within seconds two crows joined the yelling, racing in from a slightly different sector, and the four pursuers rallied around the spot where the hawk landed. Although the Pileateds lit in a treetop several trees over, the crows, perhaps showing the greater bravado of the two attackers, zeroed in on the hawk. Within seconds, the hawk's silent cover blown by the aggressive screaming and yelling, it lifted up and flew in the direction from which it came. The crows went instantly quiet; the Pileateds followed suit. Warring efforts in the avian world sometimes join unlikely comrades, and who would think a pair of Pileateds and a pair of crows would fight on the same team. Quite a sight! Quite an effort for a successful effect! Quite a behavior!

September 13

Missing the Notes

Stepping outside in the already warm mugginess at 7:15 a.m., I heard music. Well, most any birdsong is music to my ears, but this was uncommon music, the music of two different birds, neither of which had spent the summer with us. Or so I thought as I listened to these new songs. But which birds were they? Checking the songs against a birding app, I tried the most likely. None matched. Then I remembered having heard the sneaker-on-the-gym-floor chirp of yesterday's migrating Rose-breasted Grosbeak. Although I never saw the bird, its call is so readily identifiable that I knew without seeing that it was here. So was this sweet, warbling song that of the grosbeak? Checking the app again confirmed the identity, but I was still puzzled by how quietly it sang. Although the bird was within 20 yards of where I stood, I could barely discern the notes—so very different from its robust springtime vocalizations. May I call the behavior noteworthy?

The other song confused me as well: "zoo zee, zoo zee, zoo zee-zee-zee-zee." I punched through the warbler app, listening to a single song from each of the possible migrants, refreshing my memory of the springtime songs, remembering that in the fall the songs can differ, grow quieter, turn off-key. But even given the variability of autumn song, nothing matched. Later this afternoon, when a Northern Parula darted around and finally lit on the bubble rock, I checked its song again. Nope. No match. True, the bird has several song variations, some of which are remarkably similar to those of other warblers. I checked those, too. No match. Finally I noticed a separate category of song labeled as "dawn songs." Hmmm. Well, I did hear the song in the morning, although it was well past dawn. And here it was 6:30 p.m., and I was hearing it again. Hardly dawn. Still, out of desperation to identify the singer, I played the first example of dawn song. Close, but not quite. Played the second example. Bingo! So this quiet little song, a little shaky, a little hesitant, sung during

A Northern Parula faces off with a Nashville Warbler, a seemingly wasted effort given the late season.

the wrong time of day, turned out to be the Northern Parula's dawn song. The parula spent the summer here. How could I not know its song?

The parula in the yard now, however, is almost certainly not the parula that spent the summer with us. Nor is it likely one of that pair's offspring. This bird is jumpy at the bubble rock, startled by the water gurgling up through the spout. That behavior is always a sure sign that a bird is new here. They become comfortable with the bubbling within minutes, but their initial behavior is one of caution, timidity. Well, sure. After all, birds that lack caution also lack long lives. Still, shouldn't a parula sound like a parula no matter where it lives? Not necessarily. Many birds have regional differences, including both plumage and song variations. Something else is in play in September when it comes to birdsong. Hormones are changing, saving birds energy during this non-breeding season. Since hormones drive song—its strength, accuracy, and tone—by mid-September the migrants' songs grow quieter, more tentative. On the flip side, in very early spring, before hormones rev up again, songs are typically off-key, sometimes just plain "wrong."

Today's music to my ears challenged me more than it should have, but I've had the pleasure of learning. With birds, there's more than a lifetime of learning, and I come very close to learning something new about them every single day.

September 14

Wishing for More

Given last night's prediction for another heavy migration, I was out early, hyped for a slew of new warblers. Well, actually, hyped for a slew of new anything. Maybe thrushes, grosbeaks, vireos, flycatchers, and, yes, warblers. Was I ever disappointed.

I shouldn't have been. There were dozens of great birds to enjoy, each engaged in its unique behavior, some foraging in high canopy, some in mid, some low, each in its preferred vegetation. Three Rose-breasted Grosbeaks foraged in the pecan trees; a Red-eyed Vireo rustled through the top of the wild black cherry tree; three Northern Parulas flitted through the yard, recognizable by their differing plumages; crows mobbed a Red-shouldered Hawk across the pasture; a Pileated Woodpecker called first from the woods to our west and then in our own little patch of woods; three Carolina Wrens sang and called back and forth from the woods to the yard, causing me to wonder about the three's-a-crowd cliché; a Magnolia Warbler popped in and out of the cypress tree; a female Blue-gray Gnatcatcher skittered through the crepe myrtle shrub; a female or a look-alike hatch-year American Redstart showed its face in the pin oak; two White-breasted Nuthatches called persistently, apparently to one another; a little flock of five Blue Jays made at least five different kinds of calls; an American Robin and two still-spotted youngsters perched briefly atop the hemlock; a Barred Owl gave three one-note calls; and at the bubble rock, a drab female Indigo Bunting took her time checking for safety, a first-year Chipping Sparrow took a long drink, a Yellow-throated Warbler made two appearances (or two made single appearances), and a hatch-year Baltimore Oriole skittered away before either a bath or a drink. Particularly I enjoyed three female or hatch-year Summer Tanagers as they wandered together around

A female or hatch-year Summer Tanager chases bees in the garden, one of three individuals lunching today on their favorite insects.

the yard for some minutes. Nothing else wears the orangey-golden color of a female Summer Tanager. Surely it's the color of some spectacularly royal fabric. Or maybe the background for a rich tapestry. Or perhaps the color of something outlandishly sumptuous to eat.

So, given all those birds romping through the yard, shouldn't that be enough? Shame on me for wanting more, but I sincerely hoped for new migrant species to pop into view at any time. None did. Not for the entire day.

Evidence of last night's migration, however, played out in another way. Hummingbird populations once again dropped dramatically, and the couple of hundred American Goldfinches that have been eating about a gallon of nyjer seed daily and pigging out in the lush seed heads in the garden surely fell by a third. I couldn't guess with any precision the number remaining, but perhaps no more than a hundred now. That's still too many for our habitat, but they'll sort themselves out, figuring out who goes and who stays. Or at least who stays for a short time versus who stays for the winter.

There was another observation today, however, a behavior that made me cock my head in dismay. Hearing Chimney Swifts overhead, I glanced up, just to verify that my ears weren't deceiving me, and wow! There were about thirty moving as a group. They weren't hunting—not flying in those erratic but generally circular patterns chasing and feeding on high-flying bugs. No, they were aiming arrow-straight across the sky, obviously on the move. The only problem: They were flying due north. The behavior puzzled me, and I finally decided to consult an ornithologist friend. She suggested the swifts were heading toward a rendezvous with others of their kind, an activity biologists refer to as staging. Once the flock is complete, they, like other similarly formed flocks, will migrate as a group to their wintering grounds in the upper Amazon River basin in Peru, Ecuador, and Brazil. Still, it was a first experience for me to see that kind of Chimney Swift behavior, their flying in that manner—more evidence that I can learn something new about birds every day!

September 15

Anticipating Berry Picking

Today's inventory of the yard's berry production leads me to believe we'll enjoy a good number of avian berry pickers! Early this spring and summer, mulberries, serviceberries, and wild black cherries drew in the crowds, especially fledglings, which loved a non-

moving target for lunch. Now I'm seeing a nice array of berries on flowering dogwood, Witherod viburnum, winterberry, pokeweed, ninebark, and an especially heavily laden American beautyberry. That berry combination will serve birds well into November. Then we'll need several freeze-thaw cycles to eventually ready the abundant American holly berries for the birds, but that may not occur until January. I look forward to birds feeding on this lavish supply of berries! After all, that's why my yard is heavily planted in natives. Birds don't necessarily recognize nonnative berries as food and can starve

A Gray Catbird makes one of its regular fall visits to the beautyberry shrub, gorging on the little lavender fruits.

to death right next to heavily laden nonnative berry producers. Since native birds evolved with native plants, they share an almost symbiotic relationship. When birds eat the seeds and either regurgitate or pass them, they replenish their own garden, planting their future meals as they move about their territories. Smart, huh?

September 16

Going Gray

Since the hummingbird feeders have to come inside every night to prevent total destruction by marauding raccoons, I'm up just before dawn each morning to re-hang feeders in time for the first hungry hummers as they come out of torpor. This morning, shortly after I returned inside, I stood at the window, cup of tea in hand, watching for the first visitors to the yard. I was really thinking hummers, maybe a few cardinals, and surely oodles of goldfinches. But there was a furtive movement where the beautyberry branches, heavily laden with berries, droop across the ground. What was that? Raising my ever-present binocular to try to brighten the view, I found myself looking eye-to-eye with a thrush. Swainson's Thrushes arrived almost a week ago, so was this another? Or could this be the Gray-cheeked Thrush, a bird that breeds considerably farther north than does the Swainson's? In fact, it's an above-the-Arctic-Circle breeder, across northern Canada and far northern Alaska, where they nest in alder-willow thickets and in the dense understory of conifer forests. So Gray-cheeks fly amazing distances from their winter range in Colombia and

Ecuador and parts of Central America. Sadly, this bird is experiencing a precipitous population decline, almost certainly from loss of habitat in both its breeding and wintering ranges.

Because it breeds farther north than the Swainson's, the Gray-cheeked typically reaches our area a week or so later than the Swainson's; today's arrival would be about the right timing. Looking more carefully, I check for an eye ring. It's not distinct, but is that because dim light isn't giving me a clear view? I check again. Ah, this bird has such a cold-looking face, gray, not the warm beige cheek color of the Swainson's. I try for a photo in near

A Gray-cheeked Thrush, tricky to distinguish from a Swainson's Thrush, heads for the berry bushes.

darkness. Blurry. But the thrush lingered to splash, drink, and preen, and finally the day brightened enough to capture a verifying image of the Gray-cheeked Thrush. It, like the Swainson's, was a regular we missed this spring when the thrush families moved through.

A group of birds bathes together in a ground-level birdbath, including, left to right, a Black-burnian Warbler, Tennessee Warbler, American Goldfinch, and female Indigo Bunting.

Now, on this little guy's return to South America, it has paused here, attracted by a bird-friendly migratory stopover filled with berries and water. It can feed in safety, fatten up a bit, take long drinks, and clean its feathers with a good bath. Sometimes all that hard work establishing habitat pays off in aces!

That was just the start of a banner day at the kitchen window! Migrants galore rushed the yard! A female Canada Warbler popped in for a quick drink, a rarity in our yard, only our third sighting; a Summer Tanager called from somewhere along the north property line; two Nashville Warblers made simultaneous appearances along the back fence; at least six female and/or hatch-year Indigo Buntings flitted to and from water and among the beautyberry branches, settling in for a good bath at the ground-level birdbath; two distinguishable Northern Parulas sang from the yard's perimeter, visiting water from time to time, one of them extraordinarily wary of the bubble; a Baltimore Oriole jetted through so quickly that in a blink I would have missed it; a Yellow-throated Warbler, an almost regular in the yard lately, cruised through several times today; and finally, late in the afternoon, a new-for-the-year Blackburnian Warbler took a leisurely splash in the ground-level birdbath. Oddly enough, he was accompanied in the bath by a Tennessee Warbler, a female Indigo Bunting, and a goldfinch, all of them likely attracted to the shady setting, especially given the 94-degree high today. Even with that peculiar combination of bathers, everyone seemed willing to share. No spats. No threats. No chasing. That behavior marks post-breeding camaraderie. Weather fronts are sending birds south.

1 Gray-cheeked Thrush
1 Canada Warbler
1 Blackburnian Warbler
Species: 116 total in the yard to date for the year.

September 17

Puzzling over Hummer Habits

Do hummingbirds prefer one kind of feeder over another? I have feeder-host friends who swear by certain feeders. I've tried the various models, alongside my other feeders, and hummers ignore the "foreigners." Over time, as manufacturers quit making a certain style and as I've needed feeders with larger capacity, I have put into service three feeder styles. One style is hourglass shaped, holding a single cup of syrup. Another is somewhat hourglass shaped, holding three cups of syrup dispensed at six protruding tubular feeding ports, surrounded by what resembles a flower. The other is straight-sided, holding three cups of syrup dispensed at six flat-faced feeding ports set off by yellow flowerlike inserts. All feeders are clear glass. All have red tops and red feeding ports. All are easily and completely cleaned.

As I watched hummers nectaring at feeders, I noticed they favor one style over another. Or so it seemed. I began to wonder if the attractiveness was the feeder style or the feeder location. Did hummers prefer feeders hanging higher or lower than the others? Since eight of my feeders hang under a trellis, four in each of two rows, I could easily rotate their positions and their height. And it seemed to matter. The feeders that had ports higher up got heavier traffic than did those hanging lower. The feeder closest to their flight path got the most traffic, regardless of height. And the feeder hanging off to the side, away from the two rows, got the second-highest traffic, no matter which feeder hung there.

Birds Do *That*?

Pigeons once provided poop to the government—literally. In sixteenth-century England, pigeon poop was the only known source of saltpeter—or more correctly, potassium nitrate—and saltpeter is an essential ingredient in gunpowder. Since the pigeon droppings were therefore a precious commodity, the government assumed the authority to collect all available. Of course, many kinds of manure are high in nitrates, but that information came along later. (Thanks to the website Pigeons for Meat for this invaluable information.)

That takes us back to my friends' favorite feeders. Why do their hummers love those varying styles while mine ignore them, nectaring exclusively at my original trio? I've actually come to believe that for hummers it's a matter of habit. This migration season, as I've watched more carefully than usual, I've also noticed that, given the same physical arrangement, different waves of migrating hummers favor different styles of feeders. The later in the season, the more frequently they prefer the little one-cup feeders. Could that possibly be because hummer hosts to our far north rarely have the need for the large three-cup feeders, and so these hummers are accustomed to the small style? Do they go to the style they're familiar with, the "look" that has provided a regularly reliable source of nectar at previous locations? I'm almost ready to bet on it—especially given the difference between my hummer-host friends' experience and mine. Hummers are creatures of habit. They travel the same migration patterns year after year. They visit the same flower patches year after year. They return to the same breeding sites year after year. They come to the same feeders year after year. Even five years after my mother moved from her home, hummingbirds continued coming to the spot where her feeders once hung. Habit is a behavior worth reckoning, especially when it comes to hummers.

September 18

Feeding Upside Down

Goldfinches naturally feed from a variety of positions, taking the best approach to whichever seeds they're aiming to eat. Frequently, they dine upside down, a position that affords them comfortable foraging and access to seeds that other birds might miss. Clever manufacturers have taken advantage of goldfinch habits by marketing an upside-down nyjer-seed feeder, one that presumably prevents other bird species from partaking of the expensive seed. Because we humans are susceptible to clever marketing strategies, we purchase the feeders and chuckle as goldfinches quickly learn to access the upside-down ports.

Today, for the second time this season, I observed a mature male goldfinch at my standard nyjer-seed tube feeder using it as if it were designed for upside-down feeding. The poor bird had to stretch, but cling he did to the perch, reaching the distance to pick seeds from the feeding port below. His behavior, however, was in my opinion more than a normal goldfinch feeding behavior. To me, it demonstrated that this bird had only recently arrived in my yard, and he had previously hung out in a yard with an upside-down feeder.

Not yet molted into winter plumage like most mature males that live here, this male had obviously come a distance and was not familiar with my standard feeder. Sometimes little quirks in behavior convey fascinating insights.

September 19

Tracking Tanagers

During occasional years in the past, Scarlet Tanagers have nested nearby, perhaps in our own little patch of woods but more often in the adjoining larger forest to our east. Scarlets prefer large forested tracts, mostly deciduous, but will also extend into deciduous-coniferous forests. Especially, however, they look for vast areas forested by truly large trees. Our neighborhood mostly falls short of their breeding demands. In the fall, however, they will wander into open areas, even parks, foraging. That behavior causes them to show up in our yard during most fall migrations. Of course, they've usually molted into their basic (winter) plumage by then, so the male is greenish yellow, not bright red. The black wings, though, make him readily identifiable. And so today, he was here! What a handsome bird—no matter the season! He's on his way now to northern and western South America, some of his kind traveling even into Bolivia, where he'll hang out on the hillsides and mountains for the winter. Wish he could talk about his travels.

A male Scarlet Tanager, now in winter plumage, is ready to return "home," a range including northern and western South America as far south as Bolivia.

A spring male Scarlet Tanager in breeding plumage gives credence to its name. Compare this plumage with the bird's winter plumage in the photo above.

Summer Tanagers, on the other hand, breed in gaps between and edges along forested areas. So they typically breed in vicinities adjoining our property. They're not quite the long-distance travelers that Scarlet Tanagers are since they wander only into Mexico and Central America. Still, they accumulate a good many frequent-flier miles making that trip twice a year. Since their primary diet is made up of bees and wasps, gardens attract them. When they're available, berries also attract Summers. That combined preferential behavior for forest edges and gardens means we see Summer Tanagers far more often than Scarlet Tanagers.

1 Scarlet Tanager
Species: 117 total in the yard to date for the year.

September 20

Giggling over Tipping

A lovely adult male Baltimore Oriole put on a show this afternoon within 4 feet of my office window. Two one-cup hummingbird feeders hang side by side from the awning edge, giving me a steady view of hummer activity anytime I look up from my desk. This afternoon the oriole found the two feeders. His problem was that the bee guards kept him from readily accessing the nectar. Not to be outwitted, however, he devised a system. He hopped to

the edge of the feeder, tipping it, spilling just a bit of syrup into the port. After sipping up that little spill, he rotated around the four-port feeder, nectaring at each, and then hopped to the opposite feeder, tipping it in the process, and completed his round at those four ports. Back and forth he went, from one feeder to the other, making the same four-port rotation at each. He stayed almost 10 minutes, never varying from his routine. I'm betting he's done that before somewhere because he didn't waste any time figuring out how to feed. Who says birds aren't innovative? What a great illustration of adaptive behavior!

A male Baltimore Oriole learns that if he jumps onto the hummingbird feeder, his weight will cause liquid to slosh out into the "flowers," allowing him to feed on the nectar.

When this little guy migrates to Central America for the winter, he will continue to visit gardens, checking out vines, trees, and other vegetation for nectar, berries, and fruit, occupying areas like gardens and shade-grown coffee plantations.

September 21

Signaling the Edge

Rain, sometimes heavy, accompanied a cold front easing through today. Minimal winds kept the drenching from being a blasting storm. Birds, seeking protection from the downpour, huddled under leaves and next to structures both native and man-made, and shook regularly to rid themselves of water droplets. As the rain slacked off, however, they returned to foraging, tolerating light rain because their metabolisms demand steady supplies of nutrition. It's on days like today that many birds find feeders especially helpful. Readily available feeder seed allows birds to exert less energy and take less time to refuel. And for hummingbirds, feeders may actually represent lifesaving resources. Rain washes away natural nectar, new flowers don't open in the rain, and food supplies dwindle quickly.

As hummers zip from flower to flower seeking sustenance and failing, they waste even more energy, using up stored fat supplies. Again, birds live on the edge. Always.

September 22

Spotting the Bandit

Visiting friends 150 miles to our north gave us the opportunity to spot a few migrants that have not yet reached us. No sooner had we walked inside and peered out their sunroom window than we caught sight of a cute little masked nuthatch. It's been two years since we've had Red-breasted Nuthatches in the yard, so seeing it was a treat. It was our friends' first sighting of the year as well.

Red-breasted Nuthatches, smaller and even more speedy than our year-round resident White-breasted Nuthatches, make their way south to our area during what biologists call "irruptive" years. When mast crops across Canada are such that birds don't find adequate food, they may "irrupt," especially to the south and southeast from the Canadian boreal forests. In other words, behavior during an irruption year is not the same as during regular migration. Sure, the birds are moving from their usual range, but the movement is not routine, not annual, and usually not predictable. Several of the northern finches along with Red-breasted Nuthatches, then, give us days of excitement, watching the unusual visitors. Sometimes the visitors hang out; sometimes they wander through to parts farther south. One year a Red-breasted Nuthatch hung out with us the entire winter, giving us a truly rare treat. He visited feeders for peanuts, sunflower seed, and suet, but he was particularly enamored with the hemlock trees and their many cones. Foraging among conifers is the Red-breasted Nuthatch's preferred dining behavior.

A Red-breasted Nuthatch is smaller than its cousin the White-breasted Nuthatch. Red-breasteds also wear a "mask" that readily identifies them.

A White-breasted Nuthatch is noticeably larger than a Red-breasted and lacks the Red-breasted's distinctive facial "mask."

Having seen this little bandit to our north, we can now watch in anticipation, hoping that over the next several days the Red-breasted Nuthatch will actually show up at our house, maybe for a few minutes, maybe for a day, maybe for a week, maybe even longer. That would be fun!

September 23

Wallowing in Warblers

What a birding adventure we had with our friends to the north! By day's end we had spotted sixty-one species, including fifteen species of warblers! Knowing that these migrants are headed back to Central and South America, traveling startlingly vast distances, I can barely take my eyes off them. What incredible migratory behavior they evidence! Of course, as usual, fall warblers challenge our identification skills. Their plumages now have changed dramatically from that in the spring, and juveniles typically look like females but often with enough variation to further complicate the puzzle. Once again, we are reminded of the reason for the cliché, "confusing fall warblers."

Mostly we wandered along a little tree-lined peninsula that juts out into a 1,400-acre reservoir. Birds fed vigorously, flitting mainly among the upper branches in typical warbler behavior. With our binoculars trained on the birds, straining to see into the highest parts of the canopy, it became quickly obvious why another cliché is part of the fall warbler watch. It's "warbler neck." Sometimes I simply have to pause, take a rest, and massage my neck before I can resume watching those high-canopy branches and the birds they hold. But what an array! Cape May, Blackpoll, Palm, Tennessee, Blackburnian, Wilson's, Bay-breasted, Black-and-white, Black-throated Green, Chestnut-sided, Golden-winged, Nashville, Yellow-throated—oh, my, all those warblers. And that doesn't even begin to acknowledge the many thrushes, vireos, and other migrants foraging there, too.

Why was that peninsula such an attractive habitat for the migrants? Bugs and berries abound along the wooded edge. And the vast majority of birds prefer to feed along edges. Think of "edge" as a place where forest meets grassland, where grassland meets wetland,

Every year around this time, Tennessee Warblers comb the cypress tree, foraging on tiny green caterpillars. Even though I look carefully, I can never find the caterpillars myself.

where wetland meets water—in short, where one kind of habitat blends into another. Add to the bug- and berry-laden wooded edge the position of the land, jutting out into the reservoir, which gives the spot prominence, much like a banner, beckoning anything flying nearby.

Birds Do *That*?

Tiny hummingbirds live in the fast lane. A Ruby-throated Hummingbird weighs one-tenth of an ounce, so if we could somehow safely (and legally) send hummingbirds via the US Postal Service, we could mail ten of them with a single first-class stamp. That's a tiny bird! Its body temperature ranges from 105 to 108 degrees, seeming to defy good health. Depending on whether it's hovering or migrating, and depending on weather conditions, a hummer beats its wings 40 to 80 times per second, an average of 52 beats per second—or 3,120 beats per minute. To keep up that kind of physical endurance, its heart beats 250 times per minute while resting and 1,200 times per minute while feeding. Of course, it has to breathe hard and fast to keep the fast-beating heart supplied with oxygen, and that respiratory rate clocks in at 250 breaths per minute. And in case you wonder how this speck of a bird can fly across the Gulf of Mexico during migration, remember it flies 30 mph during a normal cruise but can kick it up to 50 mph to escape danger. All these details are summarized by Lanny Chambers, a St. Louis, Missouri, hummingbird bander and website host for hummingbirds.net.

September 24

Seeing Swarming Hummers—Still

Knowing that the cold front two nights ago brought those huge numbers of migrants to the peninsula yesterday, I fully expected that here at home it pushed most of the hummingbirds out. After all, it's late September now. Instead, I came back to mostly drained nectar feeders. Rushing to fill them in time for heavy late afternoon and evening feeding, I was buzzed repeatedly as I re-hung them. This has been the longest, heaviest hummingbird migration I can remember. It started early and made me think hummers had had a poor breeding season, had given up, and were going home. Then another surge the last week of August made me believe that the migration was early this year because of the really late spring migration. I concluded that the late migration caused birds that typically raise two broods to give up after one, but that they had had a remarkably successful single-brood season. Then a huge surge the first two weeks in September—the normal hummer peak migration—made me change my mind yet again, figuring that the hummers had actually had a fabulously productive year. And now, with the migration surge continuing well beyond the normal first weeks of September, I'm convinced that not only did hummers have a fabulous year, they surely had an astoundingly fabulous year. In my mind, that's the only interpretation of their behavior that makes sense.

September 25

Watching a Floor Walker

Already we've had 2.25 inches of rain over the past two days, and today rain showers continued. The day was dark, dreary, damp. Although my desk lamp was on, I had turned off the kitchen light, knowing I'd not be doing anything more than passing through. As I wandered out for yet another cup of morning tea, I paused at the kitchen window as I always do. (I may walk by the window with a load of laundry in my arms, but I will still, always, stop to scan the yard for movement.) Immediately I spotted a bird walking. Because of heavy cloud cover and dense shade, I could see no color, but I dropped what I was doing, grabbed my ever-present binocular, and focused. Any bird that is walking instead of hopping needs attention. This bird walked along the edge where a split-rail fence is fronted by ostrich ferns and where a hemlock tree, branches to the ground, sweeps the top of the fence. Behind is an unmowed patch of "woods"—pine, hemlock, and cypress trees, densely planted, branches nearly to the ground, and pine needles matting the floor.

Ovenbirds are almost always on the ground, and in my yard they come walking out from under the evergreens—always walking, not hopping.

Binocs focused, I saw what I suspected: Ovenbird. Named for the shape of its nest, the Ovenbird lives on the ground. I've never seen it anywhere other than walking on the forest floor, foraging for invertebrates. It even nests on the ground. That's the Ovenbird's unique behavior. While it resembles a little thrush, it's actually a warbler, and its most charming feature, other than its loud Carolina-Wren-like song, is the orange stripe that runs down the center of its head. Because it's secretive and habitat-specific, I'm always pleased to see it in the yard. Makes me believe our habitat is, after all, special.

1 Ovenbird
Species: 118 total in the yard to date for the year.

September 26

Staring in Disbelief

It's been fifteen years since I've recorded a Blue-winged Warbler in the yard, so today's visit was a surprise, and a much appreciated one. As the Blue-winged has pushed northward in its breeding range, it has hybridized with Golden-winged Warblers, threatening the Golden-winged population. Breeding throughout much of the eastern half of the United States, Blue-winged Warblers are heading now to Central America and to some of the Caribbean Islands for the winter. Most references say good habitat of native shrubs attracts their attention, both during breeding and during migration, so habitat restoration is paying off.

A Blue-winged Warbler wings in for the first time in fifteen years, visiting the bubble rock.

A good many other activities have played out today, too, given this peak time of migration. The Ovenbird remained, still foraging on the ground under the pines and hemlocks. A Red-eyed Vireo stopped by the bubble rock. Although it breeds here, its secretive behavior means it rarely comes out of the woods. Like other species, it's more willing to wander about now that nesting season is over. At least one Magnolia Warbler showed its face today, so that species continues to straggle through, the first one sighted several weeks ago. A Wilson's Warbler also returned, or more likely another arrived, this time foraging in the pokeweed, then turning to our monster cedar tree, and finally working its way to the top of the old apple tree, the three plants adjoining one another for a convenient buggy buffet.

As late in the breeding season as it is, our year-round residents continue to show intermittent evidence of ongoing breeding activity. Unlike migrants, they have no travel deadlines. Their only deadline is to prepare fledglings for independence by winter's arrival. So true to form, today I spotted a male Northern Cardinal feeding a fledgling. Shortly before, I saw a male American Goldfinch feeding its fledglings. They've had a good year, these two species, obviously finding time to produce a second, or perhaps even a third brood. Currently, about forty to fifty goldfinches are feeding in the yard, mostly among the seed heads in the garden. They won't stay, of course, because the garden will be depleted, but it's fun watching their foraging behavior among the stalks.

At last light this evening, between forty and forty-five hummers visited my nine feeders for a last-minute bedtime snack, guzzling enough sustenance to last them the night. To guesstimate the population of visiting hummers, one traditional rule of thumb says to multiply by six the highest number of hummers seen at any one time. That would put the count here now at about 200. That's a dramatic drop from a week ago, but in another week tonight's count will also drop dramatically. It's a crazy time, this migration, when literally billions of birds take to the skies every night. Such a miraculous event! Such astounding behavior!

1 Blue-winged Warbler
Species: 119 total in the yard to date for the year.

September 27

Thinking about the Times

For the first time since last May, temperatures last night dropped into the low 50s. We've also had another 2.75 inches of rain beyond the 2.25 inches we had a couple of days ago. So it's chilly and wet. Birds are moving. Oh, it's not the cold temperature that makes them move. It's the weather fronts, the wind, especially northerly winds, tailwinds, that send birds south.

Today was an especially notable day for flycatchers. All three species sighted in the area, although not necessarily in our yard, but they also breed to the north so could be distant

A Willow Flycatcher engages in its dart-out-and-grab bugging technique, preparing for its trip to Central America.

migrants. Two Eastern Wood-pewees worked the yard, surely different from the one that foraged here for weeks. A newly molted Eastern Phoebe hunted here, too, its lovely yellow belly challenging me to decide if the little guy was really a phoebe or instead a Yellow-bellied Flycatcher. The absence of an eye ring and the presence of a long, broad tail made it an unmistakable phoebe. The nice surprise, though, was the Willow Flycatcher working from the utility wire, behaving in typical flycatcher fashion: darting out from the wire, sallying across the neighbor's backyard, and returning to the wire. Although it sang its "fitz-bew" song only once, it was clear enough to separate it from the "pizza!" song of the similarly plumaged Acadian Flycatcher that nests in the woods.

Several late Chimney Swifts zigzagged across the sky, their foraging behavior distinctive. Grosbeaks still call and occasionally visit feeders for sunflower seed, their varied plumages making them individually recognizable. A Gray Catbird bugged its way under and then up through the old apple tree, secreting its way as catbirds do. A Summer Tanager called from the backyard. A very late House Wren picked through the goldenrod, hunting bugs. Judging by its timid behavior, I'd say it's unlikely one that nested here. A Yellow-rumped Warbler, Common Yellowthroat, and Palm Warbler made their first appearances since spring but gave me only quick views. A Black-throated Green Warbler foraged through the pin oak, obviously finding lots of little green caterpillars. Their drawn-out migratory behavior almost guarantees I'll see many more of these common warblers. Sixteen Blue Jays flew overhead, southward, as a group. Although some winter with us, some also migrate. These were obviously on a mission, an unmistakable behavior.

Woodpeckers seemed to be gathering for winter roost sites, notably a pair of Pileated Woodpeckers, hammering on trees in both the neighbor's yard and in ours. Northern Flickers returned today as well! They've been away, not far, but in some secret place to raise their young. They do that every year, a distinctive behavior of theirs, but they usually come back to spend the winter in and around our yard.

At about 6 p.m., the Barred Owl sang its full song, the "Who-cooks-for-you? Who-cooks-for-you-allll"—music to my ears! After hearing the Great Horned Owl call late this summer, I feared that it had taken over the Barred Owl's years-long-held territory, possibly even had the Barred for lunch. The Great Horned is, after all, the Barred Owl's major predator. The past four rain-soaked days had threatened the owls. They can't fly in the rain because they don't have oil on their feathers like most other birds. Because they aren't waterproof, they get plain soaking wet, feathers nearly useless, and they sometimes succumb to the conditions. Complicating their livelihood even more, they can't hunt in the rain because they can't hear their prey. As nature would have it, though, owls can't be both silent fliers and waterproof. So they're silent fliers, or more accurately, silent killers of the night. "Our" Barred Owl will be on the hunt tonight!

I worry about owls, especially in the fall. When weather chills and mice seek cozy winter hideouts, some homeowners grow nervous. At the first sight of a mouse, or maybe even before, they reach for the rodenticide, or rat poison. Unfortunately, a mouse doesn't die the instant it eats the poison, instead rushing about to further prepare for winter. Its rushing attracts owls and hawks, but because its movements are slightly slowed by the beginning effects of the poison, the mice are easy prey. As the owls and hawks catch multiple such mice, the poison accumulates in their own bodies. Rodenticides kill by affecting the victim's circulatory system; poisoned rats and mice bleed to death internally. The owls and hawks that eat the poisoned rodents suffer the same consequences. There are alternative safe means of ridding a home of rodents.

1 Willow Flycatcher
Species: 120 total in the yard to date for the year.

September 28

Indicating the Season
On September 2 I spied my first-of-season Ruby-crowned Kinglet, noting then that the winter visitor had arrived early, really early. Today I caught up with another behaving in typical kinglet fashion, this one foraging for about 10 minutes in the old apple tree. They're such crazy busy little birds, smaller than Carolina Chickadees by a quarter inch, and never still, instead scurrying here and there, flitting branch to branch, sometimes flying straight up (how do they do that?), and sometimes hanging upside down, always foraging for bugs. On an otherwise relatively quiet evening, this little guy's flighty behavior attracted my attention, so how could I not follow it? Challenged to get a photo, I moved from spot to spot trying for the perfect angle. Very soon I gave up on "perfect" and just tried to get an in-focus shot of this frenetically moving target. Finally, after almost one hundred shots I managed a reasonable photo, just to put it in the record.

Here in southwestern Indiana, we're on the very northern edge of the Ruby-crowned Kinglet's winter range, so most likely the early September sighting as well as today's are of birds that will continue southward, perhaps all the way down to the Gulf Coast, maybe even into Mexico. Still, at some point a few will stop, hanging out here for the winter, not in bunches like American Goldfinches or White-throated Sparrows, but in ones and twos, motivated to test our weather conditions, perhaps to get a jump start on the spring

A Ruby-crowned Kinglet forages in its usual frenetic manner, picking through the leaves and bark for bugs in the old apple tree and then dropping into the goldenrod. Fortunately for the birds, we never use insecticides, so they find ample food.

migration. Starting here in southern Indiana rather than in, say, central Mexico, they gain the advantage of becoming first arrivals on their breeding grounds across Canada. They're tiny little fluff balls (they weigh less than a quarter of an ounce) that fly fast and far, regular little dynamos. And tonight one foraged right here, first in our old apple tree and then dropping into the goldenrod, treating me to the little drama of its arrival. I wonder where all it's been since I saw it here back in April.

September 29

Monitoring Warring Factions

A Cooper's Hawk stationed herself amid the pine boughs, a behavior suggesting she no doubt hoped to conceal herself for a surprise attack on some unsuspecting songbird. The Blue Jays, however, decided otherwise. Six of them, behaving in aggressive Blue Jay fashion, ganged up, mobbing the hawk, diving down to peck its back, swooping across its shoulders, attacking on wing and on foot, hopping, darting, sashaying. They literally screamed. Attracted by the commotion, a couple of cardinals and at least one titmouse arrived on the scene to check out the melee. They, however, didn't stay long. In hawk attacks, size matters, and the jays had an advantage the cardinals and titmouse didn't. Nonplused, the pack of jays, however, continued harassing the Cooper's until they drove it 100 yards or so to the pecan tree. There, unrelenting, the jays continued their behavior, attacking full on. In desperation the Cooper's hopped up a limb, down a branch, easing this way and that, flipping front to back, attempting to find protection from the onslaught within the foliage. She flew another 20 yards to another tree, moving higher in the canopy, but to no avail. The attack continued, the screaming readily audible through my closed windows.

I wondered how long the battle would last. For at least 15 minutes, the jays screamed and the hawk refused to leave their territory. Sure, she moved from place to place but not far enough to vacate the premises that the jays deemed their own. Finally, however, she apparently moved just far enough that the jays gave way, returning to the backyard, calling "jay, jay, jay," as if to say, "Okay, we drove her off. We can all eat in peace now." But the jays were wrong. Within a half hour, I saw her once again ducking into the pine boughs, no doubt scouring the territory for lunch. The jays had either exhausted themselves or missed her return, but I'd bet exhaustion made them give way. No jay still living ever misses anything. I never saw her catch her prey, but somewhere, sometime, somehow, I'm fairly certain she managed satisfactory sustenance. It's what she does. It's how she survives. It's her behavior.

This evening, less than an hour before dark, I birded along the north property line, at the foot of the hill, alongside a 20-foot row of 5-foot-tall native switchgrass and around the super-size goldenrod patch now in full bloom. My reasoning: If I always bird where I've always birded, I'll always see what I've always seen. Moving to different habitat might give me a glimpse of something new and interesting. Indeed, no sooner had I eased into the area adjoining the switchgrass than some tantalizing little something caught my eye foraging amid the seed-laden stalks. Although it never revealed itself sufficiently for me to identify the specific little dark creature, I did find others, including an Indigo Bunting foraging in the goldenrod and a Common Yellowthroat hiding out in the tangles. Tomorrow I plan to go for an earlier start in the area, perhaps discovering what else is hiding there. Every bird has its preferred habitat, from ground level to the highest canopy. It's how they behave.

September 30

Witnessing a Banner Day

I heard it first. Then the Red-breasted Nuthatch scooted down the sweetbay, onto a stick next to the bubble rock, then onto the rock, drinking its fill. I hadn't seen the little guy in the yard in almost two years! And little it is. Much smaller than the White-breasted Nuthatch, it's also cuter—at least in my opinion. The little bandit-like face mask distinctly sets it apart from the White-breasted, perhaps a surprising distinction, given its name. Certainly we might expect the red breast to be the deciding characteristic, but sometimes the "red" is a mere wash, especially on females and even more so on hatch-year females. So it's always the mask that catches my eye, that and the fact that it scoots about as if it's on slippery ice after a dose of steroids. Given my "cuteness" rank for the bird, I found myself taking photo after photo and watching its behavior. Well, its behavior surely falls in the category of antics.

Red-breasted Nuthatches breed across Canada and along mountain ranges, coming here only in winter, but not during all winters. Fond of insects and seeds, this mostly solitary bird typically hangs out a day or so and then moves on. Two winters ago, however, it stayed here the entire season. Today I saw only one but heard another at the same time. There's a second one nearby!

A mature Red-breasted Nuthatch, likely a female, lacks the brighter breast color of a male.

An immature Red-breasted Nuthatch, molting into adult plumage, looks a bit ragged around the edges.

Birds Do *That*?

Bar-tailed Godwits fly 7,000 miles nonstop. Each fall these long-legged wading birds travel from Alaska, where many of them breed, to New Zealand, where they winter. While other birds travel farther—the Arctic Tern, for instance, migrates from the Arctic to the Antarctic and back every year—only the Bar-tailed Godwit travels so far without stopping to rest, eat, or drink. According to Dr. Clive Minton of the Australasian Waders Study Group, satellite tracking verified that at least four tracked birds flew 6,851 miles over nine days. Yes, nine days. Another took a different—and longer—route, traveling 7,258 miles. Nonstop. What unbelievable behavior!

The winds that brought in the nuthatch also brought in some additional migrants. Hummingbirds are departing in droves, but enough remain that I added a little syrup to a couple of empty feeders. I find it interesting that the hummers arriving now are fat. I mean, they're really fat. Wherever they came from, or wherever they hatched, they had ample food. Some autumns, especially in years of drought, they arrive here so thin and so late that I worry they'll feel driven to depart before they gain enough grams to fly another 100 miles.

The Ovenbird reappeared, but after a two-day absence, this may well be a different individual. A Gray Catbird showed up again, but as with the Ovenbird, it's been absent for some time. This, too, then, is likely a different individual. A really gray-plumaged phoebe was flycatching in the backyard, an adult that has only just arrived. Rose-breasted Grosbeaks continue to move through, and given their very different stages of molt, I think at least six wandered about the yard today. They've had a long, drawn-out migration this year. Of course, our unseasonably warm weather may be contributing to their lingering. The high today was 83 degrees, approaching a record for this time of year.

Some common birds tend to abandon us for the summer, only to return in the fall for our berries, a behavior that annoys me, since I wish they'd also stay the summer. Something in our habitat, though, doesn't meet their summertime needs. For birds, habitat is always the end-all/be-all. Of course, only so many birds can survive in a habitat, so maybe our yard actually suits birds just fine, but it's too crowded for yet another nesting pair with hungry babies needing bugs. Today, however, the Northern Mockingbird returned, as it usually does, preparing no doubt to feast on the dogwood berries now and be nearby later when the American holly berries ripen. Already, I caught sight of a robin yanking dogwood berries from the upper branches of the backyard tree, another bird that abandons us until berries are ripe.

This evening I decided to bird our little locust grove. Part of what makes the grove attractive to birds is the abundance of grapevines, laden now with little wild grapes. The other part of what makes the little grove attractive in late afternoon and early evening is its location, situated so that bright sunbeams illuminate the trees and keep bugs active until last light. Still, I didn't really expect anything spectacular since I figured most warblers have moved through. How wrong I was! For over an hour I watched seven species of warblers foraging heavily, moving over and through the grove, eating little green caterpillars and oodles of spiders and the bugs ensnared in their webs. A Yellow-rump, at least three

Magnolias, several Nashvilles, a Bay-breasted, one American Redstart, two Northern Parulas, and an out-of-character Ovenbird atop a snag among the vines all entertained me as I tried to keep up with their varying behaviors and count their numbers. Joining them was a Ruby-crowned Kinglet and a Field Sparrow, although the sparrow stayed low, foraging for seed among the goldenrod stalks. As I headed back to the house, movement attracted my eye, and I spotted seven Common Nighthawks sky hunting, moving generally southward. Their numbers are worth reporting since the birds are in decline. I was happy to see them migrating.

2 Red-breasted Nuthatch
Species: 121 total in the yard to date for the year.

October

A Song Sparrow lives up to its name, singing nearly year-round, here from amid autumn foliage.

Autumn is a second spring when every leaf is a flower.

—Albert Camus (1913–1960)

October 1

Surveying the Mix

When the calendar rolls over to October, I know we're near the end of fall migration activity. The birds that nested here and to our north are moving south, migrating by the millions—some would say billions—in nighttime skies. Already some winter visitors have arrived, but more will come over the next few weeks. Then, by month's end, we will likely have settled into a winter routine.

The catbird arrived first today, behaving the way catbirds usually do, foraging furtively in the American beautyberry bush. During the course of the day, I gave up counting how many times it darted in, disappeared among the drooping branches, and worked its way through the lavender fruits. The only way I could follow its progress was by watching which branches wiggled and shook. My, how that bird loves those berries, packing on the energy.

The catbird's behavior, however, was only one small sign of the changing times. Noisy Blue Jays spent the morning plucking acorns and caching them wherever they found a convenient spot, many in the garden mulch, storing sustenance against a cold winter's day. One had filled its gullet with three acorns, then dropped its stash next to a hiding spot, burying one and picking up the other two in search of another hiding spot. A Hairy Woodpecker plucked dogwood berries, deviating from his usual diet of bugs. A few Chimney Swifts still flew generally southward, but displaying altered behavior, flying high, really high, bugging along the way. A single male goldfinch still in breeding plumage visited the nyjer feeder, the remainder of his kind almost fully molted into winter plumage. I have to wonder where he came from, but it had to have been some distance to the north where breeding duties kept hormones pumping. Grosbeaks in many stages of molt visited, too, preparing to head farther on their southward journeys.

A wide range of migrants, including those that spent the summer with us, also made appearances, and each time I see them now I have this niggling feeling I won't see them again until next spring. Shortened days are tugging them south. Two caused me to ask a question for which there is no answer. A handsome male Summer Tanager and a winter-plumaged male Scarlet Tanager both popped by. I always find it curious that male Summer Tanagers retain their red plumage season to season after reaching adulthood but Scarlets go green every winter. Why is that? Seems such a waste of energy!

Everything needs water, so behavior among and between species visiting the bubble rock merits some attention. Today, a Tennessee Warbler took its place among the chickadees and goldfinches, keeping a wary eye on its bigger companions. Size matters in behavior. Cardinals and grosbeaks also vied for places, the feisty cardinals, accustomed to having their way, showing aggression toward the grosbeaks. Mostly the grosbeaks backed off, perhaps giving way to resident birds. Sometimes visitors take the back seat, so to speak, a behavior that keeps the peace. Indigo Buntings, both females and hatch-year birds, show up daily and hop in among the goldfinches, usually each showing brief intolerance toward the other but each backing off a bit to avoid conflict. Buntings fall in the finch family, so maybe it's a cousin-to-cousin courtesy. Today, however, an Indigo Bunting and a Yellow-throated Warbler squared off but quickly backed down, deciding after all that neither was a threat to the other, sipping quietly, having moved a few inches farther apart. Of course, if a dove,

A female Indigo Bunting (left) shows aggression toward a Yellow-throated Warbler at the bubble rock.

jay, or flicker flies in, all little birds scatter, showing deference to size without any attempt at reconciliation. Better to wait for a safe opportunity than to fight a losing battle.

This evening, though, even with breeding season over, I witnessed ongoing territorial behavior. A group of a half dozen crows discovered something they didn't like, perhaps an owl on its day roost or a hawk perched in predatory preparation. At any rate, the crows made more noise than I would ever expect six of them could make, and they flew into and through a single high-rise tree, cawing all the while. Whatever the crows mobbed must have decided against a standoff, apparently exiting the backside of the tree out of my line of sight, for as suddenly as the noise began, it quit. One by one, the crows moved off, all now deemed safe in the neighborhood.

October 2

Continuing the Survey

Hummingbird populations decline daily and will continue to do so quickly over the next two weeks, but their crazy territorial battles continue to rage. Why won't these migrating hummers, with ample feeding ports readily available, simply nectar peacefully? But no, they're always at war with one another, even here, even now. The current hummers in the yard most likely hatched in Michigan or even Canada, so they're only a fraction of their way on their journey to Costa Rica. There are no territories for them to defend here. They won't return here, except perhaps in passing during next spring's journey to their ancestral breeding grounds. But they battle on. It's just routine hummer behavior.

A hatch-year male Ruby-throated Hummingbird shows accumulated fat around the base of his neck, a good sign of his preparation for migration.

Perhaps the most telling example of hummingbirds' viciousness, however, comes from a birding friend's observation in his yard. A few of his photos verified for me the otherwise unbelievable scenario, a battle unlike anything I've ever seen, surely a fight to the extreme. In the course of the two hummers' respective attempts to commandeer a single feeder, one hummer managed a two-footed grip on the other's beak. They battled to the ground, lifted up a few inches, crashed back to the ground, arose from the grass then fought to the ground again, wings whirring on both birds, each time the two-footed grip remaining in place, each time the other's beak ensnared. Not only was the battle surely exhausting for both birds, but I have to puzzle over how any given hummingbird could manage to get both feet wrapped around another's beak. Given the obvious midair attack, that would be an acrobat's savviest move. The scenario leaves little doubt about the hummer's warrior-like behavior. Another friend who bands hummingbirds for the national database likes to say that if hummers were big enough, they'd eat us. Hmmm.

The good news about their feeder battles is that many hummers now show obvious signs of packing on the fat. We humans tend to think of fat around the middle—ballooning waistlines and bulging hips. Hummers, though, store much of their visible fat rolls around the base of their necks. Some look almost as if they're wearing a boa!

Today, a year-round resident Northern Flicker, a bird that was absent from the yard during breeding season, showed up at the on-ground birdbath. Nothing unusual about that, except today he actually needed a bath. His beak was coated with mud! Not to be concerned, though. After all, a flicker's favorite meal is a mouthful of ants and beetles. This guy had been poking in the soil for a dandy supper.

A migrating Blackburnian Warbler gave me an identification test this morning. Confusing fall warblers often only remotely resemble their spring selves, having molted from alternate (breeding) plumage into basic plumage. Blackburnian is one of them. A bird's molt pattern is part of its behavior, albeit an uncontrolled behavior, but behavior nevertheless. How a bird changes appearance, particularly from season to season, makes for dramatic observation, each species wearing a unique and identifiable result. So here's the deal: In spring the Blackburnian male's fiery orange-red throat, its signature field mark, makes it pure eye candy. In fall, however, the throat shows barely a yellow blush—all because of molt patterns and their variations. Other feather colors and patterns change as well. But in the Blackburnian's case, two definitive field marks make identification certain. First, pale braces on a Blackburnian's back are unique among warblers, so if this was definitely a warbler (and it was), then it was definitely a Blackburnian. Second, a yellowish patch on the forehead is also unique to Blackburnians. Photos showed both field marks, and my ID was confirmed! How incredible, though, that seemingly nondescript and insignificant

A Blackburnian Warbler shows distinctive back and facial field marks, unique identification clues to one of fall's confusing warblers.

markings could be so telling, such an integral part of the molt pattern. It's yet another example of how bird behavior is so amazing.

A migrating Black-throated Green Warbler foraged through the cypress tree this afternoon, momentarily causing me to puzzle over its identification. It had no namesake black throat! Even females have a spattering of a black throat. So what's up with this little guy? It was just that—a little guy, a youngster—in the early stages of molt. Ah, yes, there's that word again! This youngster had not yet molted into adult plumage that will give it the namesake black throat. But come spring, look out. He or she will be gorgeous, decked out in breeding plumage. Nothing unusual, though, about this youngster's arrival now. Hatch-year birds are among the last of their species to head south. Just weeks out of the nest, they need a little time to develop their flying and foraging skills to survive the arduous migration on their own. Mind-boggling, isn't it, that they make these long-distance journeys alone, only weeks old, the route hardwired into their brains.

After seeing a Black-and-white Warbler here on May 2, I enjoyed seeing it, or another of its kind, return this fall on August 30. Seeing one again today, two months later, however, says something about Black-and-white behavior, but I'm not sure exactly what. Okay, true, fall migration is a protracted affair. Arriving two months later than another of its kind may indicate nothing more than a migrant taking a leisurely trip home. Black-and-whites, though, nest in an incredibly wide geographic range, from central Canada south almost to the Gulf Coast. So these two Black-and-whites could be coming from anywhere—or nowhere. They may, in fact, have nested right here in the area. Of course, as we've noted before, not all birds of a species finish nesting duties at the same time, depending on how far the bird migrated to breed, how soon it reached its breeding territory, how many broods it raised or tried to raise, and whether or not it experienced nesting success. But here's another complication: The Black-and-white's winter range covers almost as much geography as its breeding range, from Mexico through Central America into Ecuador. So some may leave late because they don't have far to go to reach their ancestral "home." Finally, since today's bird is a "female," it could in fact be a youngster. If it fledged with a second brood, perhaps here in this area, it may only now be mature enough to migrate. So many "ifs"! So many possible explanations for this bird's behavior! How I wish we could know exactly where it's been, this little winged wonder that makes our yard home for a few days.

October 3

Disregarding Weather Clues

Today's record high of 88 degrees and strong sustained winds from the southwest caused birds to spend much of the day tucked in. With no north wind and no weather front to move birds south, very little migration activity is predicted for tonight.

So today merely revealed ongoing signs of the times—with one delightful winter visitor's arrival: a Yellow-bellied Sapsucker, a bird whose plumage indicates it hatched just this summer and already has flown from somewhere in central Canada to southwestern Indiana. Imagine that. It could be as young as five weeks out of the nest! Perhaps it will stay the winter (we're on the very northern edge of its winter range), but more likely it will continue farther south with possibly another sapsucker taking its place. At least that's my hope. It's

the only migrating woodpecker in the East. In size, it's exactly between a Downy Woodpecker and Hairy Woodpecker. It's also the only eastern woodpecker, male or female, with a red throat. I get a kick out of watching the behavior of these relatively quiet woodpeckers, clinging to the old sugar maple, drilling rows of little round holes across the trunk. The holes become sap wells that accumulate daily nutrition for the appropriately named sapsucker. In spring, before nectar becomes plentiful, the sap wells also provide nutrition for early hummingbirds. While the rows of holes may look threatening, they really don't harm the tree, but they certainly provide lifesaving sustenance for those two species.

Given this week's extraordinarily warm weather, however, isn't it surprising that migrants are pouring through, that winter visitors are arriving daily? Shouldn't the warm weather keep them in place? Isn't it surprising that the most recent previous photograph I have documenting the arrival of a Yellow-bellied Sapsucker is dated October 4, only a single

A hatch-year Yellow-bellied Sapsucker, the only fully migratory woodpecker in eastern North America, makes a one-day visit to the yard during its fall migration south, heading perhaps as far as Panama.

day later than this year's arrival? Well, no. Birds migrate according to internal clocks set by length of day, the times of the rising and setting sun. Temperatures are irrelevant. Thus, birds mostly arrive right on schedule, year after year. That's another reason why climate change will dramatically affect migrants. They will arrive at the times they usually do only to find the bug bloom past, handicapping them in feeding their young. When Mother Nature's clock gets out of sync, as it has and will with climate change, all kinds of things go awry.

> 1 Yellow-bellied Sapsucker
> **Species:** 122 total in the
> yard to date for the year.

October 4

Spotting Flocks

Today's yard hosted more than the usual number of Brown-headed Cowbirds, a species I'm never happy to see. While they weren't here in a huge flock, at least a dozen splashed in the on-ground birdbath, drank from the bubble rock, and gobbled sunflower seed and peanuts from a feeder. Perhaps I'm to blame for their gathering. Since I don't offer much in the way of commercial feed this time of year, adding the sunflower seed and peanuts in hopes of attracting an array of Rose-breasted Grosbeaks possibly triggered the arrival of the cowbirds. Just knowing they're here, though, makes my stomach churn. They're murderously destructive to over 200 species of other birds, parasitizing their nests. Cowbirds don't raise their own babies and can lay fifty or more eggs per season in other nests, thus destroying those other birds' broods while increasing their own populations by leaps and bounds. So, yes, I find their presence stomach wrenching.

The onset of winter—at least according to the length of day—also sees the formation of other flocks. On several occasions over the past few days I've spotted flocks of European Starlings, groups numbering in the hundreds. After breeding season ends, extended families join forces, including the still-brown youngsters, and forage together, aiding the food-finding efforts and simultaneously teaching the youngsters the ways of survival. Grackles and Red-winged Blackbirds are famous for their massive winter flocks. Robins leave our yard and join roving flocks for the same purpose: More eyes spy more food, and youngsters learn from adults. Sometimes the flocks are of mixed species, and some of those are particularly fun to watch and follow. Chickadees and titmice, especially, join with Downy Woodpeckers and sometimes Yellow-rumped Warblers and kinglets to forage along forest edges. Anytime I hear chickadees in winter, I check to see who is roaming with them, sometimes finding a surprising array of companions, sometimes not.

All these flocking behaviors simply clarify that winter is nigh.

October 5

Distinguishing Distance Fliers

Oddly, this afternoon I spotted among the little flocks of foraging backyard birds one adult male American Goldfinch and one adult male Indigo Bunting, both still in breeding plumage. While goldfinches and buntings remain regulars at feeders and water, seeing these two still in breeding plumage was a bit of a surprise. I suspect, but cannot prove, that these two are long-distance migrants, possibly birds that nested at the northern edge of their breeding ranges. While American Goldfinches have an expansive year-round territory across most of the middle and northern United States, some do roam into southern parts of Canada to breed, departing the area as winter arrives. Indeed, those parts of Canada

A male Indigo Bunting makes a late-in-the-season yard visit, surprisingly still in breeding plumage.

have already had snow, so this breeding-plumaged female may have nested there, only now arriving here, perhaps to stay for the winter, perhaps only to feed and rest before moving still farther south. On the other hand, buntings nest across the entire eastern half of the United States up to the Canadian border, creeping into the southern rim of Canada here and there. They winter, though, from southern Florida to northern South America. So this guy may be less than a third of the way along his journey. What awesome behavior!

October 6

Meeting Returning Sparrows

Bingo! It's winter! No matter that the temperatures are still at record highs, hovering daily near 90 degrees, no matter that the record warm lows fail to cool the scorched land at night, no matter that the calendar says early October, no matter that the trees are still mostly green! No, in my book, when the winter sparrows arrive—well, it's winter. Today a spiffy White-throated Sparrow made its first appearance of the season. Every year I think I'll pinpoint the last White-throated visitor to leave in the spring. They tend to linger with us later than any of the other winter visitors, and when they leave, they leave in ones and twos, not in flocks. So the end-of-season sightings are far more tricky to record than first-of-season, like today. About all I can say is that my final reference to them last spring was May 5. Since then they've been as far north as the Arctic Circle and back, although this first returnee probably bred closer, perhaps only in southern Canada.

During one of our earlier birding forays into Canada, hubby and I found ourselves on the northeastern shores of Newfoundland, ambling among the dense evergreens called tuckamore. About shoulder- to head-high, the conifers grow so tightly together that no human could maneuver through, not even in a crawl. Among the vast, dense growth, however, we watched White-throated Sparrows flitting about, seemingly oblivious to our presence (although birds are never oblivious to anything in their surroundings). This, then, is their summer habitat, their nesting preference. No wonder when they visit here for the winter, I tend to find them in the densest vegetation in the yard!

When I think about the effort we exerted and the time we spent getting to the far shores of Newfoundland, it's a bit mind-boggling to look at this pretty little feathered creature, weighing in at less than an ounce, and try to imagine what its life (or at least that of one of its kind) has been like since it left here five months ago. Did it find a mate and raise a family? Did the offspring survive? Did it struggle on this current journey with bad weather? Flee predators? Nearly starve before finding food in new places? How long did it take for it to fly the distance? How did it find water? How did it know the way? How did it find my yard? How does it decide whether to stay or move on?

Then I pause. Is it possible, even by the wildest stretch of imagination, that this same sparrow wintered in my yard last year?

Of all the questions about this species' behavior, only one has much of an answer, and that's the one about knowing its way. The set of directions that bring White-throated Sparrows to and from their winter range and their breeding grounds are hardwired in their brains, information passed down over thousands of generations, as automatic for this fluff of feathers as breathing and blinking. The rest, though, try as we might, remains largely lost on scientists. Yes, banding studies or geolocators could perhaps reveal some secrets, but scientists don't work from my yard.

Friends stopped by for a visit this afternoon and were greeted by the newly returned Northern Mockingbird. Because it sings a boisterous, full-fledged mimic song, I suspect it's a male. In any case, it's highly territorial. Why now? Mockers stake out winter feeding territories in the same way they stake out breeding territories, and I'm fairly certain this one has staked out our yard as his own personal winter dining area—or for at least as long

A White-throated Sparrow makes a first-of-season appearance, joining us for the winter.

as the berries last. The mocker's greeting, however, was not welcomed by our friends. Somehow, within minutes, the mocker discovered his perfect reflection in their auto's windows. Sensing an "intruder" in his reflection, he began his territorial defense. He flew against the window, fluttered down, took refuge on the side mirrors, and repeated the routine. And repeated and repeated and repeated. Worse yet, each time he fluttered and took refuge, he pooped. By the time our friends departed an hour or so later, their vehicle was seriously painted by the droppings, on the mirror, on the window, down the side of the door, on both sides of the vehicle. By necessity, we pulled out a hose to clean the mess. I fear our friends were seriously offended. At least I hope they're still our friends. What a test of friendship.

October 7

Borrowing Time

Among the last warblers to wander through during fall migration are the pretty little Black-throated Green Warblers. I glimpsed the first one on August 31, and today at least several individuals foraged through the bald cypress tree in the backyard. How do I know there were multiple individuals? Not because we watched them off and on for most of the day (although we did), and not because I saw several at one time (although I did). No, it was because in spite of their all being the same species, they didn't look alike. They were identifiable by their plumage variations. While spring breeding males tend to have a namesake fully black throat, and spring breeding females lack anything much more than a few streaky suggestions of a black throat, in the fall, hatch-year birds can wear almost limitless variations of blackness. The adults likely came through earlier, so most if not all of the birds we saw today were youngsters. Watching carefully, then, lets me know for sure that various Black-throated Greens had stopped by for breakfast, lunch, and dinner. Photos confirmed the variations.

Some references refer to this species as rather "tame and confiding," and I agree. Their behavior suggests they're undisturbed by our big-eyed binoculars or camera lenses pointing their way, and they forage easily and readily throughout the mid-level vegetation,

Fall warblers are typically difficult to identify accurately by age and sex, but this is likely a hatch-year male Black-throated Green Warbler.

Showing pale plumage, this is likely a hatch-year female Black-throated Green Warbler. Compare with the male in the photo at left.

harvesting what appear to be plentiful little green caterpillars (although when I check branches similar to the ones on which the birds are foraging, I never find any). Given the abundance of food, the birds may stay a few days, but they have a long way yet to go, wintering in Central America.

October 8

Registering Change

Hummingbird populations continue to drop, now down to countable numbers. This morning, I saw no more than nine at any one time. Yes, I know the rule of thumb. To figure how many hummers sip nectar at feeders, one multiplies by six the number counted at any given moment. But I think that rule is likely invalid now, late in migration, especially in early morning and late evening, when hummers feed (mostly) peacefully side by side, virtually all of them youngsters only weeks out of the nest just trying to figure out how to survive this journey they've been sucked into, hardwired into their very being. Most look

Birds Do *That*?

Birds use made-to-order, built-in goggles. A third eyelid, called a nictitating membrane, closes front to back, as opposed to the other two lids that, like those of most animals, close top down and bottom up. Since the nictitating membrane is translucent, it serves birds well by protecting their eyes while still allowing them to see, at least reasonably well. Birds close the third eyelid when coming in contact with prey, while feeding young, and while diving through the air or into water. Think of this third eyelid as a pair of goggles, offering safety. According to The Peregrine Fund website, the nictitating membrane is the lid that birds blink with, keeping their eyes moistened and clean, and is critical for survival. Blind birds, even those blind in only one eye, don't live long.

healthy, even a little chunky, suggesting they've found adequate sustenance along the way. As a result, these individuals likely won't stay long. They don't need to spend days here preparing for farther flights; they're already fat, the bulges along the base of their necks holding visible stored fat.

October 9

Forming a New Normal

With warbler migration nearing its end, I'll surely get back to my normal daily chores! I've been glued to the window or to hot spots in the yard, feeling certain that if I miss even a minute I might miss the few seconds that a migrant visits the garden, the berries, the bubble rock, the ground-level birdbath, or the bug-laden boughs of their favorite foraging spots. Maybe now I'll feel less galvanized to the drama outside the window, assured that I need no longer watch minute by minute, that whatever is here will remain for some time.

Still, today I caught sight of a late migrating Bay-breasted Warbler splashing in the bubble rock. Bay-breasted populations fluctuate with budworm infestations, crashing when budworms crash, so seeing it here, late though it is, might suggest they've had a good year. Ironically, though, had I not walked past the window at that moment, I would have missed its entire 60-second visit. Likewise with the Magnolia Warbler that foraged through the lower branches of the bald cypress tree, behaving in typical Magnolia fashion, foraging on the outer edges of the tree, poking under leaves for little green caterpillars. Again, though, had I not paused while I was making a pot of tea to study the boughs for movement, I would have missed its 2-minute visit. Now I have to wonder: What did I miss today by not maintaining my usual vigil?

Later, a dozen Chipping Sparrows in a variety of plumages, from adult to near-adult to juvenile to winter, all bounced in together, foraged in the gone-to-seed grasses and splashed in both water sources. After a half hour or so, they departed together, not in a single liftoff but in ones and twos in quick succession. So these little sparrows have flocked together, perhaps an extended family, no doubt in preparation for winter, aiming to forage together, keeping an eye out for one another, multiplying their protection twelve times over. Smart behavior.

A Chipping Sparrow in winter plumage investigates a water feature.

Another new normal for the immediate season comes from the berry eaters. At the moment, a few American Robins and a lone Northern Mockingbird are routinely munching lunch in the dogwood trees, the berries slowly disappearing without any obvious moment-by-moment riddance. Many more berries—dogwood, winterberry, pokeweed, cedar, holly, and viburnum—remain, so more feeding frenzies are yet to come.

A male Northern Flicker, identified by his black moustache, stops for a drink at the bubble rock.

Finally, the new normal means the woodpeckers are returning to their winter routines. A male Pileated Woodpecker checked out the old tulip-tree snag and scooted up the cypress trunk before checking the platform feeder. He was glamorously handsome, obviously in brand-new plumage. While I saw only the single bird, I heard another calling, apparently from the other side of the house. He flew that direction when he left.

Meanwhile, the flickers have returned, making their daily visits. Well, at least two of them have. I recall the seven that hung out here last winter during the worst of the weather. Actually, while I enjoyed their presence during those drab days, I hope these don't face similarly severe weather this winter. Crowding into each other's territory, even in winter, seems all wrong.

October 10

Monitoring Fronts

The strong weather front, predicted for days now, brought about three-quarters of an inch of rain today. We needed the soaking to break the heat spell and bring more seasonable weather. Meteorologists are calling for a low tonight in the low 40s, a real shocker of a change from recent lows in the low 70s. But it's time. Past time. And the birds are already responding to the change. Weather always affects their behavior.

A few Rose-breasted Grosbeaks linger, feeding as usual on sunflower seed and now adding dogwood berries to their diet, benefiting from the rich nutrients, preparing for the remaining flight to Central America, perhaps into northern South America. They aren't the same birds each day; they wear different plumages. While the fall males lack the pizzazz of spring adult males, I think they're quite lovely. (See the spring male Rose-breasted Grosbeak on April 30.)

This morning brought only six hummingbirds to feeders, and I'm willing to bet that by tomorrow morning, they'll be absent. More have been feeding on flowers than at feeders simply because as new arrivals, they more readily find flowers than feeders. Some authorities believe that during this time of year, the hummers we see today are not the hummers we saw yesterday. It's possible, however, that hummers finding themselves short on energy may linger an extra day or so when they find ready resources like garden abundance. Then, over the course of a couple of days, they also find feeders, probably by watching other hummers. At least I feel comfortable knowing that when they leave here, they're as prepared to move on as they choose to be.

It is with serious reservations that I think about migration now. Hurricane Michael hit the Florida Panhandle today as a Category 5. Although it will veer northeast and continue moving quickly across the Southeast and offshore, many

A male Rose-breasted Grosbeak returns to the yard this fall wearing mostly winter plumage. Compare with his spring breeding plumage on April 30.

Spring female Rose-breasted Grosbeaks are readily identifiable, but in fall, immature birds, males and females, all look like spring females.

migrants—not just hummers—will find themselves directly in the path of that storm. I wonder how they will survive. Or if they will.

October 11

Scanning the Garden

The yard and garden are oddly changed today, the front having blown through last night, dropping temperatures so significantly that today's high is lower the any of the previous ten days' lows. The steady breeze, sometimes fairly strong, has a nip to it, making the sudden shift even more obvious to mere humans wandering out and about. But the birds know.

This morning I missed my bet about the hummers. Five hummingbirds joined together at feeders, although they buzzed singly to and from feeders all day long. Otherwise, the yard seemed empty of migrants. Not even a grosbeak showed its face today. Cardinals, however, seemed to have joined forces, more of them than ever foraging in the backyard, checking out the beautyberries and dogwood berries, dashing to and from the water sources, and checking for sunflower or safflower seed on the platform feeders.

Buttonbush seed heads have recently attracted chickadees.

The front garden, however, is quite the hotbed of activity now, passing cold front or not, but the activists aren't migrants. They're our year-round residents. American Goldfinches lift off by the dozens anytime I approach the garden. They're foraging in the dense, prolific black-eyed Susan seed heads. They're equally busy plucking seeds from the washes of native liatris and purple coneflowers, sweeps of prairie dock and prairie coneflower, and smaller clusters of native perennial seed heads as well as the nonnative tall verbena. This morning, however, I was surprised to find more than just the overwhelming numbers of goldfinches. Carolina Chickadees made me stop for a double take as I watched them foraging on the native buttonbush seed balls, hanging upside down to feed, a common behavior for them. Buttonbushes produce odd little seed balls, somewhat reminiscent of sycamore balls but smaller and harder. Seems to me, though, that the balls are way too green to offer suitable nourishment, but apparently the birds know better! I'm rethinking the importance of buttonbush in my garden!

October 12

Wishing Them Well

Before I crawled out from under the extra covers this morning, I saw a single hummingbird zip past the window to the front feeder. By the time I managed my slippers and robe and headed to the kitchen, I spotted an additional hummer hunched on the feeder at the window, fluffed up into an almost perfect ball, the sphere distorted only by beak and tail. The outdoor thermometer read 39 degrees, an achy-joint-inducing drop from the 90s in which we've been broiling. So this poor hummer was fluffed to retain heat (think wrapping up in a fluffy down comforter), but doubtless feeding without stirring from its perch, maintaining as best it could the little body warmth it had, and gradually coming out of torpor. Since normal hummer body temp ranges between 105 and 108 degrees, keeping warm must be a serious challenge. Given sufficient food, however, they do quite well at even frosty temps. I'm glad the feeders are fresh.

Although I was away from home most of the day and thus don't know what kind of activity I missed, I did not see any hummers feeding at dusk this evening. Knowing that they're flying into Hurricane Michael's totally denuded landscape, I fear for their survival.

October 13

Deciphering Differences

Today's winter-like temperatures made spotting winter visitors like Ruby-crowned Kinglets seem almost routine—already!—even though a single hummingbird huddled at the feeder early this morning. To me, though, the most interesting sighting was a cute little Red-breasted Nuthatch, a bird of the northern forests, visiting the safflower feeder at least a dozen times this evening. I'm not sure if it could have eaten every seed it snatched up, given the speed with which it grabbed them, dashed away, and returned, so perhaps it was actually stashing a few of them in the bald cypress tree bark. At least that's where it headed each time it zipped from the feeder. That behavior raises an interesting question: Would a bird stash seed in a place where it had no intention of staying? Of course, I can't be certain it was stashing anything, but I like anticipating the answer to the question.

This brightly colored Red-breasted Nuthatch, photographed October 1, had already molted into new plumage.

In retrospect, I've spotted a Red-breasted Nuthatch on two previous occasions already this fall, but this one gave me pause. It was much paler than one I photographed on October 1, so this one is either a female or a juvenile. In addition, this evening's visitor is obviously molting. I have an additional set of images made on October 6 that appear to show a third individual. Put together, the photo series suggests that a number of Red-breasted Nuthatches are moving through our area now. Supporting that observation is today's social media post from the

This pale, ragged-looking Red-breasted Nuthatch, photographed October 13, is molting and may be a hatch-year bird transforming into adult plumage.

northern part of the state noting "numerous up-close-and-personal encounters with Red-breasted Nuthatches" during a morning outing. Perhaps this is a year for a nuthatch invasion! We may enjoy the little bandits all winter. Fingers crossed!

October 14

Getting the Berry Bunch

The dogwood berries look ripe for the plucking to me, and I've wondered why more birds weren't joining the occasional robin and mockingbird to take their dinners in the trees. Today, however, the fruits must have reached perfection, perfectly ripe for the picking, and a bit of competitive bird behavior resulted. At least fourteen American Robins moved in, shaking branches as they yanked off berries, one after another in quick succession, then bouncing to another branch, bobbing with their own weight, plucking more fruits. A crowd of European Starlings waded in as well but lifted off shortly, possibly because I clapped my hands to scare them off. The robins remained, attuned no doubt to the rascal

An American Robin forages through flowering dogwood berries, instinctively seeking the high-fat nutrition to prepare for winter. Native berries provide essential foods to birds in the fall and winter.

starlings' ways. Two Northern Mockingbirds fussed over who had control of this feeding territory, and one abruptly left. A single Gray Catbird stopped to check the dogwood but continued on its way to its preferred beautyberry bush. Several Northern Cardinals chose a limb farthest away from the hungry robins to feed at their leisure. After about 45 minutes, the frenzy came to a halt and everyone left. They'll return. I can bet money on that. Dogwood berries, known to be prized by at least thirty-five species of birds, are high-fat fruits, nutritionally perfect to help birds stay warm.

All the activity, the chatter of the starlings and the tut-tut-tutting of the robins, however, attracted the attention of a Cooper's Hawk, likely accounting for the other birds' sudden departure. It sallied across the property from the northeast and lit atop the tallest pine tree. Instantly, a Blue Jay began screaming. At first I thought the behavior and the timing had to be coincidental, but I was wrong. Another jay flew to the wild cherry tree next to the pine and hopped from branch to branch, obviously spying on the whereabouts of the hawk. Meanwhile, two Carolina Wrens joined the scolding. The Cooper's called once and apparently flew out the back, out of my line of sight, heading no doubt for somewhere where its cover wouldn't be blown the instant it arrived. Then, with the "inspector" jay apparently reporting the hawk's departure, the cacophony of scolding ceased. Instantly. Ah, yes, Blue Jays are the watchdogs of the avian neighborhood! What an important behavior!

White-throated Sparrows have streamed into the yard, meaning that the most recent arrivals likely came the farthest. They've surely been on the wing for at least two months, possibly longer. Starting with a single bird on October 6, now at least a dozen skittered through the tangles behind the house, here for the winter. Several showed their faces in the backyard, but they're a bit shy still. Over time, more will overcome their hesitancy, change their behavior, and forage closer to the house. To my pleasure, however, this evening a few of them sang. It's a song I haven't heard for almost six months, so the melody cheered me. Granted, the songs were a bit wavering, perhaps because the singer is young.

Birds Do *That*?

Cedar Waxwings pass berries to their friends. Given that every bird must survive on its own, perhaps it seems strange that one waxwing would pass food along to another waxwing as if seated at a dining room table, politely passing the applesauce or mashed potatoes. But that's exactly what they do. When perched adjoining one another, one bird may pluck a berry and pass it to the left. If the berry gets to the end of the row of perched birds without being eaten, the last bird may choose to down it; or the last bird may return the berry, sending it to the right, back down the line. When the berry gets squishy enough that passing it farther makes no sense, some individual will finally swallow it. Numerous social media videos show the phenomenon in action.

October 15

Itching to Find an Orange-crowned

Two days ago a birding buddy taunted me with his sighting of Orange-crowned Warblers in his yard. Indeed, it's time. They're usually the last fall warblers to come through these parts, a behavior explained by their not having as far to go as those with destinations deep into South America. Well, okay, some fly into Mexico, but the bulk hang out along the Gulf Coast. Most of my previous years' records tell me, yes, they should be here now! Right now! I'm watching, watching, watching.

This evening, my dedicated watch-sit paid off, although not with an Orange-crowned Warbler, but instead with a Blue-eyed Vireo! It's a strikingly patterned bird, and my heart skipped a tiny beat when I first caught sight of it. As forest birds, they're mostly solitary, their typical behavior putting them in mid- to upper-level trees, and like warblers, gleaning insects and eggs and larvae from leaves. This little guy (or gal—the sexes look alike) has come here most likely from breeding habitat in central Canada. Some breed in the Appalachians, but those birds would unlikely head west to go south. South for this species may mean no farther than the coastal states, but some winter as far

A Blue-headed Vireo, wearing its distinctive "spectacles," forages through the sweetbay, following its usual behavior of showing up about this time every year.

south as Costa Rica. In fact, one Blue-headed Vireo banded in Ontario was recaptured in Guatemala! Sometimes in spring I hear its song, but mostly I have trouble discerning it from that of other vireos. Seeing, though, is believing, and this one came through the backyard, probably attracted by the little grove of mixed coniferous trees, which it prefers. It checked out the bubble rock but didn't accept the gurgling invitation to drink and bathe. Still, it was here long enough for me to gasp, ohhh and ahhh, and snap a dozen photos.

Meanwhile, I was surprised to catch sight of a lone hummingbird this morning and again late this afternoon—probably the same bird both times. I always wonder when I see a hummer this late in the season: Will this be the last sighting of the season? My record-late sighting is October 24, but today's may be this year's record.

> 1 Blue-headed Vireo
> **Species:** 123 total in the yard to date for the year.

October 16

Teaming Up

What a crazy day! And not just in my yard. Fellow birders boasted on social media how many birds they saw today. To keep up with all the feathered phenomena here, hubby and I teamed up. He watched out the north windows and I watched out the south, windows open, our voices silent or subdued, cameras ready. The passing weather front last night gave a good push, and late October typically marks the last of the pushes. It's a heady time, and I'm almost dizzy trying to take in all the migration behavior. Photo records over many previous years clearly verify a common occurrence: a big, exciting wave of migrants and then the passers-through are gone, gone, gone. Here's how the behavior played out— fast-paced, busy, and, yes, a bit crazy.

Two hummers lingered today, but any appearance after October 10 is icing on the cake. Ironically, in the past few weeks I've seen more hummers in the garden than at the feeders—a significant observation. Their behavior reminds us that they need protein, too, not just nectar, and they're obviously finding bugs in the garden.

Both kinglets, Ruby-crowned and Golden-crowned, foraged in the shrubs, today being this season's first sighting of the Golden-crowned.

Black-throated Green Warblers splash in our little front-yard water feature, bathing extensively.

Back again (or still), Black-throated Green Warblers, our most common pass-through migrant, aren't considered backyard birds and don't come to feeders, but yards with mature trees, like our huge hemlock, pine, and especially cypress trees, attract their attention. Three splashed together in the front-yard water feature, so I'd bet additional individuals roamed nearby. Knowing how many wander the yard on any given day would be an impossible challenge. Let's just say "many."

A Tennessee Warbler, wearing the greenish tinge of winter plumage, bathes in our water feature, instinctively seeking clean feathers for better flight. Compare this photo with the same species in spring plumage shown on May 1.

At least two Yellow-rumped Warblers, inconspicuous in winter plumage, foraged through the yard. They breed not too far to our north, as close as Michigan, and we're along the northern edge of their winter range. If weather doesn't turn too nasty, they may stay the season with us, but usually they don't.

A very late House Wren wiggled through the beautyberry. The late migrants behave differently than those that nested here, more cautious, more furtive—probably younger. At least two Tennessee Warblers visited the water feature and foraged in the maple tree. My efforts to make at least one of them into an Orange-crowned Warbler failed. A Nashville Warbler flicked about among the Russian sage stalks and then dove into the crepe myrtle. A female Black-throated Blue Warbler gave me a headache trying to make its ID, but finally a photo showing the undertail pattern solved the mystery. The fall female isn't much to look at, but I'm delighted to have had the challenge of sorting through the field marks. A truly bright Red-breasted Nuthatch confirmed that more than one is foraging through the yard now, the other one, either a female or hatch-year bird, extraordinarily pale.

Each of these birds shared a behavior unique to its species—how it moves, what it eats and where and how it feeds, where it drinks, if and where it hides, and how and with which other birds it interacts—all fascinating to watch.

Amid all the hubbub of migrants, hubby came to my window post, grinning, ready to show me a photo. I knew he was up to something, especially when he claimed he couldn't ID the bird he'd just photographed. Of course, I knew better, so I waited to see the image. Dark-eyed Junco! The first of the season had just now arrived in the yard. And hubby got the pic! They've flown perhaps a thousand miles or more from central Canada to be here, in our yard, and they'll stay for the winter. So, yes, these so-called "snowbirds" bring the snow!

A Dark-eyed Junco makes its first appearance of the season, here to spend the winter with us.

As the dizzying afternoon of bird watching grew cooler and dimmer, I heard the final surprise of the day coming from our little patch of woods: Two Barred Owls called, one higher pitched than the other, clarifying a male and female dueting. Can they be picking mates and staking out breeding territory already? That's my guess. Owls, including Barred, are the first to nest, usually picking nest sites by late December and getting the nursery ready for mid-February eggs. Crazy, isn't it, that we're only just talking about birds returning home after breeding season, and already we're talking about the first nests of the new season?

October 17

Following Kestrels

Last winter (see February 17) I wrote about the kestrel pair hunting from the utility wires alongside the road we take to town. The pair sometimes parted ways, perching a mile or more from each other, but still hunting for mice and shrews among the harvested grain fields, using the same strategies. Today, after a long-term absence over the summer, probably off to some favorable breeding spot, the male is back on the utility wire, behaving the same way, striking the same pose, facing downward, watching the recently harvested grain field for mice. I hope I'll soon see his mate. Of course, I really won't know for sure if whatever female I see is his mate or his offspring or just some other kestrel wandering through that took up a satisfactory hunting perch. Here's hoping, whatever it is, that another individual comes along to keep him company. Maybe he'll breed again in the area, especially if he's found hunting successful. Because of the loss of cavity-nesting habitat, however, these birds are in serious trouble in some parts of the country.

October 18

Gritting My Teeth

A Red-shouldered Hawk perched atop a shepherd's hook in the front garden, causing songbirds to go on alert. They rarely flee from this big gal because seldom is she hungry enough to waste energy on a songbird chase. She hardly gets enough nutrition from a little songbird to replace the energy expended in the chase. Songsters seem to know that. Today, though, she seemed somehow different. I banged shut the front door to send her on her way. She barely looked my way. So I stepped out on the sidewalk and waved my arms. She did not respond. Then I walked across the driveway, approaching within 10 feet of her, still waving my arms. Finally, at her leisure, she lifted off, flying only into the neighbor's yard to our east, his feeding station now her target. What strange behavior!

With no other viable alternative, then, I returned to my spot at the kitchen window to watch the morning's bird activities. A mockingbird guarded a branch of dogwood berries. Two female Eastern Towhees dropped down to forage under the hemlock's overreaching branches, the first towhees of either sex I've seen in some weeks. Both Red-breasted Nuthatches fed on safflower seeds, and a Black-throated Green Warbler bugged its way through the branches of the bald cypress. The junco population has increased. Most foraged under the seed feeder, and one bathed at the ground-level bath.

Then a flash, and out of the corner of my eye I saw something big drop down. There was no sound, only movement. When my eyes focused and my brain kicked into gear, sorting through the details before me, I understood. Oh no! The Red-shouldered Hawk had returned and now dropped down on the unsuspecting bathing junco. A flurry of feathers fluttered from the hawk's beak as she plucked the hapless songbird. Then she ripped the remains apart, downing every smidgen of anything bird. When she left, I checked. Only a few feathers remained. No head, no beak, no legs, no feet, no bones, nothing.

Why didn't the junco flee in terror when the hawk sailed into view? Maybe the hawk had slipped in and perched quietly above, making no movement to alert the junco. Maybe, because it was bathing, the junco simply didn't see the hawk. Is it perhaps possible that the junco didn't recognize the predator? Red-shouldereds, after all, don't live where juncos breed. If this was a young junco, maybe it hadn't yet figured out all the real threats in its new winter territory. Perhaps a bird only weeks out of the nest simply wasn't sufficiently alert. But wouldn't fear of a hawk be ingrained in a little bird's brain? In any case, hawks take the weak, the sick, the slow, and the slow witted, this junco apparently falling somewhere on the list.

But back to the hawk herself. A big (and thus, most likely female) Red-shouldered Hawk taking a junco that weighs at best about seven-tenths of an ounce? How much energy did she expend to capture seven-tenths of an ounce of lunch? The statistics point to a very hungry Red-shouldered Hawk. And to me that's a surprise. The recently harvested agricultural fields adjoining our property have to be full of mice and shrews, and the

A female Eastern Towhee reappears after a months-long post-nesting dispersal.

After a Red-shouldered Hawk snared and consumed a Dark-eyed Junco, only a few feathers remained.

A healthy Red-shouldered Hawk with its captured prey, a small rodent, probably a field mouse.

recently mowed hayfield contains grass too short to fully conceal any little rodents. So why is this hawk so desperate? The thought crossed my mind that she may be blind in one eye, perhaps stabbed by a branch or other obstacle while on the hunt. Possible blindness in one eye could account not only for her hunger in spite of the plenty but also for her tolerance of my close proximity when I approached her at the garden's edge. Maybe she simply didn't see me. If that's the case, she won't live long.

October 19

Identifying by Elimination

Nearly certain that a Northern Waterthrush visited the yard this morning, I set out to convince myself, without the benefit of a photograph, that my identification was correct. Complicating the identification is time of year. During migration, almost anything can show up almost anywhere. Habitat is not necessarily a determining factor, and molt can dramatically affect appearance. But sometimes, by eliminating everything else, a firm ID can result. Sometimes, of course, the elimination process only narrows the field to two or more.

This morning's elusive bird made identification more complicated by showing itself only from the back as it moved away from me, always perpendicular to my position. It lifted up from the shrub adjoining the little front-yard pond, flew within a foot of the ground into another shrub about 12 feet away, sat for a short time in clear view, maybe 30 seconds, constantly bobbing its tail, and then ducked straight ahead into a dense juniper less than 4 feet away, entering at near ground level, never to be seen again. No view of the face. No sight of the beak. No glimpse of the breast. Anytime I have only a brief look (and no photo) of a mystery bird, I jot down immediately what I saw. That keeps me from distorting the memory while I research the possibilities. Today's notes read, "back all-over dark brown," "no markings on back," "rather chunky, plump, broad shouldered," "broad tail ending in scallop," "constantly bobbing tail," "always on or near ground."

I began the elimination process by comparing birds that are known to conspicuously bob their tails: four warblers, including Palm Warbler, Ovenbird, and Louisiana and Northern Waterthrushes; a flycatcher, the Eastern Phoebe; Hermit Thrush; our smallest falcon, the American Kestrel; and some shorebirds. Since I would never have shorebirds in my yard, I eliminated all those possibilities immediately. Kestrels are never on the ground unless they just slammed down on prey. Not the case here. With the obvious eliminations done, I started methodically down the list. Eastern Phoebe is gray, not brown, and rarely would it hunt from ground or near-ground level. It's a flycatcher and behaves accordingly. Hermit Thrush is, indeed, brown, but it's a reddish, rusty brown, especially on the tail. So wrong color. Palm Warbler is a tiny bird, just under 5 inches long from tip of beak to tip of tail. Too small for the bird I saw. Likewise, Ovenbird is about the same size, smaller than a bluebird. Although Ovenbird walks with a herky-jerky motion and often cocks its tail, it doesn't truly bob its tail as did my mystery bird.

That leaves the waterthrushes, both of which are about 5.5 inches long, noticeably bigger than either an Ovenbird or a Palm Warbler. Louisiana Waterthrushes breed here, so that would make it a possibility. Because they do breed here, however, when the breeding season ends, they're off and on their way. They're gone early, rarely lingering beyond

An unusual warbler here, Northern Waterthrush, as its name implies, prefers watery habitat.

mid-September. If one has dawdled, it would now be more than a month late. They also have some light streaking on their backs, but the dreary day could possibly have disguised such markings today. Except for the fact that they're surely already gone, Louisiana Waterthrush seems a possibility. Northern Waterthrushes, on the other hand, as the name implies, breed well to our north, in Canada, and typically migrate through here after their Louisiana cousins have gone. Their backs are a solid dark brown. Its scalloped tail is sometimes inconspicuous, but it is broad, especially at the end. So I turned to my warbler app, clicked on Northern Waterthrush, and scrolled to the high-definition rotation section that allows me to move the bird into the exact position in which I saw it. To my eye, it was a perfect match.

That left the habitat and further behavior issues. Unlike Louisiana Waterthrushes, which typically prefer moving-water habitats, Northern Waterthrushes like slow-moving, even still water, and forage for insects alongside those waters. Initially, that's where this morning's bird was poking about—alongside our little yard pond where slow movement makes just enough sound to attract a water-loving bird's attention. Within the open reservoir area, however, relatively still water might be attractive to Northern Waterthrushes, especially migrating individuals no longer focused on specific breeding or wintering territory but merely looking to forage and fatten up before moving on. Both waterthrushes, however, are ground feeders, typically remaining at or near ground level, no matter the season.

So given that this is migration season, given the bird's breeding area and migration pattern, given its behavior, given its ground-level presence, given its chunky overall appearance, given its dark brown non-patterned back, and above all, given its persistent tail bobbing, I felt reasonably safe—by process of elimination—listing Northern Waterthrush for this year's yard list. It's not a new bird to the yard, so there's also some history here to help verify its presence—along with that of the Louisiana Waterthrush during some spring seasons. If this were some sort of formal birding competition, though, I'd be stretching the rules. Interesting, isn't it, how many details about the bird's behavior help make the ID. Such identification exercises always help me hone my own identification skills. I'm always learning.

1 Northern Waterthrush
Species: 124 total in the yard to date for the year.

October 20

Counting on the Forecast

The Ontario Field Ornithologists, headed by Ron Pittaway, post annually what they title the "winter finch forecast," a reference that includes far more species than just finches. The report arrived in my email box today. Typically, in addition to Purple Finch, the forecast takes into account Common and Hoary Redpoll, White-winged Crossbill, Pine and Evening Grosbeak, Pine Siskin, and Red-breasted Nuthatch. Together, these species make up a group of birds that typically live in the Canadian boreal forest foraging on spruce, fir, alder, pine, birch, and other natural seeds produced by trees. Some years, however, the cone and seed production in the far north falls short, perhaps because of drought, but also because some are biennial crops. The years in which the seed crops fail or are minimal, birders to the south of the boreal forest look forward to what's called an "irruption year." The finch family that habitually stays in the forest will, out of desperation, move south in search of food. This year is deemed an irruption year. The forecast applies, as the ornithologists themselves claim, mostly to Ontario and adjacent provinces and states. While that would seem to exclude places like southwestern Indiana where I live, generally we enjoy a few extraordinary species during irruptive years. One telling comment was in the prediction: "Red-breasted Nuthatches have already pushed south in large numbers, an early indicator that other species may follow." My first Red-breasted Nuthatch sighting was September 30. More excitement may, indeed, be on the way—especially given the strong weather fronts moving through now.

October 21

Reckoning the Changing Seasons

The frost is on the pumpkins. This morning I awoke to see that the first freeze of the season turned the neighbor's pumpkin patch into a sad state of blackened vines but left the pumpkins as glowing globes across the field. It's truly winter now, after 90-degree temperatures less than two weeks ago.

To be sure, the yard also looks more and more like winter. White-throated Sparrow and Dark-eyed Junco populations continue to grow into larger flocks that forage across

the property. Activity in the garden, birds of many species foraging under the drooping frosted stems, amid the mulch, and along the seed heads, shows the value of the hundreds of native plants. Seeing so much activity there is my reward for the time and effort we've put into the habitat.

This evening, I noticed the Northern Cardinal population has also increased, with at least sixteen roaming the backyard, getting a last few bites, a few sips of water, or a quick bath before bedtime. Their quiet little conversational chips to one another make me think of a soft, nighty-night lullaby.

A male Dark-eyed Junco, foraging in the yard, shows the deep charcoal color of its sex.

Birds Do *That*?

Birds of prey hold their heads still when their bodies move. Think of an American Kestrel perched on a utility wire, the wire swaying in the wind. The bird's body sways with the wire, but its head remains in a relatively fixed position. The behavior makes raptors look spooky, even threatening, as if they're nodding and stretching, ogling to line up for an attack. There's good reason, though, for the strange-looking behavior. Most birds can't move their eyes in their heads because their eyes are huge relative to their heads. In fact, most birds' eyes weigh more than their brains. As a result of the monstrous eye size, there's no room for the musculature needed to support eye movement. To stay focused on prey, then, they move their heads instead of their eyes. By comparison, if humans had eyes of equal proportion, they would be the size of hefty oranges.

October 22

Remembering a Rhyme

This morning's cold, lovely sunrise reminded me of a rhyme: "Red skies in morning / Sailors take warning / Red skies at night / Sailor's delight." Perhaps we must take warning! And the thought crossed my mind that, given the crazy weather patterns, we could expect most anything. And sure enough, a birder friend called this evening to let me know that as he finished the front nine holes at a local golf course that adjoins a nature preserve, he saw a flock of about fifty Rose-breasted Grosbeaks, some still showing rosey breasts, moving through the highest branches of the preserve's virgin forest. Now that's amazing behavior! Wish I could have witnessed the sight.

October 23

Realizing the Prediction

A single male Purple Finch popped in for a few nuggets of sunflower seed this evening. My first silly reaction was, "Wow, look at the really bright male House Finch." Well, duh. Where was my mind? Certainly not on the potential for Purple Finches in late October! True, after breeding across Canada and along the northern fringe of the United States, they wander across much of the eastern half of the country. And true, our area isn't far from the southernmost areas where they nest. But it's October and early for their usual arrival. On the other hand, birder friends a few miles to our north texted that they had five Pine Siskins foraging in their yard this evening. No siskins here, but wait! Is the winter finch forecast starting to play out here already? Now, while the calendar still says October? Well, apparently so. Pine Siskins and a Purple Finch seem to confirm it!

Late this afternoon, we also had six Turkey Vultures perched in a dead tree along our road. What was that behavior about? Why were they there? We eased back to watch, to see what attracted them to the spot. Soon one dropped down. Then another. Then a seventh

A Turkey Vulture, rendered slightly golden in the late afternoon sun, perches overhead, waiting for us to leave, allowing it to return to its road-kill lunch.

flew in. They rummaged about in the shallow ditch alongside the road, but we couldn't see the target of their interest. Edging forward, we obviously disturbed them, and they lifted up, back into the dead tree immediately above. Hoping we wouldn't be the target of excrement, we checked the area where we had seen them rummaging and spotted the attraction: a road-killed raccoon. Given the seven of them, I have to wonder how quickly they'll devour the carcass. Typically they're unable to open the carcass on their own and have to wait for it to split or for something else to make the first tear. Okay, that was probably more than you want to know, but it does explain why they may need more than the expected time to do away with dinner.

October 24

Catching the Wave

This morning's first excitement came when I realized that among the many House Finches at the hanging platform feeder were five feeding Purple Finches, including one lovely raspberry-colored male. I had been distracted by the return of a little flock of robins feasting on the dogwood berries, obviously making quick work of the abundant fruit. I watched their behavior, how they jerked at the berries to break them loose and then tossed them back and down the way Old West movie cowboys tossed back whiskey. While studying them, my binocular crossed a bird that—oops!—was not a robin. Indeed, it was a Purple Finch. The berries provide a rich nutritious substitute for the failed mast crop to our north. Seeing one foraging on the berries made me do a quick head-swivel to the platform feeder, finding the little group pigging out on sunflower seeds.

This afternoon the second round of excitement flew in. Nine Pine Siskins, erratic nomads that show up in masses one year and skip us entirely the next year, performed their usual camouflage act today by blending in perfectly with winter-plumaged American Goldfinches and female House Finches. They attracted my attention first as they fed among the gold-finches on the nyjer-seed feeder. Soon, how-

A male Purple Finch visits the yard. Some years a male visits; some years only females show up. And some years I don't seen Purple Finches at all.

ever, I realized they were actually most active in the hemlock tree, foraging among the tiny cones. I'd be surprised, frankly, if the cones are mature enough to have much nutrition, but obviously the birds know best. Hanging upside down in their usual acrobatic fashion is their preferred foraging behavior.

While the new migrants garnered most of my excitement today, just before dusk another dropped in to remind me that one of the warblers may also hang out here all winter (although it doesn't usually hang out right here in my yard). A Yellow-rumped Warbler stopped for a quick drink. Maybe it's one that has been regularly irregular in the yard the past two months, or maybe it's brand new, having just found the habitat and stayed to check it out. Either way I was pleased to see it and hope it, as well as the Pine Siskins and Purple Finches, will honor me with their liveliness for at least part of the winter.

A Pine Siskin, showing its distinctive sharp beak and yellow wing-feather shafts, is a possible clue that the winter-finch forecast for abundant irruptions may be right on target.

A Yellow-rumped Warbler, the only warbler that sometimes winters with us, forages on sweetbay magnolia berries.

October 25

Scouting for the Hideaways

After watching out the window for almost an hour without any success on this chilly, drizzly afternoon, I shrugged into a jacket, grabbed binocular and camera, and headed out to a backyard hot spot—brambles, a little grove of locust trees, a patch of goldenrod, and a substantial row of full-seeded switchgrass. There I expected to find the missing-in-action winter sparrows and finches.

Wrong. After about 45 minutes of standing mostly stock still, creeping ahead occasionally a step at a time, listening, watching for any wiggle among the stalks or bounding of a twig, I saw only a single bird, a Ruby-crowned Kinglet foraging in the chest-high goldenrod. As I trudged up the hill, discouraged, I glimpsed activity among the windbreak grove of forty-year-old eastern red cedars. Cardinals and White-throated Sparrows flitted through the dense shelter, occasionally chipping to identify themselves among the deep shadows of an already dreary day. Everything was hidden, taking shelter, I suppose, against the light drizzle. Where were the sparrows and juncos? Had they moved on, all of them? Not even a chip from the White-throats, much less their delightful song.

A White-throated Sparrow hides amid the tangles, apparently feeling comfortably at home.

As I crested the hill, movement ahead caught my eye, low, mostly on the ground. Aha! There, foraging in the grass, were several dozen White-throateds and probably an equal number of juncos. Stopping to study them, I raised my binocular to see. Although they mostly foraged in the short grass, they never ventured more than a half dozen feet from cover. A cluster of low-growing eastern red cedars stands about knee high, covering a space about 10 feet by 8 feet, low, dense, and compact. The sparrows and juncos darted into the dense protection, ventured out cautiously, shot back in, hopped out briefly to forage, and zipped back into hiding, constantly returning to cover, although not all birds returned simultaneously. Within 2 or 3 yards beyond the cluster of cedars, a patch of fragrant sumac offers a similarly dense ground cover. Equally skittish activity occurred there: the sparrows and juncos dashing in, creeping out to forage, returning post haste to cover.

Their edgy behavior suggested two possibilities: First, these are birds that arrived here from the boreal forest, perhaps having lived or grown up in dense conifers. Now, they've found something similar in my yard—the dense junipers and the dense ground-cover sumac. They've made themselves at home. Second, however, these birds have surely been frightened by the marauding Red-shouldered Hawk, and in response they are now ever cautious. These two observations combined could well explain their behavior this afternoon. Instinctive. Smart.

October 26

Perusing the Garden

The sunless dreary day, dampened by off-and-on drizzle all morning and afternoon, left me seeking solace by watching birds. No matter the weather, pleasant or not, birds must eat. Because songbirds always live on the edge with few reserves, feeding hourly during all daylight hours is mandatory, constant, without exception, if the birds are to survive. Thus, in spite of the drizzle, in spite of a chilly breeze, in spite of dreariness, the birds foraged.

Knowing the sparrows and juncos were huddled in the junipers and sumac yesterday, scooting out to forage before zipping back to cover, I looked for repeat behavior there today. Well, they fooled me again. Amid and around the ground covers, there were no birds. Not in the cedars. Not in the ground-cover sumac. None. Zip. Zero. Preferring to stay warm and dry during my search, I stayed indoors this afternoon, moving from window to window through the house. Finally, I found the little guys. They had moved to the native flower garden, a patch that now includes dozens and dozens of gone-to-seed plants—perennials, vines, shrubs, and grasses. Today, their favorite foraging spot seemed to be buttonbushes with their sycamore-like balls of seed, and birds bobbed among the branches, foraging on the seeds. From time to time, a few individuals bounced among the blades of switchgrass, but mostly they seemed to be using the grass stems as momentary perches before launching toward a buttonbush. Later, perhaps when grass seeds mature, it will be fun to watch the little guys ride the grass stems to the ground in order to feed on the seeds. Again, I'm finding it worth the time and effort to continue expanding the already wide array of native plants. As a result, now I also have a wide array of birds. Hooray!

October 27

Tracking Evening Sounds

At about 4:30 p.m., I took up my perch along the south edge of the garden overlooking the edge of our little patch of woods. This small corner of the world seemed peacefully quiet, the distant church bells having just sounded for early mass.

Sometimes bird behavior is heard rather than seen, birds' calls and songs being unique to their species. This evening, my goal was to identify birds by listening, knowing that early winter calls and songs differ from those in spring and summer. Expecting a challenge, I began tallying what I could identify amid the quiet, the soft chips, the muted calls, the weak songs. A pair of Barred Owls called to each other from the woods to our west, reassuring me that the pair is truly defending territory. Several dozen crows cawed intermittently across the skies, scattered from northeast to southwest, most likely aiming for their community roost. Goldfinches sounded their "potato chip" flight song as seven flew over. Both nuthatches tooted what sounded like little toy horns, the Red-breasted's toot faster and higher pitched than that of the White-breasted. Chickadees scolded and a titmouse chimed in, the two species seeming to echo one another. That, of course, was only my imagination; two species don't respond to one another's calls unless the calls sound an alarm. Then all species tune in and chime in, raising a combined ruckus.

A male Red-bellied Woodpecker shows red from his beak all the way over his head and down to his neck, with only a slight tinge of red on his belly. (See the female Red-bellied Woodpecker on March 16.)

In our little patch of woods, two flickers called their "keow" calls, and as I turned their direction, they flew out, overhead, and toward the sycamore tree along our west property line. I could hear their weak chatter in flight and then their weak, quiet musical notes to one another, something akin to mewing when they were near. A couple of Red-bellied Woodpeckers clamored their "chi-chi-chi" calls from the woods, and then the male flew out to the utility post, checking first me and then the flickers, gauging the coast to be clear for the pair to move through the yard to the old snag in the back.

White-throated Sparrows gave their quiet, very high-pitched chips from a variety of shrubs and tangles. Had the evening been less quiet, I would have missed them entirely. But invariably they give away their secret locations with these early evening calls. Listening always helps me understand where they like to hang out, what kind of habitats they prefer for roosting, and when they're ready to call it a day. They told me everything this evening, their chips occasionally drifting into a weak and tentative "Oh, Sam Peabody, Peabody, Peabody" song.

Juncos sang out a few weak "tew-tew-tew" calls, keeping mostly to the ground or in low vegetation. Cardinals chipped from the native honeysuckle vine and crossvine, with their noisy wing whirs readily identifiable as they moved off toward a more likely roost. I happened to catch sight of the Hairy Woodpecker feeding silently at the seed cake, but the tapping Downy made its location known. Two Pileated Woodpeckers called from the north. Robins "tut-tut-tutted" from the backyard, probably finishing off a few more dogwood berries before bedtime. Two Blue Jays scolded their way across the sky to take up a perch in our woods. Then, as time passed, they too passed from tree to tree to tree, steadily working their way westward out of our woods and through the neighbors' woods until they moved out of earshot.

As the breeze picked up, the silence was broken, and my ability to catch every chip and scold rapidly diminished. At the same time, though, darkness crept in, the birds grew quiet, and a few final notes drifted by. House Finches chittered at one another at the feeder as they grabbed a few final seeds. A Carolina Wren sounded what surely must have been a "Where are you?" call, because another answered from the east, each moving toward the other, likely to a common nighttime roost. A mockingbird scolded once and then went quiet, perhaps securing its solitude for the night.

Birds' late-evening behaviors differ remarkably from their robust daytime routines. It was time to find my own nighttime spot—indoors.

October 28

Bracing against Wind

With stiff 25 to 35 mph winds, I could barely keep my balance outside, especially when sudden gusts of 40-plus upped the ante. While the sunny 66-degree day seemed ideal, the bluster forced my retreat, and I placed my stool tight against a south-facing wall, protected from the northwest winds. From that vantage point, I could watch birds and how they behaved in the strong wind. As goofy as it may sound, some birds—notably cardinals, goldfinches, and chickadees—actually joined me in the lee. Perhaps my being motionless helped encourage them to join me, but mostly I suspect they were merely eager to find comfort, only slightly concerned about my non-threatening presence.

Of course, birds have to feed, no matter what. Crows flew across the skies sideways, their bodies pointing north but their movements mostly easterly, on their way to forage in the harvested fields. Flying leaves, flashing horizontally across the landscape, competed with flying birds, the birds recognized mostly by flight paths angling in some direction against the grain of the flying leaves. Mostly birds flew only from one spot of safety to another, immediately tucking in upon landing. And landing seemed to require a trick of dexterity. Thus, a bird flying with a tailwind from the northwest had to make a sudden U-turn to land, jockeying its body quickly to face into the wind. Like airplanes, birds must face into the wind for both takeoff and landing. Or maybe it's more accurate to say that like birds, airplanes must face into the wind for both takeoff and landing. Airplanes, after all, came well after birds, and no doubt designers watched bird behavior before they managed true flight.

But I digress.

Occasionally a bird misjudged its landing spot and, blasted by the wind, had to flit off a short distance, steady its flight, regain its composure, and make another try. Landing on the perch of a swinging tube feeder seemed to require especially practiced skill. In fact, I suspect those birds that found themselves making a second—or third—try, were probably youngsters, not quite agile yet at their maneuvering skills.

Surely, too, wind ruffling feathers forward must to birds be something like a cat or dog having its fur rubbed the wrong way. They'll avoid the situation if possible. On a cold day, feathers blown forward would also translate into a highly chilling effect. Today, however, temperatures weren't a serious issue, although 66 degrees would feel chilly to a bird with a typical body temperature of 102 degrees. What tough little guys they are! After 30 minutes I was ready to find shelter indoors.

Wind ruffles the feathers of a Dark-eyed Junco.

Birds Do *That*?

Woodpeckers don't get headaches. In spite of the fact that they slam into tree trunks at what seems like 1,000 times the force of gravity, their brains suffer no damage. According to Eldon Greij, ornithology professor emeritus, four characteristics of a woodpecker's structure save their brains—and their lives. First, the bill has a self-sharpening chisel-like design, so it penetrates the wood rather than pounding bluntly against it, thus absorbing part of the blow. Second, woodpecker brains are rather tightly packed inside their skulls, preventing their sloshing around as human brains do under jarring circumstances. Third, strong neck muscles help soften the blow. And finally, the orientation of the brain in the skull spreads out the effects of the blow, adding yet another means of protection.

October 29

Wondering about "One Eye"

The Red-shouldered Hawk whose nonchalant behavior puzzled me eleven days ago showed up once again in the front yard, obviously watching songbirds in preparation for lunch. She seemed a bit disheveled, as if she hadn't preened carefully, her feathers too fluffy for a bird having only recently molted and for an unseasonably warm morning. She had no cause to be fluffed against the cold—unless, of course, she was weak and malnourished, thus struggling to maintain body temperature. This bird displayed the same odd behavior as it did nearly two weeks ago, showing no fear when I stepped out the front door, standing no more than 20 feet away. Of course, I had been purposely quiet, slipping out the door, but certainly my presence was in no way hidden or disguised. As happened eleven days ago, the bird showed no reaction as I approached. Although last time I was waving my arms and clapping my hands in an effort to send the terrorist on its way, this time I made no aggressive movement. I wanted an answer to my question: Was this bird perhaps blind in one eye? Could she thus see my approach from only one side? Is that why she showed no reaction to my presence?

I'd already managed several photos from inside the house, attempting to capture images of both sides of her face, hoping a clear image might verify the condition of her eyes. But since she remained perched on the feeder pole, I was curious about how close I could approach for perhaps a better photo. Then, maybe because she heard something or maybe because she was being cautious, she turned her head, saw me, and lifted off, flying easily across the front yard to the east. The sun's glare allowed her to escape without my being able to follow her flight, so I don't know how far she flew.

Back inside, I checked the photo images. The left side of her face looked perfect, the eye bright, reflecting light in a perfectly shaped retina. Images of the right side of her face, however, revealed something quite different and confirmed my suspicion. Indeed, she appeared to be blind in her right eye. I'm truly sorry that such a magnificent animal faces what is surely a dismal future. But it's Mother Nature's way: Eat or be eaten. Mother Nature is not

A Red-shouldered Hawk likely faces a bleak future as a result of its damaged right eye.

known for gentle kindness. In the brutal wild world of birds, only the healthiest, smartest, and fastest survive.

Later in the day, after the Red-shouldered sallied off, birds returned to the yard. Sparrows and finches foraged throughout the grassy areas, mostly, I think, feasting on smartweed. Among them, a standout, an immature White-crowned Sparrow foraged among the flock. But this White-crowned Sparrow wore a brown crown. While it's tempting to think of a brown-crowned sparrow as a female of the White-crowned species, adult male and female White-crowneds actually look alike. This bird's brown-and-tan-striped crown told me it was a hatch-year bird. Only weeks out of the nest, this little creature began its arduous journey south, winging its way from the far northern fringes of Canada, well north of the Arctic Circle, to my yard in southwestern Indiana. Some individuals may travel

An immature White-crowned Sparrow is identified by its brown-and-tan-striped crown.

Mature White-crowned Sparrows, both males and females, wear white-and-black-striped crowns.

farther south, as far as the Gulf Coast or well into Mexico. In fact, the individual in my yard may very well continue its journey farther south, or it may linger in the area all winter. The mystery, of course, is how any one individual decides whether to stay here, move a few hundred miles south, or move way, way south.

Most likely, individuals are hardwired to retrace the patterns of their ancestors. I'm ecstatic that this one found my habitat attractive enough to stop for at least a respite before moving on. If it stays, I'll be even more thrilled.

> 1 White-crowned Sparrow
> **Species:** 125 total in the yard to date for the year.

October 30

Confirming the Reports

Because folks know my interest in birds, in part because of my newspaper columns and social media posts and in part because of the ongoing bird classes I teach, I'm fortunate to hear from friends and strangers alike about what they're seeing and what puzzles them. Over the past several days, the queries have been mostly along the lines of, "Why are owls hooting in the daytime?"

Only two owl species in our area hoot: Barred Owls and Great Horned Owls. By contrast, Screech Owls most often whinny, very much like a horse, and Barn Owls shriek, similar to the haunting calls in Halloween soundtracks. Of the two "hoot owls," only the Barred Owl regularly calls during daylight hours, generally fairly early in the morning or in mid- to late afternoon. Recently, 3:30 p.m. seems to be the preferred startup time, not only here in our little patch of woods but in places where friends and strangers are listening. In most situations, including here at home, folks hear two owls calling, as if one is answering the other, one higher pitched than the other. When that happens, we're getting a clue that breeding season is approaching. The female owl protects her territory year-round, inviting

A Barred Owl at dusk begins its evening hunt.

a mate in only when the time is right. Think of the calls as pillow talk. She will be the first of our birds to start her family, very soon after the first of the year.

October 31

Keeping an Eye on Bathers
Unseasonably warm weather and off-and-on easy rains have been the rule for the entire day today. Watching birds react to the gentle rains, however, has brightened the otherwise all-day dreariness. Birds, in fact, seem to have enjoyed the pitter-patter—especially, I think, the cardinals. They first attracted my attention perched in the buttonbushes. As the raindrops fell, the cardinals fluttered, stretched their wings, fanned their tails, shook themselves, and repeated the process. They seemed to relish the water droplets rolling off their plumage, perhaps washing off dust and dirt particles in the course.

Other species, including White-throated Sparrows and Dark-eyed Juncos, followed suit, but cardinals seemed most persistent in their rain bathing. In fact, once I expanded my watchfulness beyond the buttonbushes, I realized that more cardinals were following a similar behavior in the native trumpet honeysuckle vine and in the native crossvine, both semi-evergreen. The cardinals took advantage of the somewhat waxy greenery and its water-holding qualities to wallow about as if splashing in a bath. They squatted, fluttered, and shook themselves repeatedly, spattering water droplets through the air as if under a real rain shower faucet head. I can't say I've ever caught them bathing quite so vigorously in such a manner, using the natural foliage as a bath. But surely that's a behavior as nature intended, right?

November

A female American Goldfinch forages among native weed seed heads.

Shall I not rejoice also at the abundance of the weeds whose seeds are the granary of the birds?

—Henry David Thoreau (1817–1862)

November 1

Catching Up with Kestrels

At last, on our usual route to town today, I spotted not one but three kestrels hunting from the utility wires. While agricultural fields edge the north side of the road where the utility wires run, a railroad separates the road from the fields to the south. The utility wires' location thus dictates that perching there gives birds a clear view of only the northerly fields. And the fields differ along the 3-mile stretch. One section is hayfield, so that part always offers ground cover. Of course, if it's been some time since mowing, the cover may have grown too tall for good hunting, but not now, after growing season has ended. Some of the harvested soybean fields remain as harvested, relatively bare, providing little or no cover but offering enough spilled beans to provide tempting morsels for rodents. Other former soybean fields, however, have been replanted in winter wheat, some of it already up. Where the wheat is tall enough to offer a hint of cover for rodents, kestrels find prime hunting. Finally, some fields currently stand in corn stubble, also perfect hunting ground for kestrels. We always know where to watch for the kestrels, if they're there at all. They'll be perched adjoining the best hunting grounds, ready to grab prey in an instant. Today, all three were spaced along the high wire edging the hayfield, facing into a south wind but with heads turned, eyeing the field behind. The hunt was on. But three is a crowd, so that matter will be ultimately resolved by whichever bird is highest on the pecking order.

A hunting male American Kestrel holds steady in a strong wind that ruffles his feathers.

November 2

Welcoming another Winter Bird

A Fox Sparrow made an appearance in the backyard today, foraging below the seed feeder, the first sighting since last mid-January. It has spent the summer in northern Canada and Alaska, ranging from east to west across the continent. Now it has ventured into its winter territory, our area being near the northern limits. Some will go almost to the Gulf Coast, taking up residence from the East Coast to mid-continent. Generally, however, Fox Sparrows skip a Florida retreat, perhaps preferring more dense vegetation. In general, they like brushy patches and thickets, usually along or in woodlands, so they should find what they like in our little patch of habitat. Still, given

A Fox Sparrow forages amid fallen pine needles while clearly revealing its inverted V breast markings.

the small size of our patch, no more than one or two would find the area satisfactory, especially since they tend to hang out with other sparrows, like the multitudes of White-throated Sparrows now wandering the property and nearby environs. There's something special about Fox Sparrows, and not just because they're that lovely foxy red color. Maybe rich chestnut would be a better description of the color. By any name, it's a one-of-a-kind attention-getter in the yard.

November 3

Listening to Change

Not only does the yard look different now, with frostbitten vegetation, colorful and falling leaves, and a different palette of birds, but the yard sounds different, too. Song takes on a new definition. In fact, few birds sing in the traditional melodic sense. Instead, I hear chips and squeaks. Carolina Wrens "chirrr," communicating with and keeping track of one another. Northern Flickers give their "wicka-wicka-wicka" calls from the woods, usually just before they fly across the yard into the old snag. Jays yell and scream as usual. Carolina Chickadees and Tufted Titmice scold more than usual. The breeding songs of both seem long lost in the hubbub of scouting out winter food sources. Our single mockingbird scolds at intruders but now rarely if ever sings. When it does, the song is weak, muted, and only a few measures long. The "tew-tew-tew" of juncos heralds their presence, but there's nothing territorial about anything, vocal or behavioral. Red-breasted and White-breasted Nuthatches give their respective toots, sometimes described as sounding like children's toy horns but perhaps more accurately depicted as "yank, yank, yank," a nonmusical nasal call. Kinglets alert me to their presence with truly high-pitched chips, almost beyond my aging

A Cedar Waxwing, its silky plumage sleek and smooth, checks out the water feature, looking for a drink after heavy berry eating.

range of hearing. Likewise with Cedar Waxwings, their very high, thin "sreee" calls typically alert me they're in the area. Today, only a single one made an appearance, alighting briefly in the little front-yard water feature for a drink. Rarely do I see a single waxwing; they're sometimes in groups of hundreds. Two Pileated Woodpeckers called "kuk, kuk, kuk" from the woods, although I've not yet discovered in which trees they're carving out their individual winter roosts. Probably only one will stay here, although the other will no doubt seek refuge as close by as possible, perhaps in the neighbor's woods to the east where I see them flying to and from. They're a mated pair, I think, so they'll likely remain in close proximity to each other.

The rising "zhreeeee" of Pine Siskins makes me look for the little guys, hard to see because of their ready-made camouflage. Usually if I follow the goldfinches' "potato chip" flight call, though, I can eventually spot the siskins. The two species seem to be constant companions, both preferring the nyjer seed or sunflower seed bits. Cardinals, two of them cleaning up the pokeweed berries, sound off with almost constant chips, and White-throated Sparrows call "see, see, see" way more often than they sing an off-key, weakened non-breeding song. In fact, one today just said, "O, Sam, Sam, Sam." Guess it forgot the last name!

Given the nonmusical chips, chirps, toots, and other calls, the music of the Eastern Bluebird's song was especially welcome to my ears. Granted, today's melody wasn't as loud or vigorous as in the spring and summer, but the identity was unmistakable—and certainly didn't go unnoticed.

November 4

Getting Glimpses

Some winter visitors move in for the duration, and some offer only occasional glimpses. In part, the daily-versus-occasional sightings are the result of populations. White-throated Sparrows and Dark-eyed Juncos, for instance, come in throngs, filling the yard with fifteen or maybe thirty individuals. They may not be the same individuals every day, but the numbers are mostly high and the sightings daily and plentiful. Pine Siskins, during irruption winters, like this winter, can show up in droves but maybe not every day. They wander in little flocks, hanging out in one place until the food runs low or they have some other reason to move on, then dashing off in flocks the same way they dashed in. At present, I see a few every day, perhaps six or eight. Someday those few may move on, perhaps roving into a neighboring yard or productive native habitat, and it's possible others will replace them. Or perhaps the yard may be absent of siskins until another troop wanders in.

On the other hand, visitors like Ruby-crowned and Golden-crowned Kinglets or Fox Sparrows treat me with only occasional sightings. I doubt that there is ever more than one of each in the yard at one time, so even if they're here day after day, I may not see them. Kinglets aren't feeder birds, and Fox Sparrows prefer to feed in private. That's just how different birds behave.

But there's more to their unique behaviors. Some winter visitors tend to show up, sometimes in numbers, early in the season and again late in the season (perhaps because they move as a group farther south), very few if any individuals lingering for the entire season. Purple Finches tend to fall into that category. Although I've seen Purple Finches over the years in every month of the winter season, typically I see more of them early and late. And typically I see more "females" than males, with the understanding that hatch-year birds, male or female, all look like adult females. It's also true that male Purple Finches leave their breeding territory earlier than females and offspring, so spotting a wandering male is sometimes more tricky than spotting a group of streaky females. Of course, part of that is also due to the fact that male Purple Finches can be readily confused with male House Finches, so it's easy to miss look-alike—or at least similar-looking—birds at feeders or even in the habitat.

Today, however, a Golden-crowned Kinglet popped into view in the front yard, flicking about the water feature, scooting through the coralberry shrubs, and hopping through the late-blooming asters. This is a bird in almost constant motion, so the quick, ongoing behavior signified I needed to watch, trying to decipher the movement into some sort of identification. It's not the first of the season, but Golden-crowneds show up here far less often than their Ruby-crowned cousins.

A Golden-crowned Kinglet returns for the winter, showing off his always-present namesake golden-crown streak outlined in stark black.

Birds Do *That*?

Birds see colors humans can't. In fact, according to Yale University ornithologist Richard Prum, birds have additional color cones in their retinas that are sensitive to ultraviolet range. Not only do they see a broader range of red or blue, for instance, but they see beyond the normal color spectrum as we humans know it. As a result, females are super aware of even minute variations in a male's plumage; it's on the basis of his good looks—and therefore his likely good health—that she chooses a mate. In short, according to Prum, "We're colorblind compared to birds."

November 5

Studying Diet

Some birds eat seeds; some eat berries; some, insects; some, nectar. Many eat a wide variety of foods. They're insectivorous, granivorous, frugivorous, carnivorous, and omnivorous. A few, like goldfinches and siskins, are strict vegetarians. They even feed their young regurgitated plant matter, usually partially digested seeds. Scientists believe goldfinches' vegetarian diet explains why cowbird babies fail to survive in goldfinch nests.

Today I was reminded, however, that vegetarian birds eat more than seeds, blossoms, and buds. They eat algae! Our little front-yard water feature includes shallow parts where string algae grows. In fact, in the hottest weather, when water plants can't keep up with the

Pine Siskins, vegetarians that they are, find high-protein nourishment in the string algae in our little yard pond.

algae growth, I'm in the habit of pulling out the algae, my effort to minimize the clogging effect of too much of a good thing. Several times when I've flipped the algae out onto the pond's rock apron, I've seen goldfinches picking through it, strings hanging from their beaks as they eat it the way some kids eat spaghetti. So there must be a reason why gold-finches would eat algae, right? Unlike those of us who eat foods for the pleasure of their taste (think chocolate, ice cream, and fried anything), wildlife eat foods mostly because something in them is in some way particularly beneficial to their well-being. Turns out, algae is high in protein. For a vegetarian bird, then, a plant protein source is particularly vital to its survival.

Today's reminder of the importance of protein, however, flew in not on the wings of goldfinches but on the wings of Pine Siskins. They were working along the edge of a flat rock protruding only slightly above inch-deep water. Algae grows there, too. So the siskins found the protein-rich vegetation ready for the supping. And eat they did. I'm always in awe of birds' adaptable—and adapting—behavior.

November 6

Pinpointing Seed Choices

Juncos fascinate me. They come in a wide variety of plumages, even within the single sub-species that ventures into our yard each winter. Ranging from a soft pale gray to deep slate gray, all wear white bellies. Some also wear a tinge of pink on their sides, and some show more pink than others. Occasionally the pink is prominent enough to raise the question: Is this individual the Oregon subspecies rather than the slate-colored subspecies most common to where I live in southwestern Indiana?

Since juncos migrate in flocks, they show up in flocks. And since they tend to winter where they've wintered in the past, I can always expect a nice-size winter flock. Often, though, the nice size turns out to be too many for my little habitat to support, so some scatter, although I'm guessing they don't scatter far. Typically, a flock forages in an area of ten to twelve acres, so our three-acre patch is only part of any flock's total winter habitat. Their social hierarchy reflects a fairly straightforward behavior. Males dominate females; adults dominate immatures; older adults dominate younger adults. What happens at feeders reflects the so-called pecking order, and younger, less dominant birds readily give way to older, more dominant birds. By readily giving way, they avoid wasting energy in battle. In general, everyone wins when nobody fights.

During the day, juncos won't remain in a single feeding area. Instead, they wander the ten- to twelve-acre territory, foraging as they go; their routine behavior is to follow the same route at about the same time each day. Lately, I've been watching where they forage. Because they relish tiny seeds, I know they will eventually ride down every single stalk of switchgrass, gleaning the seeds as they hold the grounded stalks in place with their weight. Now, though, the switchgrass seeds stand untouched, perhaps not yet ripe enough for the junco's satisfaction. Instead, the birds are gleaning other tiny grass seeds, especially along edges where the mower and weed whacker both missed. Particularly attractive are the tiny pink-berried smartweeds. But they'll also strip off crabgrass seed, the only good reason I can think of for allowing it to grow.

A Dark-eyed Junco forages on tiny grass and weed seeds.

At night the flock roosts together, usually in a dense conifer or in other thickly protective vegetation where they can find shelter from the elements. With numerous eastern red cedars, hemlocks, evergreen hollies, and pines, our yard has the advantage of offering juncos what they need to survive. I've never followed them to roost to see which of the evergreens they choose (I fear I would disturb them), but I know the ready shelter available here is an attraction to the flock. Of course, they don't necessarily use the same roost every night. They're too smart to allow habitual behavior to make them potential targets of predators.

Their flashing outer white tail feathers always let me identify juncos when they alight or lift off, and sometimes when they're foraging. Some authorities speculate that the flashing white tail feathers also help juncos locate the flock when it's time to settle in for the night. Their quiet calls surely help as well.

November 7

Interpreting Crests

Now that the Blue Jays have returned to the yard on a regular basis, I've once again begun offering shelled peanuts, one cup every morning, tempting them back to their regular routine. In previous winters, they've habituated themselves to checking for my daily peanut distribution, yelling at their comrades that breakfast is served at the Sorenson residence. Jays are smart, and I enjoy their clever behavior, always hoping to catch them doing something particularly witty. Sometimes they cache their peanuts, especially in the fall, preparing against bad-weather days. That's when I enjoy their antics most. I'm always amazed at how often, after burying a cache and tamping it in place with their beaks, they will make a thoughtful decision to conceal the fresh dig. So I guess I should admit it: I'm tempting them, hoping to watch their behavior again this fall.

A Blue Jay, with a whole pecan in its beak, wears its crest flattened, suggesting the bird finds itself in a comfortable, non-aggressive situation.

Now, however, I'm noticing yet another interesting behavior among the jays: the use of their crests to communicate. Several species have crests and are so named, such as Tufted Titmouse, Great-crested Flycatcher, or Double-crested Cormorant. Other birds, like Blue Jays and Northern Cardinals, wear crests but are not so named. Why is it, though, that sometimes crested birds have hardly any crest showing? How is it that they choose to flatten the feathers and appear slick-headed? Or conversely, how is it that they choose to lift the feathers and sport a fully erect crest?

A Blue Jay, with at least one peanut already in its beak, wears its crest raised, suggesting the bird feels threatened or is assuming an aggressive position in order to sneak a few more peanuts.

It turns out that in general birds hold a crest erect when they're excited, aggressive, or frightened. Does that hold true with jays as well? I think so, and here's why. I've watched jays feeding peacefully alongside one another, their crests flattened. The feeding group is likely an extended family, and each bird knows its place. When they're at the bubble rock or other water feature, bathing or drinking, their crests lie flat. No one is excited, aggressive, or frightened. When I do see jays with crests erect, they're usually on the attack, scolding a stranger or an intruder, such as a hawk or an owl, both threats to their nests and contents. But I've also seen a jay

A Blue Jay, squatting, crest raised, is most likely an invader in the territory.

approach the proffered peanuts with crest erect. What's that about? My best guess is that it's an intruder, trying to move in on the local family to gather its own share of the loot. Intruders are known to crouch down, fluff their body feathers, erect their crests, and await the opportunity to assuage the territory holder. If all goes well, the crest begins to flatten and the intruder, if it's accepted, has an opportunity to feed. Often though, that opportunity seems to occur only after the extended family has fed to satisfaction and is willing to tolerate the intruder. My, what stories the crest tells!

November 8

Recounting Orange-crowneds

I've given up hope. My written and photographic records show that over the past ten years Orange-crowned Warblers have wandered through here between October 10 and October

An Orange-crowned Warbler, whose orange crown rarely shows, visited our water feature last year on October 16. So far this year, it's been a no-show.

18. While they habitually linger during fall migration (as do many migrants on their lackadaisical way back home), we're now nearly a month beyond their usual estimated arrival time. So I've given up hope for seeing one in the yard this year. For some unknown reason, I seem to spot them only every other year. Since one cruised through last year, I guess this is my year off. Phooey.

November 9

Startling a Flock

As I stepped out the back door to fill a nyjer-seed feeder this morning, thirty to forty Cedar Waxwings lifted off from the top of the maple tree, squealing as they flew. In fact, it was the high-pitched flight call that made me look up, just to verify with my eyes what I thought I sensed with my ears. Yep, a whole flock of them! Rarely do I see a single or even two or three waxwings; they're almost always part of a crowd. Sometimes the crowd numbers in the hundreds, the size dependent on how many berries are ready for the plucking wherever the birds have gathered. I'm guessing they were here to forage on any remaining dogwood berries, but if that was the case, they were disappointed. The dogwood berries are gone. Robins, cardinals, House Finches, mockingbirds, and bluebirds have taken their fair shares, and no doubt the waxwings managed a few dinners as well. Of course, they could also have been here this morning to scout out the readiness of winterberries and holly berries. Or maybe they were here only to get a good long drink. When birds eat berries, I've noticed they drink more than usual, probably to aid digestion.

Actually, all birds have fed heavily today. They know: A shift in the weather is hard on our heels with winter on the way, our first hard freeze predicted tonight (low of 23 degrees) along with possible snow flurries. While we'll see nothing more than a few flakes, our neighbors to the north are expected to see an accumulation. As a result, some birds that have moved south from Canada over the past two months or so may be pushed farther south by snow cover. Shifts in populations are tricky to detect, but fewer juncos and White-throated Sparrows roam the yard now than did a month ago. Maybe all of the first arrivals have moved on, replaced by later arrivals. Or maybe some of the first arrivals have stayed, forcing later arrivals to travel farther. Without banding studies, there is no way to figure out who's come to stay and who's moved on. In any case, tonight's winter blast may well shift populations again. Whether the newest arrivals will stay or simply move through, leapfrogging over, is beyond my ability to determine, but populations do shift. In another month, however, birds will likely have settled in for the remaining winter months—assuming the habitat continues to offer the necessary food, shelter, and water for their survival. BirdCast shows almost no migration in our area for the next three nights, a clue that perhaps migration is over, or at least nearly so. Instead, birds are merely wandering about, seeking the perfect spot for wintering.

November 10

Feeling the Change

This morning's low of 21 degrees seems to have made the yard a little crazy. Falling leaves, frozen stiff, rattled as they fell. Ground-covering redbud leaves, curled in autumn's grip, held snow pellets in their cups. Birds were everywhere—in the garden, in the backyard, in the front yard, at the bubble rock, at the little yard pond, in the trees, in the shrubs, in the mulch, in the grass, at the feeders, everywhere. All were foraging in their preferred manner: Two Red-bellied Woodpeckers showed up to pound on the old tulip-tree snag; a couple of White-breasted Nuthatches scooted down the same trunk; at least a dozen White-throated Sparrows foraged beneath the coralberry bushes and under the low-hanging hemlock boughs; a dozen or so Dark-eyed Juncos picked their way through grass seeds and smartweed seed heads; the usual fifteen or so cardinals hung out around and under the sunflower-seed feeders; a robin relished a good long drink at the little yard pond; Pine Siskins—too many to count—checked out the nyjer-seed feeder but mostly hung upside down feeding on the tiny hemlock cones; a couple dozen goldfinches clung to the nyjer-seed feeders; four doves waddled about under the seed feeders; three Blue Jays sounded their hawk-mimic screams to clear feeders for their own foraging; several chickadees zipped in to pluck single safflower seeds and then flew off to pound them open; a Song Sparrow flitted through the now-frozen aster blossoms; several titmice slipped in to snag a few sunflower seeds; a Carolina Wren called to its mate from the low cedars; a single mockingbird gorged on beautyberry berries; two Red-breasted Nuthatches zipped to and from the sunflower-chip feeder to the cypress tree; a solitary Field Sparrow explored the little yard pond but never drank or bathed; two Downy Woodpeckers picked at the seed cake. Crazy busy. Weather changes birds' behavior. Always.

Carolina Chickadees, this one hammering open a seed held between its feet, regularly roam the yard. Their populations fluctuate with the season, winter bringing them in for fast-food meals at feeders.

A Brown Creeper, in its first-of-season appearance, forages in the old tulip-tree snag, spiraling up, returning to the bottom, and spiraling up again, hiding in plain view wearing its camouflage plumage. It may stay a few days, a week, a month, or not at all.

Most interesting to me, however, was the Brown Creeper that spiraled its way up the trunk of the old tulip-tree snag. Ironically, I posted last night on social media that folks should be on the lookout for these little guys. They're tough to see, the little feathered creatures that look exactly like a piece of moving bark. But I didn't mean to suggest that they would arrive in less than 12 hours or to imply that I have some sort of psychic powers. Nor did I expect, even in my wildest dreams, that my own sighting the next morning would substantiate my prediction. Made me feel a little spooky!

Birds were reacting today exactly as I've seen them behave in the past when temps drop suddenly. They fed heavily yesterday, somehow knowing what would happen overnight, and they fed heavily again this morning to replenish their dwindling fat supplies, which were expended last night keeping warm in the bluster, snow flurries, and cold. And they fed heavily this evening, knowing better than I what to expect tonight.

November 11

Remembering Grosbeaks

The so-called winter finch forecast has called for an irruption this winter; already now in mid-November, it seems fairly obvious the forecast was right on. Several dozen Pine Siskins are roaming the yard now, stopping at nyjer-seed feeders but more often gleaning seed from the hemlock cones. Although Red-breasted Nuthatches obviously aren't in the finch family, their irruption typically coincides with that of the finch family. Three have made appearances in my yard, readily identifiable by their plumage differences. I've mentioned the presence of the "little bandits" already, their masks and small size separating them from White-breasted Nuthatches. What makes their presence noteworthy, however, is the trio. In the fifty-plus years I've lived here, I've never seen more than a single Red-breasted Nuthatch at a time. Recently, other folks have also posted multiple sightings, and some have reported not just multiples, but multitudes, especially in woodland edges. In fact, a fellow birder who hiked less than 2 miles along a trail in a nearby state fish and wildlife area yesterday reported twenty-nine Red-breasteds along the way and emphasized that his reported number represented a serious undercount. Wow. That's a bunch of Red-breasteds. In short, however, these reports and counts, especially the large number of them, verify not only the irruption prediction but give promise of more to come.

For instance, folks who have never previously seen Common Redpolls in their yards are now reporting them, especially in areas through Wisconsin and northern Michigan. While it's unlikely anyone as far south as here in southwestern Indiana will also see Hoary Redpolls (they typically remain farther west), range maps show Common Redpolls throughout our area—albeit the maps all show them as rare, and only in winter. I would also add only in the winter of irruption years! How cool it would be to add Common Redpoll to my yard list. While I enjoyed watching them foraging upside down in conifers when we birded in Alaska, I've never seen one in Indiana, much less in our little corner of the state. I know the odds are long, but I'll be watching.

The prediction for a major finch irruption this year makes me wish for Common Redpolls, birds we saw in Alaska.

Grosbeaks, however, are also part of the finch forecast. In spite of their name, some grosbeaks are actually large, heavyset finches, separated from other finches by their massive cone-shaped bills. The Rose-breasted Grosbeaks that sail through here during every spring and fall migration, however, fit into a different family. Only Pine Grosbeaks and Evening Grosbeaks are part of this predicted finch family irruption. Along with Red and White-winged Crossbills, Pine Siskins, Purple Finches, and the two redpolls, the Pine and Evening Grosbeaks round out the most likely irruptive species in our part of the world.

As a kid, I remember Evening Grosbeaks flocking to the feeder outside our kitchen window. They never came in ones and twos; they arrived by the dozens, multitudes, fighting at the feeder, hanging on to the edges awaiting a chance to snatch a seed or two, squabbling over a spot at the feeder ledge. My family didn't know anything about bird migration or why these amazing birds made an appearance so infrequently in our yard. We had no idea where they came from or where they went. Field guides were unknown to us. But I remember them as stunningly beautiful birds. Since then, I've seen an Evening Grosbeak only three times: once in central Michigan in 2016 where a couple of pairs were breeding, and twice in my own yard—a single bird in December 2012, and thirty-seven years earlier, according to my now-faded records, four males and two females.

Beyond the namesake monster beak, these birds also wear flashy plumage, including broad, bold white bars on otherwise black wings. The female also wears a series of debonair white tail spots that males lack. Where he's gold, however, she's gray, sporting only a mustard-yellow shawl across her shoulders.

Evening grosbeaks wander south only during winter, after spending their breeding season in western mountains and north through Canada. Their migration, however, is irregular, depending, scientists think, on food supplies. That's what this year's irruption business is all about—a mast crop failure through central Canada, a result, we're told, of drought.

Historically, however, there's an odd chronicle to Evening Grosbeaks' behavior. These primarily western and northern birds didn't show their big-beaked faces on the East Coast until the early 1900s, drawn east by seeds of box-elder trees and by outbreaks of spruce budworm, both favorite grosbeak foods. Since then, however, their populations have plummeted, by an alarming 91 percent since 1967, likely because of the shrinking boreal forest and extensive pesticide applications to kill spruce budworm. Other possible causes for their decline include harvest of old forest, climate change, and perhaps parasites and disease.

Given their decline, wouldn't it be special to have one—or more!—again this winter? There's hope. Multiple reports of Evening Grosbeaks have already been posted from northern Indiana.

Given the prediction for a major finch irruption this year, an Evening Grosbeak is on my wish list, like this male, photographed last summer on breeding territory in central Michigan.

Birds Do *That*?

Mourning Doves sit in the open for safety. Really? Wouldn't sitting half asleep away from concealing branches or clumps of grass make them prime targets for a raptor's lunch? Habitually, doves loaf about, right in plain view, apparently even dozing in winter's sun, seemingly oblivious to whatever may lurk above or around them. According to ornithology professor David Bird, however, all birds, not just doves, stay on the alert 24/7, even sleeping with one eye open— literally. And because they're always targets for predators, both two legged and four legged, they survive by employing a keen sense of sight and sound, sensing way more than seems likely as they loiter in plain view. Add to that, however, the fact that Mourning Doves fly with such speed and agility that nothing can catch them in a tail chase, and the safety factors seem clear. So contrary to what seems obvious to us pokey landlubber humans, doves sitting in the open never suffer a sneak attack.

November 12

Recommending a Road Trip

Certain flocks of birds put on seasonal extravaganzas. In early winter, one such grand show is the congregation of staging Sandhill Cranes at Jasper-Pulaski Fish and Wildlife Area in northwestern Indiana, named for the fact that the area straddles the county line between Jasper and Pulaski Counties. Okay, it's not Nebraska's Platte River, where a half-million Sandhills gather before moving south to Texas and surrounding environs. For me, however, reaching the Platte River is a three-day drive; J-P is about 4 hours.

Most years about now, the J-P flock peaks at about 10,000 birds, staging there, gathering forces, before moving farther south for the winter, typically to Tennessee, Georgia, and perhaps as far south as Florida. As of today, however, the count already exceeded the usual peak, with 12,700 cranes on the refuge, up from just over 5,000 last week. While they're hanging out at J-P, they fill the skies each evening, gathering in the field in front of the viewing stand, greeting one another, dancing with mates, and generally seeming to talk over the day's events before lifting off to fly into the nearby marsh to roost, standing in shallow water overnight. The next morning at dawn, they reverse the process, flying from the marsh back to the pasture, seemingly making plans for the day, renewing bonds with lifelong mates, and then, the morning visit over, drifting off in family units to forage for the day on private lands, preferring harvested corn fields. Their in-flight bugles carry for over a mile, depending on wind direction, so it's relatively easy to track their meanderings throughout the day.

Sometimes the birds hang out at J-P for most of a month, their presence determined by weather. They don't mind the cold, but snow deep enough to prevent their foraging for grain, bugs, and small invertebrates forces them to head south. Snow to the north has already shepherded the flocks into Indiana, so their numbers have ratcheted up dramatically over the past week. When they do move south, we see them V-ing across our skies, although I almost always hear them well before I see them. How cool would it be to have Sandhill Cranes as a yard bird?

Sandhill Cranes mate for life and sometimes live twenty years or more. Here, a pair forages in corn stubble.

Sandhill Cranes fly from daytime foraging fields into the marsh at sunset and remain safe overnight by roosting (i.e., standing) in water, a safety barrier against predators.

November 13

Calculating the Flocks

Fall behavior differs from spring in how and why birds amass in flocks. In fall, some bird species form massive flocks, some to migrate and some to form foraging and/or roosting flocks. For instance, Purple Martins and Tree Swallows gathered in ancestral staging areas, preparing for their leap across the continent to South American wintering grounds. That happened in early fall, back in August. Now, in November, in addition to the Sandhill Cranes that are staging for a mass migration from the Jasper-Pulaski FWA, Snow Geese and Greater White-fronted Geese formed vast flocks in the Arctic, probably in early September, and moved, en masse, our way. Already several thousand Snows and White-fronteds have gathered in the wetlands across the Ohio River in northern Kentucky. Thousands of ducks have joined the geese, but they typically don't migrate in masses, only in family units of maybe a dozen.

Other bird species form huge winter flocks but without plans for migration. Black-colored birds—especially Red-winged Blackbirds, European Starlings, Common Grackles, and Brown-headed Cowbirds—form mixed flocks of thousands. They forage together through harvested fields, lift off and fly together for miles, and roost together in convenient places. At dawn they reverse the process, lifting off their nighttime roosts and flying into fields near and far, typically in groups of hundreds or thousands. Some even estimate their numbers in the millions. During several Christmas Bird Counts, we estimated flocks of 9,000 to 12,000 birds. And we found several such flocks over the course of the early

Flocks of black-colored birds, here mostly Red-winged Blackbirds, amass sometimes by the tens of thousands, foraging and roosting together for mutual protection over the winter.

morning. Apparently the huge populations offer safety in numbers, with many eyes and ears offering 100 percent surveillance for the flock. Likewise, apparently more eyes readily find more grain amid the thousands of acres of farmland. An hour or so before sunset, stationed alongside fields stretching into the distance, an observer can watch what appear to be undulating ribbons of birds stretching from horizon to horizon, the flock returning to roost somewhere miles away. So while these flocks of birds don't truly migrate, they may well wander, searching out new food sources as nearby foraging grows thin.

In spring, some bird species remain in flocks, migrating together back to their breeding grounds. Snow Geese and Greater White-fronted Geese, for instance, migrate in massive flocks back to the Arctic before breaking off in family units to set up territory and breed. By contrast, non-migratory bird species, like the black-colored birds, break from the local flocks, wander off to suitable breeding territories, and set up housekeeping. Mostly, paired birds prefer territories to themselves, so that competition for food with other pairs and their nestlings won't add stress during the breeding season.

November 14

Checking Food Supplies

Winter is early. We're having record cold for this time of year, lows in the low 20s, a full day with below-freezing temperatures, windchills in the low teens. Birds need more than their usual food supply to stoke their furnaces, to maintain their metabolism, and to survive the night. Apart from those that may find backyard feeders a regular source of energy, what do wild birds find to meet their demands?

Some cling to seed heads, gleaning seeds from perennials and grasses, both in the wild and in native gardens. Since seed heads spill some of their riches onto the ground below, birds forage there, too, under plants and amid leaf litter. So folks who rake up all the leaves, cleaning every nook and cranny, deprive birds of their instinctive means of survival. Without leaf litter, birds are left with no place to forage, no native seeds to feast on, no grain to forage, and no ready protein that's always tucked away, hidden in the leaf litter. Other birds go for fruit, berries that may be dried but still viable for nutrition. Winter fruits like American holly, winterberry, inkberry, and beautyberry offer rich nutrition for hungry birds. Larger birds, of course, can deal with larger morsels, like acorns, pine nuts, even pecans and pig nuts—but they need special beaks strong enough to crack open the prizes. Perhaps the most valuable morsels are those that provide protein: insects. Of course, bitter winter weather puts insects into dormancy—all the easier for birds to "catch." But insect eggs and larvae, mostly those of certain moths, beetles, and borers, help chickadees, nuthatches, woodpeckers, and creepers survive the tough winter. The dormant insects and their eggs and larvae are most likely also buried among the leaf litter or perhaps burrowed into mulch, loose soil, tree bark, and rotting wood either still standing or on the ground. Note what all this means in terms of how we tend our yards and gardens!

Finally, carrion provides a great source of protein. Okay, yes, roadkill makes a dandy feast for the likes of vultures and hawks, although once carcasses freeze, few birds can hack into the vittles. Given fresh or at least not frozen roadkill, even the little guys like chickadees and titmice will partake in the protein-rich matter. Not that I'm recommending that folks serve up roadkill or other meat, but I do know a few brave souls who put out the turkey carcass after Thanksgiving. To each his own.

The idea that all these kinds of foods feed all kinds of birds, however, may be slightly misleading. It's clear that not every bird can eat seeds, for instance, because they lack the bill structure to crack them open. In short, what a bird eats is determined by its beak. Hummingbirds leave because their bill structure won't allow them to eat anything other than nectar and tiny insects, neither of which they can find here in winter. Flycatchers leave because their foraging behavior requires bugs in flight, their bill structures designed to snag bugs from the air, not to crack open seeds or pop open fruits. Like the humming-birds, they can't find flying bugs here in winter, so they return to their ancient origins in the south. Mourning Doves don't migrate, but their beaks are designed not to crack open seeds but to pick them up and swallow them whole. Thus, they tend to congregate in or near harvested agricultural fields, foraging for spilled soybeans and corn. In short, what visits our wintertime backyard is determined by not only what's available for them to eat but also what's available that they *can* eat.

November 15

Coping with Early Winter

Last night's ice storm and snowfall, albeit only a few inches, has seriously stressed and in some cases damaged trees, especially those still leaf-laden. While our maple is bare, many trees, like our oaks, pecans, dogwoods, gums, and others, still hold most of their foliage. Ice followed by snow has pulled limbs into a deep droop, and I fear for their return to a natural upright position. Our sweetbay magnolias, semi-evergreen in this part of their range, have suffered the most, their broad leaves gathering way too much ice to be healthy for their stature. Although temps never rose above freezing today, tomorrow should bring a thaw. The sooner the branches are relieved of their weight, the more likely they'll spring back.

Watching the birds today reminded me that for hatch-year youngsters, this is their first experience with ice and snow. What must they think? They fly to a branch, land as they always do, and slide sideways or flip over, righting themselves only on the wing, then struggling again to find traction. Mostly, they foraged on the ground, skittering for protection under the drooping evergreen branches now brushing the ground. Birds seem more skittish than usual, perhaps because of the ice and snow or perhaps because of a hawk in the neighborhood. I never saw one—neither the Red-shouldered Hawk nor the Cooper's Hawk—but bird behavior suggested the presence of one or the other. Among the brave, the Fox Sparrow, back for the third consecutive day, did its

A Carolina Chickadee finds safflower seed to its liking, offered here in a homegrown gourd cut out for birds' easy come-and-go feeding.

usual double-footed scratch to loosen snow from spilled seed, and Pine Siskins used their sharp little beaks to poke into the snow for scattered seed. Both, though, were quick to duck under cover at the least movement. Even my shadow across the window sent them scurrying. Maybe the snow made for a stronger shadow or made me more visible from the outside. For whatever reason, skittish behavior ruled the day.

November 16

Understanding Feeding Habits

Cardinals take up a position at a feeder and munch away, selecting seeds, hulling them, and swallowing them. They're ever watchful as they eat, their heads pivoting to keep track of their surroundings. But they stay in one spot, feeding until satisfied. Goldfinches and doves feed in a similar fashion, eating at the food source. Unlike those three species, jays behave differently, snatching a craw full of seeds and darting off to eat some and cache some. During most of the year, however, when they're only feeding rather than feeding and simultaneously hiding seeds against bad weather, jays clasp seeds between their feet and hammer them open. Like jays, chickadees and titmice also snag one seed at a time and fly off to hammer it open, securing the seed between their feet. Once the seed is shelled and downed, they fly back to the seed source for another. Back and forth, back and forth. Zip, pick, zip, eat, zip, pick, zip, eat. Wouldn't it be far more energy efficient if they'd just stay put, hammer open the seed where they found it, eat it on the spot, and then pick up another? Aren't they wasting lifesaving calories engaging in this back-and-forth feeding behavior, calories that would help them survive bitter winter nights? How many more seeds must they find and eat to make up for the back-and-forth flights?

Their back-and-forth behavior, however, is not a matter of energy expended—or saved. Instead, their behavior is about safety. When cardinals and goldfinches eat seeds, they're rolling the seeds around in their beaks, hulling them. All the while they keep their heads up, observant, ensuring against sneak attacks. Doves likewise eat heads-up, but they swallow seeds whole and unshelled, their beaks too weak to hull seeds. When jays, chickadees, and titmice hammer seeds open, however, their heads are down, the view of their surroundings obscured. They're at risk. By leaving the feeding area and flying to a sheltered spot to pound open seeds, however, they put themselves in a protected position. So their feeding behavior is really about survival.

A Tufted Titmouse hammers open a seed held between its feet. In that position, it's highly vulnerable to predation; thus, it flies from feeders to a safe place to eat.

November 17

Watching the Hawk Dive

From the corner of my eye, I caught sight of a Red-shouldered Hawk tearing through the front yard, diving into the coralberry shrubs. Because I scatter sunflower seed under these bushes, I knew instantly what was happening, and I feared the worst. What would the hawk snatch this time? A cardinal? They feed regularly there. A White-throated Sparrow? They scratch in the leaf litter under the bushes, flipping leaves into the yard while uncovering morsels. A junco? They scoot in while the others forage, knowing they'll find seeds as well. No sooner had the names of those candidates flashed through my mind than the hawk ripped off to the west, circling across the top of the dogwood tree and into the red cedar. Limbs shook. Birds scattered. The hawk flew on, across the hayfield, out toward the neighboring woods. I think the hawk missed its catch.

I know that it was a Red-shouldered Hawk only because I had a good look at its tail, heavily barred, as the bird tipped sideways, dodging the bushes before circling away. While I expected a Cooper's Hawk to be patrolling the yard, recently the Red-shouldered has been the more frequent terrorist. It's not common to have both hawks in the yard. They're two very different models. Red-shouldered Hawks, like Red-tailed, Broad-winged, and Rough-legged Hawks, are buteos—short-tailed, broad-winged birds that soar on rising thermals. They're raptors of open spaces like hayfields, meadows, and other grasslands. Think of them as the massive semis that cruise the interstate highways, rolling ever onward along the open road. On the other hand, Cooper's Hawks, like Sharp-shinned Hawks and Northern Goshawks, are accipiters—comparatively long-tailed raptors with short, rounded wings.

A light adult Rough-legged Hawk, a high-Arctic breeder, soars above southwestern Indiana grasslands only in winter.

Their shape makes them especially agile, able to rip through woodlands, dodging trees and careening through branches. Think of them as ATVs, compact but powerful, pounding their way through the woods. Given our little patch of woods and the neighbors' adjacent woodlands, Cooper's are at home here. At the same time, given the adjoining hayfield, pasture, and agricultural lands, Red-shouldereds find themselves equally at home. Our yard, situated exactly in between grasslands and woodlands, hosts buteos and accipiters equally well. Hawks keep the songbird gene pool strong.

November 18

Catching the Wave

Thousands upon thousands of waterfowl now routinely fill the morning and evening skies, and massive flocks of Snow Geese turn harvested agricultural fields white. Late this afternoon, as we were puttering with fall chores in the yard, I heard the calls. And way above our heads, in what I call our sky-high yard, strings of Snow Geese and Greater White-fronted Geese flew due south, in usual V formation, headed, no doubt, to the wetlands to roost overnight in the shallow waters. Several reports have drifted in over the past few days about arriving flocks, but the reports haven't reflected the vast numbers I saw this afternoon.

Last January 28 we ventured across the Ohio River to investigate which species of waterfowl and shorebirds might still be on the refuge. Numbers were already down then, and I'm sure the remainder departed shortly thereafter, returning to their breeding grounds in the

A trio of Greater White-fronted Geese in flight reveal why they get the nickname "Speckle Belly."

Arctic. With the breeding season having ended probably in early August, the birds began their long trek back here for the winter. It's a several-months-long journey for these strong fliers, but surely they're eager to settle in to forage in the harvested fields and loaf in the marsh.

1,000 (estimated) Greater White-fronted Geese, flyovers
Species: 126 total in the yard to date for the year.

Birds Do *That*?

Shorebirds can see behind themselves—without turning their heads. You've seen them, those little sewing-machine-like birds that needle down in mudflats and sandy shores, drilling long bills down until their faces almost nudge the mud. Imagine the focus problems we'd have with our eyes that close to the ground. But Mother Nature takes care of that. Shorebird eyes are set near the backs of their heads. So while they're poking about for tasty morsels in the mud, they're watching above, surveying their surroundings for predators. And you thought your third-grade teacher was the only being with eyes in the back of the head!

November 19

Noting New Arrivals

Right on the heels—or should I say webbed feet—of the Snow and Greater White-fronted Geese at area wetlands, Tundra Swans made their first-of-season appearances today. These pure white birds were originally dubbed "whistling swans" by Lewis and Clark in the first written description of these big birds that boast a 5.5-foot wingspan. While the name whistling swan lingers, a reference to their whistle-like calls, the more accurate Tundra Swan refers to their breeding habitat in the remote Arctic tundra. Our most numerous swan species, Tundras are slightly smaller than our only other native swans, Trumpeter Swans. (Mute Swans are nonnative and a threat to native swans. Introduced in the early 1900s, they're highly aggressive, attacking and killing other swans over nesting competition. They also destroy feeding areas since they consume 4 to 8 pounds of aquatic vegetation per day and yank up and destroy a similar amount.) There is an annual, regulated hunting season for Tundra Swans, but their populations are stable. In fact, according to AllAboutBirds.com, their biggest threat continent-wide is lead poisoning, resulting from the birds' ingesting spent shot, fishing sinkers, and mine wastes deposited in sediments. Tundras do face outbreaks of avian cholera, but their larger threat stems from the deterioration of their breeding habitats due to oil and gas drilling in the Arctic and loss of wetlands at migratory stopover sites. Given all that, I'm pleased that our local refuge will protect this wintering site forever.

I try to imagine what would happen if the local wetlands refuge to our south suddenly disappeared. Tundra Swans may live twenty years or more. Their cygnets learn the migration route from the remote Arctic to northern Kentucky by following their parents, a

A mated pair of Tundra Swans flies with this-year's cygnet (on far right).

migratory behavior that sets them apart from, say, warblers that have the migration route hardwired in their DNA. Every year, for their entire lives, these individuals and then their offspring make the arduous round-trip journey to winter here. In my mind, if for some crazy reason bulldozers destroyed the refuge or protections were lifted, the Tundras that habitually winter here would likely not survive. They mate for life, hanging out together year-round, not just during breeding season. Range maps, however, don't reflect their presence in our area. While they hang out and roost on the local refuge, I see them regularly grazing the harvested agricultural fields in Indiana. After all, from a swan's perspective, a flight across the river is only a few flaps away. They don't recognize geographic boundaries.

Separating Tundra Swans from Trumpeter Swans sometimes presents a challenge for bird watchers, but one characteristic usually clears up the confusion: Tundras float, swim, and fly straight-necked. Trumpeters, on the other hand, typically float and swim with their necks in a slightly S-curved posture. Even though Tundras are a tad smaller than Trumpeters, they're still big birds, weighing between 9 and 23 pounds, depending on age and sex. When they fly directly overhead, their wing beats exert an audible whoosh of air, confirming the strength of their flight, their hefty bodies moving smoothly forward as if effortless. Surely, though, the effort is tremendous—all the way from the remote Arctic.

November 20

Checking Hummingbird ID

This is the time of year when unusual hummingbirds tend to visit nectar feeders left out purposely for stray birds in dire need of a good meal. Several reports have come in over the past few days, some scintillating, suggesting perhaps a rarity. Most often here in south-western Indiana, late fall or early winter rarities turn out to be Rufous, Black-chinned, or Calliope Hummingbirds. And sometimes they turn out to be our regular Ruby-throated Hummingbirds, somehow caught up in a delay that puts them at our feeders way beyond the usual season. Such was the case today when a photo reached me that showed a hum-mer with a very short tail and wing feathers that extended beyond the tail. Wow! Could it really be a Calliope? Well, as it turned out, after much photographing of the extended wing feathers, this was a Ruby-throated Hummingbird that had somehow lost its tail. Poor baby! No wonder it's late going home, handicapped in such a manner. Knowing it tanked up at a local feeder for several days, however, gave the host the satisfying comfort that she had helped this little gal survive.

On the other hand, in a typical year in November or December, four or five Rufous Hummingbirds make their way into Indiana record books. Rufous hum-mers, western birds, breed in Oregon, Washington, parts of Idaho, and along the western coast of Canada to the south-ern edge of Alaska. Its usual migration route takes it south into Mexico, follow-ing age-old migratory routes that extend almost into the Rocky Mountains. But sometimes they cross the Rockies (What a feat for a hummingbird!) and meander their way across the continent to the East Coast.

In late November several years ago, a Rufous Hummingbird, a rare visitor to southwestern Indiana, nectared at our feeder.

Why do hummingbirds make these out-of-character appearances in out-of-range places? Have they changed their migratory pattern? Or do more folks leave feeders out—and keep an eye on them—and thus now spot birds that have always wandered through? No one really knows, but the latter may be the case. As more and more folks understand that they should leave nectar feeders out and keep them fresh until early December, we record more and more Rufous Hummingbirds. Interesting, huh?

November 21

Surveying Our Sky-High Yard

Wicked southwest winds led me outdoors today to watch bird behavior. While I espe-cially hoped to see migrants like Sandhill Cranes, Snow Geese, Greater White-fronted Geese, and Tundra Swans, instead the skies held—nothing. Since we'd seen a scattering of

Bonaparte's Gulls, this one in winter plumage, make regular appearances in southwestern Indiana during migration.

Bonaparte's Gulls sailing through windy skies earlier this morning about 10 miles from our house, I even entertained the potential for adding a new species to our sky-high yard list. But winds from the southwest do not treat birds kindly, especially those daytime migrants moving ever so slowly, day by day, southward. As it played out, rather than taking to the skies, birds tucked in, hiding behind tree trunks, feeding only on the lee sides of plants and feeders, staying mainly to the north side of the house and other buildings. What few birds meandered the property flew low and darted from protective shrub to protective shrub. Those that ventured higher and farther, perhaps aiming to fly a straight distance to a nearby foraging spot, found their efforts rebuffed, literally. Winds shifted them sideways, redirected their typically straight paths into drunken wobbly ways. One trio of Red-winged Blackbirds simply twisted in the wind and let it take them wherever it would, ultimately settling into the tops of the nearest trees in their uncharted path.

November 22

Declining Goldfinches

As American Goldfinch populations rise and fall at the nyjer-seed and sunflower-seed feeders, I'm left with either too much or too little of the seed supply. At the moment I have too much; populations have crashed. It's not an unusual phenomenon, these population fluctuations, as goldfinches from farther north leapfrog over locals, heading farther south, fleeing our sudden temperature drops that catch them by surprise. Only banding studies would reveal for sure whether some of our present goldfinches are, in fact, year-round residents. Best estimates reckon today's goldfinch numbers barely topped a dozen. Two feeders filled with about a gallon of nyjer seed may well go sour before it's consumed. And the 20-pound bag in the garage is at risk as well. Today's minuscule population certainly doesn't represent our breeding population. Far more than a dozen goldfinches brought their "dah-deet, dah-deet, dah-deet"-calling youngsters to the yard three months ago. Meanwhile, however, Pine Siskins, House Finches, and an occasional chickadee will pick at the nyjer seed. Kernels they flick to the ground will serve juncos and a few White-throated Sparrows. Now a social media contact in Tennessee claims he's inundated by goldfinches. Wonder if the nyjer seed in my now-idle feeders energized their journey there.

November 23

Tracking Turkeys

Although we have a little flock of turkeys that hangs out with us throughout most of the spring and summer, come fall and early winter, they disappear. True, toms and hens form separate flocks at the end of their breeding season, the hens keeping track of the poults until maturity. And true, we see the two flocks meandering the hayfield, plucking bugs from the grass, throughout the summer and into the fall. But what happens in late fall or early winter that takes both hens and toms off to some distant land? The first time both groups disappeared, I feared a coyote or a reported cougar somehow destroyed the flock, scattering the remaining individuals to parts unknown. Striking such fear in these birds typically means they've departed for good, never to return to such threatening environs. But return they did.

Nine Wild Turkey hens in a summer flock (one partially hidden at far right) have now joined ranks with other hens to form a large flock that roams neighboring oak-filled woods.

And now they're gone again. This time, though, I understand why. And where. Today I spotted a large flock of turkeys, mostly hens as far as I could tell, about a mile away, along the edge of a vast woodland. They've simply joined forces for the winter, foraging in larger congregations, more protective and more watchful groups, the better to be safe. I love solving behavioral mysteries!

November 24

Venturing Out

Given a relatively warm, sunny day, we ventured out to a wetlands management area where wintering Snow Geese, Greater White-fronted Geese, Tundra Swans, and assorted ducks fill the skies at dusk as they depart their feeding areas and move back to roost overnight in the marsh. Best estimates suggest between 8,000 and 10,000 geese, mostly Snow Geese, flew across our view. While about 2,000 or so were loafing in shallow waters near the road when we arrived, a female Northern Harrier flew low across the shallows, causing the birds to lift en masse, cackling and screeching, creating such a din that anyone for miles around knew something was amiss. The geese circled, swirling, whirling, gaining altitude, then breaking into layers, forming Vs that diverted in every direction of the compass. Because their alternate directions occurred at different altitudes, they seemed to fly in total disarray. In reality, though, they had sorted themselves into individual groups, perhaps extended family groups, gaining their sense of direction.

Some of the estimated 3,000 Snow Geese lift up as the result of a Northern Harrier flying over.

As the white geese turned and wheeled in the sunlight, they went from gray to bright white, flashing and flickering as a group—quite the light show in the low afternoon sun. As the Vs reached higher and higher altitudes, the groups of 80 became 180 or 380. Then the Vs broke into branches, reformed, changed leadership, creating Vs within the Vs, sometimes becoming a long waving thread as Vs merged, blended into 800, 1,800, 2,800, all flying in unison. Their calls defined their proximity, but sometimes it took minutes to find them in the high sky as they materialized out of nowhere. Focusing on their undulating formations, tracking their paths to the marsh, we distinguished the calls of the Greater White-fronted Geese "barking" among the Snows. Mingling with the geese's calls, however, the witch's-laugh call of Bald Eagles surely made the geese wary.

November 25

Puzzling over Flocks

Barometric pressure dropped precipitously this afternoon, driving warm weather into a distant memory and blasting this little corner of the world with rain and freezing cold. And birds knew. Late today I watched their behavior. Flocks of starlings circling, swarming, seeming to seek a group sense of direction, a group of several thousand landing finally in the tallest trees along the north edge of our property. Most interesting, however, was that the masses behaved as separate units, hundreds lifting up to fly to the east, followed by a pause as others seemed to consider their options, and then hundreds lifted up to fly to the northwest. Before the scenario ended, birds seemed to have headed off to every compass direction. In the course of the random group departures, some returned to the tallest trees. At least I think some arrivals were returnees—not new additions to the already impressive mass. After more than an hour, the last of the flock made their final departures, leaving the tallest trees empty of birds. Surely they ultimately decided where to find safety for the night, no doubt roosting en masse somewhere protected.

Birds Do *That*?

Okay, so a bird eats like a bird. What does it mean to "eat like a bird"? How much do birds really eat? Like most other animals, birds don't all eat the same proportionate amounts, depending on a number of variables. The colder the weather, the more a bird needs to eat to keep warm. The more active the bird—while feeding nestlings, for instance—the more it needs to eat to maintain its energy and metabolic levels. The smaller the bird, the more it eats in proportion to its weight, usually because little birds are fairly hyper and can't store as much fat in reserve. Of course, the more nutritious the food, the less of it a bird needs to eat. Thus, according to AllAboutBirds.com, a Black-capped Chickadee may eat 35 percent of its weight on an average day but a Blue Jay may need only 10 percent and a Common Raven only 4 percent. On the other hand, a hummingbird may consume 100 percent of its weight on any given day. So a 135-pound human who eats like a hummingbird, well . . .

November 26

Preparing for the Night

An early dusk crept in tonight, cloud cover darkening the skies well before the usual sunset. The weather prediction calls for a low of 22 degrees tonight, below-freezing temps for tomorrow's high, and even colder for tomorrow night. Knowingly, birds fed heavily, foraging late. One of the busiest of the late feeders came in the form of a little bandit, the Red-breasted Nuthatch. Three seem to have taken up residence here in the yard, at least for the time being. They typically feed across tree trunks, moving up, down, or sideways, likely unconcerned about which way is up. Unlike woodpeckers, they don't rely on stiff tail feathers to prop themselves up while hitching up and around tree trunks, instead depending on long toes and sharp toenails to keep themselves attached to their foraging spots. Tonight, though, they abandoned their natural behavior of foraging on tree trunks and were instead feeding steadily on the sunflower seed chips in a protected feeder on the south side of the house. Feeding away from a 40-mph wind surely makes for more pleasant dining!

November 27

Explaining Cardinal Numbers

Just at dusk, I can count on a special viewing pleasure: an abundance of Northern Cardinals. The biggest numbers come late, at a time when the females blend so perfectly with the shadows that they're a trick to count, camouflaged until they move. Still, somewhere

At least twelve Northern Cardinals gather at dusk to grab a few last morsels before going to roost.

around twenty of them tend to forage in the backyard then, snatching up the last sunflower kernels of the day, plucking a few extra safflower seeds, or visiting the bubble rock for a last drink. Rarely do I see them bathing at dusk, but frequently they stop to drink.

I'm reminded, however, of the folks who ask, "Why don't I have such a fine number of cardinals in my yard?" One who asked recently prefaced by explaining that she lives in a lovely forest, dense, deep, and well protected by a nearly solid canopy, only the roof of her small house forcing an opening to the sky. In her innocence, she explained exactly why she does not have cardinals. They're not forest birds. They're birds of the forest edge, preferring shrubby areas, places that are semi-open but with abundant vegetative cover. The cover need not be tall, just ample.

Two other friends, both former residents here in southwestern Indiana, bemoaned the absence of cardinals in their new locations, one in Colorado and the other in Oregon. Oops! No cardinals in those parts of the United States! Those of us accustomed to seeing cardinals on a daily basis, often in sizable numbers, sometimes forget they're not common—or even present—throughout the entire United States. They have moved northward over the decades, finally reaching Chicago, but only when railroad construction opened a pathway through the forest. Yet another acquaintance in northern Vermont wondered why he has no cardinals—never in twenty years—while his buddy 20 miles away sees the birds daily. But this acquaintance lives in the forest, and I'm guessing his buddy doesn't. Still, northern Vermont represents the cardinal's farthest range northward, so although the birds are found in the area, their numbers would likely be scant.

November 28

Wondering about Siskins

Most days at least a dozen Pine Siskins roam the yard, some visiting nyjer-seed feeders, some picking out crumbs in sunflower-seed feeders, and others preferring to forage among the tiny hemlock cones. How I wish I could know if the daily visitors over the past month or so are the same or different individuals. Are they hanging out here to fatten up, preparing to move farther south? Are they leapfrogging over one another as some move through while others stay briefly? Are they here for the duration, enjoying satisfactory winter habitat with adequate food for the group? It's the same ol' saw: Without banding studies, we can't know. But I have at least a few current clues, all from social-media friends who are now reporting

A Pine Siskin, apparently newly arrived for the winter, explores the water feature, a bit skittish in its approach.

large groups of Pine Siskins at their feeders in Tennessee and Georgia. Do I dare hope that some siskins will stay the winter, allowing me to enjoy their high-pitched rising calls for the season? Or will all of them ultimately move south, preferring a bigger variety of seed cones for wintertime sustenance? We'll all be watching their behavior.

November 29

Noting Vanishing Goldfinches

Yesterday morning's low of 14 degrees marked the coldest 24 hours since last February, a record for late November. Vicious winds put the chill factor into the single digits, and as expected, birds reacted. Their behaviors made clear the effect of bitter weather. True, they tucked in for most of the day, making only quick sashays to feeders. Most remarkable, however, is the now-total absence of American Goldfinches. For two days, none have visited feeders, none gave their "potato chip" flight call, none visited the water features, none made forays between shrubs and evergreens. Vanished! Their behavior marks yet another example of how so-called year-round birds aren't truly year-round everywhere. While we tend to have goldfinches all year (although certainly not at the moment), somewhere in that definition of "year-round," we have to account for their dramatically varying population numbers. I'm betting there will be a spell of absence. Then, when the next big cold front blows through, a few will find their way to the feeders, joining me for some period of time, maybe weeks, maybe days. Wanderers, without question!

November 30

Enjoying Bluebirds

Two males and a female Eastern Bluebird spent about 15 minutes this afternoon checking out the bluebird nest box mounted along the west end of the garden. Each of the three ducked in and back out, inspecting the interior and then seeming to study the general surroundings. No, they're not planning a midwinter nesting, not at the beginning of winter with below-freezing temps, but they are planning ahead, this time only as far ahead as upcoming severe winter nights. They readily use nest boxes as winter roost boxes, finding protection from biting winds and falling precipitation. To further protect themselves, multiple birds huddle together in a single box. In fact, one early morning some years ago, I watched eight bluebirds pop out of a single nest box after a bitter winter night. That's a crowd!

A female Eastern Bluebird perches near a nest box, checking the area's safety. Birds commonly use nest sites as overnight winter roost sites.

December

A Barred Owl on its day roost gets a once-over from a curious fox squirrel.

There is something infinitely healing in the repeated refrains of nature—the assurance that dawn comes after night, and spring after winter.

—Rachael Carson (1907–1964)

December 1

Gaping at Flocks

Pre-dawn heavy rain and strong winds marked another fast-moving weather front. And weather fronts, especially strong ones, almost always affect bird behavior. This morning, sheer numbers created the drama. Big numbers. Best estimate: 10,000 to 15,000. The massive flocks settled onto harvested grain fields, carpeting acres and acres and acres as far as I could see. And since we live on the highest point in the area, we can see several miles. By photographing the distance, I could fairly closely estimate the number of individuals captured in the image, but the count of those outside the image—too far to the left or right—remain only wild guesstimates. Thus, it's possible that the flocks exceeded 15,000.

By photographing the birds closest to us, the several hundred that landed in the hayfield adjoining our property and then in the abutting harvested corn field farther north, I could analyze at least several hundred—a mighty tiny portion—of the massive flocks' composition. Most were Red-winged Blackbirds and Common Grackles. Those identifications were evident even without looking but by listening to the racket. Beyond the obvious, a few Brown-headed Cowbirds hung out among the thousands. Probably a smattering of European Starlings were tucked in the group, but I couldn't pick out any in the photos. Most interesting, however, were the many Rusty Blackbirds and a few possible Brewer's Blackbirds. Because photos did not fully verify Brewer's, however, and because they are rare here, I'm leaving that species off the list. Tempting, but not verifiable. Rusties, however,

Hundreds of thousands of black-colored birds swirled through the neighborhood today, filling the sky from horizon to horizon and covering fields with black carpets, only a small portion of which are shown here.

Among the thousands of black-colored birds, I was able to identify one hundred or so Rusty Blackbirds, distinctive in their winter plumage.

while not as abundant as they once were, were readily identifiable, especially in their distinctive winter plumage, ironically more definitive than their summer plumage.

Beyond the dramatic flocks, the weather front produced some less spectacular changes in the yard. The goldfinches and siskins returned. At least a dozen goldfinches frequented the feeders, and a handful of siskins sashayed between feeders and hemlock trees. Probably more than a handful are here, but keeping track of which birds are which during their dizzying dashes across the property leaves me too befuddled to name a precise number. No matter the number, it's fun to have both species back.

100 (estimated) Rusty Blackbirds
Species: 127 total in the yard to date for the year.

December 2

Worrying about Wrens

Several days ago, as we finished fall yard chores and put away equipment and lawn furniture for the winter, I chased a Carolina Wren from the tool shed. Little stinkers! It's their usual behavior, always poking around inside buildings, checking out any little cavity for a potential nest or roost site, pecking for bugs, eggs, or larvae. Fortunately, as I walked into the shed, arms laden with stuff to hang from the tool racks or stack on the shelves, I caught sight of the little scamp. Alarmed by my arrival, I suppose, it fluttered at the back window, hoping to escape. So I stopped, edged toward the back corner, and waited until it flitted out the open door.

Back to work, I finished mulching and stored pitchforks and rakes. Ready to call it quits, I closed the shed, latched the door, and retreated to the warmth of the house and a cup of tea.

This morning, four days later, I found myself wondering aloud about the wrens. I hadn't heard them sing recently, and that's the one thing I love most about the busy little creatures: They're here, singing, year-round. Then I stopped dead in my tracks, feeling the heat rise in my face. Did I lock one of the pair in the shed? I hadn't looked around that late afternoon, only closed and latched the door. Could the wren have returned in my absence to further nose around for tasty morsels? Since I didn't go back inside when I stopped to lock up, had it sat quietly, hiding, perhaps in plain sight? Did I even look? I couldn't remember. I also couldn't remember if I had heard or seen either of the pair since then. I didn't think so.

Maybe because the wrens were on my mind, later today I heard the wren's song, the loud, cheerful melody. And there it was, poking about in a protected feeder, snacking on peanut crumbs. But was it alone? Was it singing to empty space? Scurrying to the window, listening carefully, scanning hopefully left to right across the yard, I watched. Then, there! Its mate sat chirring, her call following his song, confirming their pair bond even now, in the depths of winter.

What a relief. Several times we've found some tiny wraith dead on the second floor of the workshop or in the back corner of the first floor, usually at the base of a window, trapped when we dropped the overhead doors, loading doors, or even the walk-in door. Trapped, and then it fluttered in its final effort to escape through unforgiving glass. A bitter lesson, the loss reminds us that we must tour the spaces before we close up, watching for any sign

Carolina Wrens like to explore any open building and any crack or crevice, sometimes to the bird's demise.

of flight, clapping our hands to startle into flight any bird perching quietly, hiding during our close-up check. Still, sometimes we're tired after an afternoon's work, leaving us less attentive than we should be to every detail, and we close up without the careful check. I'm grateful that my inattention to detail a few days back didn't result in yet another dead bird on my conscience. I understand the birds' behavior, but I can't always justify my own.

December 3

Sighting the Kestrels

Along our usual route to town, the kestrels remain as fixtures on the utility wires paralleling the road. They perch facing the wind, but when the wind comes from the south, they peer over their shoulders to watch the hayfield at their backs. Today's southerly winds probably gave them a crick in their necks as they hunted. On every trip along this road, including today's, we watch, hoping to verify the kestrels' presence and well-being. Today we were especially pleased to note that one of them held a little rodent in its toes, tearing at the creature with that surprisingly sizable hooked beak, a reminder that while it's small, this little kestrel is nevertheless a mighty falcon. I can visualize the romp that led to the capture, a fast flight to the spot, perhaps a brief hover as the kestrel honed in on the prey, planning an attack that avoided interference, and the final dive and snap of the spine. Fortunately, the bird's hunt did not involve contact—most likely deadly contact—with an automobile. Instead, since the utility wire runs along the same side of the road as the hayfield,

Birds Do *That*?

Pigeons once delivered the news. In fact, they delivered the names of the winners of the first Olympics in 776 BC. The Rothschild family used carrier pigeons to communicate among their many banks, a financial business established in the 1760s. And pigeons brought the rest of the world the news of Napoleon's defeat at Waterloo in 1815. During both World War I and II, pigeons saved lives and earned medals of honor for their work. History earns pigeons their due respect.

harvested corn and soybean fields, and winter wheat fields, the kestrels usually fly away from, not into, the road. It brightens my day each time I see them both.

December 4

Ratcheting Up the Numbers

As snow deepens to our north and winter turns the world brittle, more and more winter residents arrive. In area marshes, Snow Geese now exceed 5,000, and several thousand Greater White-fronted Geese fill the fields, feeding on fallen grain. More than one hundred Tundra Swans have settled in at the wetlands across the river. A few more are likely still on their way. Numbers of Short-eared Owls are slowly increasing at the reclaimed strip mines

White morph and blue morph Snow Geese stand on the ice (foreground) or paddle about, keeping water open for protection.

to our north, a rolling, treeless area the owls find comfortably like their home on the Arctic tundra. Once the owls move in, Rough-legged Hawks and Bald Eagles wander in, looking for prey the owls might miss.

As snow flurries swirl, melting on still-warm ground, junco numbers multiply, Red-breasted Nuthatches stay busy at feeders, and White-throated Sparrows show up more regularly in the yard, otherwise hiding in brushy growth along the yard's edges.

Winter residents continue to arrive, chased here by worsening weather to the north, remaining only until worsening weather here drives them still farther south. It's routine behavior for them.

December 5

Catching Regular Creepers

In our yard, Brown Creepers have always been regularly irregular. Most years I catch sight of them a few times, usually during the transition seasons. This year, however, I'm seeing one almost every day, and almost always in the same place: on the old tulip-tree snag. Watching it again today, I now understand that I see it regularly there for two reasons: First, my unobstructed view of the bare snag means if the creeper visits, I'll likely see it, right out in the open. Second, the creeper is consistently finding something yummy on its daily spiral up the tree, thus encouraging its regular revisits. Given the state of the snag's decay, surely beetle eggs and larvae aplenty reside inside the bark's grooves, perhaps even under the rotting bark's loose edges. Frequently, after the creeper scuttles from bottom to top of the snag, it flies 30 feet to a bald cypress and scours that bark bottom to top as well, apparently finding means to satiate its hunger there, too. Clues help explain the bird's behavior!

I truly believe that on the days I don't see it, I've simply not been looking during the few minutes when it visited. This afternoon, for instance, it spiraled up the snag, dropped back down to the suet cake, poked around a bit, then dropped to the ground. There it picked up what appeared to be a sunflower-seed hull, rotated the empty hull briefly in its beak, and then dropped it, returning to the snag, spiraling upward, past the suet cake, making its way to the top. Then it dropped to the base of the snag and repeated its spiral, moving along a slightly different path, making its way once again to the top. Then, surprise! A second creeper joined the first! That was a milestone for our yard—two Brown Creepers at once! Habitat draws 'em in!

What if I hadn't been at the window during those 5 minutes?

December 6

Dodging Robins

At a strip mall today, a flock of perhaps 100 to 150 robins fluttered in, around, and under the crabapple trees edging one side of the parking lot. The crabapple fruits, small ones in this case, just about the right size for a robin to swallow whole, have endured several hard freezes and are now soft. Falling-off-the-tree-at-a-touch soft. Mushy soft. Translation: rotten. Unfortunately, when birds, typically robins or Cedar Waxwings, find these softened fruits, they think they've found a bonanza. Great eating and plenty of it. But here's the problem: Most of the rotten or rotting fruits have undergone some degree of fermentation. Think alcohol. The more the birds eat, the more alcohol they consume. And the drunker they become. While some folks find their drunken activities amusing, it's a particularly dangerous situation for the birds—especially given the traffic in a pre-holiday grocery-store parking lot. The birds fly in wobbly form, landing on the roadway, on vehicles, on grocery carts. Sometimes they miss their landing target altogether and fly into moving vehicles. I'm sure I need not explain the consequences. Although I saw no deadly crisis at today's scene, I have seen previous crises.

December 7

Speculating about Pigeons

Pigeons, more accurately called Rock Pigeons, live mostly in cities, sometimes to the chagrin of city fathers who would prefer the birds roost elsewhere, other than atop favored statues, historic architecture, and prized tourist attractions. Introduced from Europe, pigeons escaped domestication (they were formerly considered a gustatory delicacy and raised for use by gourmet chefs) and thrived amid ornate buildings where they found perfect nesting quarters. Occasionally, a rural farmstead still hosts pigeons, sometimes because owners enjoy the birds' company, encouraging their presence, and sometimes because the pigeons find suitable food and loft quarters, choosing to move in without an invitation. In any case, living in a rural community as we do, pigeons rarely find their way here. Yes, I have pigeons on my yard list, but they're rarities—and always only flyovers.

Considered city-sidewalk birds, Rock Pigeons are targets of certain raptors, including Peregrine Falcons.

All this in mind, I found myself watching the pigeons as I traveled along the expressway into town. Mostly they roost on the high-mast light poles lining the roadway, but sometimes they gather instead by the hundreds along utility wires, always, of course, facing into the wind. Today, however, they were in flight, whirling, diving, obviously all astir about something, seemingly in a panic. Although I could see no obvious cause (but I was, after all, driving highway speed), a thought came to mind that I could not put down: Peregrine Falcon.

Habitat loss and pesticides like DDT decimated the Peregrine Falcon population so that by 1965, no Peregrines nested east of the Mississippi River. Indiana participated in a reintroduction program, releasing sixty young falcons between 1991 and 1994 in Indianapolis, Fort Wayne, South Bend, and Evansville. Tall city buildings had been found to be satisfactory substitutes for the birds' preferred cliff-side nest sites. The birds moved about,

A Peregrine Falcon perches on its favorite pigeon-eating roost, feathers from previous lunches now tangled in cobwebs draped from the "K" of one of the city's "Bank" signs.

however, choosing their own preferred locations. In recent years a bird or two has been sighted locally. And their preferred diet? Pigeons.

Although a quick tour of promising city-building facades yielded no Peregrine sightings today, I still had that niggling feeling one was somewhere, likely munching on pigeon.

December 8

Sighting Sumac

Staghorn sumac grows readily along roadsides and railroad tracks, but there's none in my yard. Yes, there's fragrant sumac, but not staghorn sumac. The difference is the fruit. What fragrant sumac lacks, staghorn sumac makes up for with a broad-based clump of fruit that tapers irregularly up to a point, a sort of upside-down ice-cream-cone shape. While the fruits are hard and fuzzy and mostly unappetizing to wildlife, when the going gets tough in late winter, sumac berries may be the sole means of survival for some birds, including bluebirds. The later in the winter, the more desperate the birds' behavior. And desperation is exacerbated by the minimal nutrition per sumac berry, meaning birds need an abundance of sumac fruits in order to down a decent meal.

An American Robin feeds on the berries of a staghorn sumac seed head, cut from the stalk and tied to a backyard feeder post.

Today, then, I started making a mental note of where the sumac shrubs are growing, hoping I won't need to know but having a Plan B in the back of my mind. Should the winter grow severe enough that birds grow desperate, I'll have a source of native, natural food. In previous severe winters, I've pruned sumac fruits, brought them home, and tied them to feeders or posts. Bluebirds, robins, and mockingbirds responded. These three species generally don't visit feeders, except perhaps suet feeders when they're desperate. But berries! Ah, they relish berries. What else is left in late March, before new growth buds out?

December 9

Renewing the Gull Watch

Here in southwestern Indiana, we're situated nearly mid-continent and conscious of oceans only as vacation destinations. Still, routine winter bird-watch reports include gulls. Most gulls that winter here migrate from their summer homes on the Great Lakes. Two major attractions draw them. First, the mighty Ohio River certainly is no Lake Michigan, but its waters are wide, fishy, and, except during a few historic winters, ice free. On the wing, miles high, the gulls can surely sight the vast, welcoming waters. Sometimes rafts of gulls in the hundreds float with the current, bobbing past those of us on the bank who are ogling their bright white. The second attraction, however, guarantees their annual return: the county landfill. Every day the birds fly the dozen or so miles from the river, where they loaf, to the landfill, where they feast, and back again.

Some days, however, they detour to dumpster dive. Then we find them on shopping center parking lots, taking up sunning positions on the warm tarmac, barely waddling aside to avoid oncoming traffic. In fact, most drivers simply steer around the dozing flocks, respecting their winter escape to our parts.

While the United States hosts upward of two dozen species of gulls, most of those that winter here are Ring-billed Gulls. Occasionally a Herring Gull joins the group, and during migration we frequently find Bonaparte's Gulls foraging in wet fields. But for the most part,

Likely having migrated from the Great Lakes, Ring-billed Gulls congregate in and along the river in winter, foraging for anything edible.

Ring-billed Gulls dominate. In part, they dominate simply because, area-wide, they're the most numerous—by bunches and bunches.

Today's sightings at one of the local malls were most certainly Ring-billed Gulls. They flew up from the parking lot near a fast-food restaurant dumpster and landed atop the flat roof of one of the big-box stores. Seeing them spoke once again to the deepening of winter. More winter birds seem to arrive daily, not only in terms of additional species but also in terms of growing numbers. After all, we're only days away from the longest night of the year.

Birds Do *That*?

Peregrine Falcons are the fastest creatures on Earth. Forget the cheetah. We're talking speeds well in excess of 200 mph. Here's how: Peregrine Falcons have a unique manner of catching prey. While flying, they cruise along, watching for signs of quarry. Once they spy a target, they fold their wings and dive, a tactic ornithologists term a "stoop." Because their bodies take on the shape of a bullet, they're aerodynamic speedsters. In a dive, they've been clocked at 240 mph. In the journal *Bio-aerial Locomotion*, scientists point out that Peregrines can fly that fast because of an amazing respiratory system that includes a one-way air flow into its lungs. Best not to make any miscalculation in such a speedy stoop, however, or the falcon could go from killing prey to being killed.

December 10

Bringing More Birds

Colder temps almost always bring an influx of birds to the yard, and the past two days have proven that fact. Instead of seeing the recently customary one or two Blue Jays during their brief forays through the yard, today at least four spent considerable time in both front and back yards, foraging on black-oil sunflower seeds and shelled peanuts and visiting the bubble rock for both a drink and a quick splash. Their interaction suggested they're members of an extended family, but one seemed more unsure of itself than the others, perhaps indicating it was the youngest of the group.

This year's now-regular Brown Creeper and three equally regular Red-breasted Nuthatches made their routine visits, and two White-breasted Nuthatches showed up simultaneously. A resident pair, they nested here this summer and fledged two youngsters, but it's not just coincidental that they don't show up together at feeders. Males tend to push females out from forag-

A White-breasted Nuthatch caches a safflower seed in the bark of the old tulip-tree snag.

ing sites, so she generally feeds alone. Of course, in winter, they tend to join little foraging flocks of chickadees, titmice, and Downys, so they're irregular winter feeder visitors. I've no way to prove it, but I think it's the same pair that has been here for a couple of years. The oldest known pair, banded and recaptured in Colorado, was nine years old.

A female Eastern Towhee scratched amid the fallen oak leaves, sometimes flipping them over herself as she foraged in the litter for bugs—eggs and larvae, I suppose—a behavior I see repeatedly among towhees. Oddly, she shared space in close proximity with a squirrel this morning but quickly scurried under the ground-sweeping coralberry shrubs anytime she felt insecure. Since I hadn't spotted her recently, I'd wondered about her well-being. Two females, most likely one of which was a hatch-year bird, visited back in mid-October,

but the male continues to make himself scarce. He'll likely show his face soon, foraging below the seed feeders as he usually does once he arrives. Of course, any of these could be different birds from those I saw earlier, perhaps having moved into the territory in the absence of others. Either way, they fill the slot of missing towhees. Meanwhile, the female zipped up into the hemlock, pausing, perching, seeming to relax and rest, perhaps taking a 15-second siesta. No bird sleeps the way we humans think of sleeping. They'd be lunch for some predator if they did.

A female Eastern Towhee roams through the back-yard, ducking into hemlock branches when she feels threatened by a hawk overhead.

December 11

Seeing Snowy Owl Reports

Already, the first Snowy Owl has been sighted in northern Indiana. Only on rare occasions does the ghostly bird travel so far from the Arctic that it reaches southern Indiana. Last year the snowies were abundant, traveling across much of the northern tier of states and spurring news media attention wherever they appeared. It was an irruption year for snowies, an event caused when abundant summertime lemmings, voles, and other tasty little animals provide adult snowies with more than the usual food supply to raise their owlets. Populations boom. Then, because more owls need more food, when early winter descends, the birds disperse, on the hunt for winter sustenance. As a result, one handsome youngster ended up at our area airport, finding the vast mowed acreage reminiscent of the high Arctic tundra—and full of mice and voles for the taking. Maybe this winter will bring one or more owls back here, but I don't have high hopes that two irruption years will occur back to back.

During some winters, Snowy Owls irrupt well south of their normal range, including this individual that, several years ago, lingered weeks in southwestern Indiana. This winter may bring more.

December 12

Responding to Questions

Someone asked me today, "What do you feed your bluebirds?" A simple, straightforward question for which the person most certainly expected a simple, straightforward answer. But I'm sure my answer wasn't what the questioner expected: I don't feed the bluebirds. At least not specifically. Yes, I understand that some folks offer dried (or even live) mealworms, some even raising their own moth larvae in various concoctions of oat or wheat bran or wheat germ, wheat flour, dried skim milk, brewer's yeast, chicken mash, oat and wheat kernels, moistened with a wedge of cabbage or half a raw potato, all layered with newspaper and burlap. Lots of effort and daily attention required. Not my bag of tricks.

Beyond mealworms, yes, I understand that some folks find success offering sunflower chips to bluebirds, and that's a surprise to me. In general, bluebirds simply aren't feeder birds and rarely eat seeds—mostly because their beaks are not designed to crack open seeds. Of course, sunflower chips need no cracking; the hull is already removed and the pieces are small enough for the bluebirds to swallow whole. Still, bluebirds' regular appearance at feeders surprises me. It's not part of their usual behavior. But back to the question.

Instead of "feeding my bluebirds," the habitat attracts and supports them. Not only has hubby built and mounted a nice little bluebird trail of eleven boxes that he monitors every three or four days during breeding season, but our native habitat provides support to native bugs. That's what feeds the bluebirds. Now, given the bug-absent cold, bluebirds, like other insect-eaters that don't migrate, turn to berries. While the yard is full of berries now, bluebirds will also wander into adjoining areas to seek out other native fruits, varying their diets.

The hard part comes in late winter, when berries and other fruits are gone, either eaten or rotted, and snow and ice make life all but impossible. That's when I put out finely chopped apples and rehydrated raisins, maybe fine crumbles of pure suet—all no larger than pea-size. Because bluebirds swallow foods whole, pea-size is max. I place these on the ground directly under a suet feeder, knowing bluebirds habitually check the spot for suet crumbles that woodpeckers inadvertently drop from the feeder. In addition, I may spread a bit of chunky peanut butter (no-sugar-added is better for birds) on the base of a tree trunk near where the fruit is scattered. In short, when bluebirds are desperate, they're attracted by the other birds feeding in the yard. That's the only time I find bluebirds near feeders, and it's the only time I offer food specifically to meet their needs (see photo on January 13). The experts say bluebirds don't come to feeders, but the birds sometimes learn to if the offerings are suitable. At my house, they've found the window feeders that hold sunflower hearts or chips.

December 13

Spotting Goldfinches

True to form, the here-again-gone-again goldfinches have once more disappeared from the yard. Nyjer-seed feeders hang idle, not even Pine Siskins or House Finches visiting the dinner spot. Once upon a time, I used to worry when the goldfinches disappeared. Did the seed get wet in the rain/snow/ice and spoil? Did it get too warm in the garage and turn buggy or rancid? Was a hawk or stray cat prowling the area, scaring off the birds? Nowadays, though, I've learned to accept the goldfinches' come-and-go behavior, knowing that the little flocks wander, that the more northerly migrant flocks come and go, displacing local populations. Sometimes in early winter, goldfinches simply edge farther south and the yard goes empty until the next flock moves in from the north, populations pushed around by weather fronts and strong winds.

Today, however, as I was out and about, I drove through a local county park and—bingo!—there were sixty-two goldfinches feeding in a single group along the auto path. The huge number made me doubt my initial identification, given their recent absence in the yard. As I watched, I soon became aware that even more scampered about in the tree

A male American Goldfinch in winter plumage, including dark bill and missing black cap, perches on a winter-bare redbud limb. Goldfinches wander seasonally, deserting feeders for weeks before rushing back in huge numbers.

above. What brought them here? Gum balls. The sweetgum tree hung full of the spiny little balls, twisting by their stems in the wind. Apparently that twisting and turning, perhaps along with the rain, had shaken the seed from many of the balls, scattering it across the pavement. Some birds continued to scavenge among the balls on the trees, no doubt causing still more of the tiny seeds to fall. No matter how seeds reached the ground, it was obviously fiesta time! Flock behavior helps birds find wintertime food, a sort of cooperative learning behavior whereby all of them together know more than any one of them alone! And this flock found the Mother Lode!

December 14

A Black Vulture perches, waiting to follow a Turkey Vulture. Because Turkeys have a better sense of smell than do Blacks, Turkeys often lead the way to ready-to-eat carrion.

Reeking of Roadkill

A road-killed squirrel attracted six vultures along our country road this morning. Nothing unusual about that, since vultures have a strong sense of smell for carrion. What was unusual, however, was that five of the vultures were Turkey Vultures, but the sixth was a Black Vulture. We don't see all that many Black Vultures in our neighborhood, but since the Blacks tend to look to the Turkeys for help finding lunch, the two species do sometimes forage together. It's probably unnecessary to explain that within 30 minutes or so, the road was clean. No fur, no feet, no tail, no skull. Nothing. Six vultures make quick work of such a small dinner.

December 15

Chuckling at Blue Jays

Now that I toss out a small handful of shelled peanuts each morning, the Blue Jays have returned to their noisy every-morning visits to the yard, calling to one another that breakfast is served. I've described earlier how they stuff their gullets with four or five peanuts, eat one, and hide the rest, digging a tiny pit, dropping in the peanut (or in other cases, the acorn, pecan, corn kernel, sunflower seed, whatever), and covering it. As a finishing touch, they conceal the fresh dig with a leaf or twig. Clever enough.

A Blue Jay fills its craw and beak with peanuts before dashing off to eat some and cache the rest.

But recently I've discovered the rest of the story. Because jays engage in this behavior regularly, researchers studied marked birds, thus identifying individual behavior. Did all jays cache the same way?

Here's what they discovered: Innocent jays, probably young ones, bury their caches, add the concealing touch, and, satisfied with the job, sail off for the next morsel. More experienced jays, however, follow a more secretive behavior. When they finish the job, adding the twig or leaf for concealment, they hop back, pause, and look around furtively, making sure no thieving fellow jay has caught them in the act. If, indeed, they suspect the hiding place has been compromised, they dig it back up and relocate. The most amusing part of the study, however, showed that only birds that themselves had stolen another jay's cache showed concern about their own caches being raided. Have to love their clever antics. Smart birds, these jays.

December 16

Puzzling over Head Bobbing

Four Northern Flickers arrived simultaneously at the front-yard water feature this morning, mostly each minding its own business. Within a few minutes, however, as a disinterested male took long sips at the water's edge and then departed, two females faced off, engaged in a head-bobbing display. Each stretched her neck up, bill pointing skyward, and bobbed up and down, forward and backward, seemingly threatening the other. One also held her wings slightly away from her body, perhaps to make her look bigger? At any rate, a bobbing period lasted perhaps 20 seconds followed by a 20-second pause, and then the two birds repeated the behavior. The whole curious affair, however, lasted a surprising 12 minutes. At that point, with neither seeming to show defeat or even deference toward the other, the two wandered off, each flying a short distance before resuming foraging. While December seems an odd time for either same-sex aggression or territorial displays, perhaps each

Two female Northern Flickers engage in a head-bobbing display, acting out aggression, perhaps an adult sending her female offspring on its way, forcing it to find its own territory.

was testing the other in anticipation of times to come. Later in the winter, such behavior becomes routine as females vie for the best territories. The question remains: Were the two females related? Sisters? Mother and daughter? No matter. Two is too many for a territory.

December 17

Touting Pure Suet

Watching woodpeckers at a suet cake today revealed interesting behavior. Here's the background: They're attracted to suet because of its high fat content, a superb source of nutrition that keeps birds warm in winter. Pure suet is a specific kind of fat, that surrounding the kidneys in hoofed animals. In its pure form, suet looks shiny and waxy, and feels smooth, hard, and crumbly, very different from plain ol' fat. Having offered suet cakes that include additives like cracked corn, millet, and milo, and then having offered suet cakes that include no additives, I've concluded that cakes serve woodpeckers best in pure form. That's because birds, including woodpeckers, that eat suet in winter are primarily birds that eat insects in summer; they're not big-time seed eaters. So adding seed to suet cakes attracts, well, seed eaters. Think especially the likes of starlings and House Sparrows. When they peck at the seed, the cakes crumble, chunks fall to the ground, and the residue attracts undesirable ground feeders, including rodents. Woodpeckers, however, can enjoy suet cakes without competition when the cakes include mostly or nothing but fat and little or no fiber (think

Birds Do *That*?

Gulls crack open shells by dropping them. When gulls pluck bay scallops from the water, for instance, they must somehow open the shell to eat the contents. Their only means of cracking the shell, however, is to drop it from some height onto a hard surface—a road, parking lot, or (heaven forbid) your automobile. Researchers at Southern Massachusetts University found that first- and second-year gulls are less successful than are third-year gulls at cracking the shells, an apparent learning curve that finally brings adult gulls to a 100 percent success rate.

"trash" or "filler"). Labels reveal the truth: Some cakes tout as much as 98 percent fat. That's good. Some have as little as 15 percent. That's pitifully poor. Those 15-percent-fat cakes may be cheap, but being stuffed with trash only makes them more profitable for marketers and less beneficial for birds. Fruit, though, is okay in suet since birds that eat insects in summer typically eat berries in winter. Still, high fat content remains key to nutritional value, so fruit should make up no more than 5 percent of the cake.

But back to the woodpeckers' behavior. Whether they're feeding at a suet cake or hammering for lunch in a decaying tree branch, they have a special technique for holding themselves in position. They use their tails. The longest tail feathers are spiny affairs, stiff and stout. Woodpeckers can prop themselves against their tail feathers, leaning back to survey the next best foraging spot. Then, as they prepare to leap upward along the trunk, the stiff tail serves as leverage for the hitch up to the next spot. Awesome adaptation, huh?

A male Hairy Woodpecker displays its stout, spiny tail, an amazing adaptation that allows woodpeckers to hitch themselves up tree trunks.

December 18

Sending Grackles Flying

The noise caught my attention: unmusical squawks and harsh tuneless clatter. At the window I was greeted by nearly fifty Common Grackles, drinking and bathing in our little front-yard water feature. They seem to have come from nowhere, arriving in a horde, staying only long enough to quench their thirst, and then dashing off in the same manner in which they came—a rush of wing whirs and flight calls. When they left, the yard seemed even more quiet than usual, in part the result of the contrast between their noise and its now absence, and in part because their mass arrival scared off everything else. I'm betting my tapping on the window glass sent them off a bit earlier than they would have gone

Shown here are about thirty of the fifty-some Common Grackles that winged in for a drink, accompanied by one European Starling.

otherwise, and that's fine by me. They're foraging in their winter flocks now, and those flocks can be overwhelming in a yard the size of ours. They need fields. Vast fields. Acres and acres of fields. Of course, those acres of fields usually lack water, and that's all they wanted here.

December 19

Checking Black-capped Chickadees

Two species of chickadees, Carolina and Black-capped, breed in the eastern United States. The Black-capped species lives to the north, while the Carolina—as the name suggests— lives to the south. They look very much alike, although their songs are slightly different. The kicker here, though, is that across the narrow ribbon of geography where the two species overlap, they learn each others' song. Yikes! Field guide range maps define each species' individual year-round ranges, but I've noticed that not every guide shows exactly the same divide. Complicating matters more, in places like northern Indiana, where the two species' ranges meet, the species sometimes hybridize. Then it's anybody's guess which is which. The separation of which species is which grows further blurred by the fact that the birds wander, and climate change has likely caused them to wander even more widely than in the past. Separating one from the other thus becomes a matter of debate among those who demand precision in the identification. Personally, I take the safe route.

Black-capped Chickadees, this one photographed in Michigan, live north of their look-alike cousins, the Carolina Chickadees.

If I'm in central Michigan, I can be fairly certain I'm looking at Black-capped Chickadees. If I'm at home in southwestern Indiana, I can be fairly certain I'm looking at Carolina Chickadees.

December 20

Bearing Out Buffelhead

As we were out and about today with birding friends, we found ourselves surrounded by waterfowl—ducks and geese. Cruising the back roads around vast wetlands—both natural and mitigated—we came upon flock after flock of these winter wonders. By day's end we had tallied a dozen species, including Gadwall, Common and Hooded Merganser, Lesser Scaup, Black Duck, Pintail, Bufflehead, Mallard, Northern Shoveler, and Canada and Snow Goose. For some species, like Pintail and Black Duck, we saw only a handful of each. For others, like Gadwall, we saw hundreds. And for still others, like Snow Goose, we saw thousands—probably upward of 10,000. Flocks that large make for difficult counts, especially when they lift up as a single blurred mass when eagles harass them or when they fly in skein after skein across the entire sky, horizon to horizon, for 10 minutes or more. We saw both phenomena today. So maybe 10,000 is barely half of what we actually saw. I really don't know.

What does all this waterfowl behavior mean? We have no ducks in summer. Oh, yes, maybe a few Mallards and resident non-migratory Canada Geese, but nothing else. Most of the ducks we studied today breed across Canada or, in the case of Gadwall, throughout pothole country in the north-central United

Buffleheads, one of our prettiest ducks, winter here after migrating from central Canada.

Gadwalls winter here after leaving their breeding range in the north-central pothole country.

Pintails, now becoming somewhat rare, winter here after migrating possibly from as far away as Alaska.

States. Some, like Snow Geese, breed in the high Arctic or, like Pintails, through Canada up to and including the Arctic. But for every one of these species, field guides denote southwestern Indiana as part of their sometimes very broad winter ranges. What's really mind-boggling is that all these many waterfowl species have traveled the distance here to find open water and ample food for the season. In late winter they'll grow restless and start edging northward, assuring themselves that they'll be on nesting territory ASAP in spring.

Waterfowl migration behavior is influenced by three big variables, all in evidence in our observations today. Right now, in December, weather conditions make the biggest impacts. Extended subfreezing temps set birds migrating south as quickly as does snow cover, both conditions seriously limiting feeding opportunities. Mallards and American Black Ducks are more cold hardy than are American Wigeon, Green-winged Teal, and Northern Shovelers. Today, only a handful of Black Ducks paddled among today's migrants, while hundreds of shovelers were in evidence. Snow and subfreezing temps to our north have just recently set in, thus affecting who's here now. Landscape conditions also influence where waterfowl eventually set down for the winter. Flooding attracts them to new foraging areas, but poor water quality that causes a loss of submersed aquatic vegetation sends them elsewhere. Wetlands restoration draws birds in by the thousands, as we saw today at the mitigated sites. Finally, food must be accessible at the perfect depth for waterfowl. Dabblers, the ones that stick their heads in the water as they dip for food, need shallow vegetation while divers need deep foraging.

December 21

Clocking the Longest Night of the Year

Because of the current warm weather, birds likely found this longest night of the year easily manageable. Given their high rates of metabolism, they need abundant food supplies to keep them warm, and on this day they have the shortest time of the year to find it. Now the minutes will start ticking upward for welcome, life-giving daylight.

December 22

Reflecting on Predators

The number of Bald Eagles at the wetlands during our recent foray clarified the adage that where there's prey there are predators. With more than 10,000 waterfowl packed in tight flocks throughout the refuge, at least some will be sick, injured, old, or otherwise infirm. Any creature not in its prime is a target for another creature that is. And Bald Eagles, both mature and immature, all apparently in their prime, were certainly in no short supply. Our best estimates ranged between twelve and fifteen eagles, but given their wide, sweeping predatory hunts, our count could be off. Since these handsome raptors nest in the area, and since other prime nest sites are well within a day's flight from the refuge, wintertime and its vast waterfowl congregations draw them in for the hunt. In turn, we're drawn in for the display, both of the hunters and the hunted. What a spectacle!

An immature Bald Eagle hunts across the wetlands where tens of thousands of waterfowl are wintering.

December 23

Catching the Chase

Although I'm not outside much this time of year, I was out long enough today to catch two American Crows taking on a Red-tailed Hawk. The hawk was soaring, relatively high on strong winds, and the crows took offense. Breeding season having ended long ago, I was surprised to see crows using valuable energy to go on the chase, but perhaps the hawk had wandered into their usual homeland. True, they're longtime enemies, but typically birds don't waste energy. Perhaps these were young crows enjoying a diversion. They're smart. They're also known to play.

December 24

Witnessing Misrepresentation

Calendars make thoughtful gifts. Some are truly works of art, paintings as realistic as a photo or as stylistic as a Charley Harper. And of course, if the subject of that art is birds, you can count on my interest. Today's gift of one such lovely art calendar prompted me to spend leisurely minutes enjoying each new page. That is, until I came to the month of August. It featured a Ruby-throated Hummingbird perched at the opening of a tiny "hummingbird house." Oh dear. Only in someone's wild and whimsical imagination do hummers use a house. Across the United States, of the approximately 914 bird species found here, only about 86 use cavities for nesting: woodpeckers, chickadees, titmice, Wood Ducks, Great Crested Flycatchers, Prothonotary Warblers, Tree Swallows, American Kestrels, some owls, and a few seabirds, for example. But most birds choose nests high or low, from ground level to high canopy, tucked in a hidden niche of vegetation. Sadly, I've spotted "hummingbird houses" in gift shops, some marketer suspecting at least some folks will succumb to the suggestion.

Hummingbirds, no matter the species, never nest in "houses" or any other cavities. Here, a Ruby-throated Hummingbird has built her nest at the fork of a small branch and under the shade of a single leaf.

December 25

Bringing the Color Purple

Not since late October have Purple Finches visited the yard—or at least none that I've seen. Today, however, two males checked out the sunflower seeds. Typical Purple Finch behavior calls for my seeing more females than males and seeing them more often. Some years slip by without my seeing either. Spotting them, then, in late December was a nice gift of the season. Perhaps they've been in the area all along, or perhaps the worsening weather to our north sent them to the relative comfort here. Still, I'm guessing they were another one-day wonder, albeit a charming one.

A male Purple Finch stops briefly to feed. Typically, the males are in my yard only during spring and fall migration, so he was a surprise.

December 26

Counting Nuthatches

The abundance of Red-breasted Nuthatches set all kinds of records in the yard this winter, and I'd venture to guess that the same has happened almost everywhere else between here and Canada during this amazing irruption year. I have no way to be certain of an accurate count, but I've now seen four individuals simultaneously. Actually, then, it's quite likely that more than four visit regularly. Just as a quick test, this morning for 3.5 minutes I counted visits to a single feeder: fourteen visits! That's an average of one every 15 seconds! Of course, it's possible that four individuals could make that many visits, but I think it's unlikely.

My usual pair of White-breasted Nuthatches continued their routine, apparently unconcerned about the appearance of their northerly cousins.

Birds Do *That*?

Starlings fly in murmurations. These whirling fluid flocks of thousands or sometimes hundreds of thousands (some might say millions?) move through the sky while the mass changes shape and direction. It's like a shape-shifting cloud. How can any bird fly in a flock in such close proximity without charging headlong into another bird or crashing to the ground in one collision after another? Scientists have been searching for an explanation for this seemingly intelligent cloud, and Giorgio Parisi, a theoretical physicist with the University of Rome, has at least a part of the answer. If one bird changes speed or direction, so do all the others, but with sometimes many thousands of massed birds, Parisi found that individuals reacted only to the seven birds nearest them. As the groups of seven ripple across the hundreds of thousands almost instantaneously, the mass moves as a single unit. Check YouTube for videos.

December 27

Shifting Attention

As a break from holiday activities, we wandered afield, finding ourselves at two area spots of interest. First was a borrow pit alongside the interstate and behind a little conglomeration of restaurants and hotels. With easy access and ready parking available, we could check out the pit, a lake known for its unusual waterfowl. And today? Well, how rewarding to find a Common Loon paddling the lake's perimeter! By necessity, loons' migratory behavior demands they find ice-free wintertime waters, so they habitually head to salt water. They may choose one of two destinations, either along the East Coast or, wandering through the Midwest, fishing, occasionally staying days or weeks, finally reaching the Gulf Coast. Like this one, they usually migrate alone. Today's loon found successful fishing, so it may stay until it fattens up or until ice edges it out.

Besides the loon, six Ring-necked Ducks and two Pied-billed Grebes were diving regularly, foraging in the fishy waters. Usually, timid winter waterfowl swim like the dickens away from anyone trying for a good view or a photo, but these guys were relatively comfortable with our watching.

The reclaimed strip mine area attracted our attention next. That destination drew us for its usual wintertime Short-eared Owl population that migrate here from their breeding grounds in the tundra. Since their usual behavior is to wait until almost dark to start hunting, we spent the earlier part of our visit driving some of the more promising roads, watching for whatever might appear. The two biggest surprises: Great Horned Owl, a year-round resident here, and Great Egret, a summertime visitor. Why a Great Egret still visits in late December is anyone's guess, but it seemed healthy and was actively fishing. Great Egrets have a varied diet, including, in addition to fish, amphibians, reptiles, small mammals, and birds, as well as invertebrates like crayfish, worms, and grasshoppers. Food is no doubt plentiful on the property, so perhaps this long-legged elegant creature is hedging its bets against an ice-up, resisting migration until absolutely necessary. Since plume hunters decimated Great Egret populations by 95 percent around the turn of the twentieth century, their recovery after the 1910 ban on hunting them has been remarkable.

And yes, we found the Short-eared Owls just at dark, engaged in their usual behavior. They swooped across the low vegetation, hunting, obviously successfully, even though Northern Harriers harassed them in the process. A single Rough-legged Hawk perched nearby, watching the activity but apparently too well satisfied to join the hunt.

A Common Loon in drab winter plumage makes a migratory stopover in the area to rest, feed, and prepare for the remainder of its travels, probably to the Gulf Coast.

December 28

Focusing on Finches and Creepers

Up and down, up and down, goldfinch numbers are now down—again. Only one came into my field of view today. But Pine Siskins have taken the goldfinches' places at nyjer-seed and sunflower-seed feeders, and hemlock trees bounced with siskins' feeding antics, hanging upside down to gain the best access to tiny hemlock cones. And the sycamore trees have garnered nearly equal attention as siskins pick at the ball-shaped seed heads. The siskins' numbers seem to grow by the day. More than a dozen perched at feeders this morning, but I was unable to count those bouncing through the trees. Another verification of finches' irruptive behavior!

In a surprising move, a Brown Creeper plucks a suet crumble from the ground.

Because at least one Brown Creeper (maybe the same one) has visited the backyard almost every day since my first sighting of it on November 10, I've zeroed in on its habitual foraging behavior. It starts just above ground level and spirals its way up the trunk of the old tulip-tree snag until it reaches the top. From there it flies to near the base of the bald cypress tree and repeats the spiraling act. Some-times, it returns to the snag and takes a different route up the trunk. Today, how-ever, when it returned for a second tour of the snag, instead of spiraling upward, it diverted from its usual habit and scooted down, head first, toward the ground. Really? What respectable Brown Creeper moves across the ground? But as this little guy reached ground level, it indeed stepped onto the soil and poked about near the base of the tree. Grabbing binocs, I took a closer look at the bird's actions. It was picking up tiny, tiny crumbs of suet that had fallen from the feeder above. Savvy birds never miss a thing, and this bird spied the tiniest of morsels and went after them—even stepping away from its normal behavior. It's called adaptive behavior. Sharp!

December 29

Counting Woodpeckers

It was a five-woodpecker day! Downy, Hairy, Red-bellied, Pileated, and Flicker all came to the same spot: the old tulip-tree snag. More than three years after the tree guys cut the biggest part of the monster branches away from the house and girdled the tree, the decay-ing branch stubs and trunk must now surely contain a true smorgasbord of bugs, eggs, and larvae. Everything loves that snag. Red-breasted and White-breasted Nuthatches cache safflower seeds there every day and then pick around for other tasty morsels. Nothing but the snag can explain the everyday months-long visits of at least one Brown Creeper, a true delight in this year's wintertime yard. In short, all manner of birds poke and pick in the deep ridges of the decaying bark, much of it now beginning to break off during strong storms, the water weighting and loosening it and the wind ripping it off. When the bark goes, the naked branch stubs and trunk show the tunnels of beetles and caterpillars, all the better for birds.

I'm gaining more and more understanding and appreciation of the birds' behavior and the importance of dead and dying trees. I used to think dead trees were for woodpeckers—and they are—but certainly not woodpeckers alone. I've noted earlier that a dead or dying tree is Mother Nature's perfect grocery store/nursery combo. It's become obvious that the benefits of having a native grocery store readily available for birds far outweighs having another feeder and another bag of commercial birdseed. As a result, it's becoming the birds' favorite buffet. Should I mention that it's also become my favorite hot spot for bird watching?

December 30

Repeating the Tally

Closing out the year the way it began, with a tally of the birds in the yard, seems a reasonable conclusion to this year's study of bird behavior, so I was up at dawn's early light, listening and looking. Given the gray day, "light" may be a poor word choice, but according to the meteorological charts, the sun had risen.

At 6:50 a.m. the temperature hovered in the low 40s, a real drop from the near-record high yesterday of 62 degrees. Yesterday's storms dumped almost 1.5 inches of rain, swelling creeks and flooding fields and roads. The morning's damp, breezy air sent a chill across my jeans-clad legs.

Within minutes the Carolina Wren called. Then an Eastern Towhee asked its quizzical "Whee?" but I couldn't be sure if it was the male or female calling. Cardinals, almost always the first to arrive in the yard, picked at sunflower seeds. As I hung out the suet feeder (I bring it in every night to prevent the rascal raccoons from yanking it down and dragging it off), the Brown Creeper barely scooted out of my way, eager, I suppose, to gather a few suet crumbles for breakfast. A Red-bellied Woodpecker called from the woods. Pine Siskins called from tree to tree as at least a dozen swarmed the upper branches. Chickadees and Red-breasted Nuthatches darted to the window feeder to snap up sunflower-seed hearts. Somewhere to the east, a Northern Mockingbird scolded.

Back inside, I slid open the window just enough to hear any bird calls or songs outside. The creeper continued scooting around looking for suet crumbles. Titmice zipped in one after another to sneak split peanuts. Somehow they know when I've added another cupful. Crows flew over, cawing to one another. From the north, I heard Eastern Bluebirds singing their quiet winter song. A Downy Woodpecker called. Juncos crisscrossed the yard, visiting the window feeder, the platform feeder, and the bubble rock. A female Red-bellied Woodpecker, perhaps the one that called from the woods, came for her share of peanuts. Meanwhile, the number of cardinals grew as the first females arrived for their share of goodies. An annoying pair of House Sparrows picked at the seed cake. A third bluebird, a male, joined the pair checking out the nest box in the front garden. The ensuing fuss no doubt meant he wasn't welcome. A female Northern Flicker clung to the suet feeder, a behavior the reference books say doesn't happen.

Now the clock struck 7:30 a.m., and a Song Sparrow foraged under the seed cake while another sang in the distance. A pair of Carolina Wrens continued their contact calls to one another from the woodland edge. At 7:40 the yard went empty and quiet, only House Sparrows chirping and water gurgling.

Within 10 minutes, though, a Blue Jay flew in, followed by four others, all five gathering around the little pile of peanuts. That apparently broke the spell, and activity resumed. Cardinals returned. Red-breasted Nuthatches resumed feeding. Overhead, a pair of Canada Geese rowed by, calling to each other along the way. The towhee repeated its call. Several House Finches arrived to check out the safflower seed.

At 8 a.m. I headed outside to look and listen. I stopped in my tracks when I heard "FEE-bee," accented on the first syllable the way an Eastern Phoebe says its name. But wait! Not now. I listened more carefully, finally understanding that European Starlings were doing their masterful mimics. Before I took another step, however, a commotion in the two holly trees diverted my attention. The upper branches of both huge trees shook with activity. The hubbub turned out to be those five jays chasing through the berries with the mockingbird in hot pursuit. They'll probably spend the day sorting out who gets what. Meanwhile, a Hairy Woodpecker hitched up the sycamore tree, and two White-breasted Nuthatches "yank-yanked" their way across the little apple orchard. A mixed flock of Common Grackles and Red-winged Blackbirds flew over, traveling southeast to northwest, likely on the path toward their daily feeding grounds. A hawk called—or so I thought—but more careful listening made me believe instead that it was a jay's imitation. So many imitators! A male towhee popped up out of the now-dead goldenrod patch, revealing his identity. And—finally!—a White-throated Sparrow called and then appeared from amid the tangles, a latecomer to the party. Above, high above the low gray clouds, I could hear Snow Geese call as they winged their way toward the Wabash River. A little flock of seven or eight American Robins "tut-tutted" across the treetops before departing for the woods.

Back inside by 8:45 a.m., chilled from the misty breezy cold and hot tea in hand, I watched Pine Siskins seemingly foraging everywhere, multiple Red-breasted Nuthatches, and, in the low-spreading evergreens, White-throated Sparrows flipping mulch into the lawn. Cardinal populations multiplied to over a dozen, activity overall slowly increasing. Two American Goldfinches, having just returned to the yard, flitted to the nyjer-seed feeder. A dove waddled in to check spilled seed. Then, just to get me back to chores at hand, a Cooper's Hawk sailed in, perched on a shepherd's hook, and sent everything fleeing.

In total, thirty-one species made an appearance this morning. Last January 1, a year ago when this record of observations began, on that frigid 3-degree morning, twenty-five species showed up. It's all proof once again how dramatically weather affects our feathered friends and how their behavior changes because of it. All in all, the morning reflected birds' typical wintertime feeding and foraging behavior, vocal behavior, sheltering behavior, and interactive behavior, each species repeating its distinctive actions and reactions with which I've become familiar this year. The birds have become like old friends, when you know what they're going to say and do before they say or do it. Well, except for the times they don't. Gotta love old friends!

Birds Do *That*?

Woodpeckers can use their tongues as spears. Really? Ouch! In fact, a woodpecker's spear-like tongue is so long (three times their bill length) that it curls up behind the bird's eyes and over the top of the brain. Since the tongue is also barbed, it works efficiently to poke into wood, rake up goodies, and then grab tasty beetle grubs. According to Eldon Greij, ornithology professor emeritus, woodpecker tongues are also coated with a sticky saliva that enables the birds to more readily hang on to buried bugs and yank them to the surface for delicious dining.

December 31

Reflecting on the Year's Observations

Watching bird behavior every day for a calendar year has brought challenges and rewards, the most treasured reward being an eye-opening education. A year that included frigid below-zero nights and sultry, blistering hot days, a year that brought too much rain followed by too much dry, a year that took us hundreds of miles from home but kept us mostly in and around the yard, was also a year filled with avian actions that demonstrated survival tactics, migratory behavior, courtship and breeding activities, nesting habits, and molting patterns with dramatic and sometimes humorous effects. Not every day burst with discovery or drama, but the seasons drove change among the birds, and day by day they revealed the stories behind their behaviors.

By year's end, our yard, planted now almost exclusively in natives, had attracted a record 127 bird species. Beyond the yard, out and about, I enjoyed still more birds, thousands more in fact, in a wide variety of habitats, from grasslands to wetlands, from forests to edges, in the open and in thickets, in and around water both still and fast, from agricultural fields to urban concrete. No matter their habitat, birds demonstrated time after time how they're irrevocably tied to the vegetation around them—for food (including bugs), for shelter, and for nesting. No forest-dependent Pileated Woodpecker, for instance, could survive on the ocean any more than a water-dependent American White Pelican could survive in the forest. Birds live in niches. Witnessing birds' dependence on their unique habitat niches ultimately led me to a clear understanding: The more diverse the native habitat in the yard, the more diverse the bird species that the yard attracts. This year's record-high yard count manifests the overwhelming significance of the message, not just for the yard but, by extension, for the global environment.

Over the year, then, as seasons changed, so bird behavior changed. And I'm changed forever because of what I've seen and heard among the avian species with whom I shared the year.

ACKNOWLEDGMENTS

Two groups of folks triggered the concept for a book about how birds behave: those who asked how and those who answered.

As a newspaper columnist, I've written the prerequisite 550 biweekly words about birds for more than a dozen years. The columns often prompt readers' questions—thoughtful, curious, and downright inspiring. Then in a cooperative venture with the local public library, we offered birding classes that ultimately evolved into monthly 2-hour sessions, ongoing now for over ten years, still available free to the public. Hundreds of folks have scanned the columns, attended the classes, scoured my website, and followed my social media posts about birds. And they've asked questions. Questions in class, questions via email, questions on social media. Good questions. So to them, I extend my gratitude for showing interest and directing my attention to the kinds of things you want to know. Thank you for your inquisitive minds.

Of course, you made me work. Good questions deserve good answers, and you sent me on the search. I owe a deep debt of gratitude to the folks and their resources that helped provide the answers. Among the invaluable online resources, the premier site is *Birds of North America Online*, this nation's definitive reference for all things bird. Thanks to Indiana Audubon Society for providing subscription access to this end-all/be-all reference. AllAboutBirds.org, Cornell University's Lab of Ornithology website, catalogs the basics about identification, habitat, and breeding. It's always the best place to begin a general search. eBird.org has become *the* source for pinpointing birds' locations during any month of the year, clarifying beyond published maps the real-time summer, winter, and migration ranges of any bird in the world. BirdCast.info, a readily accessible seasonal radar site, predicts three-day migration patterns, a dandy aid for planning watch days.

Years-long subscriptions and memberships have brought commercial magazines and professional journals to my desk, every issue replete with details about how birds behave. Favorites include *BirdWatcher's Digest*, *Bird Watching* (formerly *Birder's World*), *Living Bird* (Cornell Lab of Ornithology), *Birding* (American Birding Association), *Bird Conservation* (American Bird Conservation), and the related *INPS Journal* (Indiana Native Plant Society), all of which have educated me for the past twenty-five years. Regular columnists in these publications pepper their works with juicy tidbits gleaned from who-knows-where. Folks like (in alphabetical order) Paul Baicich, David Bird, Kevin Cook, Julie Craves, Lara Erickson, Don Freiday, Eldon Greij, George H. Harrison, Dawn Hewitt, Alvaro Jaramillo, Kevin Karlson, Brian Sullivan, Connie Toops, and Julie Zickefoose become my go-to writers in every issue. I've met only a couple of these experts, but I feel that I know them all and hold them all in high regard for teaching me.

Other favorite writers, whose nearly 200 books line my shelves and who have given me hours and hours of pleasure and an all-but-free education, providing more answers than I can credit, include Jennifer Ackerman, for sharing the research in *The Genius of Birds*; Miyoko Chu, especially for her *Songbird Journey: Four Seasons in the Lives of Migratory Birds*; Pete Dunn, for his witty commentary in every book he's done but especially *Essential Field Guide Companion*; Bernd Heinrich, for writing reams about birds in layman's language; Kenn Kaufman, not only for his field guides but also for his regular outpouring of advice and information in numerous columns and articles; Donald Kroodsma, for his remarkable research and writing about birdsong, especially *The Singing Life of Birds*; Roger J. Lederer, for explaining how birds adapt their behavior, especially in *Beaks, Bones and Bird Songs*; John M. Marzluff, for his contemporary look at human impact on birds, especially in *Welcome to Subirdia*; Roger Tory Peterson, not just for his early ground-breaking approach to identifying birds but also for his clear, poignant writing and lifetime commitment to birds; David Sibley, for his thorough field guides in both print and on my now-favorite birding app as well as his concise writings in multiple publications; Alexander Skutch, for his unusual topics, especially *Birds Asleep*; Doug Tallamy, for introducing me to the research about the importance of native plants to birds' survival, inspiring me to further restore our yard to native, thus providing the springboard for me to write *Plant Natives to Attract Birds to Your Yard*; and Scott Weidensaul, for his prolific writings, especially those triggering my ongoing education about migration.

In addition, organizations' regular monthly, bimonthy, or quarterly publications and websites have always been standard go-to references when drilling down for details, including especially those for the National Audubon Society, the National Wildlife Federation, and The Nature Conservancy. Thanks to them for the services they provide. Memberships help them continue their services.

A special thanks to Judith Schnell, Stackpole Books editor, for guiding the direction of this book and seeing it through to production.

And finally, a heartfelt hug to Charles, my lifelong companion and husband of more than fifty years, for his tolerating my time away from him to teach, write, research, and answer all the thoughtful, curious, and inspiring questions. His photographs have added an immeasurable quality to this work. Thank you, babe.

May you, my readers, enjoy the fruits of the labors of all these incredibly knowledgeable folks as their efforts have now filtered through my own, enabling me to share my meager yearlong role in observing and explaining how birds behave.

INDEX

pelicans: Brown, 31, *31*, 38. *See also*
American White Pelican
Peregrine Falcon, 314; decline of and
threats to, 379–80; flight, 230, 382;
hunting sources and behavior, 230, *230*,
379, *379*, 380, *380*; immature, 230, *230*;
migration and range, 230
pesticides, 142, 148, 229, 230, 354, 379
Peterson, Roger Tory, 199
pet hair (for nests), 183, *183*, 220
Philadelphia Vireo, 153, 268–69, *269*
phoebes. *See* Eastern Phoebe
Pied-billed Grebe, 88, 89, 153, *153*, 396
pigeons: manure use historically, 290;
as news carriers historically, 377;
Passenger, 30; Peregrine Falcons eating,
379, 380, *380*; Rock, 69, 290, 377, *379*,
379–80
Pileated Woodpecker, 286, 400; defensive
and aggressive behavior, 71–72, *72*, 284;
feeding sources and behavior, 43, *43*,
52–53, *53*, 263, 298, 316, 397; hawks
attacked by, 284; molt for, 71; nesting/
breeding behavior, 225, 233; plumage,
43, 71; Red-shouldered Hawk conflict
with, 284; song/calls, 334, 344; territorial behavior, 2, 71–72, *72*, 268; winter
food for, 43, *43*, 397
Pine Siskin, 5, *371*, 398; American Goldfinch companionship with, 344; feeding
sources and behavior, 3, 6, 21, *21*, 25,
35, *35*, 36, 51, *51*, 67, *67*, 83, 84, 147,
149, *149*, 331, *346*, 346–47, 352, 360,
367, 371, 375, 397; hemlock importance
for, 44, 51, *51*, 66, 331, 351, 371, 375,
397; during irruption years, 331, *331*,
345, 352, 397; migration and range, 14,
36, 66, 74, 87, 128, 141, 147, 329, 331,
345, 353, 371, 397; plumage, 331, *331*;
song/calls, 44, 344
Pine Warbler, 119–20, *120*, 122, 125
Pintails, 78, 391, 392, *392*
Pittaway, Ron, 328
plants. *See* berries/berry bushes; gardening
and plants

poisons: insect, 101, 119, 165, 189, 250,
300; pesticides, 142, 148, 229, 230, 354,
379; rodent, 299
Prairie Warbler, *272*; migration and
range, 259, 261, 272; plumage, 133,
258, *258*
predators: Blue Jay response to, 300–301,
320, 349, *349*; in bunny death mystery,
237–38; cats as, 9; Dark-eyed Junco
response to, 80, 325, 332; Downy
Woodpecker response to, 80; Eastern
Towhee response to, 383, *383*; foxes
as, 178, 184, 186; nest boxes guarded
for, 117, *117*; nest failure and, 178, 184;
Northern Cardinal response to, 80;
raccoons as, 63–64, 74, 117, 125, 184;
shelter from, 6; shelters for, avoiding,
9; skunks as, 125; snakes as, 117, 125;
song detection by, 85; turtles as, 184;
for waterfowl, 393, *393*. *See also* Bald
Eagle; Cooper's Hawk; Red-shouldered
Hawk; Red-tailed Hawk
preening, 180, 186, 197–98, *198*, 226
Prothonotary Warbler, 155, *155*
Prum, Richard, 346
Purple Finch, 5, *331*, 395; feeding sources
and behavior, 3, 98; House Finch con-
trasted with, 98; migration and range,
97–98, *98*, 102, 214, 328, 329, 330–31,
345, 353, 395; molt for, 3; plumage and
identification, 3, 98, 114, *114*, 345
Purple Martin: feeding sources and
behavior, 83, 165, 168; identifying,
178; migration and range, 64, 67, 81,
357; nesting/breeding behavior, 64, *64*,
67–68, *68*, 179; song/calls, 168

R
raccoons, 13; feeders raided by, 77, 262,
287, 398; hummingbird feeders raided
by, 262, 287; Northern Cardinal brave
behavior with, 62–64, 77; as predators,
63–64, 74, 117, 125, 184; suet feeders
raided by, 398
ravens, 62, 196, 228, 369